SECRET A

BRITAIN'S COLLUSION WITH RADICAL ISLAM

MARK CURTIS

NEW UPDATED VERSION

A complete catalogue record for this book can
be obtained from the British Library on request

First published in 2010 by Serpent's Tail
First published in this updated edition in 2012 by Serpent's Tail
an imprint of Profile Books Ltd
3A Exmouth House
Pine Street
London EC1R 0JH
website: www.serpentstail.com

ISBN 978 1 84668 764 8
eISBN 978 1 84765 301 7

Designed and typeset by folio at Neuadd Bwll, Llanwrtyd Wells

Printed and bound in Great Britain by CPI Group (UK) Ltd, Croydon
CR0 4YY

10 9 8 7 6 5 4 3 2 1

Special thanks to John Pilger, Tom Mills for excellent research assistance, my agent Veronique Baxter, numerous people at Serpent's Tail, especially Pete Ayrton, Stephen Brough, Ruthie Petrie, Rebecca Gray, Valentina Zanca and Diana Broccardo. And, above all, to my wife, Florence.

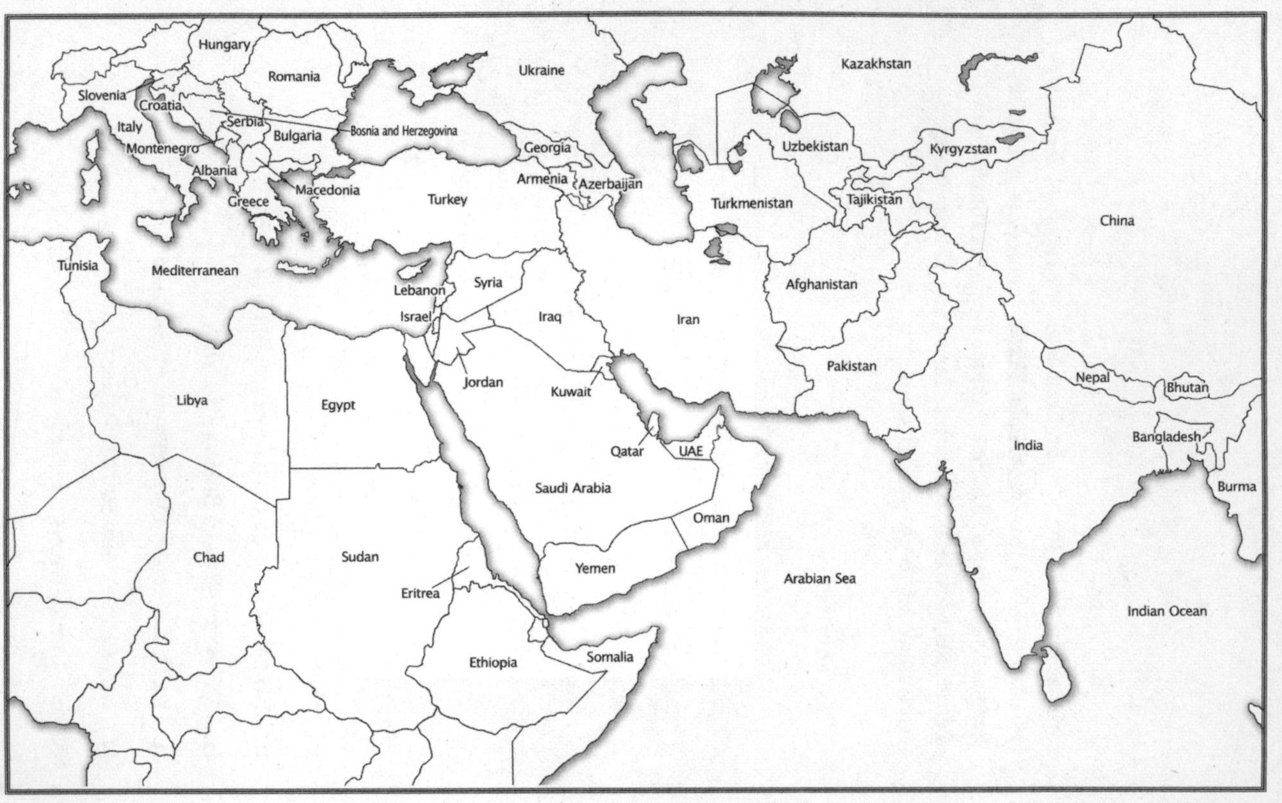
Hungary
Romania
Ukraine
Kazakhstan
Slovenia
Croatia
Serbia
Bosnia and Herzegovina
Italy
Bulgaria
Montenegro
Georgia
Uzbekistan
Kyrgyzstan
Albania
Armenia
Azerbaijan
Macedonia
Greece
Turkey
Turkmenistan
Tajikistan
China
Tunisia
Mediterranean
Syria
Afghanistan
Lebanon
Israel
Iraq
Iran
Pakistan
Nepal
Bhutan
Jordan
Kuwait
Libya
Egypt
Bangladesh
Qatar
UAE
India
Burma
Saudi Arabia
Oman
Chad
Sudan
Yemen
Arabian Sea
Eritrea
Indian Ocean
Ethiopia
Somalia

Contents

Introduction

DURING THE RECENT upheavals in the Middle East, known as the 'Arab Spring', one important aspect of British foreign policy has been ignored by the mainstream media: British collusion with radical Islamic actors to promote oil and other commercial or strategic interests. Indeed, this policy has a long history, which this book will tell, and has contributed not only to the rise of radical Islam itself but also to that of international terrorism, which the British government's new *National Security Strategy* identifies as the country's biggest threat.[1]

The intelligence agencies say they have prevented twelve terrorist plots in Britain over the past decade, and claim there are 2,000 known terrorist suspects organised in 200 networks.[2] Counter-terrorism officials have also warned of a 'huge spectacular', and shooting and hostage-taking raids involving gunmen with bombs.[3] The extent of this threat is all too easily exaggerated for political purposes – the former director of MI5, Stella Rimington, has, for example, accused the government of 'frightening people in order to be able to pass laws which restrict civil liberties'.[4] But Britain, along with many other countries, clearly does face a threat from radical Islamic groups. The July 2005 London bombings, which killed 52 people, constituted the first 'successful' attack by Islamists in Britain, and the British courts have convicted over 80 individuals who planned to kill British citizens in acts of terrorism. Meanwhile,

Britain's most senior military figure has called the threat posed by Islamist extremism 'the struggle of our generation – perhaps our Thirty Years' War'.[5]

How we got to this point has been the subject of much speculation as to how 'home-grown' British citizens can turn to terrorist violence and be prepared to blow themselves up. Right-wing commentators typically blame liberal culture, arguing that laws have not been tough enough to clamp down on extremism, or even that multi-culturalism has made it impossible to challenge people of a different faith.[6] The government has been widely attacked since 7/7 for failing to clamp down on a number of Islamist radicals in Britain – most notoriously, Abu Hamza, the former preacher at the Finsbury Park mosque in north London, who was allowed to openly encourage numerous young Muslims to espouse violent jihad.[7]

For others, and many on the political Left, the terrorist threat has been fuelled by British military interventions in Iraq and Afghanistan and Whitehall's siding with Israel in its conflict in occupied Palestine. These are surely major factors: in April 2005, for example, the Joint Intelligence Committee stated, in a report leaked the following year, that the Iraq conflict 'has exacerbated the threat from international terrorism and will continue to have an impact in the long term. It has reinforced the determination of terrorists who were already committed to attacking the West and motivated others who were not.'[8] This followed a joint Home Office/Foreign Office report, called 'Young Muslims and Extremism', which was also leaked and which stated that there was 'a perceived "double standard"' among many Muslims in Britain who believe that British foreign policy, in places such as Iraq, Afghanistan, Kashmir and Chechnya is 'against Islam'.[9]

But there is a big missing link in this commentary, and Britain's contribution to the rise of the terrorist threat goes well beyond the impacts its wars in Afghanistan and Iraq have had on some individuals. The more important story is that British governments, both Labour and Conservative, have, in pursuing the so-called 'national interest' abroad, colluded for decades with radical Islamic forces, including terrorist organisations. They have connived with them, worked alongside them and sometimes trained and financed them, in order to promote specific foreign policy objectives. Governments have done so in often desperate attempts to maintain Britain's global power in the face of increasing weakness in key regions of the world, being unable to unilaterally impose their will and lacking other local allies. Thus the story is intimately related to that of Britain's imperial decline and the attempt to maintain influence in the world.

With some of these radical Islamic forces, Britain has been in a permanent, strategic alliance to secure fundamental, long-term foreign policy goals; with others, it has been a temporary marriage of convenience to achieve specific short-term outcomes. The US has been shown by some analysts to have nurtured Osama Bin Laden and al-Qaida, but Britain's part in fostering Islamist terrorism is invariably left out of these accounts, and the history has never been told. Yet this collusion has had more impact on the rise of the terrorist threat than either Britain's liberal culture or the inspiration for jihadism provided by the occupation of Iraq.

The closest that the mainstream media have got to this story was in the period immediately after 7/7, when sporadic reports revealed links between the British security services and Islamist militants living in London. Some of these individuals were reportedly working as British agents or informers while being involved in terrorism overseas. Some were apparently being protected by the British security services while being wanted by foreign governments. This is an important but only a small part of the much bigger picture which mainly concerns Britain's foreign policy.

Whitehall has been colluding with two sets of Islamist actors which have strong connections with each other. In the first group are the major state sponsors of Islamist terrorism, the two most important of which are key British allies with whom London has long-standing strategic partnerships – Pakistan and Saudi Arabia.

Foreign policy planners have routinely covertly collaborated with the Saudis and the Pakistanis in their foreign policy, while both states are now seen as key allies in what was until recently described as the War on Terror. Yet the extent of Riyadh's and Islamabad's nurturing of radical Islam around the world dwarfs that of other countries, notably official enemies such as Iran or Syria. As we shall see, Saudi Arabia, especially after the oil price boom of 1973 which propelled it to a position of global influence, has been the source of billions of dollars that have flowed to the radical Islamic cause, including terrorist groups, around the world. A good case can be made that al-Qaida is partly a creature of Britain's Saudi ally, given the direct links between Saudi intelligence and Bin Laden from the early years of the anti-Soviet jihad in Afghanistan in the 1980s.

Pakistan, meanwhile, has been a major sponsor of various terrorist groups since General Zia ul-Haq seized power in a military coup in 1977 – military support brought some groups into being, after which they were nurtured with arms and training. The 7/7 bombers and many other would-be British terrorists are partly the product of subsequent decades of official Pakistani patronage of these groups. And today it is the Pakistan-based networks which pose the largest threat to Britain and which are at the centre of global terrorism, having become perhaps even more important than al-Qaida, despite the Western media's focus on Bin Laden.

Both Pakistan and Saudi Arabia are partly British creations: Saudi Arabia was bloodily forged in the 1920s with British arms and diplomatic support, while Pakistan was hived off from India in 1947 with the help of British planners. These countries, while being very different in many ways, share a fundamental lack of legitimacy other than as 'Muslim states'. The price paid by the world for their patronage of particularly extreme versions of Islam – and British support of them – has been very great indeed. Given their alliance with Britain, it is no surprise that British leaders have not called for Islamabad and Riyadh to be bombed alongside Kabul and Baghdad, since the War on Terror is clearly no such war at all, but rather a conflict with enemies specially designated by Washington and London. This has left much of the real global terrorist infrastructure intact, posing further dangers to the British and world public.

The second group of Islamist actors with whom Britain has colluded is extremist movements and organisations. Among the most influential of the movements that appear throughout this book is the Muslim Brotherhood, which was founded in Egypt in 1928 and has developed into an influential worldwide network, and the Jamaat-i-Islami (Islamic Party), founded in British India in 1941, which has become a major political and ideological force in Pakistan. Britain has also covertly worked alongside the Darul Islam (House of Islam) movement in Indonesia, which has provided important ideological underpinnings to the development of terrorism in that country. Though Britain has mainly collaborated with Sunni movements in promoting its foreign policy, it has also at times not been averse to conniving with Shia forces, such as with Iranian Shia radicals in the 1950s, and before and after the Islamic revolution in Iran in 1979.

Britain has, however, also worked in covert operations and wars with a variety of outright jihadist terrorist groups, sometimes linked to the movements just mentioned. These groups have promoted the most reactionary of religious and political agendas and routinely committed atrocities against civilians. Collusion of this type began in Afghanistan in the 1980s, when Britain, along with the US, Saudi Arabia and Pakistan, covertly supported the resistance to defeat the Soviet occupation of the country. Military, financial and diplomatic backing was given to Islamist forces which, while forcing a Soviet withdrawal, soon organised themselves into terrorist networks ready to strike Western targets. After the jihad in Afghanistan, Britain had privy dealings of one kind or another with militants in various terrorist organisations, including Pakistan's Harkat ul-Ansar, the Libyan Islamic Fighting Group, and the Kosovo Liberation Army, all of which had strong links to Bin Laden's al-

Qaida. Covert actions have been undertaken with these and other forces in Central Asia, North Africa and Eastern Europe.

Although my argument is that Britain has historically contributed to the development of global terrorism, the current threat to Britain is not simply 'blowback', since Whitehall's collusion with radical Islam is continuing in order to bolster the British position in the Middle East. Planners not only continue their special relationships with Riyadh and Islamabad, but they have also recently been conniving with the Muslim Brotherhood in Egypt and Islamists and their supporters in Libya. In a different way, the British are now also in effect collaborating with elements of the Taliban in Afghanistan in a desperate effort to find an exit from an increasingly disastrous war.

The roots of British collusion with radical Islam, as we will see in the first chapter, go back to the divide and rule policies promoted during the empire, when British officials regularly sought to cultivate Muslim groups or individuals to counter emerging nationalist forces challenging British hegemony. It is well known that British planners helped create the modern Middle East during and after the First World War by placing rulers in territories drawn up by British planners. But British policy also involved restoring the Caliphate, the leadership of the Muslim world, back to Saudi Arabia, where it would come under British control, a strategy which had tremendous significance for the future Saudi kingdom and the rest of the world.

After the Second World War, British planners were confronted with the imminent loss of empire and the rise of two new superpowers, but were determined to maintain as much political and commercial influence in the world as possible. Although Southeast Asia and Africa were important to British planners, largely due to their raw material resources, it was the Middle East, due to its colossal oil reserves, over which London mainly wanted to exert influence. Yet here, a major enemy arose in the form of popular Arab nationalism, led by Egypt's Gamal Abdel Nasser, which sought to promote an independent foreign policy and end

Middle Eastern states' reliance on the West. To contain the threat, Britain and the US not only propped up conservative, pro-Western monarchs and feudal leaders but also fomented covert relationships with Islamist forces, notably the Muslim Brotherhood, to destabilise and overthrow the nationalist governments.

As Britain withdrew its military forces from the Middle East in the late 1960s, Islamist forces such as the Saudi regime and, once again, the Muslim Brotherhood, were often seen as proxies to maintain British interests in the region, to continue to destabilise communist or nationalist regimes or as 'muscle' to bolster pro-British, right-wing governments. By the 1970s, Arab nationalism had been virtually defeated as a political force, partly thanks to Anglo-American opposition; it was largely replaced by the rising force of radical Islam, which London again often saw as a handy weapon to counter the remnants of secular nationalism and communism in key states such as Egypt and Jordan.

After the Afghanistan war in the 1980s spawned a variety of terrorist forces, including al-Qaida, terrorist atrocities began to be mounted first in Muslim countries and then, in the 1990s, in Europe and the US. Yet, crucially for this story, Britain continued to see some of these groups as useful, principally as proxy guerilla forces in places as diverse as Bosnia, Azerbaijan, Kosovo and Libya; there, they were used either to help break up the Soviet Union and secure major oil interests or to fight nationalist regimes, this time those of Slobodan Milosevic in Yugoslavia and Muammar Qadafi in Libya.

Throughout this period, many jihadist groups and individuals found refuge in Britain, some gaining political asylum, while continuing involvement in terrorism overseas. Whitehall not only tolerated but encouraged the development of 'Londonistan'– the capital acting as a base and organising centre for numerous jihadist groups – even as this provided a de facto 'green light' to that terrorism. I suggest that some elements, at least, in the British establishment may have allowed some Islamist groups to operate from London not only because they provided information to the security services but also because they were seen as useful to British foreign policy, notably in maintaining a politically divided Middle East – a long-standing goal of imperial and postwar planners – and as a lever to influence foreign governments' policies. Radical Islamic forces have been seen as useful to Whitehall in five specific ways: as a global counter-force to the ideologies of secular nationalism and Soviet communism, in the cases of Saudi Arabia and Pakistan; as 'conservative muscle' within countries to undermine secular nationalists and bolster pro-Western regimes; as 'shock troops' to destabilise or overthrow governments; as proxy military forces to fight wars; and as 'political tools' to leverage change from governments.

Although Britain has forged long-standing special relationships with Saudi Arabia and Pakistan, it has not been in strategic alliance with radical Islam as such. Beyond these two states, Britain's policy has been to collaborate with Islamist forces as a matter of ad hoc opportunism, though it should be said that this has been rather regular. Time and again, the declassified planning documents reveal that British officials were perfectly aware that their collaborators were anti-Western and anti-imperialist, devoid of liberal social values or actually terrorists. Whitehall did not work with these forces because it agreed with them but simply because they were useful at specific moments. Islamist groups appeared to have collaborated with Britain for the same reasons of expediency and because they shared the same hatred of popular nationalism as the British. These forces opposed British imperialism in the Middle East just as they do the current occupations of Iraq and Afghanistan, but they have not generally opposed the neo-liberal economic policies pursued by the pro-Western, British-backed regimes in the region.

Crucially, British collusion with radical Islam has also helped promote two big geo-strategic foreign policy objectives. The first is influence and control over key energy resources, always recognised in the British planning documents as the number one priority in the Middle East. British operations to support or side with Islamist forces have generally aimed at maintaining in power or installing governments that will promote Western-friendly oil policies.

The second objective has been maintaining Britain's place within a pro-Western global financial order. The Saudis have invested billions of dollars in the US and British economies and banking systems, and Britain and the US have similarly large investments and trade with Saudi Arabia; it is these that are being protected by the strategic alliance with Riyadh. Since the period of 1973–75, when British officials secretly made a range of deals with the Saudis to invest their oil revenues in Britain, as we shall see, there has been a tacit Anglo–American–Saudi pact to maintain this financial order, which has entailed London and Washington turning a blind eye to whatever else the Saudis spend their money on. This has been accompanied, on the Saudi side, by a strategy of bankrolling Islamist and jihadist causes and a 'Muslim' foreign policy aimed at maintaining the Saud family in power.

In promoting its strategy, Britain has routinely collaborated with the US, which has a history of similar collusion with radical Islam.[10] Given declining British power, Anglo–American operations changed from being genuinely joint enterprises in the early postwar years to ones where Whitehall was the junior partner, often providing specialist covert forces in operations managed by Washington. At times, Britain has acted as the de facto covert arm of the US government, doing the dirty work which Washington could not, or did not want to do. This said, the British use of Muslim forces to achieve policy objectives goes back to the empire, thus predating the US. Equally, in the postwar world, Whitehall has sometimes acted independently of Washington, to pursue distinctly British interests, such as the plots to overthrow Nasser in the 1950s or the promotion of Londonistan in the 1990s.

My argument is not that radical Islam and violent jihadism are British or Western 'creations', since this would overstate Western influence in regions like the Middle East and Southeast Asia, where numerous domestic and international factors have shaped these forces over a long period. But British policy has contributed to the present threat of terrorism, although this dare not be mentioned in mainstream British culture. It is only the anti-Soviet jihad in 1980s Afghanistan that is well-known as contributing to the emergence of terrorist groups. Even here, much more attention has been paid to the covert US role than the British. As for the rest of history, there is virtually complete silence, similar to the darkness that prevails over other episodes in Britain's recent foreign policy, where less than the noblest of intentions were in evidence. The British public has been deprived of key information to understand the roots of current terrorism and the role that government institutions, who pose as our protectors, have played in endangering us.

My understanding of Islamic radicalism is based on the definition of the widely-respected French expert, Olivier Roy, in that it involves a return of all Muslims to the true tenets of Islam (usually called 'Salafism' – 'the path of the ancestors' – or 'fundamentalism') and a political militancy that advocates jihad, in the sense of a 'holy war' against the enemies of Islam, who could include Muslim rulers. Roy defines Islamism as a brand of modern fundamentalism that seeks, through political action, to create an Islamic state by imposing Islamic ('sharia') law as the basis for all society's laws. Islamists see Islam not merely as a religion, but as a political ideology which should be integrated into all aspects of society.[11] With this analysis in mind, throughout this book I use the terms 'radical Islamic', 'Islamist' and 'fundamentalist' interchangeably. 'Jihadists' are understood as those engaged in violent activities to achieve Islamic states.

This book results partly from several months' research at the National Archives in London, where I looked at the British declassified files on policy towards countries in the Islamic world. The research for a subject as large as this can perhaps never be exhaustive, and there are also many unknowns in British policy in some of the episodes considered here. I invite others to complete the picture in these areas.

CHAPTER 1

Imperial Divide and Rule

THE ROOTS OF British collaboration with radical Islamic forces in the postwar world are found in the policies of empire. The first step towards British empire in the Muslim world came in 1765 when the Mughal emperor in the rich province of Bengal granted the British East India Company the right to raise revenue and administer justice there. Britain subsequently took control of the Indian subcontinent, defeating Tipu Sultan, the last significant Muslim power in India, in 1799. By the late nineteenth century British power had moved far beyond India, and had become a major influence over the world's Muslims. The formal empire, along with Britain's 'protectorates' (colonies in all but name where Britain controlled defence and external relations) encompassed more than half the Muslim peoples of the world.[1] Winston Churchill, then secretary of state for war, remarked in 1919 that, with the 20 million Muslims in India, Britain was 'the greatest Mohammedan power'.[2]

British imperialism often came into direct conflict with Muslims and Islamic power, and was regularly challenged by jihadist movements, such as the religious tribesmen, or *ghazis*, who fought the British during the Second Afghan War in 1880, or the Islamic revivalist Mahdist movement in Sudan, which in 1881 promoted an uprising against the Egyptian ruling class, capturing Khartoum from the British general, Gordon, and establishing an armed theocracy. In his first book in 1899, on the British reconquest of the Sudan, Churchill had written of Islam that 'no stronger retrograde force exists in the world' and that 'Mohammedanism is a militant and proselytising faith'.[3] Some Islamic movements arose in direct response to British colonial rule, two of which went on to have huge influence in the development of modern radical Islam. One, the Deoband Sunni religious revivalist movement was named after a town in modern Uttar Pradesh in northern India, where a religious seminary, or *madrassa*, was founded in 1866. It brought together Islamic clerics hostile to British rule in India who were intent on promoting religious learning away from the corrupting influences of Westernisation. Another Sunni organisation which sprang up was the Muslim Brotherhood, established in Egypt in 1928 by a twenty-two-year-old school teacher, Hassan al-Banna, whose ideology rejected British occupation of the country and Western cultural and political influences, calling for a strict adherence to the Koran in all aspects of human life.

The British feared not only Islamic radicalism but also pan-Islamism – the prospect of united global Muslim action against the British empire. In India, pan-Islamism was exemplified above all in the 'Khilafat' (i.e., Caliphate) movement, which emerged in 1919 under the leadership of Muslim clerics seeking to challenge the British Raj and shore up the disintegrating Muslim Ottoman empire after the First World War. By also reaching out to Hindu nationalists, the Khilafat movement became for a time the greatest protest movement against British rule since the rebellion by Indian troops and civilians during the 'mutiny', or civil war, of 1857.[4]

Critically, however, the British empire was not always in confrontation with Muslim forces, but also often ruled through them, by proxy. After Britain's Maxim guns brutally defeated the Islamic Sokoto Caliphate in northern Nigeria in the early years of the twentieth century, the British ruled through the Sultan of Sokoto, his emirs and the structure of Islamic government that existed under their authority. Northern Nigeria provided the classic model of 'indirect rule', as described by the governor, Lord Lugard, which was subsequently exported to other colonies. In Sudan, the state established by the Mahdist movement was eventually defeated by Britain in 1898, and by the 1920s London had come to view Mahdist leader, Sayyid Abd al-Rahman, as an ally who could ensure the loyalty of many Sudanese.[5] In various other colonies and protectorates, Britain sought to uphold 'traditional' Muslim authority as a bulwark of its continuing authority, and Islamic law was often allowed to continue in its more conservative forms. Even in directly ruled British India, Muslim personal law, an important aspect of the sharia, continued to flourish. This co-option of Islamic elements had profound consequences; it helps explain the failure of Muslims in many British-ruled territories to respond to the call of Turkey's Ottoman empire for jihad against the British at the beginning of the First World War.[6]

In the 'Great Game' of nineteenth century competition with Russia for influence in Asia, Britain propped up the region's decaying Islamic regimes as a buffer between Russia and British India, its most important possession. In particular, the British sought to keep Russia out of Afghanistan. Then, the concerns were mainly strategic and to do with British 'great power' status; by the early twentieth century, oil had entered the picture, and control of the Middle East's vast resources revitalised the Great Game.

In India, the British built up hundreds of conquered Princely States, most of which were Hindu, as forces of conservatism and stability. But at the same time the Raj showered official patronage on favoured Muslim leaders in the community, seeing Muslim India partly as a counter to Hindu nationalism. It has long been argued that the British construction of knowledge about India, including academic research, was deliberately sectarian, building up the distinctions between Muslims and Hindus, and that the category of 'Muslim' was partly a product of the colonial state's discourse.[7] George Francis Hamilton, the secretary of state for India, once wrote to Lord Curzon, the governor general from 1895–1904 and subsequently viceroy, saying that he:

> should so plan the educational textbooks that the differences between community and community are further strengthened ... If we could break educated Indians into two sections holding widely different views, we should, by such a division, strengthen our position against the subtle and continuous attack which the spread of education must make upon our system of government.[8]

Muslim revivalist and jihadist movements challenged British rule in India in the nineteenth century, and further contributed to the British construction of India in religious terms, sharpening perceptions of difference between Hindus and Muslims. These factors helped sow the seeds of communal antagonism that culminated in the 1857 'mutiny', which was partly a religious war. After 1857 the British promoted communalism, creating separate electorates and job and educational reservations for Muslims. '"Divide *et impera* [divide and rule]" was the old Roman motto,' declared William Elphinstone, the early nineteenth-century governor of Bombay, 'and it should be ours.'[9] This view pervaded and became a cornerstone of British rule in India. Secretary of State Wood wrote in a letter to Lord Elgin, governor general of India in 1862–3, that 'we have maintained our power in India by playing off one part against the other and we must continue to do so. Do all you can, therefore, to prevent all having a common feeling.'[10] Another secretary of state for India, Viscount Cross, informed the viceroy, Lord Dufferin, that 'this division of religious feeling is greatly to our advantage',[11] while British civil servant, Sir John Strachey, observed in 1888:

> The truth plainly is that the existence side by side of these hostile creeds is one of the strong points in our political

> position in India. The better clashes of Mohammedans are already a source to us of strength and not of weakness ... They constitute a small but energetic minority of the population, whose political interests are identical with ours.[12]

Some analysts have argued that the British did not follow a consistent, coherent doctrine to promote communal hatred as official policy.[13] This may well be true, but as noted by Francis Robinson, an academic specialist on the British empire and Muslim identity, the policy of divide and rule remained 'very much in the minds of late-nineteenth century administrators'.[14] British decision-makers were pragmatists, adapting policy to particular circumstances at the time, often to achieve specific, short-term objectives – and in this, a policy of promoting communal divisions appears with considerable frequency.

CREATING THE MODERN MIDDLE EAST

This British strategy of colonial divide and rule, and reliance on Muslim forces to promote imperial interests, reached its apogee in the Middle East during and after the First World War. The carving up of the region by British and French officials has been endlessly commented on – though less so as an illustration of the long-standing British 'use' of Islam, which then took on a new turn. The Middle East was seen by British planners as critical for both strategic and commercial reasons. Strategically, the Islamic territories were important buffers against Russian expansion into the imperial land route from British India to British-controlled Egypt. But oil had by now also entered the picture, with the founding of the Anglo–Iranian Oil Corporation in Persia in 1908, the discovery of oil in Iraq soon after, and its increasingly important role in powering the military during the First World War. British planners viewed control over Iraqi and Persian oil to be 'a first class British war aim', Sir Maurice Hankey, secretary of the War Cabinet, said towards the end of the conflict.[15] By

November 1918 the general staff in Baghdad wrote that 'the future power in the world is oil'.[16]

British foreign policy had, since the sixteenth century, supported the Ottoman empire of the Muslim Turks, the largest and most powerful Muslim entity in the world which, at its height in the seventeenth century, had spanned North Africa, southeast Europe and much of the Middle East. Britain was committed to defending 'Ottoman integrity' against Russian and French imperial designs, which involved de facto support for the Turkish Caliphate – the Ottoman sultan's claim to be the leader of the *ummah*, the Muslim world community. After Britain captured India, the Ottoman empire was seen as a convenient buffer to keep out rivals along the military and trade route to the jewel in the crown. London often cast itself as the saviour of the Turkish sultan: in the Crimean War of 1854–6, one of the bloodiest conflicts in modern European history, Britain and France fought on behalf of the Ottomans against Russia. The 'Eastern Question' – the imperial struggle for control in the lands dominated by the decaying Ottoman empire – was a process in which Britain essentially tried to shore up the last great Muslim empire against its great power rivals. By the time Ottoman Turkey made the fateful choice of siding with Germany in the First World War, it was already a declining power but still controlled much of the Middle East, including present-day Syria, Iraq, Jordan and Palestine, which it had ruled for 400 years. After its defeat, the European powers, led by the British, fell upon its carcass and divided it up between them.[17]

During the First World War Britain appealed to the Arabs in the Middle East to join it in overthrowing Ottoman rule of their territories, in exchange for British guarantees of postwar independence. In its 1914 proclamation 'to the natives of Arabia, Palestine, Syria and Mesopotamia', the British government stated that:

> One of [the government's] fundamental traditions is to be a

> friend of Islam and Muslums [sic] and to defend the Islamic Khalifate even if it was a Khalifate of conquest and necessity as the Turkish Khalifate which England had defended with money and men and influence several times … There is no nation amongst Muslums who is now capable of upholding the Islamic Khalifate except the Arab nation and no country is more fitted for its seat than the Arab countries.[18]

In May 1915, Britain also proclaimed to the 'people of Arabia' that 'the religion of Islam, as history proves, has always been most scrupulously respected by the English government', and that, despite the sultan of Turkey having become an enemy, 'our policy of respect and friendliness towards Islam remains unchanged'.[19]

A huge amount has been written on the 'Arab revolt' against Turkish rule, including the romanticised heroics of Lawrence of Arabia and Britain's subsequent betrayal of its guarantees of 'independence' for the Arabs; these guarantees, to the British, meant not granting Arabs national sovereignty but allowing the presence of exclusively British advisers to administrate Arab countries which would become British 'protectorates'. One striking aspect of the call to Arabs was Britain's appeal to Islam in its promises to the then ruler, or *sherif*, of the holy city of Mecca, Hussein bin Ali. Hussein, whose religious authority and position derived from his supposed descent from Muhammad, agreed to lead the Arab revolt in return for British recognition of him after the war as the ruler of a vast territory stretching from present-day Syria to Yemen, thus encompassing all of modern Saudi Arabia. The British government wrote to Hussein in November 1914, stating that:

> If the Amir [ie, Hussein] … and Arabs in general assist Great Britain in this conflict that has been forced upon us by Turkey, Great Britain will promise not to intervene in any manner whatsoever whether in things religious or otherwise … Till now we have defended and befriended Islam in the

> person of the Turks: henceforward it shall be in that of the noble Arab. It may be that an Arab of true race will assume the Khalifate at Mecca or Medina, and so good may come by the help of God out of all the evil that is now occurring.[20]

This last momentous sentence was Britain promising to help restore the Islamic Caliphate to Arabia and for Sherif Hussein to be the new caliph, the successor to the Turkish sultan. It was Medina, in modern Saudi Arabia, which was the first capital of the Caliphate after the prophet Muhammed died in the seventh century, following which it had been claimed by a variety of dynasties, latterly the Ottomans. London promised to Hussein that Britain 'will guarantee the Holy Places [at Mecca and Medina] against all external aggression and will recognise their inviolability.'[21] Lord Kitchener, the secretary of state for war, noted in March 1915 that 'if the Khalifate were transferred to Arabia, it would remain to a great extent under our influence.'[22] The coastline of the Arabian peninsula could be easily controlled by the British navy. By championing an Arabian kingdom under British auspices, Britain was exerting its dominance over the spiritual leadership of the Muslim world. Indeed, Britain was helping Islam to reclaim its roots and return to its origins.

However, some British officials during and after the war also feared that the Caliphate could be used as a rallying point for anti-colonial movements, to undermine British rule in India and Egypt. In particular, they feared the prospect of a Muslim holy war against Britain, something the Turkish sultan had proclaimed on entering the First World War. In his analysis of the Middle East during and after the First World War, David Fromkin notes that British leaders believed that Islam could be manipulated by buying or capturing its religious leadership. They believed, in short, that whoever controlled the person of the caliph controlled Sunni Islam.[23]

Sherif Hussein came out in revolt against the Ottoman empire in June 1916, recruiting a small Arab force of a few thousand men to fight in the Hijaz region, the western coastal area of Arabia containing the cities of Jeddah, Mecca and Medina. The writer, Gertrude Bell, who was to become an imperial architect of Iraq, noted that with the fighting at Mecca 'the revolt of the Holy Places is an immense moral and political asset'.[24] However, Hussein's revolt achieved only minor victories over the Ottoman army and failed to mobilise people in any part of the Arab world, despite being subsidised by the British to the tune of £11 million (around £500 million in today's money). British officers served as military advisers to Hussein's revolt; one such was Colonel T. E. Lawrence 'of Arabia', an aide to Faisal, Sherif Hussein's son, who was appointed to command the latter's military forces.

One month before the Arab revolt broke out, Britain and France secretly agreed to divide the Middle East between their zones of influence, in the Sykes-Picot Agreement, named after their respective foreign ministers. This abandonment of the commitment to Ottoman territorial integrity – overturning a mainstay of British foreign policy – was frankly explained by British officials. Lawrence, supposedly the great 'liberator' of the Arab world, wrote an intelligence memo in January 1916 stating that the Arab revolt was:

> beneficial to us because it marches with our immediate aims, the break up of the Islamic 'bloc' and the defeat and disruption of the Ottoman Empire, and because the states [Sherif Hussein] would set up to succeed the Turks would be … harmless to ourselves … The Arabs are even less stable than the Turks. If properly handled they would remain in a state of political mosaic, a tissue of small jealous principalities incapable of cohesion.[25]

After the war, Lawrence wrote a report for the British Cabinet entitled 'Reconstruction of Arabia', arguing that it was urgent for the British and their allies to find a Muslim leader who could counter the Ottoman empire's attempted jihad against them in the name of the caliph:

> When war broke out an urgent need to divide Islam was added, and we became reconciled to seek for allies rather than subjects ... We hoped by the creation of a ring of client states, themselves insisting on our patronage, to turn the present and future flank of any foreign power with designs on the three rivers [Iraq]. The greatest obstacle, from a war standpoint, to any Arab movement, was its greatest virtue in peace-time – the lack of solidarity between the various Arab movements ... The Sherif [Hussein] was ultimately chosen because of the rift he would create in Islam.[26]

The benefit of division in the Middle East – a key point in all these documents – was also recognised by the foreign department of the British government of India: 'What we want', it stated, 'is not a United Arabia, but a weak and disunited Arabia, split up into little principalities so far as possible under our suzerainty – but incapable of coordinated action against us, forming a buffer against the Powers in the West.'[27]

BIRTH OF THE SAUDI ALLIANCE

Following the Arab revolt and Britain's defeat of the Turkish armies throughout the region, Hussein proclaimed himself King of all the Arab countries, including the Hijaz, but the British government was prepared to recognise only his control of the latter. Confrontation over the future of Arabia ensued between Hussein and another British protégé, Abdul Aziz Ibn Saud, an emir and rising power in central Arabia whose forces had captured the Nejd region with its capital at Riyadh. British officials had been split on who to champion as the leader of the revolt against the Turks – the British government of India had feared British sponsorship of an Arab caliph who would lead the entire Muslim world, and the effects this might have on Muslims in India, and had therefore favoured Ibn Saud, whose pretensions were limited to Arabia. In contrast to Hussein's orthodox Sunnism, the future founder of Saudi Arabia sat at the head of an ultra-conservative Sunni revivalist movement, now known as Wahhabism, which professed a strict adherence to the tenets of Islam, and which had developed in the eighteenth century based on the teaching of the theologian, Mohammed ibn Abdul Wahhab, born in 1703. Ibn Saud's military forces were the Ikhwan, or Brotherhood, a militia of Bedouin tribesmen instructed by religious teachers who were committed to the purification of Islam and the advancement of government based on strict Islamic law.

Britain had already provided arms and money to Ibn Saud during the First World War, signing a treaty with him in 1915 and recognising him as the ruler of the Nejd province under British protection. By the end of the war, he was receiving a British subsidy of £5,000 a month[28] – considerably less than the £12,000 a month doled out to Hussein, whom the British government at first continued to favour. That some British officials were pinning their strategic hopes on Ibn Saud during the war is evidenced in a memorandum from one British soldier, a Captain Bray, on the 'Mohammedan question' in 1917:

> At the present moment agitation is intense in all Mohammedan countries ... The reports of agents and others confirm ... the extreme vitality of the movement [pan-Islamism] ... It is ... essential that the country to whom Mohammedans look should not be Afghanistan. We should therefore create a state more convenient for ourselves, to whom the attention of Islam should be turned. We have an opportunity in Arabia.[29]

In 1919 London used aircraft in the Hijaz in support of Hussein's confrontation with Ibn Saud. It was to little avail: after accepting a temporary ceasefire in 1920, Ibn Saud's 150,000-strong Ikhwan advanced relentlessly, and by the mid-1920s had gained control of Arabia, including the Hijaz and the Holy Places, defeating Hussein for supremacy in the region. Ibn Saud established 'Saudi' Arabia in an orgy of murder. In his exposé of the corruption of the Saudi ruling family, Said Aburish describes Ibn Saud as 'a lecher and a bloodthirsty autocrat ... whose savagery wreaked havoc across Arabia', terrorising and mercilessly slaughtering his enemies. The conquest of Arabia cost the lives of around 400,000 people, since Saud's forces did not take prisoners; over a million people fled to neighbouring countries. Numerous rebellions against the House of Saud subsequently took place, each put down in 'mass killings of mostly innocent victims, including women and children'. By the mid-1920s most of Arabia had been subdued, 40,000 people had been publicly executed and some 350,000 had had limbs amputated; the territory was divided into districts under the control of Saud's relatives, a situation which largely prevails today.[30]

The British recognised Ibn Saud's control of Arabia, and by 1922 his subsidy was raised to £100,000 a year by Colonial Secretary Winston Churchill.[31] At the same time, Churchill described Ibn Saud's Wahhabis as akin to the present-day Taliban, telling the House of Commons in July 1921 that they were 'austere, intolerant, well-armed and bloodthirsty' and that 'they hold it as an article of duty, as well as of faith, to kill all who do not share their opinions and to make slaves of their wives and children. Women have been put to death in Wahhabi villages for simply appearing in the streets. It is a penal offence to wear a silk garment. Men have been killed for smoking a cigarette.'[32]

However, Churchill also later wrote that 'my admiration for him [Ibn Saud] was deep, because of his unfailing loyalty to us', and the British government set about consolidating its grip on this loyalty.[33] In 1917 London had dispatched Harry St John Philby – father of Kim, the later Soviet spy – to Saudi Arabia, where he remained until Ibn Saud's death in 1953.[34] Philby's role was 'to consult with the Foreign Office over ways to consolidate the rule and extend the influence' of Ibn Saud. A 1927 treaty ceded control of the country's foreign affairs to Britain. When elements of the Ikhwan, opposed to the British presence in the country, rebelled against the regime in 1929, Ibn Saud called for British support. The RAF and troops from the British-controlled army in neighbouring Iraq were dispatched, and the rebellion was put down the following year. Ibn Saud highly appreciated Britain's support for him, especially during the rebellion, and this paved the way for the development of relations between the Saudi kingdom and the West that became the core of Saudi foreign policy.[35]

Following the consolidation of the Saudi–British alliance, Ibn Saud relegated the Ikhwan's role to that of educating and monitoring public morality. But the power of Wahhabism had already transformed Bedouins into mujahideen – holy warriors – for whom devotion to the *ummah* transcended tribal affiliations. In subsequent decades, the Ikhwan's jihadist conquest of the Arabian peninsula by the sword and the Koran would be constantly invoked in Saudi Arabian teaching.[36] Officially proclaimed in 1932, and to a large extent a British creation, Saudi Arabia would go on to act as the world's main propagator of fundamentalist Islam, providing the ideological and financial centre of global jihadism. Indeed, Saudi Wahhabism has been described as the 'founding ideology' of modern jihad.[37]

The new state of Saudi Arabia, its regional authority underpinned by a religious fundamentalism, gave Britain a foothold in the heart of the Islamic world, in Mecca and Medina. More broadly, Britain had succeeded in achieving its goal of a divided Middle East and a 'ring of client states' out of the ashes of the Ottoman empire. The Gulf states ringing Saudi Arabia, in Aden, Bahrain and Oman, were all feudal regimes underpinned by British military protection. Meanwhile, Britain continued to exploit its other potential clients: Faisal, who, with the Allies had captured Damascus in 1918, was made King of Iraq in 1921, and Abdullah, Sherif Hussein's other son, was dubbed King of Transjordan, which became 'independent' under British 'protection' in 1923. Finally, there was Palestine, which had also been captured by British forces towards the end of the war. Here, however, Britain was committed to creating what Foreign Secretary Arthur Balfour outlined in 1917 as a 'national home' for the Jews. In April 1920, at a conference in the Italian resort of San Remo, the newly formed League of Nations formally handed Britain a mandate to govern Palestine.

Balfour had also said that what Britain needed in the Middle East in the early years of the twentieth century was 'supreme economic and political control to be exercised … in friendly and unostentatious cooperation with the Arabs, but nevertheless, in the last resort, to be exercised.'[38] The regimes that Britain had created were puppets, essentially law-and-order governments allied mainly with the traditional ruling classes of Islam. In turn, these favoured sultans, emirs or monarchs saw British rule as providing protection against the dangers of instability or emancipatory nationalist movements that had begun to stir, notably in Iraq.

CENTRAL ASIA AND IRAQ

But it was not only in Arabia that Britain was building up forces who claimed authority in the name of Islam. As already mentioned, British leaders had, since the late nineteenth century, seen a Muslim nexus of states as a counter to Russian expansion in the Middle East and Central Asia. When the Bolsheviks overthrew the tsar's regime in the 1917 revolution, the new rulers in Moscow signed treaties with Turkey, Persia and Afghanistan, which the British saw as threatening their supremacy in the region. At the same time, British officials believed that anti-colonial pan-Islamic movements in the region were being inspired by Germany as well as Russia.[39] To regain the initiative and reassert its influence in Asia, Britain provided covert support to Muslim forces challenging the new Soviet regime. A year after the Russian revolution, in August 1918, Britain sent its military into Central Asia to fight with Turkmen tribesmen and the rebel government in Ashkhabad (capital of modern-day Turkmenistan) against Bolshevik forces moving south. British military planning for the mission noted that 'officers should be accompanied, if possible, by persons qualified to conduct Muhammadan propaganda in favour of the allies, and every endeavour should be made to exploit anti-Bolshevist and pro-autonomous sentiments'. The British feared that Soviet propaganda and their agents would spread into Persia and Afghanistan, and that Turkey and Germany would attempt to undermine the British position in India and Iraq. Britain's intervention had the effect of bogging down Soviet troops in the region and putting off, for a while, the imposition of a communist regime there.[40]

In April 1919 British troops were withdrawn from Central Asia; in their place London provided support to Muslim guerrilla groups which had sprung up across the region to resist the Bolshevik advance. These rebels, called Basmachi ('bandits') by the Soviets, formed part of the army of the Bukhara emirate, the last bastion of Turkic independence in Central Asia, located mainly in modern-day Uzbekistan, near the frontiers with Afghanistan and China. During 1919, the British government in India provided camel caravans of arms and ammunition to the Basmachi via their leaders in the Afghan capital, Kabul. After the Soviets captured the city of Bukhara in 1920, Basmachi groups took to the hills to promote a guerrilla war. The following year, Moscow dispatched an Ottoman general, Enver Pasha, to pacify the rebels, but who then proceeded to switch sides and join them. Pasha proclaimed his goal to be the creation of an independent Muslim state, Turkestan, in Central Asia; his strong Islamic message won him the support of the mullahs, who rallied to his cause alongside the Muslim emir of Afghanistan. The Russians, meanwhile, declared him an agent of the British.[41]

Enver's revolt initially scored some successes, but a Soviet campaign in 1922 killed him and destroyed most of his forces, though the Basmachi rebellion dragged on and was only finally crushed in 1929.[42] Fifty years later, in 1979, British and other arms would flow to the region, again to counter a Soviet advance; in the ensuing war against the Afghan mujahideen, Soviet troops would often call the jihadists Basmachi.[43]

In British-administered Iraq, meanwhile, London at times promoted either Sunni or Shia religious leaders to maintain control over the territory. After capturing Mesopotamia from Turkey during the First World War, Britain was to exercise de facto hegemony over Iraq until the nationalist revolution of 1958. Its authority was promoted through a small Sunni urban elite, while the Shia population, comprising some 55 per cent of Iraq's people, was excluded from political power. However, Britain also had a long history of backing Shia religious figures in Iraq as well as in neighbouring Iran. For more than a century after 1850, Britain channeled funds to hundreds of clergy in the Shia holy cities of Najaf and Karbala in order to exercise influence over them, through a financial mechanism called the 'Oudh Bequest'.[44] In 1903, when Britain was vying with Russia for influence in Iran, the British minister in Iran noted that the Oudh Bequest was an excellent means of 'cultivating friendly personal relations with the chief priests as would enable us to use them if necessary as a lever should Persia follow an unfriendly policy or show signs of contracting a fresh Russian loan'.[45] This suggested use of religious forces as a 'lever' was to recur in subsequent decades. During and after the First World War, Britain used the bequest to try to counter Ottoman efforts to organise a mass jihad movement against British rule in Iraq. British policy failed, however: by 1915 jihad was being preached in every mosque in Iraq, and the religious leadership, the *ulema*, had mobilised some 18,000 volunteers – the first time that Shia leaders had led an armed resistance against a Western power.[46]

Another uprising in southern Iraq in 1920, encouraged again by Shia clerics, was brutally suppressed by the British by early 1921; two years later, the Shia leadership was deported to Iran. During this rebellion, the British promoted the religious leader of the Sunni community in Iraq, known as the Naqib, in the person of Abdal Rahman al-Gaylani. The Naqib was a supporter of the British administration of the country in the face of the Shia threat, and in 1920 London made him the first prime minister of Iraq, while Gertrude Bell became a personal friend.[47] Some British officials even regarded the Naqib as a potential king of Iraq, but in the end they plumped for Faisal, whom they eventually persuaded the Naqib to support – a British policy of garnering the support of establishment Islam for royal rulers also pursued elsewhere. In July 1921 the Council of Ministers, headed by the Naqib, unanimously adopted a resolution declaring Faisal to be the constitutional monarch of Iraq; he was crowned the following month after a British-sponsored plebiscite produced 96 per cent in favour of his assuming the throne – a figure which would have impressed the new Bolshevik rulers of Russia.[48]

PALESTINE AND THE MUFTI

Britain's promotion of the leader of the Sunnis in Iraq was echoed in Palestine at the same time. The background was that Britain's new mandate over Palestine was seen as crucial to its interests in the region, providing a foothold in the Eastern Mediterranean, a buffer between the Suez Canal and possible enemies to the north, and opening up a clear overland route to the huge oil reserves of British-controlled Iraq.[49] Whitehall's stated policy in Palestine was to carry out the Balfour Declaration and create a home for the Jewish people, but 'without prejudice' to the Arab inhabitants. Much has been written about British objectives in making the declaration. Proclaimed some weeks before Britain captured Palestine from the Turks in December 1917, Prime Minister David Lloyd George said that the declaration was designed to secure the support of the Jews in the First World War. The historian, Barbara Tuchman, remarks that the declaration 'allowed Britain to acquire the Holy Land with a good conscience'; British planners were set on seizing Palestine anyway 'but they had to have a good moral case', and the declaration was issued 'to dignify that approaching moment'.[50] Britain also saw the Jewish national home as creating a reliable client population in a strategically important region, and to keep the French, the controllers of neighbouring Syria, out of a territory bordering the Suez Canal area and close to the Arabian peninsula.[51]

British rule in Palestine lasted for thirty years until the military withdrawal in 1948. It was continually confronted with the competing claims of the majority Arab population, which feared displacement by increasing Jewish immigration, and the Jewish population, whose Zionist vision was the consolidation of a homeland as promised by the British. London's policy under the mandate came to be condemned by Jews and Arabs alike. To a large extent, that policy was set by officers of the military and colonial administration on the ground, some of whom favoured Arabs, others Jews. Then there were those, like General Sir Wallace Congreve, a senior British military commander, who said that 'I dislike them all equally ... Arabs and Jews and Christians, in Syria and Palestine, they are all alike, a beastly people. The whole lot of them is not worth a single Englishman.'[52]

Overall, however, British strategy in Palestine clearly favoured the Jewish population throughout the 1920s and 1930s in its sponsorship of immigration into Palestine. This changed the demographic balance in Palestine from 600,000 Arabs and 80,000 Jews in 1917 to one million Arabs and 400,000 Jews by 1938.[53] The basic policy was set by the 1922 White Paper, drawn up by Colonial Secretary Winston Churchill, whose concern was to ensure that no Arab majority could stand in the way of Jewish immigration. Churchill – a lifelong Zionist[54] – regularly spoke against the possibility of the Arabs in Palestine achieving self-determination and representative government.[55] He also regarded Arabs as 'a lower manifestation' than the Jews, who, he contended, accomplished much more economically in Palestine and were 'a higher grade race' compared to the 'great hordes of Islam' who were unable to cultivate the land.[56]

Within this basically pro-Jewish context, however, the British also worked to build up Arab religious forces to maintain order and British control of the territory. The first violent anti-Jewish street riots by Arabs broke out in Jerusalem in April 1920, leaving five Jews and four Arabs dead and hundreds wounded. What became known as the 'Easter Riots' had been incited by several leading Arab figures, including Haj Amin al-Husseini, the son of the Grand Mufti of Jerusalem, religious leader of the Arabs.[57] The title of Grand Mufti was an invention of the British, who sought to promote a single authority representing Palestine's Muslims with whom they could negotiate, and through whom they could govern. This move had the effect of turning what was formerly a simple Muslim legal dignitary into the actual leader of the Muslim Arab community in Palestine.[58]

During the Easter Riots, the British authorities sought to arrest al-Husseini for incitement, and he was sentenced *in absentia* to ten years in prison, after escaping to Syria. However, following the death of his father, the Grand Mufti, British High Commissioner Herbert Samuel took the extraordinary step of pardoning the twenty-six-year-old al-Husseini and appointing him mufti, in April 1921, on condition that he promised to cooperate with the British authorities. Through him, the British now worked to dilute Arab anti-colonial sentiment and counter a developing radical, popular protest movement against British policy and its sponsorship of Jewish immigration. The mufti headed up the Supreme Muslim Council, established under British sponsorship in 1922 as the main body responsible for Muslim affairs in Palestine, and which enjoyed considerable influence over the Arab judicial, educational, religious and political systems. In his analysis of Palestine under the British mandate, Tom Segev argues that al-Husseini was a 'vocal advocate of terror against Zionism' and that his appointment as mufti by the British did not soften his view, although he turned in public to more legitimate political means to further the Arab cause.[59]

Further Arab riots and attacks on Jews broke out in August 1929, killing dozens and injuring hundreds, which were also widely believed to have been inflamed by al-Husseini, while the British police held back from intervening.[60] Following these riots, violence and political terrorism became persistent, normal features of life in Palestine, targeted at both Arabs and Jews and, from the early 1930s on, the British themselves, as they continued to sponsor further waves of Jewish immigration into Palestine.

In 1931, al-Husseini convened an Islamic Congress in Jerusalem and travelled widely in the Muslim world, raising funds and building support, always under overall British protection.[61] By the mid-1930s, after Hitler's assumption of power in Germany, Jewish immigration rose again, and by this time a significant Palestinian protest movement had developed, promoting a general strike in 1936 and a wave of further strikes, boycotts and violence. For three years, a full-blown rebellion – the first Palestinian intifada (uprising) – raged, challenging a British army of over 50,000 in the country. Around 10–15,000 Arab rebel fighters took control of much of the countryside and occupied many of the urban centres, an episode that figures little in British history books but which was brutally suppressed by British forces, with mass arrests, shootings, indiscriminate killings, the destruction of hundreds of houses, collective punishment and the internment of thousands without trial.[62] Al-Husseini, realising a turning point had been reached, and wanting to maintain himself as mufti, eventually turned towards championing and leading the rebellion and adopted a completely anti-British stance. In so doing, he now became *persona non grata* to the authorities, who dismissed him as president of the Supreme Muslim Council. After supporting al-Husseini for fifteen years, the British authorities now even forbade any official mention of his name and circulation of his picture.[63] He escaped to Lebanon in 1937, from where he continued to lead the Palestinian uprising.

By 1939, however, the prospect of war with Germany was looming and the British perceived the need to maintain good relations with the Arab states and to try to appease the Palestinians. Prime Minister Neville Chamberlain told a Cabinet meeting in April 1939 that it was of 'immense importance ... to have the Moslem world with us' and that 'if we must offend one side let us offend the Jews rather than the Arabs.'[64] Thus after brutally defeating the rebellion, the British government enacted a White Paper in May 1939, which gave in to many Arab demands and restricted Jewish immigration into Palestine, giving the Arabs an ability to prevent the emergence of a Jewish majority. This policy, widely interpreted as repudiating the Balfour Declaration, embittered Jews everywhere and would lead to Jewish confrontation with the British after the war.

Two years after the crushing of the intifada, al-Husseini fled to Iraq, where in April 1941 he helped orchestrate an anti-Jewish pogrom that left over 400 Iraqi Jews dead during a Nazi-backed military coup against the pro-British government.[65] The mufti called for a holy war against the British but the Iraqi coup collapsed after a British military intervention re-instated a pro-British government. Al-Husseini now fled again, this time to Berlin, where he met Hitler and other leading Nazi officials, developing a close relationship with SS chief, Heinrich Himmler. The mufti had long supported the Nazis, based on his anti-semitism and a desire to secure their support in Palestine; some German aid had been sent to the Palestinians during the intifada. Al-Husseini now helped the Nazis recruit Muslims from the Balkans to be formed into a variety of Muslim SS Divisions in Eastern Europe. With hundreds of thousands of Muslim soldiers in the Nazi war machine, Himmler adopted a policy of using Islam as a bulwark against Nazi enemies – orthodox Serbia and Russia: the strategy was an echo of the British use of Islam against the Bolsheviks and would be repeated by the British and Americans against nationalists in Bosnia and Kosovo in the 1990s.[66]

At the end of the war, al-Husseini escaped from Germany, possibly with the help of the Allies, and was put under house arrest in France by the French authorities.[67] He then escaped to Egypt, where he was given political asylum by King Farouk's pro-British regime after appeals on his behalf by the Muslim Brotherhood.[68]

Requests to the British by Jewish groups to have him indicted as a war criminal were rejected by London for fear that moves against the still popular al-Husseini would increase unrest against the British presence in Egypt. Indeed, in 1946, al-Husseini began to work for the British once more, with sources suggesting that he was employed by the Arab News Agency, an MI6 front established in Cairo to spread British propaganda in the region.[69] Thus, nearly a quarter of a century after first collaborating with al-Husseini, Britain was still prepared to regard the mufti as an instrument of British policy, despite his role in the intervening period in leading the rebellion in Palestine and collaborating with the Nazis. This expedience in British policy, sketchy though many of the details are, was a precedent for the subsequent more extensive use of Islamists.

EGYPT AND THE MUSLIM BROTHERHOOD DURING THE WAR

The war years witnessed the continuing growth of the Muslim Brotherhood, which developed under Hassan al-Banna's leadership into an Islamist mass movement. It had become the largest Islamic society in Egypt and had set up affiliates in Sudan, Jordan, Syria, Palestine and North Africa. Aiming to establish an Islamic state under the slogan 'The Koran is our constitution', the Brotherhood preached strict observance of the tenets of Islam and offered a religious alternative to both the secular nationalist movements and communist parties in Egypt and the Middle East – forces which were becoming the two major challengers to British, and US, power in the region.

Britain had regarded Egypt as a linchpin of its position in the Middle East ever since it declared a 'protectorate' over the country at the beginning of the First World War. British firms dominated foreign investment and the commercial life of the country, while the British military base in the Suez Canal Zone had become the largest in the world by the time of the Second World War. British dominance of the country was, however, increasingly challenged both by a growing nationalist movement and by the religious forces of the Muslim Brotherhood, while London's ultimate ally in the country was its ruler, King Farouk, who assumed the throne in 1936.

The Brotherhood had called for jihad against Jews in the 1936–9 Arab Revolt in Palestine, and had sent volunteers there after an appeal from the mufti; it had also been assisted by German officers in constructing its military wing.[70] The organisation regarded the British as imperialist oppressors in Egypt, and agitated against the British military occupation of the country, especially after the Palestine rebellion. During the early years of the Second World War, British strategy towards the Brotherhood in Egypt mainly involved attempts to suppress it. Yet at this time the Brotherhood, which was allied to the political right, also enjoyed the patronage of the pro-British Egyptian monarchy, which had begun to fund the Brotherhood in 1940.[71] King Farouk saw the Brothers as a useful counter to the power of the major political party in the country – the secular, nationalist Wafd Party – and the communists. A British intelligence report of 1942 noted that 'the Palace had begun to find the Ikhwan useful and has thrown its aegis over them.'[72] During this time, many Islamic societies in Egypt were sponsored by the authorities to oppose rivals or enhance the interests of the British, the palace or other influential groups.[73]

The first known direct contact between British officials and the Brotherhood came in 1941, at a time when British intelligence regarded the organisation's mass following and sabotage plans against the British as 'the most serious danger to public security' in Egypt.[74] That year al-Banna had been jailed by the Egyptian authorities acting under British pressure, but it was on his release later the same year that the British made contact with the Brotherhood. According to some accounts, British officials offered to aid the organisation, to 'purchase' its support. Theories abound as to whether al-Banna took up or rejected the offer of British support, but considering the relative quiet of the Brotherhood for some time after this period, it is possible that British aid was accepted.[75]

By 1942 Britain had definitely begun to finance the Brotherhood. On 18 May British embassy officials held a meeting with Egyptian Prime Minister Amin Osman Pacha, in which relations with the Muslim Brotherhood were discussed and a number of points were agreed. One was that 'subsidies from the Wafd [Party] to the Ikhwan el Muslimin [Muslim Brotherhood] would be discreetly paid by the [Egyptian] government and they would require some financial assistance in this matter from the [British] Embassy.' In addition, the Egyptian government 'would introduce reliable agents into the Ikhwan to keep a close watch on activities and would let us [the British embassy] have the information obtained from such agents. We, for our part, would keep the government in touch with information obtained from British sources.'[76]

It was also agreed that 'an effort would be made to create a schism in the party by exploiting any differences which might occur between Hassan al-Banna and Ahmed Sukkari,' the two leaders. The British would also hand over to the government a list of Brotherhood members they regarded as dangerous, but there would be no aggressive moves against the organisation. Rather, the strategy decided upon was that of 'killing by kindness'. Al-Banna would be allowed to start a newspaper and publish articles 'supporting democratic principles' – this would be a good way of, as one of the attendants put it, 'helping to disintegrate the Ikhwan'.[77]

The meeting also discussed how the Brotherhood was forming 'sabotage organisations' and spying on behalf of the Nazis.[78] It was described as 'a narrow religious and obscurantist organisation', but one which 'could bring out shock troops in a time of disturbance', including 'suicide squads'. With an estimated 100–200,000 supporters, the Brotherhood was 'implicitly anti-European and in particular anti-British, on account of our exceptional position in

Egypt'; it therefore 'hoped for an Axis victory, which they imagined would make them the dominant political influence in Egypt.'[79]

By 1944, Britain's Political Intelligence Committee was describing the Brotherhood as a potential danger, but with a weak leadership: al-Banna, it felt, was the 'only outstanding personality', without whom 'it might easily crumble away'.[80] This rather dismissive analysis of the Brotherhood would be revised in the years to come, as the British cultivated and collaborated with it in the face of growing anti-colonialism in Egypt.

Thus, by the end of the Second World War Britain already had considerable experience of colluding with Muslim forces to achieve certain objectives, while officials also realised that these same forces were generally opposed to British imperial policy and strategic objectives: they were temporary, ad hoc collaborators to achieve specific goals when Britain lacked other allies or sufficient power of its own to impose its priorities. This policy of British expediency would significantly deepen in the postwar world as the need for collaborators increased in a much more challenging global environment.

CHAPTER 2

Partition in India and Palestine

FOLLOWING THE END of the Second World War, Britain was confronted with three major challenges to its world position: first, the financial drain of the war had left Britain near-bankrupt and suffering a domestic economic crisis; second, Whitehall was losing its hold on the empire and faced increasing nationalist demands for independence in various colonies; third, two new superpowers, the United States and the Soviet Union, had emerged as the primary strategic beneficiaries of the war. However, British planners were desperate to maintain as much of their great power status as possible and to continue to use the resources of the colonies for Britain's own benefit. Initially, they pursued the idea of acting as a 'third force' alongside the two superpowers, a strategy involving the super-exploitation of the colonies to shore up Britain's declining global influence.[1] Yet by the end of the 1940s, as US and Soviet power rose while Britain's continued to diminish, the 'third force' idea was recognised as simply not viable, and Whitehall plumped for a special relationship with the US as its key strategy. This was seen as the best means to retain British power, counter the Soviet Union and organise the postwar global economy according to British and Western commercial interests.

However, Whitehall certainly did not want to rely only on the special relationship to exert its influence, recognising that in some areas of the world Washington sought to replace rather than enhance Britain's influence. British policy-makers wanted to preserve a military capability to intervene unilaterally around the world, and also developed atomic weapons, as much to uphold their global status with the Americans as to deter the Soviets. In key areas of the world where Britain had important military and commercial interests, notably the Middle East and Southeast Asia, the British had to play a delicate balancing act, enlisting US support while not ceding all influence to Washington. The US accepted British pre-eminence in some areas where it did not see itself playing a major role, notably Africa, instead backing ongoing British colonial control.[2] In the Middle East, however, the US had already started to encroach on the British position before the war, with control of oil as the key prize. Active collaboration between London and Washington, both covert and overt, took place alongside an uneasy rivalry as the two aimed to reshape the region to their interests.

The weakness of Britain's postwar position was immediately evident in two territories which had, in different ways, been key to British power in the pre-war world. In both India – the jewel in the empire's crown – and little Palestine – a strategic asset in Britain's dominance in the Middle East – British rule was confronted by popular anti-colonial movements that proved too powerful for Britain to counter. Postwar, a weakened Britain lacked the ability to deploy the overwhelming military force that would have been required to suppress these rebellions and which it had sometimes done in the past. Although Whitehall tried for as long as possible to hold on to India, officials eventually came to the realisation that, as in Palestine, the game was up. Knowing that formal colonial rule would soon be over, British policy-makers sought to salvage what they could for the post-colonial future. Lacking other means of influence, they took advantage of the religious and ethnic divisions in the rebellions in India and Palestine, and in both cases resorted to using Muslim forces to achieve specific objectives. The consequences of this British policy were far-reaching: out of the Palestinian and Indian conflicts emerged new states that would reshape South Asia and the Middle East. Moreover, these states would, in very different ways, contribute profoundly to the development of radical Islam throughout the world.

'KEEP A BIT OF INDIA'

In 1947 the partition of colonial British India into two new states, India and the Muslim state of Pakistan, involved massive population transfer and a bloodbath: up to a million people lost their lives in the communal violence that accompanied partition. Indian nationalists, and a good many others, have constantly charged Britain with having deliberately promoted partition and the creation of Pakistan to secure its strategic interests. A huge amount has been written on this subject, and there remains much debate and controversy. Much of the historical evidence is contradictory, and the issues involved are clearly complex, but there is considerable evidence to support the view that Britain indeed used the 'Muslim card' for its own purposes.

In 1886 a group of northern Indian Muslims, led by the educationalist and social reformer, Sayyid Ahmad Khan, set up the All-India Muhammadan Educational Conference in order to build bridges between Islam and science, and between Muslims and the colonial state. Known as the Aligarh movement, after the city in modern Uttar Pradesh where it was founded, the conference made a point of not supporting the Indian National Congress, the organisation of Indian nationalism – thus endearing itself to colonial officials, who provided it with moral and material support. In 1906, the movement's representatives, largely landowners from the Muslim nobility, asked the viceroy, Lord Minto, for special political representation for Muslims in new provincial legislative councils announced by the British; separate electorates were duly established for Muslims who voted for representatives from their own community, and with extra seats, over and above their proportion of the population, in certain provinces. Minto thus secured the continuing loyalty of the Muslim elite; his wife recorded in her diary that her husband had prevented 'sixty-two million people from joining the ranks of the seditious opposition'.[3] On 20 December the same year the Aligarh movement gave birth to the Muslim League, whose first article was 'to promote among the Mussalmans of India, feelings of loyalty to the British government'. The League was looked on favourably by British officials; then Labour MP and future prime minister, Ramsay Macdonald, wrote in his 1910 book, *The Awakening of India*, that the leaders of the League 'were inspired by certain Anglo-Indian officials, and that these officials pulled wires at Simla [the colonial 'summer capital' in northern India] and in London and of malice aforethought sowed discord between the Hindu and the Mohammedan.'[4]

By the 1930s the idea of a separate 'Pakistan' – meaning 'land of the pure', an acronym of Punjab, Afghan (i.e., the people of the Northwest Frontier province), Kashmir, Sind and Baluchistan – gained ground within the Muslim League. In 1939, the viceroy, Lord Linlithgow, worked with Muslim League leader, Muhammad Ali Jinnah, to try to counter the Congress Party's demand for full Indian independence from British rule and to urge the League to come up with an alternative. Linlithgow told Jinnah in September 1939 that if the Muslim League regarded it as unsuitable for India to become a dominion within the Commonwealth, a major British demand, 'then the escape from the impasse is partition'. When the two met again in March 1940, Linlithgow continued to press Jinnah to produce an alternative to Congress' plan.[5] Linlithgow considered that the demand for a separate Pakistan might give the British some useful leverage over the Hindu nationalists, who feared any break-up of India, and was, as Patrick French notes, 'playing a complex game of political brinkmanship which was to have lasting consequences for the future of Asia'.[6] On 23 March, ten days after this meeting, and backed by the British secretary of state for India, Lord Zetland, the Muslim League adopted the Lahore resolution, declaring as its official policy the establishment of a separate Muslim state in northern India.[7]

Whitehall had long opposed demands for Indian independence of any description, but the popular power of the nationalist movement led by Gandhi, coupled with Britain's weakened postwar position, made the end of the Raj inevitable by the mid-1940s. By then, crucially, the British realised that, post-independence, Indian nationalists would withdraw India from the Commonwealth and deny Britain military and political influence in the region. It was at this point that, much evidence indicates, London sought to detach the northwest part of the country to establish a separate Muslim state. The proposed state of Pakistan was strategically located, bordering Iran, Afghanistan and China, and close to the southernmost areas of the Soviet Union – the site, indeed, of the nineteenth century Great Game. Britain now deliberately set out to partition India to achieve important strategic objectives in the area.[8]

Field Marshall Wavell, the British viceroy in India from 1943, was the principal proponent of partition, realising soon after his arrival that the Congress Party was not interested in post-independence military cooperation with Britain. By 1944, Wavell was determined to build up Jinnah's Muslim League and withdraw British military forces into the strategic northwest, where they would seek to retain their bases. Pakistan, he envisaged, would become a dominion within the Commonwealth; the rest of India would be left to its own devices. Prime Minister Churchill had long rejected any form of Indian independence, but by March 1945, Wavell remarked that Churchill's position was shifting: he 'seems to favour partition of India into Pakistan, Hindustan and Princestan' – Hindustan referring to the Hindu regions of India, and Princestan to the numerous princely states which Britain had long cultivated to ensure colonial control. That August, Churchill, now in opposition following Clement Attlee's landslide Labour election victory in July, had a further meeting with Wavell, who was in London to discuss India with the new ministers. According to Wavell, Churchill left the meeting with the parting words: 'Keep a bit of India'.[9] Thus, although Lord Mountbatten, the last viceroy, has often been blamed for partition by decisions made in

1947, the division of India appears to have already been shaped two years earlier.

Attlee and other ministers also initially opposed partition, holding out for retaining a united India that would cooperate with Britain after independence. When it became obvious that this was never going to happen, Attlee agreed to support partition as long as the Congress Party also acquiesced with this solution – thereby absolving Britain of any responsibility for it. When it became plain that Congress would not support partition, Attlee went ahead anyway, in April 1946 authorising the government to work towards the creation of Pakistan, 'if it seems to be the only chance of an agreed settlement'.[10]

By 1947, the British military chiefs of staff had become enthusiastic proponents of Pakistan, seeing its creation as providing several valuable functions, including obtaining air bases in the new territory and 'to ensure the continued independence and integrity [of] Afghanistan'. 'The area of Pakistan', the chiefs noted, 'is strategically the most important in the continent of India and the majority of our strategic requirements could be met.' Britain would also be able to 'increase our prestige and improve our position throughout the Muslim world, and demonstrate, by the assistance Pakistan would receive, the advantages of links with the British Commonwealth.'[11]

Field Marshall Montgomery, now the chief of the imperial general staff, noted that it would be 'a tremendous asset' if Pakistan remained within the Commonwealth, since 'the bases, airfields and ports in northwest India would be invaluable to Commonwealth defence'. A document in his papers provides a precise analysis of Pakistan's strategic importance, post-independence:

> The Indus Valley, western Punjab and Baluchistan [the northwest] are vital to any strategic plans for the defence of [the] all-important Muslim belt … [and] the oil supplies of the Middle East … If the British Commonwealth and the

> United States of America are to be in a position to defend their vital interests in the Middle East, then the best and most stable area from which to conduct this defence is from Pakistan territory. Pakistan [is] the keystone of the strategic arch of the wide and vulnerable waters of the Indian Ocean.[12]

Patrick French argues that no leading British civil servants favoured the dismemberment of the Indian empire at independence or believed that the creation of Pakistan would be beneficial. He writes that 'the claim that the British had secret plans all along to partition India … cannot be supported from the internal memoranda and documentation of Whitehall officialdom.'[13] However, French's account did not apparently benefit from consulting the documents from the chiefs of staff, which are recounted in the analysis by Narendra Sarila, a former aide-de-camp to Mountbatten. It is true that the British did not 'prefer' to dismember India up to, say, late 1945 or early 1946, and therefore did not have 'secret plans' to partition India all along. Yet by the time it became obvious that Britain would not obtain an agreement on its terms – i.e., a united India which would preserve strong ties with Britain – planners quickly opted to promote a separate Pakistan. The British had long tried to use the Muslim card to exert leverage over the Hindu nationalists, since they had few other means to maintain British power in the face of a popular movement against it – there were no other major political forces to turn to, and overt military intervention was out of the question.

Another key aspect of Britain's policy towards partition concerned the north Indian region of Kashmir, which London wanted annexed to Pakistan. Pakistan invaded and occupied Kashmir in October 1947, and throughout the ensuing border war with India, Britain maintained a strongly pro-Pakistan stance. The Commonwealth secretary noted, five days after Kashmir acceded to India in October, that 'it would have been natural for Kashmir to eventually accede to Pakistan on agreed terms'.[14] At the

UN, Britain lobbied in favour of Kashmir's becoming a Pakistani province, based on the argument that 77 per cent of the population was Muslim. Foreign Secretary Ernest Bevin told US Secretary of State George Marshall that 'the main issue was who would control the main artery leading into Central Asia.' Indeed, Pakistan was, as the then Chancellor of the Exchequer Hugh Dalton put it, central to Bevin's ambition to organise 'the middle of the planet'.[15]

The Times heralded Partition Day, 15 August 1947:

> In the hour of its creation Pakistan emerges as the leading state of the Muslim world. Since the collapse of the Turkish empire that world, which extends across the globe from Morocco to Indonesia, has not included a state whose numbers, natural resources and placc in history gave it undisputed pre-eminence. The gap is now filled. From today Karachi takes rank as a new centre of Muslim cohesion and rallying point of Muslim thought and aspirations.[16]

Two years after partition, its key proponent, Field Marshall Wavell, made an address to the Royal Central Asia Society, outlining the strategic importance of Central Asia and the Persian Gulf. Wavell stated that 'the next great struggle for world power, if it takes place, may well be for the control of these oil reserves.' These regions might be the battleground not only for the material struggle for oil but also 'of the spiritual struggle of at least three great creeds – Christianity, Islam, Communism'. Therefore, 'the Western powers must surely be in the Middle East.'[17]

The partition of India had immediate terrible human consequences. With an estimated 20 million people crossing the new border in both directions, in search of new homes, there was an almost total breakdown in law and order, and massive violence in the border areas. The process created a country that, like Saudi Arabia, would become a perceived strategic asset for Anglo–

American planners. Pakistan would go on to become a 'balance' to neutral, non-aligned India, joining the US-backed Baghdad Pact military alliance in the 1950s and offering the US air base facilities to spy on the Soviet Union. In the 1980s, it was to act as a forward base for intervention in Afghanistan – precisely its utility as seen by British military chiefs over thirty years earlier.

Partition also created a state that had little to bind it together other than an adherence to Islam, and which, under military rulers lacking any other domestic legitimacy, would later propagate extremist versions of Islam and nurture jihadist groups. Kashmir's division between India and Pakistan not only became a constant source of conflict between the two states; Pakistan's Islamist cause to 'liberate' Kashmir from part-Indian control would help advance the jihadist movement far beyond the sub-continent. Thus would Pakistan go on to become an epicentre of Islamic radicalism and, in the present, pose the largest terrorist threat to Britain. While these are complex processes, working over a long time-scale, they can be traced back to the very creation of Pakistan, in which British policy-makers, seeking to promote their own interests, played an important role. Perhaps ironically, clerics of the revivalist Deobandi movement, which would be patronised by Pakistan's later military rulers and would back jihadist forces in Pakistan, largely opposed the creation of Pakistan at the time, arguing that a Muslim national state was not needed to create their Islamic world.[18] Narendra Sarila notes that 'the successful use of religion by the British to fulfil political and strategic objectives in India was replicated by the Americans in building up the Islamic jihadis in Afghanistan', to which we come in Chapter 8. Overall, 'many of the roots of Islamic terrorism sweeping the world today lie buried in the partition of India.'[19]

PARTITION AND WAR IN PALESTINE

While British planners were using Muslim forces to further their interests in India, they were confronted by the outbreak of a Jewish uprising against British rule in their Palestine mandate. This led to a series of momentous events that shape the present-day Middle East: the British decision in February 1947 to withdraw from Palestine, the UN's decree in November 1947 to partition the territory, the Jewish declaration of the state of Israel in May 1948 and the first Arab–Israeli war, in which Israeli forces annexed much of Palestine by December of that year. Like the partition of India, these events remain the subject of intense debate; the focus here is on British policy, first towards the Jewish uprising and then towards the Arab–Israeli war.

Near the end of the Second World War, the leadership of the Yishuv, the Jewish settler community in Palestine, headed by David Ben-Gurion, embarked on a campaign to push the British out of the country. A wave of terrorist attacks was conducted against British forces and Palestinian Arabs, in response to which the British declared martial law, enacted draconian emergency regulations and undertook brutal collective punishments on local Jewish communities. Jewish antagonism towards Britain was shaped partly by London's policy on Jewish immigration from Germany and elsewhere which, in deference to Arab objections, Britain was now trying to restrict. During the last three years of the mandate, 40,000 illegal immigrants succeeded in entering Palestine, but shiploads of Jewish refugees regarded as illegal were intercepted at sea. In 1946 the Royal Navy turned back 17 ships carrying refugees to their ports of origin, while MI6 was instructed to sabotage some of the transport ships while in port.[20] The policy continued throughout 1947, and by December of that year over 51,000 passengers on 35 ships had been intercepted and interned by the British in Cyprus.[21]

By this time, the Attlee government had decided to give up on finding its own solution to the rebellion and had resolved to relinquish the mandate and hand the problem over to the recently-formed United Nations. At a time when Britain was faced with numerous demands on its resources, the Jewish uprising was clearly not going to be overcome quickly or cheaply, and Prime

Minister Attlee regarded Palestine as 'an economic and military liability'.[22] Britain now began to promote the partition of Palestine into Jewish and Arab states, a policy supported by the Jewish leadership but which immediately undermined the interests of the Palestinians, who at the time made up around two-thirds of the population, compared to one-third of Jews.[23] In November 1947, the UN passed General Assembly Resolution 181, partitioning Palestine and awarding the Jews a state that comprised over half the country, against the will of the indigenous majority population.

In his outstanding analysis of the 1948 Arab–Israeli War, Israeli historian Ilan Pappe notes that a month after the UN resolution, the Jewish leadership embarked on the 'ethnic cleansing of Palestine', beginning with a series of attacks on Arab villages following the vandalisation by some Palestinians of buses and shopping centres in protest at the resolution. The same month the Arab League decided to form an Arab volunteer force to 'liberate' Palestine. Known as the Arab Liberation Army (ALA), and consisting of around 5,000 volunteers from Syria, Iraq, Egypt and Jordan, the force began operations in Palestine against Jewish forces in January 1948.[24] As warfare among Jews and Palestinians increased, the Jewish leaders' plans culminated in a meeting in March 1948 which decided on a 'Plan D', the 'systematic expulsion of the Palestinians from vast areas of the country'.[25] When the British withdrew from Palestine in May, the Jewish Agency declared independence and the regular armies of the Arab states invaded Palestine; brutal fighting ensued between an estimated 98,000 Jewish forces and 50,000 Arab forces.[26]

Not all Arab states opposed Israel, however. Transjordan's King Abdullah, the British-backed monarch still reigning after being installed by London a quarter of a century earlier, entered into a tacit alliance with Israel not to join in any pan-Arab military operations against the Jewish state, and to quietly recognise its existence. In return, Abdullah would be permitted to annex most of the areas allocated to the Arabs under the partition resolution, the lands on the West Bank of the river Jordan. This unwritten agreement, reached in January 1948, resulted in the neutralisation of the Arab world's most effective fighting force, the British-backed Arab Legion, based in Transjordan and commanded by the British officer, Sir John Bagot Glubb.[27] In May, the same month that the state of Israel was founded, the British ambassador in Transjordan, Sir Alex Kirkbride, wrote to Foreign Secretary Bevin, reporting that 'there have been negotiations between the Arab Legion and the Hagana [the Jewish paramilitary force] which have been conducted by British officers of the Arab Legion. It is understood that the object of these top secret negotiations is to define the areas of Palestine to be occupied by the two forces.' Bevin replied: 'I am reluctant to do anything that might prejudice the outcome of these negotiations.'[28]

Bevin's response was typical of the line the British were now taking on Israel–Palestine. In late May 1948, the British supported the Arab states in opposing a ceasefire resolution at the UN accepted by the Israelis, who had by now annexed a large amount of Palestinian territory and were content to consolidate their gains. The reason for British policy was the hope that Abdullah's forces would soon capture the West Bank; once it became clear in late May that they had annexed the territory, Britain lifted its opposition to the ceasefire (which later broke down).[29] The formal unification of the two banks of the river Jordan occurred two years later, in April 1950; Britain was one of only two states, along with Yemen, which then recognised the enlargement of Abdullah's kingdom.[30] British support for 'Greater Transjordan', now the Foreign Office's chosen method for solving the Palestine problem, was intended to make Abdullah, London's closest ally in the Arab world, the heir to Arab Palestine. If Britain was not able to maintain its own presence in the region, it aimed to do so by proxy through its client state – a strategy typical of postwar British foreign policy.

As British planners focused on this territorial aim, they became deeply implicated in the Israelis' ethnic cleansing of other parts of Palestine. The British commander in the territory, General Sir Gordon Macmillan, had 50,000 troops in Palestine but was under strict directives from London not to get embroiled in military action against either Arabs or Jews, so long as they did not interfere with Britain's plans for withdrawal.[31] Ilan Pappe notes that the British probably knew of Plan D, and even announced, soon after it began to be implemented, that their forces would not be responsible for law and order in the areas where they were stationed but would simply protect themselves: this meant that huge areas of Palestine, notably the towns of Haifa and Jaffa but also numerous rural villages, could now be taken over by the Israelis without fear of a British response. British forces stood idly by as Israeli forces destroyed Arab villages and forced out their inhabitants.

In April 1948, British forces, which had hitherto acted as a buffer between Jewish and Arab forces in Haifa, the largest port town, announced to the Jewish authorities there that they would be withdrawing. This sent a green light to proceed with the city's 'de-Arabisation', which involved expelling its 75,000 Palestinian residents, and is described by Pappe as 'one of the most shameful chapters in the history of the British empire in the Middle East'. The same fate befell the city of Jaffa, which was taken in May 1948 after a three-week long siege by Israeli forces, who succeeded in expelling the entire population of 50,000 with the 'help' of British mediation. In parts of Jerusalem, the British even disarmed the few Arab residents defending themselves against Jewish attacks on their neighbourhoods.[32] The British also aided Israel's annexation of Palestine in other ways, such as handing over land ownership deeds for villages, which provided vital information to aid the depopulation process.[33]

Yet Britain also provided some support to the other side, though it is unclear if this was a policy set in London or the result of officials' choices on the ground. The Arab Liberation Army was commanded by Fawzi al-Qawqji, a Beirut-born army officer who had fought with the Palestinians against the British in the Arab Revolt of

1936–9. Many of the ALA's volunteers were Muslim Brothers from Egypt, inspired by Hassan al-Banna's call to participate in the Palestinian jihad; many also owed allegiance to the mufti, Haj Amin al-Husseini, the exiled leader of the Palestinians living in Cairo. One of the leaders in the volunteer force was the Egyptian, Said Ramadan, personal secretary to al-Banna, who would later become the chief organiser of the international Muslim Brotherhood and help establish Brotherhood branches around the world.[34] The first batch of up to 2,000 Egyptian Muslim Brothers reached Palestine in April 1948; crossing the Egyptian border they attacked Israeli forces in the Negev Desert.[35] The British-backed Egyptian government's position on the Brotherhood was ambivalent; although supporting the Brothers' infiltration into Palestine, King Farouk proceeded to ban the organisation within Egypt, fearing its revolutionary tendencies. When regular Egyptian troops moved into Palestine in May, they forced the volunteer Muslim Brothers into camps, and gave them the choice of either laying down their arms and returning to Cairo or staying at the front and assisting the Egyptian army, which many subsequently did.[36]

The ALA's activities were being extensively monitored in British intelligence reports.[37] As the British pulled out of Palestine, they handed over many of their arms and forts to Arab forces, who often received notice of impending moves from sympathisers in the Palestine police or the British army. Thus Iraqi volunteers were reportedly inside the Allenby Barracks in southern Jerusalem a week before British forces had given up the camp. In April 1948, the British also handed over three police stations to the ALA in the northern city of Safed, near the Syrian border – an area allocated to the Arabs under the partition plan – which greatly strengthened the Arab forces' position in the face of a Jewish offensive.[38]

British policy vacillated between allowing ALA incursions into Palestine and trying to prevent them, with decisions apparently left to local commanders on the ground.[39] When the ALA made its first attack on Jewish settlements in the Palestinian West Bank in January 1948 the British at first protested to Syria, but this was ignored and ALA incursions intensified.[40] In contrast, Sir Alec Kirkbride persuaded Transjordan's King Abdullah not to allow the transfer of Arab volunteers through his kingdom, fearing they might be used to mount a coup against his regime; in early 1948 Abdullah even sent his army to block the entry into Transjordan of Saudi volunteers trying to get to Palestine.[41]

Although individual British officials sometimes acquiesced in small-scale incursions into Palestine by Arab forces, the British Cabinet decided in February 1948 to oppose a large-scale invasion by Arab states.[42] But the regular Arab armies that did intervene in May after Britain's withdrawal, those of Egypt, Iraq and Jordan, were all commanded by British-backed monarchs and equipped with British arms. Britain declared an arms embargo on both sides fighting in Palestine, which had the effect of crippling the Arab forces by not allowing them to replenish their stocks; at the same time, the newly-formed Israeli army received a large shipment of heavy arms from Czechoslovakia and the Soviet Union in May.[43] This British policy has been interpreted by some analysts as allowing London to control the effectiveness of the Arab armies by supplying or denying them arms at key points.[44] The Egyptian political analyst, Mohamed Heikal, later a key adviser to President Nasser, noted that Britain provided Egypt with enough arms 'to enter the war, but not enough to win'.[45] However, RAF photo-reconnaissance squadrons based in Egypt also mounted numerous clandestine flights over Israel in 1948, photographing Israeli military movements which may have been passed on to the Arab states.[46]

By December 1948, the Palestinian and Arab forces had been defeated and Israeli troops had captured the territory designated to it under the UN partition plan, plus around half of the territory designated for the Arabs. Around half of Palestine's native population, 800,000 people, had been uprooted and over 500 villages destroyed.[47]

Over sixty years on from the first Arab–Israeli conflict, there remains disagreement as to whose 'side' Britain was really on – indeed, whether British policy-makers themselves knew what they were doing in the later chaotic stages of withdrawal from Mandate Palestine. To some analysts, British policy was marked by a mixture of incoherence and indecision.[48] Said Aburish argues that British strategy helped shape the outcome of the war and that the Arab Legion's policy was 'an extension of British policy ... to avoid bitter fighting between the two sides so as to prevent the derailment of common plans to award most of Palestine to the Jews.'[49]

British policy was consistent in some respects, aimed at promoting its major ally in the region, Jordan, which was bent on annexing the West Bank. The official policy of 'non-interference' had the effect of assisting the stronger side, meaning acquiescence in Israel's take-over of most of Palestine and 'ethnic cleansing', which included the 'transfer' of Palestinian Arabs into Jordan. At the same time, however, Britain's support for some Arab military activities was intended to avoid jeopardising relations with its Arab clients and to strengthen British influence in the region after the conflict. Overall, Britain appears to have attempted to establish some kind of 'balance' in the conflict and in the region, to serve ongoing interests. Whitehall's acquiescence in, and sometimes support of, the Arab volunteer forces, which included their Muslim Brotherhood component, can be seen as a lever to help the Arab side achieve this 'balance'. The more overt British 'use' of such Muslim forces would, as we shall see, be stepped up in the 1950s.

THE DILEMMAS OF PAN-ISLAM

In May 1947 Sir Alec Kirkbride, Britain's top diplomat in Amman and one of the architects of British policy in the Arab–Israeli war, had reported to Foreign Secretary Ernest Bevin on a recent visit to Jordan by Abdel Hakeem Abdeen, the secretary general of the Muslim Brotherhood. 'I know a number of the leaders of the local branch' of the Jordanian Brotherhood 'personally', wrote Kirkbride; 'I do not regard them as being politically objectionable.'

On his visit Abdeen was, according to Kirkbride, 'shown marked favour' by Transjordan's King Abdullah. Abdullah told Kirkbride that the Brotherhood was 'praiseworthy in that it recalled the younger generation to their religious duties and obligations and was, therefore, of value in checking the spread of communism to Transjordan.' Kirkbride replied that if the Brotherhood's activities were limited to religious affairs 'there might be a great deal of truth in what the King had said, but it appeared from reports that the motives of the founders of the Brotherhood were as such political as they were religious.' The king agreed to keep the Brotherhood 'on more correct lines' (meaning to keep it out of politics) but that there would be 'no intervention at present'.[50]

By 1949, King Abdullah was proposing to the shah of Persia, the king of Iraq and the president of Turkey the establishment of a pan-Islamic movement, to increase cohesion and cooperation among Muslim states. The idea came to very little, but the response to it by Foreign Office officials is interesting. In October 1949 one official noted that:

> In so far as a modern Panislamic movement is designed to create a common front against Communism it is evident that we should do everything in our power to assist it … I suggest … that a Panislamic movement if properly guided into channels of social reform … can be a boon to the peoples themselves and should offer no threat to the Western world. The fact that such movements in the recent past have had their foundations in xenophobia should not alarm us. If its aims are simply political it will inevitably fail: if it takes the form of a religious revival we must do all we can to direct and help it into the channel of social service; under such conditions it would transcend nationalism and dynastic and other rivalries.[51]

The memo was a response to one from Sir John Troutbeck of the

British Middle East Office in Cairo. Troutbeck had argued that 'we should go very slowly in encouraging this conception' of a pan-Islamic movement. He wrote that although 'its one attraction to us would presumably be that Islamic cooperation might form a bulwark against the spread of communism', the problem would be that 'it would train its biggest guns against Western imperialism, of which we are still regarded as the strongest protagonists.' Therefore, 'I cannot believe that we should find anything more constructive in an association of Muslim countries.'[52]

In a further memo, this time to Ernest Bevin, Troutbeck also argued that the Muslim states were not currently an economic unit, but should they become one, 'the effect on British trade could not fail to be damaging'. Troutbeck ended with a further thought: Christian minorities would become alarmed by Muslim cooperation 'for they know by bitter experience that where two or three Muslims gather together as Muslims, their thoughts are likely to turn sooner or later to the alluring prospect of massacring unbelievers.'[53] Bevin replied to the British embassy in Cairo, saying:

> [The] dangers to which Troutbeck calls attention are very real ones. Nevertheless I feel it would certainly be impossible for us to discourage any move towards greater cooperation between Islamic countries and that provided cooperation were based on a community of practical interests and not on political achievements, it would have valuable results both in increasing confidence of governments concerned and in developing potential wealth of the area.[54]

These memos contained an important theme of British policy towards Islamic forces. They showed that British officials viewed the Muslim Brotherhood and the pan-Islamic movement as useful domestic and international 'bulwarks' against 'communism' (a term understood very broadly by British planners to mean a variety of anti-British forces); but also that, as a united force, pan-Islam would likely challenge British strategic interests. While British officials were, then, prepared to back individual Muslim leaders or groups to achieve specific objectives, as in India and Palestine, they did not regard 'Islam' as a strategic ally, a view that would be consistent throughout the postwar era. This view enabled British collusion with Islamic actors to enter a new phase, as ad hoc partnerships began to deepen with radical forces in covert operations.

CHAPTER 3

Shock Troops in Iran and Egypt

THE EARLY 1950S were a testing time for British planners. They sought to reshape the postwar world to their interests by upholding as much of their former imperial status as possible and by playing second lieutenant to the US, on whom they were increasingly dependent. Their ambitions continued to be confronted, principally by nationalist movements in various countries which espoused independent foreign policies between the superpowers, and domestic economic policies that challenged the dominance of Western companies. Added to this was the Cold War with the Soviet Union, which was now in full swing, and, in the Far East, the ascendant force of Chinese communism following the 1949 revolution. The Attlee government, following President Truman in the US, began a massive rearmament programme in early 1950 to consolidate Western power globally.

Britain continued to conduct various military and covert interventions, the biggest deployments being in the Far East, where thousands of British troops had begun fighting an insurgency in Malaya after the British declaration of a state of emergency in 1948, and in Korea where British forces began a three-year-long campaign following the invasion of the South by the North in June 1950. In October 1952, Britain, with Winston Churchill having succeeded Attlee as prime minister, declared a state of emergency in another colony, Kenya, and fought a brutal war against the

'Mau Mau' nationalist movement demanding the redistribution of the country's unfair land holdings. In 1953, British warships were dispatched to overthrow the democratically elected government of Cheddi Jagan in British Guiana, who principally challenged British commercial interests in the country.[1]

The 'problem of nationalism' was described in a Foreign Office paper of that title in June 1952. It noted the distinction between 'intelligent and satisfied nationalism' and 'exploited and dissatisfied nationalism'; the latter was seen as likely to 'undermine us politically' and challenge Britain's position as a world power. The report observed how this hostile nationalism had five key characteristics, all of which were inimical to British interests:

> (i) insistence on managing their own affairs without the means or ability to do so, including the dismissal of British advisers; (ii) expropriation of British assets; (iii) unilateral denunciation of treaties with the UK; (iv) claims on British possessions; (v) ganging up against the UK (and the Western powers) in the United Nations.[2]

A month after this paper was written, nationalist army officers overthrew the pro-British King Farouk and seized power in Egypt, Britain's major military base in the Middle East and still a de facto colony. The Egyptian Revolution represented the start of a serious challenge to British power in the region and to the traditional Arab elites which administered it by proxy. By this time, British interests were also being threatened in another key Middle Eastern state – Iran, whose parliament voted to nationalise British-controlled oil operations in the country in March 1951, a policy which was implemented by the government of Mohammed Musaddiq in May.

Both Nasser and Musaddiq were recognised by British planners as being 'avowedly anti-communist'. The problem with Nasser was, the Foreign Office stated, that 'the neutralist position [neither support for the West nor the Soviet Union] fits in with the desire of the regime to show that Egypt can stand up to the Western powers on equal terms'[3] – that is, act independently of, and challenge the policies of, the colonial master. Nasser's Egypt became the chief proponent of what was being described by a Foreign Office official as the 'virus of Arab nationalism'.[4] The fear was that the regime would inspire nationalist movements to overthrow British-backed monarchies elsewhere and that it could *unite* the Arabs. Foreign Office officials described 'the essence of the problem' as being that 'Nasser has committed himself to uniting the Arab world and to getting rid of "foreign imperialism".'[5] This fear had long stalked British planners, as when they created, in the aftermath of the First World War, a series of separate states in the region that would remain 'disunited' and under overall Western control.

In response to the challenges posed by Musaddiq and Nasser, Whitehall sought to remove both regimes. Before resorting to the outright invasion of Egypt in 1956, however, Britain took to covert manouvering with Islamist actors within both Egypt and Iran. The forces of the Shia Ayatollah Kashani in Iran and the Muslim Brotherhood in Egypt, although regarded as anti-British and strategic liabilities in promoting Whitehall's long-term interests, were regarded as temporary allies for a Britain desperate to retain postwar influence in the region in the face of its obviously declining power.

WORKING WITH THE AYATOLLAH

The story of the joint MI6/CIA coup in Iran in 1953, which deposed Prime Minister Musaddiq and installed the shah in power as absolute ruler, is well known. In most accounts the CIA is regarded as the prime mover behind the 1953 coup, yet Britain was in fact the initial instigator and provided considerable resources to the operation, accurately known as 'Boot'. One hardly known aspect of the story is the British plotting with leading radical Shia Islamists in Iran, the predecessors of Ayatollah Khomeini.

In the early 1950s the Anglo–Iranian Oil Company (AIOC), or

BP as it is now known, was run from London and owned jointly by the British government and British private citizens. It controlled Iran's main source of income, oil, and by 1951 had become, according to one British official, 'in effect an *imperium in imperio* [an empire within an empire] in Persia'.[6] Iranian nationalists objected to the fact that the AIOC's revenues from oil were greater than the Iranian government's, with company profits amounting to £170 million in 1950 alone. The Iranian government was being paid meagre royalties of between 10 and 12 per cent of the company's income, while the British government received as much as 30 per cent in taxes. Britain's ambassador in Tehran, Sir Francis Shepherd, had a typically colonialist take on the situation: 'It is so important to prevent the Persians from destroying their main source of revenue ... by trying to run it themselves ...The need for Persia is not to run the oil industry for herself (which she cannot do) but to profit from the technical ability of the West.'[7]

Of course Iran was, as it proved (and as the British were surely well aware), perfectly capable of running its own oil industry. In March 1951 the Iranian parliament voted to nationalise oil operations, take control of the AIOC and expropriate its assets. In May, Mohammed Musaddiq, the leader of Iran's social-democratic National Front Party, was elected as prime minister and immediately implemented the bill. Britain responded by withdrawing the AIOC's technicians and announcing a blockade on Iranian oil exports; moreover, it also began planning to overthrow Musaddiq. 'Our policy', a British official later recalled, 'was to get rid of Mossadeq as soon as possible.'[8] Following the well-worn pattern of installing and backing compliant monarchs, the British preference was for 'a non-communist *coup d'état*, preferably in the name of the shah', which 'would mean an authoritarian regime'. The ambassador in Tehran preferred 'a dictator' who 'would carry out the necessary administrative and economic reforms and settle the oil question on reasonable terms' – meaning reversing the nationalisation.[9] The military strongman chosen to preside over the coup was General Zahidi, a figure who had been arrested by the British for pro-Nazi activities during the war.

Despite British propaganda, Musaddiq's government was privately recognised by British officials as generally democratic, popular, nationalist and anti-communist. One difference between the National Front and other political groupings in Iran was that its members were, as Britain's ambassador in Iran privately admitted, 'comparatively free from the taint of having amassed wealth and influence through the improper use of official positions'. Musaddiq had considerable popular support, and as prime minister managed to break the grip over Iranian affairs exercised by the large landowners, wealthy merchants, the army and the civil service. As British planners put it, in typical fashion, Musaddiq was 'regarded by many of the ignorant as a messiah'.[10]

The popular nationalist threat posed by Musaddiq was compounded by his alliance of convenience with the pro-Soviet Iranian communist party – Tudeh. As British and US covert planners met throughout 1952, the former tried to enlist the latter in attempting a joint overthrow of the government by deliberately playing up the scenario of a communist threat to Iran; one British official noted in August 1952 that 'the Americans would be more likely to work with us if they saw the problem as one of containing communism rather than restoring the position of the AIOC'.[11] However, neither the British nor US planning files show that they took seriously the prospect of a communist take-over of the country; rather, both primarily feared the dangerous example that Musaddiq's independent policies presented to Western interests in Iran and elsewhere in the region.[12] By November, an MI6–Foreign Office team was jointly proposing with the CIA the overthrow of the Iranian government. British agents in Iran were provided with radio transmitters to maintain contact with MI6, while the head of the MI6 operation, Christopher Woodhouse, put the CIA in touch with other British contacts in the country. MI6 also began to provide arms to tribal leaders in the north of Iran.

Anglo–American plotting also involved the Islamic clergy. The most important religious figure in Iran was the sixty-five-year-old Shia cleric, Ayatollah Seyyed Kashani. Kashani had helped German agents in Persia in 1944, and a year later had helped found the unofficial Iranian branch of the Muslim Brotherhood, the Fadayan-e-Islam ('Devotees of Islam'), a militant fundamentalist organisation. The Fadayan was involved in a number of terrorist attacks against the shah in the late 1940s, including an assassination attempt in 1949, and killed the shah's prime minister, Ali Razmara, in 1951; around this time, it appears that Kashani broke with the organisation.[13]

By the early 1950s, the Ayatollah had become the speaker in the Iranian parliament, the Majlis, and a key ally of Musaddiq. A US intelligence report noted that, like Musaddiq, Kashani had a large popular appeal and strongly supported the National Front's policies of oil nationalisation, the elimination of British influence in Iran and the 'replacement of the political power of the traditional governing groups by that of the "people" expressed through a "truly national" Majlis'.[14] However, by early 1953 relations between Kashani and Musaddiq became strained, notably over the latter's proposals to extend his powers, and in July of that year Musaddiq dismissed Kashani from the post of speaker. Tensions between Musaddiq and Kashani and other religious supporters of the ruling National Front were further stirred up by two of the principal British agents in the country: the Rashidian brothers, who came from a wealthy family with connections to the Iranian royals. Instrumental in securing the shah's endorsement for the coup, the Rashidians also later acted as go-betweens among army officers distributing weapons to rebellious tribes and other ayatollahs, as well as Kashani.[15]

In February 1953 rioting broke out in Tehran, and pro-Zahedi supporters attacked Musaddiq's residence, calling for the prime minister's blood. MI6 expert, Stephen Dorril, notes that this mob had been financed by Ayatollah Kashani and was acting in collaboration with British agents.[16] Kashani's potential for attracting the Iranian street had been noted by the British Foreign Office, which remarked on his 'considerable following in the bazaar among the older type of shop-keeper, merchant and the like. This is the chief source of his political power and his ability to stage demonstrations'.[17] British pay-offs had secured the cooperation of senior army and police officers, deputies and senators, mullahs, merchants, newspaper editors and elder statesmen, as well as mob leaders. 'These forces', explained MI6 officer Woodhouse, 'were to seize control of Tehran, preferably with the support of the shah but if necessary without it, and to arrest Musaddiq and his ministers.'[18]

The British also operated agents inside the Tudeh Party and were involved in organising 'false flag' attacks on mosques and public figures in the party's name.[19] CIA officer Richard Cottam later observed that the British 'saw the opportunity and sent the people we had under our control into the streets to act as if they were Tudeh. They were more than just provocateurs, they were shock troops, who acted as if they were Tudeh people throwing rocks at mosques and priests.' All this was intended to frighten Iranians into believing that a victory for Musaddiq would be a victory for communism and would mean an increase in Tudeh's political influence.[20]

A secret US history of the coup plan, drawn up by CIA officer Donald Wilber in 1954, and published by the *New York Times* in 2000, relates how:

> CIA agents gave serious attention to alarming the religious leaders at Tehran by issuing black propaganda in the name of the Tudeh Party, threatening these leaders with savage punishment if they opposed Mossadeq. Threatening phone calls were made to some of them, in the name of the Tudeh,

> and one of several planned sham bombings of the houses of these leaders was carried out.[21]

The report refers to this 'campaign of alleged Tudeh terrorism' which involved organising 'gangs of alleged Tudehites on the streets with orders to loot and smash shops … and to make it clear that this was the Tudeh in action.'[22]

British declassified files show that both the British and US governments considered installing Ayatollah Kashani as a client political leader in Iran following the coup. In March 1953 Foreign Office official Alan Rothnie wrote how Foreign Secretary Anthony Eden had discussed with the head of the CIA, General Bedell Smith, the possibility of dealing with Kashani as an alternative to Musaddiq. Rothnie noted that 'they would be glad to learn whether we have any information which would suggest that the United States and United Kingdom could find a *modus vivendi* [way of living] with Kashani once he was in power. They feel that Kashani might be bought, but are doubtful, once he was in power, whether he could be held to a reasonable line.'[23]

The British and US consideration of Kashani as a future leader is itself instructive; yet the answer that came back both from the US State Department and the British Foreign Office was that Kashani would be a liability: he was seen as far too independent. The Foreign Office stated that Kashani 'would be of no use to us, and almost certainly a hindrance, as a successor to Dr Musaddiq, both generally and in an oil settlement.' It regarded him as even more anti-Western than Musaddiq, describing him as 'anti-British' and as nursing a 'bitter enmity towards us' after being arrested for helping the Germans during the war. The Foreign Office termed him 'a complete political reactionary … totally opposed to political reforms'. 'He would conceivably … accept Western money', it noted, but he would not follow 'a reasonable line about an oil settlement'. 'If he came to power it would be impossible to reach a *modus vivendi* with him … We could not count on Kashani giving Persia that minimum of order and stability which is our basic need,' the Foreign Office concluded.[24]

However, written comments appended to this report show other Foreign Office officials pondering 'the idea of Kashani as a stop gap, or a bridge to some more amenable regime'. One official questioned whether Britain should work to replace Musaddiq with Kashani 'before we can expect something better in order to produce the necessary public revulsion'.[25] The British view was that if Kashani could not be entrusted with power, his forces could still be used as shock troops to change the regime. The evidence suggests that British and US support was provided to this 'complete political reactionary' both before and after the report noted above was written, in March 1953. Thus the episode shows how British policy-makers were prepared to work even with completely unreliable – indeed anti-British – forces to achieve immediate objectives against an even greater enemy (in this case, a democratically-elected government). This theme recurs throughout the postwar world, as Britain was later to connive with even more anti-Western forces.

In late June 1953, the US gave the final go-ahead for the coup, setting the date for mid-August. The initial coup plan was thwarted when Musaddiq, having been warned of the plot, possibly by the Tudeh Party, arrested some officials plotting with Zahedi and set up roadblocks in Tehran, causing the shah to panic and flee abroad. In order to trigger a wider uprising, the CIA turned to the clergy and made contact with Kashani via the Rashidian brothers. Footing the bill for this joint Anglo–American operation, the US gave Kashani $10,000 to organise massive demonstrations in central Tehran, together with other ayatollahs who also brought their supporters out onto the streets.[26] Amidst these demonstrations, the shah appointed General Zahidi as prime minister and appealed to the military to come out in support of him. Wider protests developed in which anti-shah activists were beaten up and pro-shah forces, including elements in the military, seized the radio station, army headquarters and Musaddiq's home, forcing the latter to surrender to Zahidi and enabling the shah to return.[27]

The CIA also helped to mobilise militants of the Fadayan-e-Islam in these demonstrations; it is not known if Britain also did. The Fadayan's principal founder and leader, Navab Safavi, is believed to have had associations at the time with Ruhollah Khomeini, a Shia cleric and scholar based at the shrine city of Qom. According to Iranian officials, Khomeini, then a follower of Kashani, was among the MI6/CIA-sponsored crowd protesting against Musaddiq in 1953.[28] Fadayan-e-Islam's members would act as foot soldiers of the Islamic revolution of 1979, helping to implement the wholesale introduction of Islamic law in Iran.[29]

After Musaddiq's overthrow, the British received a report from the new Iraqi ambassador in Tehran, telling how the shah and Zahedi had together visited Kashani, 'kissed his hands, and thanked him for his help in restoring the monarchy'.[30] The shah soon assumed all powers and became the 'dictator' preferred by the British ambassador; the following year a new consortium was established, controlling the production and export of Iranian oil, in which the US and Britain each secured a 40 per cent interest – a sign of the new order, the US having muscled in on a formerly British preserve. Kashani, meanwhile, faded from political view after 1953, but he acted as Khomeini's mentor and the latter was a frequent visitor to Kashani's home. Kashani's death in 1961 would mark the start of Khomeini's long rise to power.[31]

Despite eventual US management of the coup, the British had been the prime movers, and their motives were evident. As a former Iranian ambassador to the UN until the 1979 revolution, Fereydoun Hoveyda, claimed years later:

> The British wanted to keep up their empire and the best way to do that was to divide and rule ... The British were playing all sides. They were dealing with the Muslim Brotherhood in Egypt and the mullahs in Iran, but at the same time they

> were dealing with the army and the royal families ... They had financial deals with the mullahs. They would find the most important ones and would help them ... The British would bring suitcases of cash and give it to these people. For example, people in the bazaar, the wealthy merchants, would each have their own ayatollah that they would finance. And that's what the British were doing.[32]

In her memoirs, written in exile in 1980, the shah's twin sister, Princess Ashraf Pahlavi, who pressed her brother to assume power in 1953, observed that 'many influential clergymen formed alliances with representatives of foreign powers, most often the British, and there was in fact a standing joke in Persia that if you picked up a clergyman's beard, you would see the words "Made in England" stamped on the other side.' Ashraf wrote that after the Second World War, 'with the encouragement of the British, who saw the Mullahs as an effective counterforce to the communists, the elements of the extreme religious right were starting to surface again, after years of being suppressed.'[33]

Although exaggerating with her 'Made in England' claim, Ashraf neatly summed up the British view of the Islamists – that they could be used to counter the threat to British interests. During the 1951–3 coup planning period, Kashani was seen by the British as too much of an anti-Western liability to be a strategic ally. But his forces could be used to prepare the way for the installation of pro-Western figures, and be dropped as soon as their tasks for the imperial powers had been performed.

COLLABORATION WITH THE BROTHERHOOD

At the same time that Britain was sponsoring Kashani in Iran, it was also conniving with Egypt's most powerful radical Islamic force, the Muslim Brotherhood, again to destabilise and overthrow a nationalist enemy. As we saw in Chapter 1, Egypt was a linchpin of Britain's position in the Middle East, with its military base in the Suez Canal Zone the largest in the world; under the terms of the Anglo–Egyptian Treaty of 1936, Britain was allowed to retain the use of the base for twenty years. But British dominance of the country was being challenged by a growing nationalist movement and the Muslim Brotherhood, while London's main ally in the country was its ruler, King Farouk.

British officials, working with the Egyptian Palace, had made their first direct contacts with the Muslim Brotherhood in Egypt in 1941, extending funds to the organisation. After the end of the Second World War, the Brotherhood was one of two mass-based political parties in Egypt, alongside the Wafd Party of moderate nationalists, and King Farouk continued to find the Brotherhood useful as a bulwark against radical economic and social ideas. The Brotherhood is known to have passed information to the government to help in its continual round-ups of real and suspected communists, especially in the unions and universities.[34] It was, however, always an uneasy co-existence amidst increasing opposition to the British presence and a stream of violence which shook Egypt after 1945.

Confrontation soon escalated between the Brotherhood – bent on expelling the foreign 'occupier' and ultimately seeking the establishment of an Islamic state – and the British and the palace. In the Suez Canal Zone, bomb attacks against British troops were common, and the authorities regularly claimed to have uncovered Brotherhood arms caches. The Brothers also attempted various assassinations: between 1945 and 1948, two prime ministers, the chief of police and a Cabinet minister were among those who died at their hands. In December 1948, following the authorities' alleged discovery of Brotherhood arms caches and a plot to overthrow the regime, the organisation was dissolved, a decision the British had apparently requested the Egyptian government to take in order to clamp down on their anti-British activities.[35] Three weeks later, Prime Minister Mahmud al-Nuqrashi, who had given the dissolution order, was assassinated by a member of the Muslim Brotherhood's 'secret apparatus', its paramilitary, and terrorist, unit that carried out bomb attacks against the British in the canal zone.[36]

By January 1949, the British embassy in Cairo was reporting that King Farouk 'is going all out to crush' the Brotherhood, with a recent sweep rounding up and arresting over 100 members. The following month Brotherhood founder Hassan al-Banna himself was assassinated. Although the killer was never found, it was widely believed that the murder had been carried out by members of the political police, and either condoned or planned by the palace. An MI6 report was unequivocal, stating that:

> The murder was inspired by the government, with Palace approval ... It was decided that Hassan el Banna should be eliminated from the scene of his activities in this way since, so long as he was at liberty, he was likely to prove an embarrassment to the government, whereas his arrest would almost certainly have led to further troubles with his followers, who would have no doubt regarded him as a martyr to their cause.[37]

Yet the alibis were already being spun. Three days after the murder, the British ambassador, Sir Ronald Campbell, met King Farouk and recorded that 'I said I thought the murder might have been done by Hassan al-Banna's own extreme followers out of fear or suspicion that he was giving things away'. King Farouk, for his part, also concocted a tale of responsibility lying with the 'Saadists' (a breakaway group from the Wafd Party, named after Saad Zaghoul, a former party leader and prime minister).[38] Britain's senior diplomat in Egypt was clearly conniving with al-Banna's murderers to cover it up.

In October 1951, the Brotherhood elected as its new leader the former judge, Hassan al-Hodeibi, a figure not publicly associated with terrorism, who made known his opposition to the violence of 1945–9. Hodeibi was unable, however, to assert his control over the organisation's sometimes competing factions. The Brotherhood renewed its call for a jihad against the British, calling for attacks on Britons and their property, organised demonstrations against the occupation and tried to push the Egyptian government to declare a state of war with Britain. A British embassy report from Cairo in late 1951 stated that the Brotherhood 'possess[es] a terrorist organisation of long-standing which has never been broken by police action', despite the recent arrests. However, the report otherwise downplayed the Brothers' intentions towards the British, stating that they were 'planning to send terrorists into the Canal Zone' but 'they do not intend to put their organisation as such into action against His Majesty's forces'. Another report noted that although the Brotherhood had been responsible for some attacks against the British, this was probably due to 'indiscipline', and it 'appears to conflict with the policy of the leaders'.[39]

At the same time, in December 1951, the declassified British files show that British officials were trying to arrange a direct meeting with Hodeibi. Several meetings were held with one of his advisers, one Farkhani Bey, about whom little is known, although he was apparently not himself a member of the Brotherhood.[40] The indications from the files are that Brotherhood leaders, despite their public calls for attacks on the British, were perfectly prepared to meet them in private. By this time, the Egyptian government was offering Hodeibi 'enormous bribes' to keep the Brotherhood from engaging in further violence against the regime, according to the Foreign Office.[41]

Then, in July 1952, a group of young nationalist army officers committed to overthrowing the Egyptian monarchy and its British advisers seized power in a coup, and proclaimed themselves the Council for the Revolutionary Command (CRC), with General Muhammad Naguib as chairman and Colonel Gamal Abdel Nasser as vice-chairman. The so-called 'Free Officers' removed the pro-British Farouk and swept aside the old guard, promising an independent foreign policy and widespread internal change, notably land reform. A conflict between Naguib and Nasser gradually led to Naguib's deposition in late 1954 and Nasser's assumption of full power. The Muslim Brotherhood, pleased to see the back of the King's pro-Western regime, initially supported the coup, and indeed had direct links with the Free Officers. One of them, Anwar Sadat, later described his role as the pre-coup intermediary between the Free Officers and Hassan al-Banna. 'He was clearly one of the Free Officers on whose association with them the Brethren counted to help further their political aims,' Britain's ambassador to Cairo, Sir Richard Beaumont, later wrote, after Sadat had succeeded Nasser as president in 1970.[42] The Brotherhood leant the revolutionary leaders important domestic support, and good relations were maintained for the rest of 1952 and throughout most of the following year.

In early 1953, British officials met directly with Hodeibi, ostensibly to sound him out on his position regarding the forthcoming negotiations between Britain and the new Egyptian government on the evacuation of British military forces from Egypt; the twenty-year agreement signed in 1936 was shortly due to expire. Since some of the British files remain censored, it is not known precisely what transpired at these meetings, but Richard Mitchell, the principal Western analyst of the Egyptian Muslim Brotherhood, has documented what the various parties – the British, the Egyptian government and the Brotherhood – subsequently said about them. Mitchell concludes that the Brotherhood's entrance into these negotiations was at the request of the British and presented difficulties for the Egyptian government negotiators, providing 'leverage for the British side'. The British, in seeking out the views of the Muslim Brothers, were in effect recognising their voice in the affairs of the nation, and Hodeibi, in agreeing to the talks, was perpetuating that notion and thus weakening the hand of the government. The Nasser regime condemned the meetings between the British and the Brotherhood as 'secret negotiations ... behind the back of the revolution', and publicly accused British officials of conniving with the Brothers. They also charged Hodeibi with having accepted certain conditions for the British evacuation from Egypt which tied the hands of government negotiators.[43]

From the limited information available, British strategy appears to be traditional divide and rule, aimed at gaining 'leverage' over the new regime in pursuit of its own interests. The British cultivation of the Brotherhood could only heighten tensions between the regime and the Brotherhood and strengthen the latter's position. Internal British memos indicate that British officials told Nasser about some of their meetings with Hodeibi and other members of the Brotherhood, naturally assuring him that London was doing nothing underhand. However, the very fact that they were taking place surely instilled doubt in Nasser's mind over the trustworthiness of the Brotherhood. At this time, British officials believed that the Brotherhood and its paramilitary groups were 'at the disposal of the military authorities' and that the Brotherhood wanted to make the regime pay some kind of price for its support for it, such as introducing an 'Islamic constitution'.[44]

The files also contain a note of a meeting between British and Brotherhood officials on 7 February 1953, in which an individual by the name of Abu Ruqayak told the British embassy's oriental counsellor, Trefor Evans, that 'if Egypt searched throughout the world for a friend she would find none other than Britain'. The British embassy in Cairo interpreted this comment as showing 'the existence of a group within the Brotherhood's leaders who were prepared to cooperate with Britain, even if not with the West (they distrusted American influence).' One handwritten note on this part of the embassy's memo reads: 'The deduction ... seems justified and is surprising.' The memo also notes that the willingness to cooperate 'probably stems from the increasing middle class influence in the Brotherhood, compared with the predominantly popular leadership of the movement in the days of Hassan al-Banna.'[45]

The apparent willingness of the British and the Brotherhood to cooperate with each other would become more important by late 1953, by which time the Nasser regime was accusing the

Brotherhood of resisting land reforms and subverting the army through its 'secret apparatus'. In January 1954, government and Brotherhood supporters clashed at Cairo University; dozens of people were injured and an army jeep was burned. This prompted Nasser to dissolve the organisation. Among the long list of accusations against the Brotherhood in the dissolution decree were the meetings the Brotherhood had held with the British, which the regime later elevated to amounting to a 'secret treaty'.[46]

In October 1954, by which time the Brotherhood was seeking to promote a popular uprising, its 'secret apparatus' attempted to assassinate Nasser while he was giving a speech in Alexandria. Subsequently, hundreds of Brotherhood members were arrested and many tortured, while those who escaped went into foreign exile. In December, six Brothers were hanged. The organisation had been effectively crushed. One of those arrested, and horribly tortured, was Sayyid Qutb, a member of the Brotherhood's Guidance Council, who was sentenced to twenty-five years hard labour, and who would by the 1960s become one of radical Islam's leading theorists, writing from Nasser's jails.

After the failed assassination attempt against Nasser, Prime Minister Winston Churchill sent a personal message to him saying: 'I congratulate you on your escape from the dastardly attack made on your life at Alexandria yesterday evening.'[47] Soon, however, the British were again conspiring with the same people to achieve the same end.

Three years into the new regime, Nasser's domestic reforms included widespread land redistribution benefiting the rural poor, and moves towards enshrining a constitutional form of government to replace arbitrary rule. In July 1955, the outgoing British ambassador to Cairo, Sir Ralph Stevenson, noted that the regime was 'as good as any previous Egyptian government since 1922 and in one respect better than any, in that it is trying to do something for the people of Egypt rather than merely talk about it.' Stevenson argued to Harold Macmillan, foreign secretary in

Anthony Eden's new government, that 'they [the Egyptian leaders] deserve, in my view, all the help that Great Britain can properly give them'.[48] Nine months after this memo was written, the British decided to remove Nasser.

The British and Americans were by now involved in a variety of coup plots against Syria and Saudi Arabia, as well as Egypt, as part of a much bigger planned reorganisation of the Middle East to counter the 'virus of Arab nationalism'. According to a top secret Foreign Office memo, US President Eisenhower described to the British the need for '"a high class Machiavellian plan to achieve a situation in the Middle East favourable to our interests" which could split the Arabs and defeat the aims of our enemies'.[49]

In March 1956 Jordan's King Hussein removed the British General John Bagot Glubb as commander of the Arab Legion, a move which Eden and some British officials put down to Nasser's influence.[50] It was then that the British government concluded that it could no longer work with Nasser and that serious British and US planning to overthrow the regime began; Eden told his new foreign secretary, Anthony Nutting, that he wanted Nasser 'murdered'.[51] This was before the latter's decision to nationalise the Suez Canal in July 1956, an act which 'would inevitably lead to the loss one by one of all our interests and assets in the Middle East,' Eden explained in his memoirs, fearing the possible domino effect of Egypt's action.[52] 'If we allowed Nasser to get away with his Suez Canal coup the consequence would be to put an end … to the monarchy in Saudi Arabia,' explained the permanent under-secretary at the Foreign Office, Ivone Kirkpatrick, fearing that nationalist forces there would be inspired by Nasser's successful defiance of the West in Egypt.[53]

Many British files on the 'Suez crisis' remain censored but some information has crept out over the years on the various British attempts to overthrow or murder Nasser.[54] At least one of these plans involved conniving with the Muslim Brotherhood. Stephen Dorril notes that the former Special Operations Executive agent and Conservative MP, Neil 'Billy' McLean, the secretary of the 'Suez group' of MPs, Julian Amery, and the head of the MI6 station in Geneva, Norman Darbyshire, all made contact with the Brotherhood in Switzerland around this time as part of their clandestine links with the opposition to Nasser.[55] Further details about these Geneva meetings have never emerged, but they may well have involved an assassination attempt or the construction of a government-in-exile to replace Nasser after the Suez War.[56] In September 1956, Ivone Kirkpatrick was in contact with Saudi officials in Geneva who told him of 'considerable underground opposition to Nasser there'; indeed, his fear was that Nasser's take-over of the Suez Canal would 'put an end to the Egyptian resistance', likely to mean the Muslim Brotherhood.[57]

Certainly, British officials were carefully monitoring the anti-regime activities of the Brotherhood, and recognised it as capable of mounting a serious challenge to Nasser. There is also evidence that the British had contacts with the organisation in late 1955, when some Brothers visited King Farouk, now in exile in Italy, to explore cooperation against Nasser. King Hussein's regime in Jordan gave Brotherhood leaders diplomatic passports to facilitate their movements to organise against Nasser, while Saudi Arabia provided funding.[58] The CIA also approved Saudi Arabia's funding of the Muslim Brotherhood to act against Nasser, according to former CIA officer, Robert Baer.[59]

In August 1956, the Egyptian authorities uncovered a British spy ring in the country and arrested four Britons, including James Swinburn, the business manager of the Arab News Agency, the MI6 front based in Cairo. Two British diplomats involved in intelligence-gathering were also expelled. They had, as Dorril notes, apparently been in contact with 'student elements of a religious inclination' with the idea of 'encouraging fundamentalist riots that could provide an excuse for military intervention to protect European lives'.[60]

In October, Britain, in a secret alliance with France and Israel, launched an invasion of Egypt to overthrow Nasser, but was stopped largely by the US refusal to support the intervention. The invasion was undertaken in the British knowledge that the Muslim Brotherhood might become the primary beneficiary and form a post-Nasser government; memos indicate that British officials believed this scenario a 'possibility' or 'likely'.[61] Yet, in an echo of their assessment of Kashani's potential as a leader in Iran, British officials feared that a Muslim Brotherhood takeover would produce 'a still more extreme form of government' in Egypt.[62] Again, this did not stop them working with these forces.

A few months after the British defeat by Nasser, in early 1957, Trefor Evans, the official who led the British contacts with the Brotherhood four years earlier, was writing memos recommending that 'the disappearance of the Nasser regime … should be our main objective'. Other officials noted that the Brotherhood remained active against Nasser both inside and outside Egypt, especially in Jordan, from where a 'vigorous campaign of propaganda' was being mounted.[63] These memoranda suggest that Britain would continue to cooperate with these forces in the near future – and indeed they would, as we see in the following chapter.

In both Iran and Egypt, therefore, Britain was prepared to secretly connive with Islamist forces, using them for imperial ends as part of its arsenal of weapons in covert action. These groups were not considered as *strategic* allies, but rather recognised as avowedly anti-British. What is striking is that Britain resorted to working with these forces in the knowledge that they were even more anti-British than the regimes Whitehall was trying to overthrow. Their utility was their muscle and ability to influence events, acting as shock troops to help a desperate Britain retain some influence in a postwar world where its power was on the wane. The resort to collaborating with forces, however anti-British or however much of an anathema to long-term interests, would recur in later decades, even when avowedly jihadist terrorist groups came into the picture.

CHAPTER 4

Islam Versus Nationalism

The latter half of the 1950s was a period of great flux and convulsion in the Middle East. The dominant conflict was between two contending forces: on the one hand, the secular, nationalist regimes in the region, led by Egypt's Nasser and including Syria, and, after the 1958 revolution that overthrew its pro-British monarch, Iraq; and on the other hand, the Islamic, pro-Western monarchies of Saudi Arabia, Jordan and Gulf states like Oman and Kuwait. Britain scrambled to shore up the latter states in the face of the very real danger that the popular, radical republican ideas, emanating mainly from Cairo, would spread to the oil-rich states, thereby depriving British and US corporations of control over the world's primary commodity, oil.

The Cabinet Office stated in 1959 that Britain's 'special interest' was 'continued control of sources of oil with consequential profits to United Kingdom.'[1] British oil companies, mainly BP and Shell, produced around one-sixth of the world's oil, mainly in the Gulf, where they had large stakes in Kuwait and Iran, and handled over one-third of the international oil trade. The companies contributed £150 million a year to Britain's balance of payments and made £100 million in profits. The major threat to British oil interests was not a complete cessation in supplies but if the companies 'were denied management of crude production and the profits arising from this which at present account for the great bulk of their total profits'; in this situation, the companies would become 'merely merchants in Middle East oil'. 'With full control over the oil at source passing to the local governments', the Cabinet Office noted, 'the West would have nothing like the same assurance of uninterrupted supplies, reasonable prices or continued development on the scale needed to meet future demand.'[2]

A particular and longstanding British concern was to keep the Middle East divided and ensure that no single power dominated the region's oil resources. As the head of the Eastern Department of the Foreign Office put it in 1958:

> Our interest lies in keeping Kuwait independent and separate, if we possibly can, in line with the idea of maintaining the four principal oil producing areas [Saudi Arabia, Kuwait, Iran and Iraq] under separate political control.[3]

The following year, Foreign Secretary Selwyn Lloyd wrote that 'the irreducible interest of the United Kingdom in Kuwait is that Kuwait shall remain an independent state having an oil policy conducted by a government independent of other Middle Eastern producers.'[4] Aside from oil, British policy-makers in 1957 highlighted four other 'essential interests overseas', which were 'maintenance of our position as a world power, the strength of sterling, ensuring continued United States participation in world affairs, the importance of our trade'.[5]

Covert actions were stepped up against nationalist forces, and Britain resorted to a tried-and-tested method of imposing its will: invasion. The failed British invasion of Egypt in 1956 was followed the next year by a military intervention in Oman, to defend the repressive sultan's regime against a popular rebellion. In 1958, the British deployed a military force to Jordan at the same time as a US intervention in Lebanon; both were intended to stave off the possibility of further nationalist upheavals following the revolution in Iraq.

The nationalist challenge to British interests was rooted in the desire of people in the Middle East, long ruled formally or informally by foreigners, to control their own resources and to become truly independent. The demand went well beyond the Middle East, as Britain was forced to preside over processes of 'decolonisation' in numerous countries, especially in Africa. In some cases, London continued to fight brutal wars against essentially nationalist movements, notably in Kenya and Malaya, where opposition forces which took to military operations against British rule were depicted simply as terrorists in increasingly sophisticated government propaganda operations. In Indonesia, as we see later in this chapter, Britain went on the offensive against a leading nationalist regime by providing covert backing to a secessionist rebellion with an Islamist component.

In the Middle East, Britain and the US opted to stem the spread of secular nationalism by buttressing the region's most conservative state: Saudi Arabia.

'THE GREAT GOOKETY GOOK OF THE MUSLIM WORLD'

When Nasser expelled the Muslim Brothers from Egypt in the clampdown in 1954 many found refuge in Saudi Arabia, whither their evacuation was helped by the CIA.[6] Welcomed by the Saudi ruling family, the Brothers' conservative, right-wing credentials allowed them to integrate quickly into Saudi society, some rising to positions of influence in banking and Islamic education. The Egyptian Brothers were soon joined by Syrians and Iraqis on the run from the nationalist regimes which had seized power in those countries during the wave of upheavals. In Europe, too, exiled Brothers began setting up networks, forming an international branch in Munich, directed by Said Ramadan.[7]

Having previously only funded the Brotherhood, Saudi Arabia now became one of the chief bases for its developing international influence. The Saudi royal family was bitterly opposed to Arab nationalism, seeing popular forces elsewhere in the Middle East as a challenge to its continued rule and the Muslim Brotherhood as a conservative, religious counter to the nationalists. Ray Close, a former CIA station chief in Riyadh, states that 'the Saudis were very tolerant of the Muslim Brotherhood and they encouraged it in Egypt, Sudan and elsewhere, but they were adamantly opposed to [Brotherhood] activity inside Saudi Arabia.'[8]

By the late 1950s, the CIA was also starting to fund the Brotherhood; it is alleged that, in conjunction with the US oil company Aramco and the Saudi authorities, the CIA sponsored the creation of small religious cells in Saudi Arabia opposed to Arab nationalism.[9] Recollecting the events of those years, a British ambassador to Saudi Arabia, Willie Morris, later wrote that 'around 1956, President Eisenhower had one of his rare political ideas and thought that King Saud might be built up as … "the great gookety gook" of the Muslim world', to rival Nasser in Egypt.[10] Eisenhower similarly wrote in his memoirs:

> A fundamental factor in the problem is the growing ambition of Nasser, the sense of power he has gained out of his association with the Soviets, his belief that he can emerge as a true leader of the entire Arab world … to check any movement in this direction we wanted to explore the possibilities of building up King Saud as a counterweight to Nasser … [Saud was] the man we had hoped might eventually rival Nasser as an Arab leader … Arabia is a country that contains the Holy Places of the Moslem world, and the Saudi Arabians are considered to be the most deeply religious of all the Arab groups. Consequently the King could be built up, possibly as a spiritual leader. Once this was accomplished, we might begin to urge his right to political leadership.[11]

London's relationship with Saudi Arabia at this time was by no means smooth. After the invasion of Egypt in 1956, the Saudis had broken off diplomatic relations. These had, however, been deteriorating for some years following an Anglo–Saudi dispute over an oasis, Buraimi, which was located in an undemarcated area claimed by Oman, Abu Dhabi and Saudi Arabia. In September 1952, a Saudi force, supported logistically by Aramco, had seized one of the villages in the area, but in 1955 the British retook the territory, following which deadlock ensued and a protracted arbitration process began. The dispute was to bedevil British–Saudi relations until diplomatic relations were restored in 1963. King Saud was also personally regarded by the British as somewhat of a liability, Britain's ambassador to Saudi Arabia later remarking that 'he seems to have had no idea that money should be spent for other purposes than his personal whims or that there was any limit to the amount that would be forthcoming'.[12]

Thus Britain's attempts to preserve its interests across the region did not always square neatly with the US–Saudi axis. Meeting Eisenhower in February 1956, Prime Minister Anthony Eden complained that Saudi money was being used 'not only against us but against Iraq', where the pro-British monarch, King Faisal, still ruled. Eden also passed on to Eisenhower, Lebanese President Chamoun's warning about the 'evil influence of the Saudi money all over the Middle East'.[13] MI6 officers are believed to have proposed to the CIA to 'undertake efforts to exploit splits in [the Saudi] royal family and possibly utilise their position [in the] Trucial states [the Gulf sheikdoms] to hasten the fall of [King] Saud.'[14] Whether these efforts were approved is not known, but is unlikely in light of Eisenhower's policy of building up Saud, in which London appears to have acquiesced as its own relations with the Saudis gradually improved.

By the late 1950s the British had become reconciled to the rise of US-supported Saudi power, since London had no other option and since it was becoming more aware of the Saudis' usefulness as an Anglo–American proxy for covert operations in the region. In 1958, the Saudis are alleged to have bribed Syrian army officers to the tune of £2 million to shoot down Nasser's plane as it was arriving in Damascus – the plot was exposed and Nasser subsequently brandished a cheque to the media.[15] According to Nasser's adviser, Mohamed Heikal, the Saudis also paid Jordan's King Hussein £5 million in 1961 to fund a Bedouin plot to assassinate Nasser in Damascus.[16] It is not known if London or Washington were involved in these plots; but they would surely have welcomed them.

THE BROTHERHOOD'S UTILITY IN SYRIA

Anglo–American plans to counter Arab nationalism took other forms than building up the Saudis. In 1956–7 there were at least two Anglo–American plots which planned to overthrow governments in Syria; although neither was ultimately carried out, the planning behind them illustrates Anglo–American willingness to work again with the Muslim Brotherhood.

The problem for Britain in Syria was that, following a series of military coups since the late 1940s, a succession of governments included officials of the nationalist Baath Party, who supported Nasser's anti-imperial policies and promoted close relations with Moscow. In February 1956, the Foreign Office's Levant department tersely summarised the situation: 'Governments [in Syria] are unstable; the army is deeply engaged in politics and increasingly under the influence of the extreme left; and there is much communist penetration. The Syrians have just concluded a considerable arms deal with the Soviet bloc. There is every reason to try and save Syria before it is too late.'[17] But, the same report acknowledged, overt action by Britain would be a dangerous move 'because of Arab nationalist reactions, international repercussions and the possible strengthening in Syria of those elements who are against us.' The Foreign Office's preference was therefore to enlist Iraq, 'a brother Arab', to the task of 'winning Syria to our camp'.[18]

The following month, the British Cabinet agreed that a serious attempt should be made to establish a more pro-Western Syrian government – to 'swing Syria on to the right path', as Britain's ambassador in Baghdad, Michael Wright, put it.[19] Working in conjunction with the US, 'Operation Straggle' was an ambitious plot to promote a coup in Damascus. As MI6's deputy director, George Young, described it: 'Turkey would create border incidents; the Iraqis would stir up the desert tribes and the Parti Populaire Syrien in Lebanon would infiltrate the borders until mass confusion justified the use of invading Iraqi troops.' The British ambassador in Damascus, Sir John Gardener, also wanted to provide funds to the anti-Left Arab Liberation Party to stifle moves to create a union between Egypt and Syria.[20] An additional feature of the British plotting was to 'attach Syria to the Iraqi state', Foreign Secretary Selwyn Lloyd told Anthony Eden. This should not be attempted now, Lloyd stated, but 'we may want to go further at a later stage in connection with the development of the fertile crescent'.[21]

As well as approaching tribes along the Syria–Iraq border, Operation Straggle involved trying to enlist the Muslim Brotherhood in creating unrest in the country.[22] British officials were well aware of the rising political power of the Syrian Brotherhood; in December 1954, Gardener told Anthony Eden, then foreign secretary, of 'monster demonstrations arranged by the Muslim Brotherhood in Syria', which took place after Egypt's clampdown against the movement. Another official noted that 'the Brotherhood have succeeded in a comparatively short time in establishing an influential position in Syria.' But the effects of this were not positive to British interests since they would 'only … increase existing tendencies to nationalism and anti-Western feeling.'[23] Thus, once again, similar to policy in Iran and Egypt, Britain was covertly conniving with Islamist forces to achieve a specific objective while recognising them as being detrimental to long-term British interests.

Operation Straggle, which had involved months of planning, was eventually foiled in October 1956 by the Syrian authorities, who arrested some of the main conspirators.[24] But British plotting with the Americans against Syria resumed soon after the failed invasion of Egypt, and by September 1957 a report entitled the 'Preferred Plan' was circulated by a secret working group meeting in Washington. The planning was boosted by the Syrian government's signing of a technical aid agreement with the Soviet Union and the appointment of a pro-communist figure as army chief of staff. Despite the misgivings about the Muslim Brotherhood, this new plan once again involved soliciting them and stirring them up in Damascus; the Brotherhood's involvement would be key to provoking an internal uprising as a prelude to the Syrian government's overthrow. Backed at the highest level in Britain, the plot envisaged arming 'political factions with paramilitary or other actionist capabilities' – which is likely to have included the Muslim Brotherhood.[25]

The Preferred Plan, carried out in coordination with the Iraqi, Jordanian and Lebanese intelligence services, again aimed at stirring up the tribes on the Syria–Iraq border and also the Druze community in the south of the country, as well as utilising Syrian MI6 agents working inside the Baath Party. The plan read: 'CIA is prepared and SIS [Secret Intelligence Service or MI6] will attempt to mount minor sabotage and *coup de main* incidents within Syria, working through contacts with individuals.' Also, 'CIA and SIS should use their capabilities in both the psychological and action fields to augment tension' in Jordan, Iraq and Lebanon. The plan also incorporated another typical feature of British agitation: violent 'false flag' operations, blame for which would be pinned on official enemies, which had proved successful in removing Musaddiq from power in Iran. Thus staged frontier incidents and border clashes would provide a pretext for Iraqi and Jordanian military intervention. Syria had 'to be made to appear as the sponsor of plots, sabotage and violence directed against neighbouring governments.' This meant operations taking the form of 'sabotage, national conspiracies and various strong-arm activities' – to be blamed on Damascus.[26]

The Anglo–American plan also involved Prime Minister Harold Macmillan authorising the assassination of key Syrian officials. 'A special effort should be made to eliminate certain key individuals', the plan read, continuing, 'Their removal should be accomplished early in the course of the uprising and intervention and in the light of circumstances existing at the time.' The head of Syrian military intelligence, the chief of the Syrian general staff and the leader of the Syrian Communist Party were all approved as targets.[27] Yet in the end the 1957 plan never went ahead, mainly because Syria's Arab neighbours could not be persuaded to take action. The plan was ditched in early October in favour of a strategy of 'containment plus', which involved enlisting pro-Western Arab states and exiled opposition groups to maintain pressure against Syria.[28]

SIDING WITH THE BROTHERHOOD IN JORDAN

By now, another crisis had developed in another key country; here, the Muslim Brotherhood would also prove useful. In April 1957, a head-on clash developed between the twenty-two-year-old King Hussein of Jordan – a pillar of Western influence in the region since the assassination of his father, Abdullah, in 1952 – and the pro-Nasser socialist government under Prime Minister Suleiman Nabulsi, which had been freely elected the previous October. Nabulsi's plan was to align Jordan with Syria and Egypt, thereby breaking Jordan's long-standing dependence on the West. In response, the CIA engaged in plots to sow disagreement between Nabulsi and Hussein and to discredit Nabulsi and Nasser in order to provide a pretext for Hussein to act against his prime minister.[29]

On 10 April, the King dismissed the government and appointed a puppet regime under his control, banning all political parties and introducing martial law. This palace coup was supported by what was now a familiar combination of conservative forces in the region: the Saudis, the British and the Americans – and the Muslim Brotherhood. The CIA helped Hussein plan his coup and subsequently began funding him.[30] Saudi leaders Faisal and Saud sent 6,000 troops in support of the king, deploying them in the Jordan Valley and Aqaba areas, and promised Hussein 'unqualified support'.[31]

The British ambassador in Amman, Charles Johnston, reported that the Muslim Brotherhood in Jordan 'remained faithful to His Majesty'.[32] Although all political parties were outlawed, Hussein allowed the Brotherhood to continue to operate, ostensibly because of its religious vocation, but in reality because it was seen by the king and his allies as the most effective counterweight to the secular leftists.[33] Brotherhood preachers called upon their supporters to assist the authorities in searching for communist supporters of the government and turn them in, while Brotherhood members in Jericho are believed to have been provided with arms by Hussein's regime to help it intimidate the leftist opposition. Johnston later wrote that 'the Muslim Brotherhood was useful to King Hussein in April as representing a "strong arm" organisation which could if necessary have taken on the Left Wing extremists in the streets.'[34]

Britain extended support to Hussein's new puppet government but was under no illusions as to its nature. The regime was, reported Johnston to Foreign Secretary Selwyn Lloyd, 'frankly repressive', and 'has much in common with Franco's Spain. It is buttressed by *qadis* [Islamic judges] and muftis instead of by cardinals and bishops.' Crucially, however, 'the Jordanian regime happens to be pro-British':

> I suggest that our interest is better suited by an authoritarian regime which maintains stability and the Western connection than by an untrammeled democracy which rushes downhill towards communism and chaos. There is also something to be said for an honestly authoritarian regime such as now exists in Jordan, in comparison with the odious hypocrisy perpetrated in Colonel Nasser's 'parliamentary elections'.[35]

This was a neat summary of Britain's preference for repressive regimes backed by the Islamic right, rather than more popular or democratic governments – a permanent feature of British policy in the region, past and present, that helps explain the regular resort to connivance with Islamist forces. This preference also came with the full knowledge that the October 1956 elections won by Nabulsi 'were the first approximately free ones in the history of Jordan'.[36] The British were also perfectly aware that King Hussein had little domestic support other than from the Muslim Brotherhood, and had always owed his position to British preparedness to prop him up. Earlier in 1957, Anthony Eden had understood that 'if Her Majesty's Government withdrew their support, it was only a question of time before the kingdom of Jordan disintegrated'[37] – by which Eden surely meant that the pro-Western regime, rather than the country, would disintegrate.

But while the Brotherhood could be useful to the Jordanian regime, it continued to be seen by British officials as basically an anti-Western, anti-British force; the same view as the British had of the Brothers in Syria and Egypt. The British embassy in Amman had noted in early 1957 that the Brotherhood's increasing activity was 'disturbing' and that its official publication – *Al-Kifah al-Islami* (the Islamic Struggle) – was identifying the British and the Christians of Jordan as the organisation's two principal targets.[38] One Foreign Office official noted that extremists in the Brotherhood had been strengthened by the October 1956 elections and that this did not bode well 'for what remains of British influence in Jordan'. Charles Johnston reported to the Foreign Office in February 1957 that 'the Jordanian Moslem Brotherhood organisation is led by a group of parochially-minded local fanatics and its following is mostly illiterate'; but it did have the virtue of being 'opposed to the powerful left-wing parties' and, as well as attacking the British and the Americans, also attacked communism.[39]

British fears of the Brotherhood proved well-founded since, within a few months of the April crisis, it withdrew its support for Hussein's new government. The reason, according to the British ambassador, was that the Brothers regarded the regime as 'too completely sold to the Americans'. But the organisation's break with the regime 'need not I think cause undue concern', he added, since the Brotherhood 'will not be an easy object for Russian, Syrian or even Egyptian propaganda'.[40] Thus Johnston was saying that although the Brotherhood was anti-Western, it was also opposed to communism and nationalism, Britain's two principal enemies.

In July 1958 the British position in the Middle East took a more decisive blow when a popular revolution overthrew the monarchy in Iraq, which had ruled since its installation by the British in 1921. The revolution, from which Brigadier Abdul Karim Qasim emerged as leader, sent shockwaves through London and Washington, which feared that nationalist fervour would overthrow King Hussein and other pro-Western monarchies. In a joint operation, British forces were immediately dispatched to Jordan and US forces to Lebanon to offset the danger. Foreign Secretary Selwyn Lloyd wrote that the British intervention in Jordan 'would serve the double purpose of stiffening the King's resolve and forming a bridgehead for such possible future action as may be necessary in Iraq', thus showing that an invasion of Iraq was also being considered.[41] In fact, Britain also drew up plans for possible military intervention to shore up other pro-British governments in Kuwait, Libya and Sudan.[42]

King Hussein's call for British intervention in Jordan provoked a critical response from the Jordanian Muslim Brotherhood, which organised anti-British demonstrations in Amman. In response, Hussein's regime arrested Brotherhood leader Abdal Rahman Khalifa (releasing him three months later) and continued to curb the organisation's political activities.[43] The episode showed that, while the Brotherhood could be useful in providing support to reactionary pro-British regimes in times of crisis, as in 1957, it was a liability when it came to Western intervention in the region.

A COVERT ALLIANCE IN INDONESIA

It was not only in the Middle East that British and American planners were busy siding with radical Islamic elements against nationalist governments. Since the end of the Second World War Indonesia, the world's most populous Muslim nation, had been led by Ahmed Sukarno, a nationalist who, in 1955, had played a key role with Nasser, India's Jawaharlal Nehru and Ghana's Kwame Nkrumah in founding the Non-Aligned Movement: this committed twenty-nine states, representing over half the world's population, to opposing imperialism and membership of any great power bloc. By the mid-1950s, Sukarno's domestic and foreign policies were presenting distinct worries to planners in London and Washington. They watched the growing popularity of the PKI, the Indonesian Communist Party, and its influence on the Sukarno government with great concern. Following the government's nationalisation of Dutch commercial interests, the Foreign Office wrote that 'clearly a serious blow has been struk [sic] at the confidence of all foreign concerns trading in and with Indonesia.' The latter 'is a country with a vast population and great potential wealth, and one in which United Kingdom interests are by no means negligible.'[44] Britain wanted to ensure that Indonesia, a strategically important country with vast mineral resources, did not further threaten Western trading interests or slide further towards communism.

By late 1957 dissident army colonels in Indonesia's outlying provinces were stirring up opposition to what they regarded as Jakarta's centralised and autocratic rule that exploited the richer provinces for the benefit of the Javanese, and were demanding greater local autonomy. By the end of the year, the government's authority did not spread much beyond Java and the northeastern area of Sumatra; elsewhere, local commanders had taken de facto control of their provinces. In January 1958 opposition forces in Sumatra and Celebes broke out in open rebellion against Jakarta, and the following month, in the Sumatran city of Padang, the rebels proclaimed a Republic of Indonesia. In response, the Jakarta government launched a military counter-attack, and by June of that year it had virtually succeeded in crushing the rebellion. Padang was recaptured and the dissidents, although still in control of large areas of Sumatra, were forced to resort to guerilla warfare.

The US managed a covert operation to support the rebellion in its early phase, with a considerable role also played by Britain. US covert planning had begun in 1957, with the authorisation of $10 million in funding, and support to the colonels was first provided in the autumn as US submarines and aircraft began ferrying covert shipments of arms from the Philippines, Taiwan and Thailand.[45] A prime mover on the British side was Sir Robert Scott, Britain's commissioner general in Singapore, who, in December 1957, lamented 'the effects of the developing crisis in Indonesia in terms of dislocation of economic interests' and that Indonesia 'may pass under communist control'. Referring to the 'anti-communist elements in Sumatra and the other outlying provinces', he told the Foreign Office:

> I think the time has come to plan secretly with the Australians and Americans how best to give these elements the aid they need. This is a bold policy, carrying considerable risks ... The action I am recommending will no doubt have little influence with President Soekarno. They are not designed to; I believe it should be one of our aims to bring about his downfall.

Scott's aims were 'to limit the mischief the communists can do in Java, to save Sumatra' and 'to win complete American cooperation both public and private'. Maintaining the unity of Indonesia, however, was also seen as imperative.[46]

In February 1958, top secret discussions took place in Washington between British, US and Australian officials. These, the Foreign Office noted, 'have revealed substantial agreement on the main lines of Western policy' in Indonesia. The three states agreed to 'discreetly support and attempt to unite anti-communist elements in Java' and 'respond where practicable to requests for help from the dissident provincial administrations'.[47] The covert operation was stepped up and, according to a comprehensive study by Audrey and George Kahin, the US supplied enough arms for 8,000 men while the CIA recruited around 350 US, Filipino and nationalist Chinese to service and fly a small fleet of transport aircraft and fifteen B-26 bombers. This air force conducted numerous bombing raids on cities and civilian shipping in support of the rebellion.[48]

The British government envisaged that ideally Sukarno would be overthrown, but, in any case, the rebels had what Foreign Secretary Selwyn Lloyd called a 'nuisance value', that is, an ability to act as a lever to influence Jakarta's policies.[49] Britain covertly provided a small quantity of arms to the rebels, while British warplanes flew reconnaissance missions over Sumatra and eastern Indonesia. When Indonesian government forces attacked a rebel position off Celebes, a British submarine was also seen, apparently rescuing US paramilitary advisers as the position collapsed. However, Britain's major role in the operation was to make available to the US its military bases in Malaya and Singapore, then still colonies; the Singapore base, for example, was used as a staging post for covert US arms drops to the rebels.

Significantly, the rebellion had an important Islamist element that was exploited and supported by Washington and London, as a radical insurgent group played a key role in the rebellion and the formation of the rebel government.[50] One of the dissident colonels supported by the British and Americans was Ahmad Hussein, a regimental commander who had taken over government in West Sumatra in December 1956. Hussein chaired the counter-government deliberations and personally declared the rebel republic in February 1958; he was also recognised by the State Department as being close to the 'fanatical Darul Islam'.[51] The Darul Islam (House of Islam) movement had been established by Muslim militias during the Japanese occupation in 1942 and was led by Sekarmadji Kartosuwirjo, a Muslim politician-turned-cleric. Since 1948, Darul Islam had held control over substantial areas of central West Java and had proclaimed an Islamic state there, recognising only sharia law, and setting itself up as an alternative to Sukarno's Indonesian republic. Other Darul Islam-associated rebellions against Sukarno's rule had broken out in the early 1950s, in provinces such as Aceh, South Sulawesi and South Kalimantan (Borneo). Darul Islam leaders had met in 1953 and formed a united front to proclaim the Islamic State of Indonesia, whose first imam was Kartosuwirjo.[52]

Arriving in Indonesia in 1953, US Ambassador Hugh Cumming initially regarded the Darul Islam movement as 'a promising phenomenon'.[53] At this time the US may have helped finance its central organisation; it certainly provided arms in the late 1950s to a kindred Islamic rebellion in Aceh province, led by the cleric Daud Beureuh. Beureuh announced that the parts of Aceh under his control now formed the Islamic Republic of Aceh, and that this was one of the ten component states in the federal structure of the new rebel republic proclaimed by the colonels.[54] Unfortunately, the British files contain few details of the backing Whitehall gave to the Islamist forces at this time.

By mid-1958, the Indonesian army had pushed back the rebels, inflicting several military defeats and increasing the pressure on policy-makers in Washington to change course. At first, the US instructed its ambassador in Jakarta to tell Sukarno that if he rooted out 'the communist threat' in his administration, the US would stop aiding the rebels.[55] This meant removing or undermining senior figures in the government who were sympathetic to or members of the PKI. But soon the US, faced with continuing rebel retreat and the possibility of losing all influence with Jakarta if the rebellion continued, changed tack entirely, cutting off all supplies to the rebels and instead undertaking to provide military aid to the Indonesian government.[56]

Even after this, however, the British allowed the dissidents to continue activities from Singapore, which had become a major base for the colonels' overseas operations and which they used to import arms and coordinate military and political activities between the provinces. Indonesian government protests to the British in 1958 were rebuffed; it was only when Lee Kuan Yew's Peoples Action Party won elections in Singapore in June 1959 – following which Singapore gained self-government on all matters except foreign affairs and defence – that the rebel activities were curtailed, the new Singaporean government seeking to improve relations with Jakarta.[57] The rebellion still continued but became plagued by dissensions within the rebels' ranks and more forceful military action by Jakarta. By the spring of 1961, commanders in the various provinces, knowing the game was now up, started to surrender, and by October the rebellion was over.[58] The colonels' rebellion was to a large degree dependent on US covert support, with key inputs from Britain, and soon petered out after it was cut off.

Darul Islam leader Kartosuwirjo was captured in 1962, and its rebellion in West Java was crushed by Sukarno's forces. However, the movement was to gradually reconstitute itself and play a role in the massacres of the PKI in 1965–66, as we see in Chapter 5. Darul Islam would also go on to produce several violent splinter groups in Indonesia, notably the terrorist group, Jemaah Islamiya.[59] Darul Islam strongholds in the 1950s are now in many cases strongholds of jihadist support in Indonesia.[60] Whether Anglo–American covert action in the 1950s contributed to the longer-term development of radical Islamist forces in Indonesia is hard to say. Certainly, Washington and London's collaboration with such forces highlights a familiar pattern: they were ready to work with reactionary, often extremist elements, with whom they had little in common other than an enemy, namely a secular, nationalist and independent government with some communist influence. The colonels and their allies in Darul Islam were seen as proxy forces, London's and Washington's shock troops, similar to the Muslim Brotherhood and the Iranian ayatollahs. Used for their 'nuisance value', they were dropped when they had outlived their utility. Undermining the main enemy was a short-term goal that, for a time at least, needed to be achieved at all costs, irrespective of the longer-term implications.

CHAPTER 5

The Global Islamic Mission

THROUGHOUT THE 1960S, confrontation in the Middle East continued between the secular nationalist regimes, led by Nasser's Egypt, and the Islamic monarchies, led by Saudi Arabia. As both sides jostled for influence throughout the region, the conflict found overt expression in a bloody, long-drawn-out war in Yemen, which lasted most of the decade. Typical of its strategy, Britain covertly joined forces with the Saudis to support the forces of the deposed Yemeni imam against a new republican regime backed by Nasser, promoting a civil war in which up to 200,000 people died. The British and Saudis feared that the Yemeni example of secular nationalism would have a domino effect, spreading throughout the Middle East – perhaps even to Saudi Arabia itself – wresting vital oil resources away from British and American control and placing them in the hands of popular governments, and more generally undermining Western influence in the region.

The stakes were high, since British companies owned 40 per cent of the oil in the Gulf, with large shares in consortia in Kuwait and Iran especially.[1] Two of the eight companies that controlled the world oil trade were British (BP and Shell) meaning that Whitehall's interests lay not only in securing access to oil but ensuring that British companies retained their commercial stake in the industry. The government accrued invisible earnings from British oil companies' production and sales in other countries amounting to

£800 million in the five years from 1961–65; by 1967, these companies had overseas assets worth £2 billion. To protect these earnings, the British government had an explicit policy to oppose governments who 'expropriate or acquire too direct a control over Western oil investments', while their broad aim was described as 'to inhibit undue governmental interference in the oil trade'.[2]

Thus the British and Saudis were also fearful of nationalist groups elsewhere in the Arabian Peninsula, especially Aden and Oman. In 1964, Britain responded to a nationalist insurgency in Radfan province of Western Aden by brutally bombing rebel villages and bribing local tribal leaders.[3] The following year, Whitehall leaped to the defence of the Sultan of Oman, who presided over probably the most repressive regime in the postwar Middle East, where wearing glasses or talking to anyone for more than fifteen minutes was banned, and where oil resources were concentrated in British and the sultan's hands while the country remained completely undeveloped. Britain began what became a ten-year war to crush the Egyptian-backed rebels who proclaimed the liberation of Dhofar province in southern Oman; the Saudis first backed the Dhofari revolt to undermine the Omani sultan, with whom they had an ongoing border dispute, but soon reverted to type in backing the regime.[4]

Aside from the control of oil, the other major British interests in the Middle East were to prevent the region falling under 'Soviet communism or other hostile domination' and 'the maintenance of substantial Arab foreign exchange reserves in sterling'.[5] Nationalist regimes posed a particular threat to the latter priority and Britain had a long-standing interest in ensuring that its client states invested their earnings in Britain and the Western banking system. In 1961, for example, the record shows that British planners – desperate to ensure that oil-rich Kuwait continued to rely on British 'protection' after it secured independence that year – fabricated an Iraqi threat to the country to justify British military intervention.[6] Officials recognised that British companies could make large profits from

Kuwaiti oil but also the advantages of 'Kuwait's readiness to accept and hold sterling'.[7] The Kuwaitis' investment in Britain meant that they would, in the approving words of one Foreign Office official, 'avoid the necessity of sharing their oil wealth with their neighbours' – a view demonstrating that British officials were perfectly aware that their priorities conflicted with the needs of poor Middle Easterners.[8]

At first, the British had some success in cracking down on nationalist forces in the region, but as the decade wore on British weakness became more apparent. In November 1967 it was forced into a humiliating withdrawal from its colony of Aden, pushed out by the forces of the National Liberation Front, which had been fighting for independence with Egyptian support since 1963. Increasing British reliance on the Saudis to maintain the pro-Western status quo, and to deter Nasserite infiltration of Arabia and the wider Middle East, coincided with a development inside the Kingdom that would have huge consequences for the eventual advance of global terrorism. At the beginning of the 1960s, the Saudis embarked on a global Islamic mission to 'wahhabise' Islam, spread Saudi influence and counter Nasser, a process that marks the beginning of the resurgence of radical-right political Islam.

THE MISSION AND ITS BRITISH BACKERS

Following an International Islamic Conference in Mecca, convened by Crown Prince Faisal, in 1962, the Saudis established the Muslim World League which, managed by the Saudi religious establishment, sent out missionaries, printed propaganda and financed the building of mosques and Islamic associations around the globe. Among its first employees were many Muslim Brothers who had found refuge in Saudi Arabia after their expulsion from Nasser's Egypt in the 1950s. Its founding members included the former Grand Mufti of Jerusalem, Haj Amin al-Husseini; Said Ramadan, the Muslim Brotherhood's chief international organiser who wrote the League's constitution; and Abdul Ala Mawdudi, the founder of Pakistan's radical Jamaat-i-Islami (the Islamic Society).[9] The League's first proclamation read: 'Those who distort Islam's call under the guise of nationalism are the most bitter enemies of the Arabs whose glories are entwined with the glories of Islam.'[10]

Faisal, who took over as Saudi King in 1964, fancied himself as the King of Islam, and on his formal assumption to power he addressed the nation with the words: 'The first thing we wish from you is devotion to God, to cling to the teachings of his religion and rules of his sharia (Holy Law) since this is the basis of our glory, the underlying factor … of our rules and the secret of our power.' The goal in foreign policy, Faisal said, would be 'to move along with the Islamic nations in everything which may achieve for Muslims their glory and the raising of their standards.'[11]

Britain played an important role in the palace coup that brought Faisal to power and which threw out his older brother, King Saud, who had been on the throne since 1953. By 1958 Faisal had taken over the running of the government, and by 1963 he had used this position to become the dominant power of the two. In December of that year, Saud ordered the deployment of troops and guns outside his palace in Riyadh to reassert his power; and a tense stand-off with forces loyal to Faisal continued into 1964, when Saud demanded that Faisal dismiss two of his ministers and replace them with the king's sons. Crucial support for Faisal was provided by the National Guard, the 20,000-strong body responsible for protecting the regime and the royal family – originally the 'White Army' or Ikhwan (Brotherhood) which had bloodily conquered Saudi Arabia for Ibn Saud. The then commander of the National Guard was Prince Abdullah, the present King of Saudi Arabia, and it was being trained by a small British military mission in the country following a Saudi request the previous year. Two British advisers to the National Guard, Brigadier Timbrell and Colonel Bromage, now drew up plans on Abdullah's express wish for 'protection of Faisal', 'defence of the regime', 'occupation of certain points' and 'denial of the radio station to all but those supported by the National Guard'.[12]

These British plans ensured Faisal's personal protection, with the aim of aiding the transfer of power to him.

Saud was viewed by the British as incompetent and opposed to introducing the political reforms necessary to keep the House of Saud from being overthrown. Frank Brenchley, the *chargé d'affaires* in the British embassy in Jeddah, had written that 'the sands of time have steadily been running out for the Saudi regime', the major factor being the nationalist revolution in neighbouring Yemen and the intervention of Egyptian troops there, which challenged Saudi authority in Arabia. Brenchley noted that, in contrast to Saud, 'Faisal knows that he must bring about reforms quickly if the regime is to survive. Hampered everywhere by a lack of trained administrators, he is struggling to speed evolution in order to avert revolution'.[13]

On 29 March 1964 the Saudi religious leadership – the *ulema* – issued a fatwa sanctioning the transfer of power to Faisal as being based on sharia law; two days later King Saud was forced to abdicate.[14] The important role played both by the British and the Wahhabi clerics in sanctioning a palace coup highlighted the two forces, in addition to the Americans, on which the Saudi rulers were dependent. Reflecting on the coup, British Ambassador Colin Crowe noted that 'what may also be serious in the long-term' about the transfer of power, 'is the bringing of the *ulema* into the picture and they may exact a price for their support'.[15] His comments would prove prescient.

Attempting to bolster his country's Islamic foreign policy, Faisal proceeded to propose a 'Pan-Islamic alliance' among pro-Western Muslim countries, and toured nine Muslim states in 1965–6 to promote the idea. By the end of the decade Faisal had helped form the Organisation of the Islamic Conference, established in Rabat in 1969 with a permanent secretariat in Jeddah, which intended to promote solidarity among Islamic states. Saudi Arabia also began to bankroll the Islamic Centre of Geneva, established by Said Ramadan in 1961, and which served as the international headquarters of the

Muslim Brotherhood, becoming an organisational nerve centre and meeting place for Islamists across the world.[16] During the 1960s thousands of Muslim Brothers moved to Europe, notably Germany, gradually establishing a wide and well-organised network of mosques, charities and Islamic organisations, hoping to win more Muslim hearts and minds.[17] Ramadan himself stayed in Switzerland until his death in 1995. Muslim Brothers also came to Saudi Arabia from across the Middle East during the 1960s. They included a Palestinian refugee named Abdullah Azzam, who, as a lecturer at Jeddah University, would mentor the young Osama Bin Laden, and in the early 1980s be at the forefront of the jihad against the Soviets in Afghanistan. Another lecturer at Jeddah was the Egyptian Muhammad Qutb, brother of the leading Islamist ideologue, Sayyid Qutb, who was languishing in one of Nasser's jails.[18] This fusion of local clerics trained in the Saudi Wahhabite tradition with the international activism of the exiled Muslim Brothers helped provide the intellectual and ideological basis for the later development of al-Qaida.[19]

The Saudis' Islamic mission and the international expansion of the Muslim Brotherhood is especially significant given long-standing suspicions that Said Ramadan may have been recruited by the CIA and MI6 in the 1950s. Ramadan had been stripped *in absentia* of his Egyptian nationality by the Nasser regime in September 1954, for distributing pamphlets pleading the cause of the Muslim Brothers. Some sources suggest that the CIA transferred tens of millions of dollars to Ramadan in the 1960s.[20] Declassified documents from 1967 in the Swiss archives show that the Swiss authorities looked favourably on Ramadan's anti-communist views, and that he was 'among other things, an intelligence agent of the English and the Americans'. Ramadan's dossier, reported the Geneva newspaper, *Le Temps*, in 2004, included several documents indicating his connections to 'certain Western secret services'.[21] German intelligence documents from the 1960s reportedly state that the US helped persuade Jordan to issue Ramadan with a passport and that 'his expenditures are financed by the American side'.[22]

The Saudis, especially after Faisal came to power in 1964, also worked with and funded the Muslim Brotherhood to promote numerous assassination attempts against Nasser. These sometimes involved recruiting officers in Nasser's special forces and smuggling arms to the Brotherhood's 'secret apparatus'.[23] In response to the increase in Saudi support for the Brotherhood and other Islamist organisations, Nasser's Egypt embarked on a new wave of repression against the organisation. In late 1965, the Egyptian intelligence services claimed to have uncovered a gigantic 'plot' of assassinations and bombings against the regime, which it accused Saudi Arabia of backing. There followed widespread round-ups of Muslim Brothers and a brutal clampdown by the security forces. After trials of the alleged conspirators in December 1965, Said Ramadan was condemned *in absentia* to forced labour for life, and a number of leading Muslim Brothers were sentenced to death and executed the following year. One of them was Sayyid Qutb, whose work *Signposts*, written in jail, went on to provide a manifesto for the Brotherhood's political activities. It also became a base text that would later inspire Ayman al-Zawahiri, Bin Laden's deputy in al-Qaida, who joined the Egyptian Muslim Brotherhood as a fourteen-year-old at this time.[24] Al-Zawahiri later wrote that 'Sayyid Qutb's call for loyalty to God's oneness and to acknowledge God's sole authority and sovereignty was the spark that united the Islamic revolution against the enemies of Islam at home and abroad.'[25] Forced underground, the Egyptian Brotherhood only re-emerged after Nasser's death in 1970.

Despite the clampdown, British officials continued to recognise the Egyptian Brotherhood as a force to be reckoned with. They regarded it as 'the main threat to the regime from the outside', and noted that 'the one force apart from the armed services, of which Nasser is really afraid, is traditional Islam'.[26] One Foreign Office official wrote that 'their negative capacity for plot and assassination makes them a force which all of us (and Nasser) should keep a careful eye on.'[27] Another official, Peter Unwin, wrote that 'I should have thought that his action [the clampdown] must add to the appeal of the Islamic League [Muslim World League]; and add support to the propaganda charge that he is no true Moslem but a Marxist stooge.'[28]

Britain still feared that Nasser's Egypt could unite the Arab world – or at least a large chunk of it – against Britain. In this light, the Foreign Office wrote in 1964 that 'it is in our political and economic interests that there should be a balance of power in the Arab Middle East rather than a concentration of power in Cairo.' The pro-Western shah of Iran's relationships with Jordan and Saudi Arabia 'have played a part in maintaining the balance of forces, and are to be encouraged', it noted, reflecting Whitehall's continuing desire to keep the region divided.[29]

British planners continued to harbour desires of 'removing Nasser from the arena', and considered direct military intervention in Egypt. However, they ultimately ruled both out since 'there is little reason to believe Nasser's successor would be more moderate or more amenable to Western influence' – an echo, perhaps, of the previous concern that the Muslim Brotherhood was even more anti-British than Nasser. Military intervention was also rejected since it would create upheaval and increase communist penetration of the region; furthermore, 'nor can we conduct a Middle East policy which is at serious odds with the Americans and they will not consider either of these two courses'.[30] The Foreign Office concluded in September 1965 'that we shall have to live with Nasser's regime'.[31]

Meanwhile, Britain and the US continued to build up the Saudis as a counter to Arab nationalism, and looked favourably on their pan-Islamic foreign policy. The CIA helped run Saudi internal security while Sayyid Qutb, before his execution, had openly admitted that during this period 'America made Islam'.[32] David Long, a retired US foreign service official and expert on Saudi Arabia and the Gulf, told author Robert Dreyfus that:

> We reinforced Faisal's support for the Muslim Brotherhood and pan-Islam. We needed them against any allies that Moscow could conjure up … Pan-Islam was not, to us, seen as a strategic threat. There were bad guys doing bad things to people on the Left, to Nasser. They were fighting the pinkos. So we didn't see pan-Islam as a threat.[33]

British offficials continued to express their preference for a Saudi regime based on Islamic fundamentalism to the prospect of an Arab nationalist one, since 'a change of regime which lined up the country with its large oil revenues with the republican Arab states would upset the whole balance of power in the Middle East'.[34]

It was in Yemen where British and Saudi foreign policy interests most coincided, in their bolstering of religious, conservative forces against the Arab nationalist threat. In September 1962, a popular coup by republican forces under Colonel Abdullah al-Sallal deposed the imam, Muhammad al-Badr, who had been in power for a week after the death of his father, a feudal autocrat who had ruled since 1948. The imam's forces took to the hills and declared an insurgency, while Britain and Saudi Arabia soon began a covert war to support them. Whitehall provided arms and money to the rebels in the knowledge that the beneficiaries could not win the war but that, as Prime Minister Macmillan informed President Kennedy, 'it would not suit us too badly if the new Yemeni regime were occupied with their own internal affairs during the next few years' – as in Indonesia a few years earlier, Britain saw such conflict as providing useful 'nuisance value'.[35]

With Nasser sending thousands of Egyptian troops to Yemen to defend the new regime, the conflict effectively became a surrogate British–Saudi war against Egypt. British officials acknowledged that the new Yemeni government was popular and more democratic than the imam's despotic regime, and there was therefore little doubt which side Whitehall would back.[36] Both Britain and Saudi Arabia feared that popular republican government would spread to the other British-controlled feudal sheikhdoms in Arabia, in particular Aden, where the British were being pinned down by Egyptian-backed nationalist guerrillas. But the Joint Intelligence Committee also judged that the Yemeni revolution had made the position of the regime in Saudi Arabia itself 'more precarious': 'if a successful revolution took place in Saudi Arabia the new regime would probably, initially at least, be pro-Egyptian and the existing order in the Persian Gulf states would be subjected to very severe strains.'[37] The war ended only when the Saudis, the chief financiers of the rebels, cut off their aid in 1969 and a treaty was signed creating North Yemen.[38]

Britain supported the Saudis' 'Islamic' foreign policy. In 1965, the ambassador to Saudi Arabia, Morgan Man, was convinced that, in the face of Nasser's threat, the regime had to enhance its status on the world stage: 'it is little use showing off her virtues only at home: she must uphold her prestige abroad'.[39] Man clearly understood Saudi foreign policy, describing how its primary aim was that of 'fostering Islamic solidarity'. Faisal, he wrote, 'is trying to use Islam as a counter-magnet to Nasser's Arab unity theme, and that he hopes to create an Islamic "bloc" which will gradually draw off a large section of those who have hitherto flocked to Nasser's standard.'[40]

British officials backed Faisal's Islamic Conference initiative by keeping a low profile. The foreign minister in Harold Wilson's Labour government, George Thomson, met Saudi Prince Sultan in February 1966 to discuss the idea. The record of the meeting states:

> This was not a pact … but a congress, which would help oppose communism and defend the faith. Mr Thomson, asked for Her Majesty's Government's attitude, said that they wished it a success, since it made for stability, but thought the best service we could render was to say nothing, since any suggestion that Britain supported these developments was bound to damage their prospects. Sultan agreed.[41]

The following month one Foreign Office official, C. T. Brant, wrote, in the context of the British need to contain Nasser, that 'Whatever we may feel about developments which may favour our interest in the Middle East, it remains generally true that the less we are seen to be connected with them, the greater will be their chances of success. This seems especially true of the recent movement for an "Islamic Alliance".'[42]

As for the Muslim World League, Willie Morris, who took over as ambassador in August 1968, noted that it 'is in practice an instrument for whipping up interest in and support for Saudi policies'. Faisal's use of Islam, he noted, was not intended to create an amorphous worldwide association of Muslim states but to extend Saudi relations with countries such as Iran, Pakistan, Turkey and Iraq 'in a group of states more congenial to Faisal's view of the world'. But Morris added that the chances of it taking shape were not great.[43]

The nature of the Saudi regime was well understood by the British. In June 1963, the British ambassador, Sir Colin Crowe, summed the country up in no uncertain terms. Saudi Arabia was, he said:

> dominated by a sect of Islam of a farouche and intolerant Puritanism, but ruled by a royal family whose extravagance and dissipation are only rivaled by its numbers. It has no modern code of laws and its criminal justice is of mediaeval barbarity. There is not even a pretence of democratic institutions and though slavery has been abolished slaves are still to be found. Corruption is widespread. The country sits on top of some of the richest oil resources in the world and enjoys a vast unearned income which has dissipated in pleasure, palaces and Cadillacs.[44]

Yet the Saudi rulers were given unqualified backing by Britain, whose policy was one of 'keeping the present regime in Saudi

Arabia in power'.[45] 'The stability of the present regime in Saudi Arabia is important to Western interests in the Middle East,' Crowe also wrote, to cite one of numerous similar notations.[46] Crowe's valedictory dispatch as ambassador in October 1964 noted that the regime 'is about as satisfactory as any we could expect' and was 'friendly to the West and strongly anti-communist', while 'its objectives, except over Buraimi, are ones with which we sympathise' (the reference being to the Buraimi oasis, the territory disputed between the Saudis and Britain's other allies, Oman and Abu Dhabi).[47]

Britain's relationship with Saudi Arabia changed little in the transition from the Conservatives to Labour in the 1964 elections. The British political elite was united in its backing of the Saudi ruling family, seeing it as a force for regional 'stability', the supply of oil and an increasingly important buyer of British arms. The British–Saudi *entente cordiale* was marked by a major new arms contract worth over £100 million, involving a dozen fighter aircraft, together with ground control and communications equipment, training and maintenance.[48] The contract was signed not only with the British Aircraft Corporation but also Airwork, a 'private' company acting as a government front, which provided 'retired' Royal Air Force officers to train Saudi pilots. Airwork was brought in by the British to avoid causing the Saudis 'political embarrassment' by being seen to rely on RAF pilots, and thus becoming 'a target of Cairo propaganda', officials noted.[49] The deal was further evidence of the lengths to which British governments were prepared to go to help defend the Saudi regime.

In 1967–8 British ministers decided to end their military commitments to Bahrain, Kuwait, Qatar and the small sheikhdoms in the Trucial states that lined the Gulf by 1971, after decades of managing their 'internal security' and 'defence'. Planners regarded the situation as stark: 'our military withdrawal will remove our capability to play a significant part in determining developments in the Persian Gulf'.[50] Britain still had major interests in the region:

by 1968, British oil companies were involved in all the oil states except Saudi Arabia and Bahrain, contributing £80–100 million a year in tax revenues to the Treasury and over £200 million a year to the balance of payments.[51] The Foreign Office thus noted that the withdrawal had 'to leave behind as stable a situation as possible in which trade can flourish, oil supplies can be assured on tolerable terms, British investments (especially through the oil companies) can be safeguarded and over-flying rights to the Far East be maintained.'[52] One possible danger was that the very large sterling balances held by Kuwait and other Gulf countries – estimated at £400 million – 'will fall into unfriendly hands'.[53] Thus Saudi Arabia became even more important to Britain, acting as a regional policeman and bulwark against nationalist and popular forces, and regarded as a 'counterweight' to Egypt and the nationalist Arab states as well as 'a buffer between them and the Gulf states'.[54]

In a letter of 8 July 1965 Donal McCarthy, a British official in Aden, wrote to the Foreign Office, noting with approval the 'very important' Saudi influence in Britain's Eastern Aden Protectorate. There were, McCarthy said, a number of Saudis with links to the region who were encouraging the government to invest in projects, to increase Saudi influence in the region to draw it 'away from possible Nasserite influence'.[55] In McCarthy's list of these notables, one name in particular catches the eye: Bin Laden, a reference to Mohammed, Osama's father, whose construction company had several multi-million contracts with the House of Saud.

THE INDONESIAN SLAUGHTER

While Saudi Arabia was building up its Islamic foreign policy, in Indonesia Islamist mobs were helping the army conduct one of the worst slaughters of the twentieth century, with British and US covert backing.

The Indonesian military had long wanted to move against the Communist Party, the PKI, which, with two million members, was the largest communist force outside the Soviet Union and China, and exerted increasing but limited influence over the regime of nationalist president, Ahmed Sukarno. On 30 September 1965, a group of army officers murdered six generals in a coup which was put down by forces loyal to General Mohammed Suharto, who proceeded to take command of the army. Blaming the PKI for the coup attempt, Suharto then began a campaign to eradicate the Party. In the orgy of murder which continued into 1966, hundreds of thousands were killed, including countless ordinary villagers not associated with the PKI. After the Party had been virtually liquidated, Suharto gradually outmanoeuvred President Sukarno and emerged as the new Indonesian ruler. He established a repressive dictatorship that would last until 1998.

Britain had long wanted to see the power of the PKI curbed and the fall of Sukarno's regime, as was evident in its covert backing of the dissident colonels in the late 1950s. From 1963, Britain was in open conflict with Indonesia after Jakarta announced a policy of 'confrontation' against Malaysia for the latter's British-backed plan to include the British colonies on the island of Borneo within the new Malaysian federation. As Indonesia deployed forces to conduct sabotage raids into Borneo, a jungle war ensued, involving thousands of British troops, together with warships, aircraft carriers and squadrons of aircraft.

British officials described the Indonesian generals' campaign against the PKI as a 'necessary task' and understood that it involved 'ruthless terror' and a 'bloodbath', receiving regular reports on the mounting death toll. Britain secretly contacted the Indonesian military, promising them that Britain would not attack them in Borneo in order to leave them a free hand in Indonesia. The British also conducted propaganda operations to blacken the PKI in the eyes of the Indonesian people, planting international media stories falsely alleging that the Chinese were shipping arms to the PKI.[56]

Islamist groups, trained and equipped by the Indonesian army, played a critical role in the slaughter. Followers of the Masyumi party, the major Islamic force in Indonesia, took an active part in the killings of PKI members, as did remnants of Darul Islam, the extremist group that had been forced underground under Sukarno, which carried out massacres of suspected communists in West Java, Aceh and North Sumatra provinces.[57] These forces benefited from US arms supplies – the US embassy in Thailand secretly procured weapons for the Indonesian military to arm Muslim and nationalist youths in central Java for use against the PKI.[58]

The Indonesian military campaign was aimed at eliminating all obstacles – communist or secular nationalist – to a military takeover of the country. It succeeded partly thanks to a twin reliance on Islamist forces, acting as the foot soldiers, and Anglo-American covert action – again working in de facto collaboration, although there is no evidence in the British files of direct British contacts with the Islamist mobs. The events set back the emergence of democracy in Indonesia for more than a generation.

After Suharto gained power, the regime instituted a 'new order' in which many of Sukarno's policies were abandoned, the confrontation with Malaysia was ended and the country was opened up to foreign investors, pleasing policy-makers in London and Washington who became staunch allies of the regime. The Islamists were not so lucky: the new military rulers refused to implement sharia law and, although they did release Masyumi leaders imprisoned by Sukarno, they did not allow them to play political roles, and more generally sought to depoliticise Islam. At the same time, however, the Suharto regime had already seen how useful Islamists could be, and was keen to keep them on side. Analyst Martin van Bruinessen comments that Ali Murtopo, Suharto's intelligence chief and key architect of the new order's first decade, 'cultivated a group of Darul Islam veterans and allowed them to maintain a network of contacts as a secret weapon against "communism" and other enemies, that could be unleashed at any convenient moment.'[59] Darul Islam members would go on to join the anti-Soviet jihad in Afghanistan in the 1980s, and it would be from those militant groups that the terrorist threat in Indonesia would later emerge.[60]

THE RECKONING IN THE MIDDLE EAST

By the late 1960s it was events in the Middle East that were to prove more decisive for the future of global Islamic radicalism. During the Six-Day War of 1967, Israel inflicted a catastrophic defeat on the Arab states, led by the secular nationalist regimes of Egypt and Syria. Israel's capture of the West Bank, Gaza Strip, eastern Jerusalem, the Golan Heights and the Sinai Peninsula is often seen as marking the defeat of secular Arab nationalism as a major force. However, the appeal of Arab nationalism was by then already waning. Although the nationalist regimes had sometimes successfully challenged Western hegemony in the region, and delivered some domestic gains for their populations, they had failed to institute genuine democracies or broad increases in living standards.[61]

British and American opposition, together with the Saudis' cultivation of an 'Islamic' bloc and more radical Islamist forces, also played a key part in the decline of Arab nationalism. For nearly two decades, since Nasser's revolution in Egypt after 1952, London had set itself against the nationalist project, destabilising or overthrowing governments, bogging them down in costly wars that diverted scarce resources, and denying them aid or international support. Who knows whether, in a different world, Western support for Arab nationalism could have staved off its worse features and enhanced its better ones. Yet the interests of the people in the region were irrelevant to British planners; there is barely a reference to them in the hundreds of documents surveyed for this research – the rights of Middle Easterners were sacrificed on the altar of pure geostrategic concerns, and deeply conservative ones at that, from which the region is still to recover.

British planners recognised the decline of Arab nationalism

as being in their interests. In particular, Britain's Saudi allies had received a boost. As Britain's ambassador to Saudi Arabia was to write five years later:

> In the sphere of foreign affairs King Faisal saw himself only two years ago increasingly isolated in the Arab world as the leftist contagion spread ... and was forced to seek a place for himself in a more friendly Islamic environment ... The opportunity for King Faisal to step into this role was created by the death of President Nasser and the absence from the Arab scene of any statesman of comparable stature ... Saudi foreign policy has continued to pursue the objective of opposing the spread of communism and subversion.[62]

At first, it appeared as if the principal beneficiaries of the decline of Arab nationalism would be London and Washington's preferred alternative – the Islamic monarchies in Saudi Arabia, Jordan and the Gulf, to which they had extended considerable backing. But it was the more radical Islamist alternative that benefited the most. British officials noted that the 1967 Arab defeat was followed by a 'noticeable religious revival' and 'a remarkable increase in religious feeling in Egypt', including widespread demands for the implementation of sharia law.[63] Islamist forces would now pose as the 'solution' to the Middle East's problems among its poor masses, aided by the massive gap in living standards between them and the secular elites. In Egypt, within three years of the 1967 war, a weakened Nasser was dead; his successor, Anwar Sadat, turned away from the nationalist model and sought to Islamise Egyptian society, partly by cultivating the Muslim Brotherhood, which Nasser had repressed for so many years.[64] By now, many Islamist groups in the Middle East had become still further radicalised, partly due to having been savagely repressed by many of the secular regimes. The stage was set for the Islamist revival that was to sweep the region throughout the 1970s.

CHAPTER 6

'Handy Weapons' in Jordan and Egypt

BRITISH FOREIGN POLICY planners were confronted with a plethora of difficult tasks in the early 1970s, notably: joining the European Economic Community on favourable terms; helping its principal ally, the US, extricate itself from its brutal Vietnam War with less than total humiliation; promoting détente with the Soviet Union while preserving Western military superiority; and fighting off demands from developing countries for a New International Economic Order, a call by developing countries to establish a more equitable international trade system.

A Foreign Office paper of 1974 entitled 'Potential Problems in British Foreign Policy' considered the ongoing challenge of nationalism, understood as meaning that most countries in the developing world were 'keen to assert their national identity and independence in both political and economic contexts'. This rising trend involved countries opposing the 'practices and rules largely laid down by the wealthy countries of the West'. An additional problem, however, was 'the weakness of the West' and that 'the ability of Western countries to exercise pressure in the third world is much reduced'. 'Few countries apart from the United States possess the means to impose their will by force and public opinion in general gives little support to "overseas adventures",' it noted.[1]

This report was written following the quadrupling of oil prices during the 1973 Arab–Israeli war, which plunged Britain into economic crisis but propelled the largest oil producer, Saudi Arabia, into a position of global power. The Saudi rulers used their stupendous new fortunes to further champion the pre-eminence of Wahhabi fundamentalism within global Islam, which contributed to the emergence during the 1970s of militant Islamist groups in most of the world's Muslim nations.[2] By the decade's end, not only was Sunni Islamic radicalism a major political force, but Shia radicalism had driven Iran's Islamic revolution, overthrowing the Western-backed shah and further challenging Western hegemony over Middle Eastern oil.

The resurgence of radical Islam presented British foreign policy planners with both threats and opportunities, and the record suggests that they often saw the opportunities as greater. After 1973, a British government becoming ever weaker on the world stage forged a still-deeper new alliance with Saudi Arabia. Yet the beginning of this tumultuous decade began with two other episodes showing how the interests of British policy-makers could coincide with those of Islamist forces.

ON THE SAME SIDE AS THE BROTHERHOOD, AGAIN

In September 1970 the pro-British, CIA-funded King of Jordan, Hussein, narrowly avoided being overthrown by Palestinian radicals. His survival was due to a familiar combination of forces – the British and American governments and the Muslim Brotherhood – and dealt another body blow to the cause of Arab nationalism. Black September, as it became known, was a bloody confrontation between Jordanian government forces and Palestinian guerrillas, who were a mixture of Nasserite nationalists, Marxist groups and members of Yasser Arafat's Palestine Liberation Organisation (PLO).[3] Numbering up to half of those living on the East Bank of the river Jordan, the Palestinians, many living in enclaves and refugee camps after being expelled from Palestine in 1948, had established a virtual state within a state in Jordan, with their own arms and some diplomatic representation abroad, and in virtual control of parts of the capital, Amman. Hundreds of clashes with the Jordanian army and police had occurred throughout 1969, and in early September 1970 several attempts were made to assassinate King Hussein. When further fighting broke out in mid-September among some Palestinian factions and the Jordanian security forces, Hussein declared martial law and unleashed government forces to re-establish control.

As the fighting spread, on 19 September over 200 tanks of Syria's Baathist regime under President Nureddin al-Atassi crossed the Jordanian border in support of the Palestinians. At this point Hussein made appeals to the US and Britain for air strikes against the Syrians, which were rejected, presumably for fear of being drawn into a direct military intervention. In the end, the Jordanians were able to counter the Syrian tanks with their own British-supplied Centurions, and pushed back the Palestinian guerrillas, killing over 3,000. Through late 1970 and early 1971, Hussein's forces brutally pursued the guerillas and crushed them by July 1971. Many escaped to southern Lebanon, where they joined other Palestinians in establishing a new base for the PLO.

The Jordanian Muslim Brotherhood was quick to demonstrate its loyalty to Hussein's regime, publicly siding with it during the September 1970 crisis and, after the defeat of the guerillas, praising the government's expulsion from Jordan of the leftist groups. Established in the then British mandate of Transjordan in 1942, the Jordanian Brotherhood had been cultivated by King Hussein's regime since the 1950s, and had played an important role in bolstering it in the 1957 crisis. In contrast to other political parties, the regime allowed the Brotherhood a wide range of political and religious freedoms, seeing it as a counterweight to the leftist groups, the pro-Syrian Baathist forces and the pro-Egyptian Nasserites. Under Hussein's protection, the Jordanian Brotherhood had also been able to forge ties with its Egyptian and Syrian counterparts, both of whom were then on the receiving end of nationalist crackdowns.[4]

The Brotherhood's demonstrations of loyalty in 1970 paid off, and throughout the 1970s and '80s it was permitted to take in and train members of the Syrian Brotherhood, then engaged in a protracted confrontation with President Assad, who seized power in Syria a few weeks after Black September. Hussein allowed Brotherhood training camps to be set up near the Syrian border and promoted some Brotherhood militants to important posts in the royal administration; in turn, they recruited other officials and administrators from within the Brotherhood.[5]

Britain provided blanket backing for King Hussein during the 1970 crisis. The Foreign Office described him on the eve of the fighting as 'a moderate and pro-Western Arab leader whose stabilising influence contributes to the stability of the remaining pro-Western regimes in Saudi Arabia and the Gulf.'[6] In early October 1970, Britain flew out two RAF Hercules plane-loads of arms specially requested by Jordan, including 25-pounder shells and 76mm ammunition; these helped replenish Jordan's Centurion tanks fighting the Syrians.[7] The US also provided Hussein with large quantities of ammunition.

At the end of October Hussein received a visit from one Neil 'Billy' McLean, a British Army intelligence officer and sometime Conservative MP who acted as an unofficial member of the Foreign Office. McLean had extensive connections in the Middle East and pops up in many British covert operations in the postwar period, notably against Nasser in Egypt and Yemen. According to McLean, King Hussein told him that Nasser's death in September 1970 'had created a vacuum in the Middle East, and Jordan with British and American help could play a constructive part in bringing to power reasonable governments in both Iraq and Syria.'[8] It may not have been a coincidence that, earlier that month, the Kuwaiti newspaper *Al-Siyasa* published a memo from Jordan's foreign minister to its embassy in London. Dated 4 October, it stated that King Hussein was directing the embassy to 'carry out urgent contacts with the British authorities regarding the grant to Jordan of a sum of 300 thousand dinars in order to coordinate the military cooperation with the Lebanese authorities for encouraging Syrian officers to expedite their armed revolution against the Baathist rule in Syria.'[9] One can only speculate whether this British funding was genuine and whether it went ahead – and indeed whether it was linked to Hussein's sponsorship of the Muslim Brotherhood to overthrow the Syrian regime. Certainly, British planners were keen to see the back of the Syrian Baathists, a nationalist force which, as had just been witnessed in Jordan, was challenging pro-Western regimes in the region.

King Hussein depended on the British for his survival. In March 1970, he had requested a British SAS team to train his special forces in 'internal security'. The Ministry of Defence noted that 'King Hussein was delighted with the results to the extent that the SAS-trained bodyguard was considered to be responsible for the King's continued existence.'[10] After the 1970 crisis, Hussein called on the British again: in January 1971, an SAS team spent two months in the country training the Jordanian army.[11] That March, a Foreign Office official noted concerns about an ongoing Palestinian threat: 'It is very much in our interests to help King Hussein to preserve his regime from subversion ... Despite recent successes against the Palestinian guerilla movement, the latter are not yet a spent force ... they may continue to try to overthrow the regime.' It was imperative, the official stressed, that British training of the Jordanian special forces in 'counter-insurgency' be kept secret, to avoid (accurate) accusations that Hussein was simply reliant on Western support.[12]

But the British relationship to the 1970 Jordan crisis did not end there and took on another aspect entirely. Out of the Palestinian defeat emerged the Black September organisation, set up by members of the Fatah group in the PLO to take revenge on King

Hussein's regime, and whose most notorious subsequent act was the kidnapping and killing of eleven Israeli athletes at the 1972 Munich Olympics. During the 1970s the British secret service, MI6, recruited as agents two arms traffickers supplying Black September terrorists with weapons. The main aim was to stop the supply of arms from Libya, which was backing Black September, to the IRA in Northern Ireland. The story provides an interesting new angle on Britain's willingness to work with terrorist groups to further short-term objectives in the Middle East.

The episode centres on a certain Leslie Aspin, a former SAS soldier turned arms smuggler who in the late 1960s and early 1970s was trafficking weapons to a variety of terrorist organisations, including Black September. Aspin also ferried dozens of instructors to train recruits at Colonel Qadafi's 'Black September training school' at Hammadah al-Hamra in northwestern Libya.[13] By 1970, MI6 already had an agent inside Black September, but also recruited Aspin, in February of that year, by offering him money and threatening to reveal to his contacts that he was already working for the British.[14] Aspin later noted in his autobiography that he was recruited by MI6 because of his years spent as an arms smuggler in the Middle East and Europe, and that his handler told him that 'we are not in the least concerned with what you have been doing – apart from the fact that you can be of great assistance to us.'[15]

Given the codename 'Kovacks' by MI6, Aspin's involvement in arms trafficking continued after his recruitment. With British knowledge, he arranged at least four arms shipments from Libya to the IRA in 1970–72 and also helped to recruit IRA terrorists to be instructed in the Libyan camp. Aspin became a key source of information for MI6 and was able to tell it about Qadafi's European associates, the identities of Irish terrorists who had been to the Libyan camp and the names of other arms dealers in the Arab world.[16]

Aspin also recounts how in December 1973 he informed his MI6 handler, codenamed Homer, that he had heard of plans by his Black September contacts to blow up a Pan Am or El Al aircraft at Rome airport before the end of the month. Homer, Aspin continued, promised to pass on this information to the three relevant governments (i.e., US, Israeli and Italian) but writes that 'I'm almost positive that he never did this'.[17] It remains unclear why, but the most obvious explanation would be that the British did not want to reveal that they had agents inside Black September. On 17 December 1973 Palestinian terrorists blew up Pan Am Flight 110 on the tarmac at Rome's Fiumicino Airport, killing 29 people; this followed the deaths of two people in the terminal lounge as the terrorists began firing at passengers. They then hijacked a plane with more hostages and landed first at Athens, then at Damascus, where the hostages were released and from where the terrorists moved on to an unknown destination.

Another figure in the arms trafficking network was Monzer al-Kassar, who worked for the Syrians and was a close friend of Rifaat Assad, the brother of the Syrian president and chief of internal security. It is alleged that it was al-Kassar who, at Syrian instigation, recruited Aspin as an arms smuggler for the Libyans, and that he was also involved in procuring arms for the PLO as well as international drug smuggling. Al-Kassar was recruited by MI6 in March 1973, and continued the arms smuggling, but now under British auspices. He became a 'supersource' of intelligence and through him, 'the British could keep track of money moving to every terrorist organisation in the world'.[18] The MI6–al-Kassar story was to rumble on into the 1980s and 1990s, as we shall see.

Britain's role in propping up King Hussein's regime in Jordan sits rather oddly with acquiescing in the supply of arms and training to a terrorist group bent on overthrowing him – even if this was apparently motivated by other factors (i.e., monitoring terrorist financing and arms deliveries to the IRA). This apparent incongruence seems less odd, however, in light of various other episodes where London has also backed both sides in conflicts, such as in the Hussein–Ibn Saud conflict in Arabia in the 1920s, the

Arab–Israeli conflict in Palestine from 1920 until 1948, and others we will come to later.

ISLAMISING EGYPT

As King Hussein was crushing the Palestinians in September 1970, Anwar Sadat, Nasser's vice president, took over as President of Egypt on Nasser's death. The Muslim Brotherhood's decision to side with King Hussein in the Jordan crisis did not go unnoticed by the new Egyptian president, who had strong personal links to the Brotherhood going back to the 1940s.[19] As President, Sadat rejected Nasser's Arab nationalism, purged the government of Nasserites and expelled Soviet military advisers in 1972. Instead, Sadat's strategy was to Islamicise Egyptian society and forge a new alliance with the US. Washington was so keen to work with Sadat in bringing Egypt over to the US side in the Cold War that policy-makers and intelligence officers 'viewed his restoration of the Islamic right benignly or tacitly encouraged it'.[20] In fact, Sadat's policies helped spark the emergence of global Islamic radicalism.

For Britain as well as the US, this was a case of the chickens coming home to roost. The British had connived with Islamist forces against Nasser, their chief Middle Eastern enemy for the previous eighteen years, and helped to defeat Arab nationalism as a major political force. Now, Whitehall joined the US in backing Sadat as he swung Egypt onto a new Islamic as well as pro-Western path, understanding that the regime was 'not very' democratic, as the British ambassador noted in 1975, but welcoming it as a 'moderate', stabilising force in the region.[21] It was anything but.

Sadat's broad Islamisation of Egyptian society included enshrining Islam as the state religion in the 1971 constitution and reversing Nasser's policy towards the Muslim Brotherhood, releasing some Brothers from jail and declaring a general amnesty for all those imprisoned before May 1971. By the mid-70s Sadat, with the support of the Saudis, was also allowing Muslim Brothers to return from their Nasser-imposed exile in Saudi Arabia, where many of them had grown rich.[22] At the same time, Sadat also established a covert relationship with Kamal Adham, the head of Saudi intelligence, representing a new Egyptian–Saudi détente and a sharp break from the bitter enmity under Nasser.

The Muslim Brothers freed by Sadat gravitated towards Egypt's universities, many of which were by the early 1970s controlled by Islamist movements which had overturned the dominance of nationalist ideology. At the same time, the Islamist intelligentsia on the campuses began to spread their ideas throughout the Muslim world, courtesy of the networks and financial clout of the Saudi Wahhabis, especially following the 1973 Arab–Israeli conflict.[23] Among the new recruits to the movement were two important social groups – the mass of young urban poor from deprived backgrounds and the devout bourgeoisie, a class hitherto excluded from political power and restricted by military and monarchical regimes.

Sadat's secret services nurtured this radical Islamist resurgence by aiding the formation of various small militant groups in order to counter the remaining student groups led by Nasserites and Marxists.[24] The Jamaat Islamiya (Islamic Associations) were formed on the university campuses with the help of a Sadat aide, the former lawyer, Mohammed Uthman Ismail, who is considered to be the 'godfather' of the Jamaat.[25] By the late 1970s, the Jamaat, espousing the importance of a pure Islamic life and organising summer camps for its cadres, involving ideological training, had driven the leftist student organisations underground. The Jamaat remained close allies, and useful tools, of the Sadat government until 1977 when the president flew to Jerusalem for peace talks with Israel.[26]

In return for Sadat's opening to the Muslim Brotherhood, the latter extended enthusiastic support to the regime's neo-liberal, free enterprise economic policies. Diametrically opposed to Nasser's nationalist policies, Egypt's economic liberalisation was propelled by a programme devised by the International Monetary

Fund, which had strong Anglo–American support, and involved reducing the state's role in the economy and promoting trade and investment policies favourable to foreign investors.[27] These policies increased inequalities between rich and poor and acted as a further recruiting sergeant for Islamist movements in the 1970s and 1980s, not just in Egypt but elsewhere in the Muslim world. Radical Islamists, although supporting the basic 'free market' project, could also speak in the name of resistance to foreign domination and exploitation of 'the people', while establishing a popular base and offering vital social services that the state no longer provided.[28]

British officials witnessed Sadat using the Muslim Brotherhood to bolster the regime as a previous generation had seen King Farouk and, initially, Nasser, do. They viewed Sadat's strategy favourably, provided that he could ultimately control those forces – precisely the concern that British covert planners had with regard to their own use of the Brotherhood in overthrowing Nasser in the 1950s. In 1971 British officials recognised that 'Sadat might be tempted to make use of such a potentially handy weapon', mirroring the long-standing British perception of the Brotherhood. The organisation was enjoying 'a renaissance' under Sadat, but the danger was that he 'might underestimate the difficulty of keeping it under control'.[29] The Foreign Office wrote that Sir Richard Beaumont, the British ambassador:

> Considers that Sadat may wish to use it [the Brotherhood] as a counter-weight to left-wing forces, but equally Sadat's performance so far does not give any reason to think he would wish to see its more fanatical aspects such as its tendency towards xenophobia become a dominant factor in Egyptian politics. On the other hand, the use of individual Moslem [sic] Brothers to leaven other political organisations, rather than the encouragement of the Brotherhood as such, might suit Sadat's book better.[30]

Thus Britain's senior official in Egypt was continuing to recognise the value of conniving with Brotherhood leaders, just as officials in his embassy had done in the 1950s. Indeed, Hassan al-Hodeibi, the Brotherhood's leader with whom Britain had then dealt, was still in his position when Beaumont penned these thoughts. Whether British officials had contacts with al-Hodeibi at this time is not revealed in the declassified government files; al-Hodeibi died in 1973.

Sadat's belief that he could manage and co-opt the Muslim Brotherhood against his leftist and communist political opponents worked to an extent, but the Brotherhood refused to openly back the regime, not least since Sadat refused to allow it to operate as a political party.[31] Sadat also failed to understand that only a complete Islamisation of society could satisfy the demands of the more fundamentalist groups.[32] In the October 1973 Arab–Israeli War – when the Arab states led by Egypt made early territorial gains against the Israeli military before reaching a stalemate – Sadat deployed the symbols of Islam to fire Egypt, in contrast to Nasser's evocation of Arab nationalism in the 1967 war. But Sadat's overtures to Israel and the signing of the Camp David Accords in September 1978, which led to a peace treaty with Israel, confirmed to the radical Islamists, bent on Israel's destruction, that Sadat was clearly no ally. His earlier patronage of the militant Islamists had by now led to the formation of a violent jihadist movement in the country. Sadat realised the threat against the regime too late; it was only in 1981 that the regime cracked down on the Jamaat Islamiya, dissolving them in September.

The following month, Sadat was assassinated by the al-Jihad organisation, which had its roots in a university Islamic group at Asyut University in Upper Egypt, similar to those formed with government help earlier in the decade. In the 1980s, members of al-Jihad were to splinter off into other groups, notably Islamic Jihad, led by Ayman al-Zawahiri, whose militants would volunteer for the war in Afghanistan.[33] Though many of their members and leaders were, like al-Zawahiri, former Muslim Brothers, these more violent organisations had become distinct from the Brotherhood. They attacked the Brotherhood for its lack of militancy and for accepting some notions of democracy rather than subjecting all powers of the state to Allah's will.[34] Violent Islamism now appeared to be on the march.

Sadat's assassination was a blow to US and British strategy in the Middle East, but his Islamisation programme in Egypt was already proving useful to one major Anglo-American covert operation. It was the radicalised Islamist elements from Egypt who were among those volunteering to fight the Soviets in Afghanistan after 1979, and who played key leadership roles there, sponsored by the Sadat regime and aided by Saudi money. Thus these forces continued to be the 'handy weapon' recognised by British officials, though far beyond Egypt itself. But before turning to these later events, we consider the momentous events of 1973 and the deepening, and rather extraordinary British–Saudi alliance.

CHAPTER 7

The Saudi and Iranian Revolutions

On the eve of the October 1973 Arab–Israeli War, Britain's position in the Middle East was seen as being comparatively rosy compared to the bad old days of Arab nationalism. That September James Craig, of the Foreign Office's Near East and North Africa department, noted that in the 1950s and '60s, the battle between the 'revolutionaries', led by Nasser, and the 'traditionalists', led by Saudi Arabia, had done harm to British interests since 'it forced us, since Nasser was "anti-imperialist" and therefore anti-British ... to support regimes which were obscurantist, reactionary and discreditable to their supporters'. However:

> What has happened now is that Egypt has declined in authority and abandoned revolution and subversion; simultaneously Saudi Arabia has gained in authority and grown (slightly) less mediaeval. As it is we have an Arab world led by a comparatively moderate Sadat and a very moderate Faisal; their main competitor for the leadership, Algeria, is growing steadily less hostile; so is Syria; the Sudan is wooing us; Jordan and the Lebanon are as friendly as ever; Morocco and Tunisia are quiet and amenable; Libya, though very troublesome, is increasingly isolated; Kuwait and the Gulf will follow their leaders; the PDRY [South Yemen] can

> be ignored; only Iraq remains to be won. So the picture is a much brighter one than we could have expected in late 1967 – largely through luck but partly through our own policies. The Israelis would say the credit is theirs.[1]

In 1979 Craig would become Britain's ambassador to Saudi Arabia. His description of Saudi King Faisal was instructive, for Faisal was anything but 'very moderate'; 'moderate', in this context, simply meant pro-Western, and Faisal was head of a state bent on exporting extremist Wahhabi ideology around the world and keeping the Saud family in power, not to mention the regime's terrible human rights abuses and aversion to anything smacking of democracy. After 1973, the Saudi strategy of exporting Wahhabism took off exponentially. So did a new and profound British alliance with – indeed, dependency on – the Saudis, which tied British economic policy inextricably to the world's pre-eminent Islamic fundamentalist state.

A 'HAPPY NEW ERA'

The armies of Egypt and Syria began a surprise attack on Israel on 6 October 1973, crossing the ceasefire lines in the Golan Heights and the Sinai Peninsula, which Israel had captured during the Six-Day War in 1967. Soon after the attack, the Organisation of Petroleum Exporting Countries (OPEC), led by the Gulf states, announced a rise in the price of oil and a total oil embargo against the US for its support of Israel. After further cuts in oil production, the price soared, more than quadrupling compared to early 1973, creating an international crisis and raising panic in Western countries.

Britain's ambassador in Jeddah, Hooky Walker, wrote that the 1973 oil price rises represented 'perhaps the most rapid shift in economic power that the world has ever seen'; the Foreign Office acknowledged that the crisis had propelled Saudi Arabia 'to a position of world influence'.[2] Britain, both before and after the crisis, was reliant on the Gulf states for 70 per cent of its oil supplies,

30 per cent of which came from Saudi Arabia. 'The disappearance of cheap oil', the Foreign Office's planning staff wrote in February 1974, 'has transformed the world in which British foreign policy has to operate.' Whereas in 1972 industrial countries had a trading surplus of $10 billion, in 1974 they were likely to have a deficit of $48 billion, while the oil producers were likely to have accrued a surplus of $69 billion.[3]

The oil price rise occurred alongside a worldwide rise in commodity prices and, in Britain, an ongoing coal dispute between the Conservative government of Edward Heath and the National Union of Mineworkers, which had reduced coal deliveries to power stations. Britain was plunged into energy shortages and the 'gravest economic crisis since the Second World War', the Cabinet was told by the chancellor, Tony Barber, announcing in December 1973 the balance of payments forecast for 1974. In response, Heath announced in parliament that the government would introduce a three-day working week to conserve fuel and electricity, that industry's access to electricity would be limited to five days per week and that television programming would end at 10.30 p.m.[4]

However, the Saudis, under the pro-Western Faisal, began to seek a lifting of the embargo as soon as possible, encouraged by the US decision in early 1974 to step up arms supplies to the regime, and worked with the US to find a face-saving formula to end the impasse between the Arabs and the West.[5] In fact, the Saudis, and also Sheikh Zayed's regime in Abu Dhabi, provided additional oil supplies to Britain in late 1973 and early 1974, to ease its energy crisis, despite the official restrictions agreed in OPEC at the time.[6] On 15 November 1973, Edward Heath wrote to King Faisal, emphasising the excellent state of British–Saudi relations, and underscoring his personal friendship with Faisal. 'During the crisis through which we have been passing and the momentous issues which it has raised for us all, I have much valued Your Majesty's understanding and appreciation of British policy in the Middle East,' Heath wrote, in apparent recognition of Saudi oil policy towards Britain.[7]

The Saudis formally lifted the embargo in March 1974. In subsequent OPEC meetings, Saudi oil minister Sheikh Yamani consistently called for low oil prices in support of the Western states.[8] At the September 1975 OPEC meeting, the Saudis resisted calls from the other members for a much greater increase in oil prices than the 10 per cent eventually agreed. The British files are full of praise for the Saudis' 'moderating role' in these meetings, and it is clear that Britain actively worked through them to achieve lower prices – a strategy 'to press Saudi Arabia to use her great strength to blunt the power of OPEC', as the new British ambassador to Saudi Arabia, Alan Rothnie, put it.[9]

Flush with oil money, the Saudis stepped up their bankrolling of Islamic organisations and charities around the world. During the 1970s the Saudi-controlled Muslim World League opened a raft of new offices abroad, while its Ministry for Religious Affairs printed and exported millions of Korans free of charge and distributed Wahhabi doctrinal texts among the world's mosques. The Saudis also instigated a massive building programme that would eventually construct 1,500 mosques worldwide.[10] In Jeddah in 1972, the Saudis added to the international Islamic associations they had founded the previous decade by establishing the World Assembly of Muslim Youth (WAMY), which sought to federate Islamist youth organisations throughout the world; WAMY would later be accused of being a discreet channel for Saudi donations to hardline organisations involved in supporting terrorist groups.[11]

At the same time, a quiet revolution was occurring in the British economy, involving the sealing of a profound economic alliance with the Saudis, the consequences of which are still evident. This was begun by Conservative ministers in the dying days of the Heath government, and enthusiastically continued by their Labour counterparts in the new Wilson government of 1974. British ministers bent over backwards to forge closer economic relations with Saudi Arabia by seeking to win contracts to participate in its petrodollar-funded economic expansion; moreover, they went out of their way to offer up Britain as an attractive place to invest Saudi oil money.

These British plans had actually begun before the October oil price rises. In January 1973 the Foreign Office had noted that, with Saudi oil wealth and plans for industrialisation in the Kingdom, there was 'a golden opportunity for British industry and for British banking if they have the energy and imagination to grasp it'.[12] By the following month, it was working on initiatives 'to nudge Saudi thinking in the direction of sensible investment abroad of their surplus revenues', and to persuade them 'of the facilities that the City of London had to offer.'[13] The Saudis were clearly being seen as potential saviours for Britain, already undergoing a deep economic crisis.

A stream of high-level meetings in Britain and Saudi Arabia began in early 1973. In February, Crown Prince Fahd, the minister of the interior, visited London to meet Edward Heath to discuss Saudi investment in Britain as well as the 'broad measure of agreement' between the two countries on foreign policy.[14] In July, Prince Abdullah, the commander of the Saudi National Guard – and another future king – visited London. Amidst the oil crisis in December 1973, Trade Secretary Peter Walker proposed to the prime minister to make 'a major effort' to persuade the Arab oil producers 'to invest part of their large surpluses over the next five or six years in British industry'. He outlined various options for 'partnership', with them entailing greater involvement of British industry in Saudi industrial development, especially in exploring new sources of raw materials or energy.[15] By the end of the year, after visits to Saudi Arabia by the governor of the Bank of England and officials in the Department of Trade and Industry, Ambassador Rothnie was noting that Britain and Saudi Arabia 'had taken the first steps towards the establishment of a new long-term relationship in the linked spheres of development, investment and oil'.[16]

British finance officials were, however, concerned about the possible impact that large Arab investments might have on the international financial system. Even before October 1973, Saudi Arabia had accrued surpluses of $3 billion from oil sales, and the Bank of England's 'prime concern was with the volatility of the large reserves which the Arab states would amass from oil revenues'.[17] By October 1974, the Treasury noted that the oil producers had accrued surpluses of $70 billion, of which the Saudis alone accounted for $26 billion, confirming the forecast earlier in the year.[18] The Treasury's concern was to handle the surpluses in a way so as 'not to dislocate international financial mechanisms and aggravate the tendencies towards recession now visible in the world economy.'[19] A key problem was that the investments were being placed in Western banks at high interest rates, accruing sums for the investors that were out of proportion to the banks' capital base, threatening to 'overwhelm' them, with 'grave consequences for the entire private financial structure of the West', the Treasury noted.[20]

The British solution was 'for a new and reformed system which might serve us in the future as Bretton Woods did in the past' – referring to the arrangements established in the mid-1940s in which countries pegged their exchange rates to the value of gold, but which collapsed in 1971 following the US' suspension of the convertibility of dollars to gold. The British now wanted to ensure that the oil producers recycled their surplus petrodollars 'to reinforce the stability of the system'; at the same time, some of these should 'come our way', the Treasury implored.[21]

The British–Saudi meetings continued into late 1974 and 1975. In December 1974, the chancellor, Denis Healey, visited Saudi Arabia to discuss Saudi investment in Britain and the global financial system, and also, as his principal private secretary put it, 'to establish good personal relationships with the powerful minority who matter in this important country'.[22] In March 1975, Fahd visited London and followed this up with a further visit in October, meeting the queen and various ministers, 'to inaugurate this happy new era' between the two countries.[23] The following month, Foreign Secretary James Callaghan paid the first ever visit by a British foreign secretary to Saudi Arabia to build on the 'tremendous momentum' of contacts between the two countries and to get more British firms participating in Saudi Arabia's massive new development projects.[24]

These British visits were exercises in obsequiousness, with Chancellor Healey's notable in this respect. When Healey met Saudi finance minister, Prince Musa'id, in December 1974, he told the latter that he did not consider the oil-producing countries to have acted immorally in raising oil prices, nor did he consider that the price increase was responsible 'by any means' for the difficulties now facing the world. The inflation that the world had experienced in 1973 had 'nothing to do with the price of oil', Healey said, adding that it was simply an 'historical accident' that the oil price increase had come just when the threat of inflation was being recognised.[25]

By January 1975, the Saudis had invested a massive $9.3 billion in Britain, of which $800 million was in the public sector – a total investment equivalent to around £20 billion today.[26] British nationalised industries' total borrowing from the oil producers was around $1.4 billion. However, the Treasury noted that 'because of the sensitivities of the Saudis we have avoided identifying them as the source' of these loans to Britain. It also stated that the oil producers' surplus funds were making a major contribution to financing Britain's current account deficit in 1974 and the first half of 1975. The Saudis were now 'very substantial holders of sterling', the second largest holders among the oil producers (after Nigeria).[27] When Harold Wilson met Prince Fahd in London in October 1975, he was briefed by his advisers to tell the future king: 'Your country now has a major stake in Britain and you will naturally be closely interested in the progress of the British economy.'[28]

Thus, within two years of the October 1973 oil crisis, the Saudis had poured huge quantities of petrodollars into the British economy, taking a sizeable stake in it. The upshot was that Britain was now economically reliant on the Saudi regime and would be in effect tied to aligning its foreign policy to the regime. British planners were perfectly comfortable with, indeed championed, the Saudis' increasingly influential regional and world role. In November 1974, a Foreign Office brief for Chancellor Healey's upcoming visit to Saudi Arabia noted the confidence with which Saudi Arabia, flush with petrodollars, was bestriding the world stage, and that it 'will retain for the foreseeable future a powerful voice in the formulation of Arab policies'. It encouraged Healey to raise the point that 'Saudi Arabia and Britain have many interests in common, not least in the maintenance of stability in the Arabian Peninsula'.[29] 'Stability' of course meant protecting the sub-region from infection by wayward notions of popular, republican or nationalist government. Britain welcomed Saudi Arabia's pre-eminence in the region, especially after having decided to reduce its own military commitments to the Gulf states a few years earlier.[30]

Both states were bent on maintaining in power the pro-Western feudal sheikhdoms elsewhere in Arabia. This applied firstly in Oman, where the sultan was still fighting nationalist forces in Dhofar province with the aid of British troops and Saudi money; and secondly in North Yemen, created after the British and Saudi-backed covert war and where a pro-Saudi military government now faced a Soviet-backed nationalist regime in neighbouring South Yemen, Britain's former colony of Aden. British and Saudi officials were especially concerned with South Yemeni backing for the Dhofari rebels and connived throughout 1975 to find ways to counter it. In October that year, James Callaghan and Saudi foreign minister, Prince Saud bin Faisal, jointly agreed that the Saudis would finance North Yemen's arms imports and that the British would arrange 'private' counter-insurgency training for the North Yemeni regime.[31]

Yet Britain did not only support Saudi foreign policy in the Middle East. Crown Prince Fahd's October 1975 visit to Britain came at a time when the Foreign Office was briefing ministers to regard the Saudis 'as valuable interlocutors' for 'exchanging views … on a wide range of world (as distinct from purely Middle Eastern) problems, including East–West relations and the world economic and monetary situation (with particular reference to a new international economic order)'.[32] This was now a global strategic alliance. And British planners could have had no illusions about just who the Saudis were otherwise supporting in their foreign policy. In the 1970s and early 1980s, Saudi Arabia financed, among others, the Palestinian terrorist group headed by Abu Nidal, Islamic militants opposed to Qadafi in Libya, Uganda's bloodthirsty dictator Idi Amin, Muslim rebels in the Philippines and the brutal Siad Barre regime in Somalia.[33]

The Kingdom's links with terrorist groups were known to the US by the early 1970s. In May 1974, for example, the US State Department warned Britain not to go ahead with its reported offer to sell Blowpipe surface-to-air missiles to Saudi Arabia, for fear of 'seepage of this type of weapon into the hands of terrorists'.[34] The US ambassador to Saudi Arabia told his British counterpart that the US had refused to sell similar equipment, the Redeye, for fear of their ending up with terrorists and being 'used against civil aircraft or similar targets'.[35]

The British continued to be responsible for the very survival of the Saudi royal family. In 1970, a British army team had trained members of the Saudi National Guard in 'special duties in connection with the personal safety of HM the King'.[36] This training team stayed throughout the early 1970s, while the Saudi oil minister, Sheikh Yamani, was protected by a team of former SAS security officers; this training followed the events of December 1975, when a group of terrorists led by Carlos the Jackal had taken OPEC oil ministers hostage at their meeting in Vienna.[37]

In May 1973, Britain signed a £250 million deal with Saudi Arabia to train its air force pilots and service its aircraft.[38] By this time, 2,000 British instructors, engineers and administrators were involved in work on various military projects around the country.[39] British military equipment was being sold to a country whose 'defence' policy was, as the then British ambassador, Hooky Walker, noted in February 1975, based on 'Jihad'. A Saudi press statement of the time stated:

> The general principles upon which the Kingdom's defence policy is founded include the doctrine that Jihad (Holy War) is something that will remain in existence until the Day of Judgment within the limits laid down by God ('Fight in the cause of God those who fight you, but do not transgress limits, for God loveth not transgressors', Koran, sura ii) and by the Prophet ('Whoever fights to raise the high word of God is doing the will of God'). The Kingdom's defence system is guided by the Shari'a rules of conduct for war that are contained in the Holy Book, the Sunna of the Prophet and the guidelines of the Four Great Caliphs.[40]

This alliance had been formed neither because British planners had any particular love for the House of Saud, nor out of ignorance as to what it was like. In May 1972, just before the deepening of the Anglo–Saudi *entente cordiale*, outgoing ambassador, Willie Morris, had observed to Alec Douglas-Home, the foreign secretary, that: 'It is a great tragedy that, with all the world's needs, Providence should have concentrated so much of a vital resource and so much wealth in the hands of people who need it so little and are so socially irresponsible about the use of it.' The leading Saudis, Morris added, 'regard the rest of the world as existing for their convenience', and they 'act with unstudied, unconscious indifference to the convenience of others or what others may think of them.'[41] Morris' words are revealing in that they describe Whitehall's closest allies in the region, with whom it had formed a strategic alliance, precisely to oppose more benign forces elsewhere. In short, the British knew exactly with whom they were dealing as the Saudis promoted any cause inside the Kingdom or overseas in the name of Wahhabi extremism and defence of the House of Saud.

The lengths to which British officials went to nurture the relationship were often extraordinary. In October 1975, for example, a Foreign Office brief for the queen in advance of Prince Fahd's visit to Britain included a section called 'topics to be avoided'. It noted two – the Arab–Israel issue and 'recent reports of bribery and corruption in Saudi Arabia'.[42] The British government also provided a 'large Jaguar and an attractively leggy blonde' for Mohammed al-Fawzan, the director of foreign broadcasting in the Saudi Ministry of Information, for his visit to London in September 1973. 'Mohammed seemed in a thoroughly anglophile mood' with these provisions, the Foreign Office commented.[43]

One senior Saudi with whom Britain also began developing relations was Prince Turki bin Abdul Aziz, an Oxford-educated vice minister of defence who, in 1977, succeeded Kamal Adham as head of the Saudi foreign intelligence service, the General Intelligence Directorate. Turki would reportedly forge close ties to MI6 and the CIA and even offer jobs to retired intelligence officers to be his eyes and ears in London or Washington.[44] Soon after his appointment, in either 1978 or 1979, Turki is believed to have first met Osama Bin Laden, then a student at the University of Jeddah who had begun to associate with Islamic radicals. It is alleged that Turki suggested to Bin Laden that he use his money to aid the Afghan resistance against the Soviets following the latter's invasion in December 1979.[45]

While these developments were taking place, there was turmoil elsewhere in the Middle East.

CULTIVATING THE AYATOLLAH

The regime of the shah, Mohammad-Reza Pahlavi, in Iran, installed in the Anglo–American coup in 1953, was a key Western ally and 'policeman' in the Middle East. It sent forces to bolster the British-backed regime of Sultan Qaboos in Oman, acted as a counterweight to nationalist Iraq, promoted pro-Western economic policies and bought Western arms. Britain consistently backed the shah's authoritarian rule, helping to train its brutal security force, SAVAK, and otherwise acting as a public apologist for the regime's increasing human rights abuses. In April 1978, then Conservative opposition leader, Margaret Thatcher, visited Tehran, and gave a speech to the Iran–British chamber of commerce. She said of the shah:

> Surely he must be one of the world's most far-sighted statesmen whose experience is unrivalled. No other leader has given his country more dynamic leadership. He is leading Iran through a twentieth century renaissance.

Iran, Thatcher added, was Britain's largest market in the Middle East, and its arms purchases 'provide many thousands of jobs' in Britain.[46] Indeed, by late 1978 British companies had outstanding orders from the shah's regime to build over 1,500 tanks worth £1.2 billion.[47] British oil company, BP, was leading a consortium of oil companies which produced and purchased the bulk of Iran's crude oil and was engaged in renegotiating its agreement with Iran signed in 1973. In July 1978, six months before the Islamic revolution overthrew the shah, James Callaghan's Labour government secretly approved the supply of CS gas to Iran to help the regime control the increasing demonstrations against it, following a request from the shah.[48]

Iran's Islamic revolution and the emergence to power of Ayatollah Khomeini came to pose the biggest challenge to British and US power in the oil-rich Gulf region and wider Middle East since the rise of Arab nationalism in the 1950s. But the record shows that Britain dropped its support for the shah before the revolution and sought to insure itself with the Iranian opposition, led by Khomeini. Once the latter was in power, Whitehall initially sought good relations with the Islamic regime, and connived with it, seeing it as a counter to the Soviet Union.

Callaghan's foreign secretary, David Owen, writes in his

memoirs that throughout late 1978 Britain was still backing the shah to restore order, but ideally hoped to replace him with a military or other figure: 'We needed someone with charisma who would only be in post for a few years, brave enough to make enemies, and ready later to step aside for the shah's son as a constitutional monarch.' According to Owen, Britain also made contact with one senior religious figure, apparently to try to uphold the authority of the shah. On 29 September the British ambassador, Anthony Parsons, met the shah and urged him to promise that elections would take place. At this point, the British embassy in Tehran contacted Ayatollah Shariatmadari – one of Iran's leading clerics, whom Owen describes as 'less radical than Khomeini', and who was known for his more liberal views – 'informing him that the British government still supported the shah'. Shariatmadari was in contact with the shah during most of 1978 through his private financial adviser; it appears that the British thought he would have some influence over the shah. Owen also notes that 'we arranged for a British expert in riot control to visit Tehran but decided against having contact with Sadeq Qotbzadeh, one of Khomeini's entourage in Paris', where he was in exile.[49] Qotbzadeh was not a cleric but a member of the revolutionary Liberation Movement of Iran then allied with the religious forces in their task of overthrowing the shah. Thus British officials considered making contact with Khomeini's entourage but were overruled by Owen, his account suggests.[50]

On 10 October, Anthony Parsons had another long audience with the shah, emphasising British support for his regime, saying: 'I made clear that, so far as the British were concerned, he need not have any worry that we were messing around with the opposition or that we were thinking of ratting'.[51] By now, however, popular opposition to the regime was mounting, involving various nationalist and communist groups but whose most powerful element was the Islamic clergy. After a dispatch from Parsons in late October describing the unrest in Tehran, James Callaghan wrote: 'I would not give much for the shah's chances. I think Dr Owen should start thinking about reinsuring!'[52] This message, imploring the foreign secretary to 'insure' Britain with Iran's likely future leaders, shows that the government was already thinking of switching its allegiance. A little over a week later, however, Owen told a Cabinet meeting: 'Whatever his faults, it was still in our interests that the shah should remain in power. A military government without him would be no improvement and a government under the anti-British Ayatollah Khomeini would be far worse'.[53]

By December, however, officials were saying that the survival of the shah was unlikely and that Iran seemed on the verge of a revolution.[54] On 4 December, Anthony Parsons – who had told the shah that Britain would never 'rat' on him – informed the shah of Britain's contacts with opposition politicians, though the declassified files give no details on which figures.[55] Later that month, Foreign Office officials went further in arguing for Britain to switch its support to the Iranian opposition. Owen writes that he told a Foreign Office meeting on December 20 that the shah was in a 'hopeless' position, but that a 'severe crackdown… might work in Iran where, given the absence of an alternative and the threat of chaos, there could be greater acceptance of the ruthless exercise of power than we in the West could not easily imagine, let alone support'. Owen's account implies that some officials argued to drop the shah and support the opposition, saying that he told the meeting that 'we would get the worst of all possible worlds if we shifted policies now'. But Owen concluded that Britain should not 'advocate or be thought to be advocating solutions, nor should we become involved in advising the shah or others about what they should do' – a comment which implies that, in a concession to the officials' arguments, Britain would adopt a middle way and allow matters to take their course, meaning that the shah would fall, and that Britain would not be seen to be supporting him. Thus the British removed their support for the regime they had placed in power in 1953. On December 29, Foreign Office officials further proposed that Owen ask the Americans to press the shah not to impose a military crackdown in the country which, Owen says, he refused – a further sign that officials, at least, were no longer prepared to back the shah.[56]

Finally, Owen notes that 'as for the BBC Persian Service, it was a liability in some ways but also a form of insurance with the internal opposition. I had taken a firm decision months earlier not to interfere with the BBC and was happy with this and felt we had this problem in its proper perspective.'[57] This comment is highly revealing; at the time, the BBC was widely known in Tehran as 'Ayatollah BBC' for its critical reports of the shah, leading many to speculate that the British were tacitly promoting the ayatollah's Islamists.[58]

The shah fled Tehran on 16 January, and on 1 February Khomeini returned from exile to Iran. Now, the British tried to 'insure' themselves further with the new Islamic regime by avoiding any association with the shah. Along with the Americans, London refused to allow its onetime placeman political asylum in Britain. 'There was no honour in my decision', Owen notes, 'just the cold calculation of national interest', adding that he considered it 'a despicable act'.[59] Callaghan wrote in justifying the decision that the shah 'is an immensely controversial figure in Iran and we must consider our future with that country'.[60]

Khomeini appointed Mehdi Bazargan, a scholar jailed by the shah and the leader of the secular Liberation Movement of Iran, as prime minister in an interim government, but real power was concentrated in the Islamic Revolutionary Council dominated by fundamentalists loyal to Khomeini. Callaghan told parliament on 12 February that his government was that day recognising the Bazargan government and 'look forward to establishing good relations' with it.[61] Opposition leader Margaret Thatcher made clear that her priorities were ensuring that arms exports ordered by the shah, notably the tank deal, would be honoured, along with 'oil, trade and other interests'.[62] However, that month the new Iranian government cancelled some of the arms orders. But this did not stop the British from seeking to curry favour with the new regime.

On 20 March, Cabinet Secretary Sir John Hunt wrote to the prime minister saying that 'in winding up the contracts, we should not give the impression that we are turning our backs on Iran'. Rather, he suggested that 'we should let the Iranians know that we are ready, if they wish, to resume the supply of routine items such as ammunition and spare parts which are essential to the basic functions of their armed forces', and that 'we should lose no opportunity to foster our relationship with the new government'.[63] The following month, an Islamic Republic was declared with a new constitution reflecting the ideals of the theocracy.

After Margaret Thatcher won the May 1979 election, she accepted Anthony Parsons's objection to granting the shah asylum in Britain, consistent with the previous government. Thatcher sent the former ambassador to Iran, Sir Denis Wright, to the Bahamas to meet the shah in exile and tell him of Britain's decision. Wright travelled under a false name to avoid any British public association with the deposed leader. Members of the shah's family were also deterred from entering Britain in case London became a centre of opposition to the new Islamic regime.[64] For his part, the shah later wrote in his autobiography: 'I have a long-standing suspicion of British intent and British policy which I have never found reason to alter.'[65]

Bazargan and his Cabinet resigned in November after militant pro-Khomeini students seized the US embassy in Tehran, taking over sixty Americans hostage, in response to the shah's visit to the US seeking medical care. Britain vehemently protested against the embassy seizure, but two weeks into the crisis, when Thatcher was asked in parliament whether she would congratulate Egyptian President Sadat on offering the shah asylum, the prime minister failed to respond.[66] When the shah died in Cairo in July 1980, the US sent former President Richard Nixon and France its ambassador to the funeral, whereas Britain sent only its chargé d'affaires; David Owen implies in his memoir that this also sent an important signal to the Islamic regime.[67]

Moreover, Britain continued to arm and train the new Iranian regime: Thatcher told a press conference in Washington in December 1979 that Britain was still supplying arms to Iran, noting that 'we have sent virtually no arms since the hostages were taken', though she contradicted herself the following April in saying that no arms had been exported since the beginning of the hostage crisis.[68] In January 1980, she informed parliament that 'fewer than 30' Iranian military officers were being trained in Britain; by April 1980 'about 28 or 30' were still being trained.[69]

On 28 January 1980, with the Soviets having invaded Afghanistan a month before, Thatcher told the House of Commons that 'we face a grave development in East–West relations'. Moscow might take advantage of the unrest and 'feeling for ethnic autonomy' in the region caused by the Iranian revolution. 'The temptation to the Russians is apparent', she noted, but 'there are signs that the Iranians themselves are increasingly aware of the danger.' She continued by stating that:

> We in this country respect the right of peoples to choose their own regimes and governments. We wish the Iranians well in their search for the political system best suited to their needs. We hope that they will emerge from their present difficulties united.[70]

The following April she added that 'the future internal government of Iran is a matter for the Iranian people', and continued to raise the 'danger of secession of some of the Iranian peoples' which 'would be contrary to the interests of the West'.[71] Thatcher was here upholding the Iranian theocracy as a counter to Soviet expansion and saw a 'united' Iran as a deterrent to it. By this time, it should be said, the nature of the Iranian regime was already apparent, not only in the taking of American hostages, but also in the numerous executions that were now taking place. Britain also saw radical Islam as a counter to the Soviets in Afghanistan, and

British covert action against the Russian occupation had already been launched, as we see in the next chapter.

Thatcher's thinking appeared to mirror that of President Carter's national security adviser, Zbigniew Brzezinski. Amidst the upheaval in Iran towards the end of 1978, Brzezinski had begun to press the idea in Washington that the region from northeast Africa through the Gulf to Central Asia was an 'arc of crisis', and to argue for what he called 'a new "security framework" to reassert US power and influence in the region'. Brzezinski envisaged deepening US military ties with Egypt, Saudi Arabia, Pakistan, Turkey and other Muslim countries near the southern borders of the Soviet Union and in the Gulf region, and mobilising Islamic forces to contain the Soviet Union.[72] Once the shah had gone, this thinking took on even greater importance, and by the summer of 1979, Brzezinski wanted a 'de facto alliance with the forces of Islamic resurgence and with the regime of the Islamic Republic of Iran', in the words of Richard Cottam, the CIA officer who had played a key role in the 1953 Iran coup.[73] Brzezinski met Prime Minister Bazargan in Algiers a few months later to advance the policy, but it was completely halted once the hostage crisis began in November.[74] Thatcher, however, continued to evoke the idea of Islamic Iran being a counter to the Soviets after the hostage crisis had begun.

Britain's de facto support for the Iranian Islamists was, however, not merely passive and rhetorical. In 1982, when Khomeini's regime had stepped up its repression and executions of political opponents, Britain engaged in an extraordinary act of connivance with it, by helping it nearly destroy the communist Tudeh Party, the main leftist organisation in the country. After initially collaborating with the Islamic regime, Tudeh withdrew its support in 1982, criticising it for continuing the war with Iraq, which had begun in 1980. The regime then sought to suppress the Tudeh, imprisoning its leaders. When Vladimir Kuzichkin, a major in the Soviet KGB, defected to Britain in 1982, he passed on to MI6 a list of Soviet agents operating in Iran, following which MI6 allowed Kuzichkin to visit the CIA and also give it the list. In October, MI6 and the CIA jointly decided to pass this list to the Iranians, in order to curry favour with the Iranian regime and reduce Soviet influence in a strategically important country. Dozens of alleged agents were subsequently executed and more than a thousand members of the Tudeh arrested, while the party was banned. In December one hundred members of the party's military organisation were put on trial, drawing substantially on the information supplied by Britain; several were sentenced to death.[75] The Tudeh was effectively crushed, though later managed to reconstitute itself and operate as an underground movement.

This episode showed that Britain was prepared to secretly collaborate with a ruthless Shia Islamist regime in pursuit of specific common interests – the repression of the Left – even though Iran was by now considered a strategic threat and overall anti-Western force. This was also in line with long-standing British policy, reflecting British collaboration with Ayatollah Kashani in the coup planning against Musaddiq thirty years before. Soon, Britain even re-started the export of major weapons to the Khomeini regime, as we see in Chapter 9.

CHAPTER 8

Training in Terrorism: The Afghan Jihad

THE WAR AGAINST the Soviet occupation of Afghanistan in the 1980s was to mark the next phase in the development of global Islamic radicalism, building on the Islamic resurgence during the previous decade. Following the Soviet invasion of December 1979, tens of thousands of volunteers from around the Muslim world flocked to join their Afghan brethren and fight the communists. During the course of the war, they went on to form organised jihadist militant groups that would eventually target their home countries, and the West, in terrorist operations. These mujahideen, and the indigenous Afghan resistance groups to which they were attached, were bolstered by billions of dollars in aid and military training provided mainly by Saudi Arabia, the US and Pakistan, but also by Britain.

Britain already had a long history of supporting and working alongside Islamist forces by the time the Soviets crossed the Afghan border, but the collusion with the mujahideen in Afghanistan was of a different order to these earlier episodes, part of Whitehall's most extensive covert operation since the Second World War. The problem with the Soviet invasion of Afghanistan, as Prime Minister Margaret Thatcher put it after six months in office, was that 'if its hold on Afghanistan is consolidated, the Soviet Union will, in effect, have vastly extended its borders with Iran, will have acquired a border more than 1,000 miles long with Pakistan, and will have advanced to within 300 miles of the Straits of Hormuz, which control the Persian Gulf.'[1] In public, the prime minister and other British leaders denied British military involvement in Afghanistan and claimed to be seeking purely diplomatic solutions to the conflict.[2] In reality, British covert aid to the Afghan resistance began to flow even before the Soviet invasion, while Whitehall authorised MI6 to conduct operations in the first year of the Soviet occupation, coordinated by MI6 officers in Islamabad in liaison with the CIA and Pakistan's intelligence service, the ISI.[3] British and US covert training programmes were critical, since many of the indigenous Afghan forces, and the vast majority of the jihadist volunteers arriving in Afghanistan, had no military training.[4] It was a policy that was to have profound consequences.

ONE, TWO, THREE AFGHAN JIHADS

In the early 1970s, the ideas of the Muslim Brotherhood had gained wide circulation in Afghanistan, as Egyptian and Afghan students, studying at Cairo's celebrated al-Azhar University, travelled to each other's countries. One al-Azhar graduate was the most prominent of the Afghan Islamists: Burhanuddin Rabbani, a Tajik university professor who, in 1972, was elected head of the Jamaat-i-Islami (Islamic Society) in Afghanistan, a political party inspired both by the Muslim Brotherhood's leading thinkers, Hassan al-Banna and Sayyid Qutb, and by Abdul Ala Mawdudi's party of the same name in Pakistan. Mawdudi, who had significant influence on generations of Islamists and jihadists, believed that modern civilisation was leading the world to doom and that only Islam could rescue it. He advanced the idea of an Islamic revolution which would lead to the creation of an Islamic state, a revolutionary goal in preparation for which the Jamaat-i-Islami aimed to educate society. Rabbani's deputy in the Jamaat-i-Islami was Abdul Rasul Sayyaf, a Kabul University lecturer who also had affiliations with the Muslim

Brotherhood, while a young Pashtun civil engineering graduate called Gulbuddin Hekmatyar was placed in charge of the party's political activities.[5]

During the mid-1970s, the Muslim Brotherhood in Afghanistan was assessed by the British ambassador in Kabul, John Drinkall, as 'conservative' and a 'potent threat' to British interests there, but, he paradoxically continued, 'I do not rate this threat very high'.[6] The Brotherhood was seen not as a centralised organisation, but was a term 'loosely applied to any group of religious enthusiasts', while it was 'unlikely' to have formal links to the international Muslim Brotherhood.[7] However, another official in the British embassy noted that the 'international "Muslim Brotherhood" ... is still active in Afghanistan, including Kabul University and the army.'[8]

The British regarded Afghanistan in the 1970s much as they had during the Great Game of the nineteenth century: it was a country where Britain's commercial interests were small, but, officials noted, 'it is worth taking some trouble to maintain the close relationship with the Afghan government' since 'Afghanistan is strategically located and the Afghan government often have interesting side-lights on the affairs of their neighbours'.[9] A pro-British king, Zahir Shah, had ruled Afghanistan since 1933 with a regime acknowledged by the Foreign Office to be 'weak and inefficient, hampered by an uncontrollable and irresponsible parliament, against a background of popular discontent, especially among students.' Political parties were banned. At the same time, the Foreign Office continued, 'our own relations with Afghanistan are now better than they have been for about 130 years', mirroring the historical pattern of British support for unpopular regimes.[10]

In July 1973, the king was overthrown in a military coup led by his brother-in-law, Mohammed Daoud Khan, a former prime minister. The coup was staged by left-wing officers, many of whom had been trained in the Soviet Union, though 'Daoud was first and foremost a nationalist and determined to preserve Afghanistan's independence and freedom of action'.[11] Daoud instituted a republic, proclaimed himself President and made agreements on arms imports and military training with the Soviet Union. To shore up the regime, Daoud soon moved against a growing Islamist movement, jailing some leading figures, including Sayyaf, while others, including Rabbani and Ahmed Shah Massoud, a Tajik engineering student, fled over Afghanistan's southern border to neighbouring Pakistan.

Pakistan, meanwhile, feared that Daoud would pursue the cause of 'Pashtunistan' – a territory under Kabul's control, encompassing an area of a majority Pashtun population in southern Afghanistan and northern Pakistan; this region had been split in two by the Durand line, the British-drawn border imposed during colonial rule of India. The Pakistani government, under Prime Minister Zulfikar Ali Bhutto, the founder of the Pakistan People's Party who led a return to civilian rule in the country, moved to counter Daoud's promotion of a Greater Afghanistan by backing an Islamist rebellion in the country. Bhutto's government authorised a secret military training programme near Peshawar in Pakistan, where Afghans were given small arms and training by the elite Special Services Group under the auspices of the ISI.[12] In July 1975, the ISI sent its Afghans into the eastern part of Afghanistan to conduct a wave of attacks on government offices and to inspire an uprising; however, this failed, owing to a lack of widespread support for it in Afghanistan.[13]

Daoud's regime became increasingly unpopular and repressive until another pro-Soviet coup was staged in April 1978 by Mohammed Taraki, of the main pro-Soviet political party in the country, the Peoples Democratic Party of Afghanistan (PDPA), which after gaining power signed a friendship treaty with the Soviet Union. During 1978, a popular rebellion against the new regime broke out during which the Islamic parties, described in US files as the 'Muslim Brotherhood', and backed by Pakistan's ISI, tried to foment a second uprising by conducting a campaign of terrorism in Afghanistan, assassinating hundreds of teachers and civil servants.[14] In July 1979, President Carter, concerned about the new regime's closeness to the Soviet Union, began sending covert aid to Islamist opponents of the regime, the third attempt by outside actors since 1975 to organise an uprising against a regime in Kabul. The operation was undertaken in liaison with Saudi Arabia and Pakistan and was part of a plan by an inter-governmental body established by Carter, the Nationalities Working Group, to promote unrest among the ethnic minorities in the Soviet Union, a strategy reminiscent of Britain's age-old policies in the region.[15] The secret aid was dispatched five months before the Soviet invasion; Zbigniew Brzezinski, Carter's national security adviser, later said that he told Carter of his hope that US aid would 'induce a Soviet military intervention' that would fail, and therefore 'give the USSR its Vietnam War'.[16]

In September 1979, after months of brutal infighting between two factions of the ruling PDPA, another coup brought Deputy Prime Minister Hafizullah Amin into power, seeking to control the PDPA as well as fight the US-backed mujahideen guerillas. With Amin's regime under pressure from the insurgency, and with Moscow fearing that Amin was not sufficiently pliant to maintain a pro-Soviet government in Kabul, the Soviets invaded on 27 December, pouring troops and tanks into the country, killing Amin and installing former deputy prime minister, Babrak Karmal, as president. Immediately after the invasion, Brzezinski sent Carter a memo stating that 'we should concert with Islamic countries both a propaganda campaign and a covert action campaign to help the rebels.'[17]

Britain also appears to have begun to secretly support the Afghan rebels before the Soviet invasion. On 17 December 1979, a 'special coordination' meeting was held in the White House, chaired by Carter's vice president, Walter Mondale, involving all key US government departments. As Soviet troops were amassing near the Afghanistan border, threatening to invade to shore up the communist regime, the meeting agreed to 'explore with the

Pakistanis and British the possibility of improving the financing, arming and communications of the rebel forces to make it as expensive as possible for the Soviets to continue their efforts'. Thus the British now began to play what had become their primary role vis-à-vis the Americans, that of junior partner in US-led covert action, a sharp contrast to the more equal role enjoyed by London in the 1950s; Britain would carry out specialist tasks such as training the Afghan resistance and dispatching covert operatives to support the fighting. Overall, the US plan was 'to cast the Soviets as opposing Moslem religious and nationalist expressions.'[18]

On 18 December, the day after the meeting, Prime Minister Margaret Thatcher, by now presumably informed of the request from the White House meeting, gave a keynote speech to the establishment US think tank, the Foreign Policy Association, in New York, entitled 'The West in the World Today'. In it, she robustly championed Islam as an alternative to Marxism. Referring to the Iranian hostage crisis that had begun the previous month, Thatcher said that 'I do not believe that we should judge Islam by events in Iran', continuing:

> There is a tide of self-confidence and self-awareness in the Muslim world which preceded the Iranian revolution, and will outlast its present excesses. The West should recognise this with respect, not hostility. The Middle East is an area where we all have much at stake. It is in our own interests, as well as in the interests of the people of that region, that they build on their own deep religious traditions. We do not wish to see them succumb to the fraudulent appeal of imported Marxism.[19]

Thatcher's willingness to put aside the Iranian militants' seizure of the US embassy in Tehran and her evocation of the contrast between Islam's 'traditions' and 'imported' Marxism was striking. This was the speech – endlessly quoted in TV documentaries –

where Thatcher, in response to those like the Soviets who accused her of being an 'Iron Lady', said: 'They're quite right, I am'. Yet a key part of Thatcher's call to counter what she described as 'the immediate threat from the Soviet Union' was a very traditional British reliance on Islamist forces in the region.

The month after the invasion, Thatcher told parliament that the term 'rebels' being used by the newspapers 'is a strange word to me of people who are fighting to defend their own country against a foreign invader. Surely they are genuine freedom fighters, fighting to free their country from an alien oppressor.' She described Afghanistan in language referring to Islam and Muslims that was striking, saying that it was 'an Islamic country, a member of the non-aligned movement and a country that posed no conceivable threat to their [the Soviets] country or their interests', and that 'the Soviet Union has driven a wedge into the heart of the Muslim world.'[20]

On a later visit to a refugee camp near the Afghan border, Thatcher told her audience that 'you left a godless country because you refused to live under a godless communist system which is trying to destroy your religion', and that 'the hearts of the free world are with you'. She added that 'we shall continue, together with Pakistan, the Islamic conference, the non-aligned movement, with the vast majority of the world's countries, to work for a solution.'[21] The invocations to Islam are again striking, showing that Britain, once again, was prepared to openly identify its own geo-strategic and oil interests with those of specifically Islamic forces.

ORGANISATION OF THE JIHAD

The US's key allies in the region – Saudi Arabia, Egypt and Pakistan – soon began organising the war of resistance, with US and British support. The Saudi regime, media and mosques drummed up support for the jihad against the godless communists all over the kingdom, while the Saudi-backed Muslim World League also played a key role in sending financial aid. The Saudis, along with the US, were the chief bankrollers of the war, each providing around $3 billion. Saudi funding was managed by Prince Turki, head of intelligence, who worked with, among others, Osama Bin Laden, the son of a wealthy businessman with close connections to the royal family. Using his own financial resources to aid the Afghan resistance, Bin Laden was among the first of the Arabs to join the jihad, arriving there in 1980 and staying for most of the war; though one analyst notes that Bin Laden also visited London in the early 1980s, delivering several sermons at the Regents Park Islamic Centre.[22] Saudi King Fahd, who assumed power in the kingdom in 1982, and Crown Prince Abdullah – the present-day king – are also believed to have met with and funded Bin Laden.[23]

Bin Laden used his own money to recruit and train Arab volunteers in Pakistan and Afghanistan and, under the approving eye of Pakistani ISI officers, cultivated good relations with Afghan commanders such as Hekmatyar and Massoud.[24] There is no evidence of direct British or US support to Bin Laden, but one CIA source has claimed that US emissaries met directly with Bin Laden, and it was he who first suggested that the mujahideen be supplied with Stinger anti-aircraft missiles.[25] American journalist John Cooley notes that 'delighted by his impeccable Saudi credentials, the CIA gave Bin Laden free rein in Afghanistan' to organise Islamist fighters.[26]

A second major player was Sadat's Egypt, which organised transport to Afghanistan for the Egyptian volunteers, including Muslim Brothers, who were to make up a large proportion of the anti-Soviet resistance. After Sadat's assassination by Islamists in 1981, some of those who had been temporarily imprisoned later made the trip, including Mohamed Atef, who became a close aide of Bin Laden. Many of the hardline Egyptian Islamists fought with Hekmatyar's Hezb-e-Islami.[27]

Pakistan, which was now under martial law following General Zia ul-Haq's July 1977 coup against the Bhutto government, organised and managed the Afghan resistance on the ground. Trained in the

British Indian Army in the 1940s and subsequently at Fort Bragg in the US, and a favourite of the US Defence Intelligence Agency, Zia had also seen service in Jordan in 1970, leading mercenaries to crush the Palestinians on behalf of King Hussein during Black September.[28] After seizing power, Zia proceeded to project himself and Pakistan as the champion of Islam, and 'narrow and bigoted religiosity became Pakistan's state policy'.[29] Lacking a popular political base, Zia sought the support of the mullahs, and went even further than Sadat in 'Islamising' Pakistani society. Zia's government implemented sharia law in 1979 and was backed by the powerful Jamaat-i-Islami (JI) which provided the main channel of Arab financial aid to the mujahideen in Afghanistan.[30] The JI's network of Deobandi religious schools, or madrassas, educated and radicalised tens of thousands of young people across Pakistan in the 1970s and '80s, aided by the massive influx of money that poured in to support the Islamist militant cause in the region.

The covert arms deliveries to the Afghan rebels were organised by and routed through Pakistan, and specifically its ISI. At a meeting with Brzezinski in January 1980, General Zia insisted on the CIA providing no direct arms supplies to the Afghans, in order to retain Pakistani control over the operation.[31] Of the huge quantities of arms exported to Pakistan, for supposed onward distribution to the Afghan groups, around a third were sold onto the black market by Pakistani forces, never reaching the intended recipients. From 1983 to 1987 the annual shipment of weaponry rose from 10,000 to 65,000 tonnes.[32]

The Afghan resistance was organised into seven main groups, known as the Peshawar Seven, after the city in northwestern Pakistan where they were based. The four most important groups were all hardline and militant, professing holy war and committed to building an Islamic society. One historian has called them the Ikhwahhabis – influenced both by the ideology of the Muslim Brothers (Ikhwanism) and by the ultra-conservative ideology of the Saudis (Wahhabism).[33] The Hezb-e-Islami was split into two factions. One was led by Gulbuddin Hekmatyar, who had broken away from Rabbani's Jamaat-i-Islami, and was dominated by Muslim Brothers; this was the most powerful of the Afghan factions and received the largest share of external aid, notably from the ISI and Pakistan's Jamaat-i-Islami. Hezb-e-Islami's other faction was led by Younis Khalis, a sixty-year-old mullah and scholar whose military commanders included Jalaluddin Haqqani and Abdul Haq, whom we encounter later. Then there was Burhaneddin Rabbani's Jamaat-i-Islami, whose military commander in the field was Ahmed Shah Massoud. The fourth group was the Ittihad Islami (Islamic Unity), led by Abdul Rasul Sayyaf, a Wahhabi with links to Saudi Arabia, which gave most of its support to Sayyaf along with Hekmatyar; it was Sayyaf with whom Bin Laden, and also Khaled Sheikh Mohammed, the architect of 9/11, first went into battle.

The non-Afghan Muslim volunteers were attached to these groups, most joining Hekmatyar's and Sayyaf's. Estimates of the numbers who trained and fought in Afghanistan vary widely, from 25–85,000.[34] Although their contribution to the military effort against the Soviet occupiers was significant at times, it was negligible compared to the Afghan forces themselves, who numbered up to 250,000 at any time.[35] The chief ideologue of the 'Afghan Arab' volunteers was Abdullah Azzam, the Palestinian Muslim Brother and university professor welcomed into Saudi Arabia in the 1960s whose teaching at Jeddah had influenced the young Bin Laden. Azzam had previously been in charge of education at the Muslim World League, which sent him to Islamabad in 1980 to teach at the International Islamic University, itself part-funded by the League and supervised by the Muslim Brotherhood.[36] In 1984, Azzam moved to Peshawar after securing the League's approval to open a branch there. This allowed him to set up the Maktab al-Khidamat (Afghan Services Bureau or MAK) to organise the jihadist volunteer force, manage its funds and propagate the idea of an international armed struggle. The Peshawar office was established with the help of Pakistan's Jamaat-i-Islami and initially financed by Bin Laden together with large donations from Saudi Arabia.[37] The MAK disbursed $200 million of Middle Eastern and Western, mainly American and British, aid destined for the Afghan jihad; its recruitment effort around the world often drew on the network of Muslim Brotherhood offices.[38]

BRITISH COVERT ACTION

The British role in the Afghan war mainly involved covert military training and arms supplies, but also extended beyond Afghanistan into the Muslim republics of the southern Soviet Union. Britain played a vital role in support of the US and acted as a de facto covert arm of the US government; its role often went beyond what US forces, faced with far greater congressional oversight than existed in Britain, were able or willing to undertake.

Thus, British covert forces, unlike those of the US, played a direct part in the war, undertaking scouting and back-up roles with the resistance groups they and their colleagues were training.[39] Indeed, during the early stages of the war British SAS commandos were going in and out of Afghanistan from Pakistan, moving supplies to the Afghan groups independently of the Pakistanis – and contrary to General Zia's demands.[40] Britain initially proposed to the US to ship Soviet-made arms to the Afghan forces in order to disguise their origin; President Carter agreed to this operation, apparently unaware that the arms were to be supplied through the network of Monzer al-Kassar, the British agent who was also supplying Palestinian radicals, noted in Chapter 6.[41] It was at the request of the US that, from spring 1986, Britain shipped 600 'Blowpipe' shoulder-launched anti-aircraft missiles, mothballed following their ineffectual role in the Falklands War, to the Afghan groups. MI6 also helped the CIA early in the war by activating long-established British networks of contacts in the country – a similar role, in fact, to that played by MI6 in the 1953 coup in Iran.[42] Thus Britain could come in very handy, although, as one British intelligence expert noted, the

Americans 'paid most of the bills'[43]; by now, the specialist British role in covert action depended on American largesse.

The SAS worked alongside US special forces in training Pakistan's Special Services Group (SSG), whose commandos guided guerilla operations in Afghanistan.[44] British and US instruction was intended to enable SSG officers to pass on their training to the Afghan groups and mujahideen volunteers. One SSG commander at this time was Brigadier Pervez Musharraf, who spent seven years with the unit and who is believed to have trained mujahideen.[45] Musharraf had been chosen by Zia as a devout Deobandi and had been recommended by the JI, according to some analysts; it was then that Musharraf came into contact with Osama Bin Laden.[46] Musharraf recently wrote in his autobiography that: 'We helped create the mujahideen, fired them with religious zeal in seminaries, armed them, paid them, fed them, and sent them to a jihad against the Soviet Union in Afghanistan.' He claims that neither Pakistan nor the US realised what Osama Bin Laden 'might later do with the organisation that we had all enabled him to establish.'[47]

US instruction of the Pakistanis and senior Afghan commanders was in areas such as the use of explosives, automatic weapons and remote control devices for triggering mines and bombs, demolition and arson – practices that would later be used in terrorist operations. The CIA provided a variety of arms to the ISI, including plastic explosives, sniper rifles and sophisticated electronic timing and detonation devices that made it easier to set off explosions from a remote location – 'dual use' items that could be used both for attacking military targets and also in terrorist operations.[48] Some training programmes also included instruction in how to stab a sentry from behind, murder and assassination of enemy leaders, strangulation and murderous karate chops.[49] Brigadier Mohammed Yousaf of the ISI later noted that training ranged from striking a 'knife between the shoulder blades of a Soviet soldier shopping in the bazaar' to the 'placing of a briefcase bomb in a senior official's office'. Afghan educational establishments were considered fair game as targets, he explained, since they were staffed by 'communists indoctrinating their students with Marxist dogma'.[50]

Britain also directly trained Afghan forces, much of which was contracted out to 'private' security firms, a policy cleared in Whitehall; the main company was KMS – 'Keenie-Meenie Services', the name given to mercenaries fighting for Britain in the brutal war in Kenya in the 1950s. KMS training, led by former SAS officers, was provided to small numbers of Afghan commando units at secret MI6 and CIA bases in Saudi Arabia and Oman; the latter bases were also used as staging or refueling points for supply flights on their way to Pakistan.[51] In 1987, the *Observer* reported a secret proposal from KMS to the CIA to send small teams of ex-SAS instructors into Afghanistan to train rebels in 'demolition, sabotage, reconnaissance and para-medicine'.[52]

Ken Connor, who served in the SAS for twenty-three years, says that he was part of a team of 'ex-SAS' soldiers who trained selected junior commanders in the mujahideen in Scotland and northern England in 1983. The Afghans were smuggled into Britain disguised as tourists, and trained in three-week cycles at secret camps. 'They were well-armed and ferocious fighters, but they lacked battlefield organisation,' Connor writes. Training involved various military activities, including the 'planning of operations, the use of explosives and the fire control of heavy weapons – mortars and artillery', 'how to attack aircraft and how to lay anti-aircraft ambushes aligned on the centre of a runway' and mounting 'anti-armour ambushes'. Connor notes that there was 'strong empathy' between the British trainers and the mujahideen but that there was little warmth between the mujahideen and the British government; 'it was strictly a marriage of convenience between two organisations that had nothing else in common.'[53]

Various Afghan groups were supported by Britain. One initially favoured force was the Mahaz-i-Milli Islam (National Islamic Front of Afghanistan or NIFA). Unusually, it was led by a layman rather than a cleric, Sayyad Pir Gailani, and supported the restoration of the former king, Zahir Shah – a policy in tune with Whitehall's historical preference for monarchs; Whitehall appears at first to have regarded Zahir Shah as a possible future leader once the Soviets had been defeated.[54] The NIFA forces trained by Britain were commanded by Brigadier General Rahmatullah Safi, a former senior officer in the royal Afghan army who, after the king had been deposed, was living in exile in Britain. Safi later claimed to have trained around 8,000 men in NIFA's camps; by the late 1990s, he was still living in London and had become the European representative of the Taliban, now in control of Afghanistan.[55]

Britain also supported the Islamist groups. One of the MI6 officers in Islamabad coordinating British assistance to the mujahideen was Alastair Crooke who, it was later reported, 'got to know some of the militants who would become leaders of al-Qaida'.[56] He was described by Milt Bearden, CIA station chief in Pakistan in the mid-1980s, as 'a natural on the frontier' and 'a British agent straight out of the Great Game'.[57] Training was provided to the forces of Hadji Abdul Haq, a military commander with the Younis Khalis faction of the Hezb-e-Islami. As a favour to the CIA, MI6 ran the operation to supply Blowpipe missiles to Haq in 1986.[58] Haq was one of those figures whom MI6 introduced to the CIA in 1981, which then had very few Afghan contacts; the CIA subsequently began a long relationship with Haq. After the latter had raised a fighting force, the CIA began shipping weapons to him and he became an intermediary between the CIA, MI6 and the Kabul front. Haq's office in Peshawar, the organising centre of the resistance in Pakistan, was often full of MI6 and CIA operatives who supplied him with maps of new Soviet targets they wanted him to hit.[59]

But Afghan resistance operations were not confined to Soviet military targets. In Hadji Abdul Haq, Britain and the US had backed somebody prepared to use terrorism to achieve his aims. In September 1984, Haq ordered the planting of a bomb at Kabul airport that killed 28 people, many of them students preparing to fly to the Soviet Union. Eighteen months later, in March 1986, he became the first Afghan commander to be welcomed to Britain by Margaret Thatcher, and subsequently held several meetings with US President Reagan.[60] Responding to British criticism of his role in the airport blast, Haq said that the purpose of the bomb was 'to warn people not to send their children to the Soviet Union'. A Downing Street spokesman said at the same time that 'the prime minister has a degree of sympathy with the Afghan cause inasmuch as they're trying to rid their country of invaders.'[61]

Another of the military commanders in Younis Khalis' faction of the Hezb-e-Islami was Jalaluddin Haqqani, who received a large quantity of US weapons, much of which were used to help equip the Arab volunteers. A later US Defence Intelligence Agency report noted that Haqqani was 'the tribal leader most exploited by the ISI during the Soviet–Afghan war to facilitate the introduction of Arab extremists.'[62] Milt Bearden later wrote that Haqqani was 'America's best friend during the anti-Soviet war.' The CIA and the ISI came to rely on him for testing and experimenting with new weapons systems and tactics. Haqqani would go on to become a leading military commander in the Taliban and the 'Haqqani network' is presently one of the major Taliban factions fighting the British in Afghanistan. Another of Khalis's junior commanders in the 1980s was Mohammed Omar, who would go on to lead the Taliban as Mullah Omar.[63]

Britain also backed Ahmed Shah Massoud, who had become a prominent military commander in Rabbani's Jamaat-i-Islami group. British support for him began early in the war and involved money, weapons and an annual mission to assess his group's needs. These missions – consisting of two MI6 officers and military instructors – also provided training to Massoud's junior commanders and English lessons to his trusted aides. Britain also supplied communications equipment. One British official with knowledge of the operation spoke of how, with British help, Massoud's forces 'had a communication system which was very nearly priceless and acquired the knowledge of how to use it and how to organise. Those were subtle things but probably worth over a hundred planeloads of Armalites or Stingers.' The CIA began to supply Massoud in 1984, and is said to have relied on MI6 for reports about him.[64]

The SAS is also believed to have trained Massoud's forces to use sophisticated weaponry such as US Stinger anti-aircraft missiles which replaced the British-supplied Blowpipes in 1986. These missiles were used by the mujahideen to shoot down several passenger aircraft, with heavy loss of life. Ken Connor notes that 'newspaper reports linking Britain with the supply of the missiles led to furious Soviet protests, but "deniability" allowed the British government to maintain an air of injured innocence.'[65] After the Afghan War, the US would spend tens of millions of dollars in a belated attempt to buy back Stinger missiles that were proving lucrative on the black market. The British-supplied Blowpipes have also since resurfaced. A quantity were acquired by the Taliban after they took power in Kabul in 1996; following the Anglo–American defeat of the Taliban in February 2002, over 200 surface-to-air missiles, including 62 Blowpipes, were recovered by US forces.[66] Even in 2005 – nearly two decades after they were first supplied – there were still reports of Blowpipes being unearthed in Afghanistan.[67]

Britain also extended backing to the extremist Hekmatyar, who was invited to Downing Street in 1986 and met Foreign Office officials in London in 1988.[68] Most US aid went to Hekmatyar – by conservative estimates, at least $600 million.[69] Hekmatyar was also a ruthless killer, famed for skinning infidels alive, while his group was responsible for some of the most horrific atrocities of the war, such as the slaughter of members of other Afghan groups that were seen as rivals. Hekmatyar worked closely with Bin Laden and took a virulently anti-Western line: Saddam Hussein's Iraq and Qadafi's Libya were also funders.[70] A US Congress task force described his group in 1985 as 'the most corrupt' of the Afghan parties.[71]

British covert action in the region went beyond Afghanistan, and involved further conspiring with Hekmatyar's forces in operations inside the Soviet Union itself. Beginning in 1984, CIA Director William Casey stepped up the war against the Soviets when the CIA, together with MI6 and the ISI, agreed to a plan to launch guerrilla attacks into the southern Soviet republics of Tajikistan and Uzbekistan, from where Soviet troops in Afghanistan received their supplies. These were the first attacks inside the Soviet Union involving US and British covert action since the 1950s. Activities included sabotage operations such as rocket attacks on villages in Tajikistan, and on other Soviet targets like airfields and vehicle convoys in Uzbekistan. Some of these operations were led by Hekmatyar, and all were equipped by Pakistan's ISI. 'Scores of attacks were made' up to twenty-five kilometres into the Soviet republics, reaching their peak in 1986, according to former Pakistani intelligence officer Mohammed Yousaf. He also wrote that 'they were probably the most secret and sensitive operations of the war', and that the Soviet Union's 'specific worry was the spread of fundamentalism and its influence on Soviet Central Asian Muslims'.[72]

Propaganda operations were also conducted, involving Afghan rebels distributing Korans in the Uzbek language, which had been printed by the CIA.[73] MI6 funded the leader of Pakistan's Jamaat-i-Islami, Qazi Hussain Ahmad – who had close links with Hekmatyar and Massoud – to pump money and Islamic literature into the Soviet republics of Tajikistan and Uzbekistan to incite the local religious circles to rebel against their communist governments.[74] British expediency was again in evidence since officials could have had few illusions as to who they were supporting. British documents of the mid-1950s had described the JI, then led by its founder, Abdul Ala Mawdudi, as an 'extreme right-wing Islamic party':

> [It] has tentacles all over the country, which might enable it to exert wide influence if a propitious occasion ever arose ... This is a revolutionary and reactionary movement led by a clever, ambitious and unscrupulous man. In theory they

> wish to establish a state in Pakistan which will be run as nearly as possible in accordance with the tenets of the Koran and Sunnah … The state they would like to establish would be virtually a dictatorship ruled by an Amir following the precedents of the earlier Caliphs … The Jamaat-i-Islami is a potentially dangerous movement, comparable in many ways with the Muslim Brotherhood.[75]

THE RECKONING

After Soviet forces were expelled from Afghanistan in 1989, and the pro-Soviet government of Mohammed Najibullah was overthrown in 1992, Hekmatyar's forces fought Massoud's for control of Kabul in the ensuing civil war, killing thousands of civilians in the process. By 1996 the Taliban had driven Hekmatyar's forces out of Kabul and soon taken control of the country, forcing Hekmatyar into exile. By now, the secular leftist political forces in the country had been eliminated and Afghanistan's immediate future would be decided only by the Islamist groups.

Most importantly, by the end of the Soviet occupation, the foreign mujahideen veterans were forging a radical and violent utopianism that called for jihad as armed struggle. This was based on the ideology of the Saudi-sponsored Wahhabis and Abdullah Azzam's call for martyrdom and the belief that Islam alone had defeated the Soviets.[76] Thousands of previously untrained volunteers had received military instruction in often sophisticated techniques while gaining first-hand experience of fighting. The Arab–Afghan volunteers, especially those from Egypt, Yemen, Indonesia, Algeria and Libya, now saw their primary objective as returning to their homelands to struggle against their own governments, while Bin Laden hoped to unite them in a global force.[77]

Bin Laden's al-Qaida organisation was a direct product of the war, set up in 1988 out of the networks that were developing between the Afghans and the foreign fighters. Tony Blair's foreign secretary, Robin Cook, would later say that the name al-Qaida (meaning 'the base') derived from 'the database' – 'the computer file of the thousands of mujahideen who were recruited and trained with help from the CIA' – and, he forgot to say, MI6.[78] Several of the Afghan camp networks built at this time with CIA, ISI or Saudi aid would be subsequently used by al-Qaida as bases for training and planning terrorist attacks, including Tora Bora, south of Jalalabad, which was constructed by one of Younis Khalis' commanders. Al-Qaida would likely not have emerged to the extent that it did, had it not been for the infrastructure of the Afghan resistance built with US and British backing. Specific British contributions included specialised military training provided to various forces, covert military supplies and support for the larger US covert role in the war; Whitehall thus made a British contribution to the imminent emergence of global Islamist terrorism.

However, it would be the emergence of new Pakistani forces from the Afghan jihad that would be just as important to the future of global terrorism as the creation of al-Qaida, and these would eventually prove more dangerous to Britain.

CHAPTER 9

The Dictator, the King and the Ayatollah

The 1980s were a decade in which the British elite under Margaret Thatcher sought to reassert British power around the world. A deepened special relationship with Washington involved Whitehall backing an extraordinary period of US military intervention in the developing world under Ronald Reagan, elected in 1980. The 1982 Falklands War ran alongside covert British operations to assist the US wars in Nicaragua and Cambodia, where London provided secret military training to guerilla forces allied to Pol Pot's genocidal Khmer Rouge.[1] The Thatcher government allowed US planes to use British territory to bomb Libya in 1986, and spoke out in lone support of the illegal US invasion of Panama in 1989, carried out under Reagan's successor, George Bush senior. Thatcher also strongly supported – indeed, in many respects propelled – a massive Western rearmament programme, forcing an arms race with the Soviet Union and, for a time, a dangerous new period in international relations.

The 'Soviet threat' was constantly invoked by Thatcher and Reagan as lurking behind all malign influences in the world, but the reality was that independent regimes remained Washington and London's primary problems. The reassertion of Western power was to a large extent a belated response to the decolonisation process that had taken off in the 1950s, challenging Western and specifically British power in Africa, the Middle East and Southeast Asia. Reagan and Thatcher's strategy entailed nothing less than an economic reordering of the world, involving the sweeping privatisation of state corporations, deregulation of the financial sector and liberalisation of trade and investment policies. Dozens of developing countries were subject to this economic interventionism, usually under the formal auspices of 'structural adjustment programmes' managed by the (essentially US-controlled) World Bank and International Monetary Fund. The primary beneficiaries were Western corporations seeking access to new markets, while poverty and levels of inequality shot up in many countries.

This new interventionism also involved a marked intensification of support for a number of radical Islamic forces. The massive covert programme in Afghanistan to counter Soviet power enhanced the proficiency and militancy of the mujahideen forces, who were forming themselves into battle-hardened organisations capable of global action. But Thatcher and Reagan also deepened their special relationships with the two major state sponsors of radical Islam, Pakistan under General Zia and Saudi Arabia under King Fahd. Whitehall also tried to enhance links with, and arm, Iran, now under Islamist rulers. These policies are invariably ignored in mainstream analyses of the Thatcher years; they show that British and American planners believed that their aims – to reshape the global economy in the interests of Western business and counter nationalist or Soviet-backed forces – could be achieved in alliance with the Islamist right, just as they had throughout the entire postwar period.

THE DICTATOR: TERROR AS STATE POLICY

Rigid Islamisation affected all areas of public life in Pakistan in the 1980s, as General Zia ul-Haq introduced draconian measures and punishments that, he declared, constituted the true implementation of Islamic law.[2] In this he was guided by the leading Pakistani religious leaders of the Deobandi Islamic revivalist movement, a school of thought with many similarities to the Wahhabi version of Islam in Saudi Arabia, and two important Islamist parties: the Jamaat-i-Islami (JI), Pakistan's largest and most resourceful organisation which played a key role in recruiting for and funding the Afghan jihad; and the Jamiat Ulema-e-Islam (Assembly of Islamic Clergy or JUI), which insisted on a strict interpretation of Islamic law and which, along with the JI, ran an increasing network of madrassas throughout the country. By the time Zia was assassinated in 1988, 400,000 boys and young men, known as 'taliban', or students, were being educated in the Pakistani madrassas.[3]

The military and the mullahs under Zia had a common domestic enemy – the secular, more liberal mainstream political parties. Indeed, it was the protest movement instigated by the religious parties in the mid-1970s against Zulfikar Ali Bhutto's government that created the conditions for Zia's 1977 coup.[4] Zia's consequent promotion of the Islamist groups was presented as a vehicle for establishing an Islamic state, and was intended to block the restoration of democracy and justify martial law.[5] This project of defying secular nationalism received strong US and British support – a continuation of London and Washington's long-standing policy preference for Islamists over nationalists or democrats, in the region.

The July 1977 coup by General Zia, then chief of the army, that overthrew Prime Minister Bhutto had in effect been welcomed by James Callaghan's Labour government. The Cabinet reported two days after the military takeover that Zia 'had announced his intention of holding elections in October and of handing power back to those elected, and there was no reason to think that he did not genuinely wish to carry out this intention' – which in fact never happened.[6] A few months later, in January 1978, Callaghan met Zia for talks in Pakistan. He told the House of Commons that 'General Zia assured me of his firm intention to restore democratic government in Pakistan at the earliest possible date and described to me how he proposed to do this.' He added: 'I have hopes, in the light of what I was told, that we shall see a full return to democracy during the course of 1978.'[7] This was complete nonsense, as Callaghan surely knew; a similar mantra was constantly repeated by British ministers concerning Musharraf's supposed commitment to the 'restoration of democracy' after his military takeover in 1999.

Once Margaret Thatcher became prime minister in 1979 she abandoned Callaghan-style pieties in favour of exuding praise for the Pakistani dictator at every opportunity. 'General Zia is a wise man', Thatcher told the House of Commons in February 1979, at a time when Zia was about to impose sharia law in the country and when a death sentence hung over the overthrown Bhutto: he was hanged two months later.[8]

Britain stepped up its arming of Pakistan and Thatcher consistently fought off accusations that London was increasing the prospects of conflict with India, by increasing Islamabad's ability to fight Indian forces in the disputed territory of Kashmir. Instead, she argued that Pakistan was now 'in the front line' with regards to the war in Afghanistan.[9] After Thatcher outlined this reason for providing arms to Pakistan at a press conference in Delhi in April 1981 she received a memo from President Reagan conveying 'profound admiration for your forthright and courageous comments to the press in India on Pakistan's defence needs and on the situation in Afghanistan'.[10]

In October 1981, Thatcher paid a visit to Pakistan and gave a speech at a banquet hosted by General Zia at Aiwan-e-Sadr, the president's official residence in Islamabad. Reflecting on her host's response to the Soviet invasion of Afghanistan, Thatcher told her audience:

> Mr President … you accepted that a historic responsibility had been thrust upon you, a responsibility to cope with and manage this situation not just in the interests of Pakistan,

> but in the interests of the international community. It is for that reason, among others, that Pakistan deserves the support of Britain and of all the nations of the world who are genuinely interested in bringing about the withdrawal of Soviet troops. On behalf of Britain, let me confirm to you – Pakistan has our support in the general problems you are facing … We deeply admire the courage and skill you have shown in handling the crisis.

Thatcher ended with a toast 'to the health and happiness of His Excellency, the president' and to the 'lasting friendship' between the people of the two countries.[11] Thatcher's penchant for dictators is usually illustrated by her friendship with Chilean President Augusto Pinochet; yet her alliance with Zia was at least as strong, while his legacy of support for Islamist groups in Pakistan and Afghanistan had much greater global consequences.

Zia's domestic Islamisation drive, along with the money, arms and training pumped into the Afghan jihad, soon led to official Pakistani sponsorship of radical Islamist groups. While Britain and the US were supporting Zia throughout the decade, two major terrorist organisations were established in Pakistan with state complicity that would have important consequences for the region and the wider world.[12] The first was the Harkat al-Jehad al-Islami (HUJI), set up early in the Afghan war, in 1980, by the JUI and the Tableeghi Jamaat, a Muslim missionary movement. Initially established to run relief camps for the mujahideen in Afghanistan, Pakistan's intelligence service, the ISI, worked with the HUJI leadership to recruit and train militants from Pakistan to participate in the Afghan War.[13] In the mid-1980s, the HUJI split, one faction establishing itself as the Harkat ul-Mujahideen (HUM), whose militants fought in Afghanistan and which recruited a further 5,000 volunteers from around the Muslim world to fight there. The initial batch of HUM volunteers was trained at camps in Afghanistan run by Jalaluddin Haqqani, of the Younis Khalis faction of the Hezb-e-Islami, which was also being covertly supported by Britain and the US. The HUM was regarded as having some of the best fighters in the jihad; the CIA provided it with Stinger missiles and trained HUM forces in their use.[14]

Under its leader, Fazlur Rehman Khalil, the HUM would go on to become one of Pakistan's most violent terrorist organisations, being especially active against Indian forces in Kashmir. It would continue to run camps in Afghanistan throughout the 1990s and send militants to the jihad in Bosnia after 1992, all the while remaining a protégé of the ISI. The London bombers of 2005 would also have connections to the HUM.

The second key terrorist organisation in Pakistan developed out of the Markaz Dawa al-Irshad (the Centre for Religious Learning and Welfare or MDI), which was founded in 1987 by three Islamic scholars, including Abdullah Azzam, the Palestinian Muslim Brother who organised mujahideen forces for the Afghan War now at the International Islamic University in Islamabad. Set up as a Sunni missionary organisation, the MDI appears to have received seed money from Bin Laden; so too did its military wing, Lashkar-e-Toiba (Army of the Pure or LET), whose creation was aided by the ISI and which recruited volunteers to join the Afghan jihad, setting up camps in eastern Afghanistan in 1987–8. The LET played a minimal role in the Afghan War, instead turning to fight in the Indian-administered part of Kashmir, for which it received ISI support.[15] It has since become Pakistan's largest jihadist organisation and one of its most violent terrorist groups.[16] The 7/7 bombers would also be linked closely to the LET.

The creation of these two organisations, with the complicity of the ISI, would be as significant for the development of global terrorism as the establishment of Bin Laden's al-Qaida at around the same time. Yet the effects of this radicalisation in Pakistan were not only felt there and in Afghanistan and Kashmir, but also in Britain. Bahukutumbi Raman, a former Indian intelligence officer and leading expert on Pakistani terrorist groups, notes that 'the seeds of the radicalisation of the Pakistani diaspora in the UK were sown during the military dictatorship of Zia.'[17] The general encouraged a number of Deobandi clerics from Pakistan to go to Britain as preachers in the mosques patronised by the Pakistani diaspora. There, they replaced the clerics of the Barelvi school of Islam, who tended to be more liberal and welcoming of Western-style democracy. Raman notes that in Britain today 'the influence of the more tolerant and not anti-Western Barelvi mullahs has been almost totally replaced by that of the more fundamentalist, anti-Western Deobandi–Wahhabi ones'.[18] He also argues that 'the intelligence agencies of the US and the UK went along with Zia's policy of Arabising–Wahhabising the Muslims of Pakistan because this contributed to an increase in the flow of jihadist terrorists' to Afghanistan.[19]

The first signs of the radicalisation of the Pakistani diaspora in Britain came in February 1984. A group of British terrorists of Pakistani origin in the Jammu and Kashmir Liberation Front (JKLF) kidnapped an Indian diplomat posted to the Assistant High Commission in Birmingham, demanding the release of the JKLF's leader, who was in jail in Delhi convicted of murder. When the Indian government rejected the terrorists' demand, they killed the diplomat. Five years later, a better-known event revealed how some elements in the British Muslim community had become radicalised, when in January 1989 a group of Islamists in Bradford burnt copies of Salman Rushdie's novel, *The Satanic Verses*, and issued a fatwa calling for Rushdie to be killed. The protest was initially orchestrated from Pakistan and India by supporters of the Jamaat-i-Islami and by the UK Islamic Mission, which had been set up in the early 1960s to, as it stated, build a society 'based on the ideals, values and principles of Islam' and to introduce the sharia into British law.[20] It also had – and maintains – strong links with Pakistan's JI. Deobandi and Barelvi associations also organised street protests in Britain and Pakistan against the novel. The

Leicester Islamic Foundation – set up by the Islamic Mission in 1973 with JI officers, and still heavily influenced by the spiritual followers of the JI – called on Muslims to sign a petition to have the novel banned; this idea had been instigated by the Chennai chapter of the JI, which was pushing Indian politicians to stop the book being published in India.[21]

The anti-Rushdie protests were supported by only a small minority of British Muslims but sadly placed the broader British Muslim community under a harsh media spotlight. It took a long time for that community to recover; no sooner had it done so than first 9/11 and then the 7/7 bombings dealt it even more severe blows. The radicalisation of elements in the Muslim community in the 1980s was already a case of 'blowback', given Britain's conniving with a Pakistani regime sponsoring Islamist and terrorist groups. The Rushdie affair should have been a wake-up call to British foreign and domestic policy-makers – yet their response in the early 1990s was the opposite: to deepen still further British complicity in Pakistan's promotion of radical Islam.[22]

THE KING: FOLLOWING THE SAUDIS

British policy also contributed to other important developments in radical Islam in the 1980s. When the Saudi regime approached its protégé, Bin Laden, to wage jihad in Afghanistan, they also asked him to form volunteer mujahideen units to fight an anti-communist insurgency in South Yemen.[23] Forged after forcing a humiliating British withdrawal from its colony of Aden in 1967, South Yemen was now a Marxist regime hosting Soviet military advisers and backing the Soviet-sponsored regime in Afghanistan. The Yemen campaign in the early 1980s was organised by Bin Laden personally overseeing the activities of a group of Arab–Afghans, supported by millions of dollars of Saudi aid and Saudi White Guards.[24]

Hardly any details of this murky campaign have emerged but, as ever, the hand of the British secret services can also be detected, running a number of covert activities in South Yemen, though the extent to which they were connected to Bin Laden's activities is unclear. Stephen Dorril notes that MI6 conducted operations in 1980 in which 'several small teams were being trained to blow up bridges', supported by the CIA.[25] In February 1982, the South Yemen government announced that it had uncovered an MI6–CIA plot against it to bomb economic installations in Aden; 12 South Yemenis were sentenced to death the following month for bringing explosives into the country, the prosecution claiming that the men had been trained by US intelligence in Saudi Arabia.[26]

Under King Fahd, Saudi Arabia pursued an openly pro-US foreign policy in the 1980s, while continuing an oil policy to pressure other OPEC members to keep prices low. The Saudis helped finance a variety of Ronald Reagan's brutal covert wars, not only in Afghanistan, but also in Angola, Zaire and Chad, while in Nicaragua they helped bankroll US support of the Contras, who were waging a brutal war against a popular elected government. King Fahd also paid $2 million to the CIA to help finance a secret operation to prevent the Communist Party from gaining power in Italy.[27] The Saudis also continued funding whoever abroad might be useful to them, including Zia's Pakistan, Yasser Arafat's PLO, Saddam Hussein's Iraq during his conflict with Iran – now Saudi Arabia's arch rival – and the Islamic movement in the Philippines.[28]

At home, following the twin 1979 shocks of the Iranian Revolution and the seizure of the Grand Mosque by radicals, the Saudis embarked on a phase of 'controlled re-Islamisation', in which public manifestations of piety multiplied while some of the most turbulent potential insurgents were evacuated off to the Afghan War. In 1986, King Fahd replaced the title of 'Majesty' with the honorific 'Custodian of the Two Holy Places' (i.e., in Mecca and Medina), thus trying to amplify the regime's religious credentials.[29] The Sunni Saudis now found themselves with a competitor for leadership of the Muslim world – revolutionary Shia Iran. Thus, in the 1980s, awash with oil wealth, Riyadh competed with Tehran to promote its fundamentalist interpretation of Islam, Wahhabism, and joined with wealthy Arabs from other states bordering the Persian Gulf in donating money to build mosques and religious schools that could preach their interpretation of Islamic doctrine.[30] The Islamic financial system, backed by Saudi money and banks established in the 1970s, also expanded significantly; Islamic banks began springing up everywhere in the Muslim world. Some private Saudi banks helped finance the resistance to the Soviet occupation of Afghanistan and would later be accused of financing al-Qaida and Islamist groups such as the Algerian Islamic Salvation Front and Hamas in the 1990s.[31]

Amidst these developments, Whitehall planners proceeded in time-honoured fashion. In April 1981, Margaret Thatcher paid the first visit by a serving British prime minister to Saudi Arabia. In a speech in Riyadh, she told her hosts that 'the purpose is to try to become closer to the government in Saudi Arabia, know their viewpoint, to try to take these things into account in planning the policies which the British government will follow.'[32] Even by Thatcher's standards of public support for dictatorial regimes, the idea that British policies would take such account of Saudi views was noteworthy.

After the British government's decision to more or less tie the British economy to Saudi Arabia after 1973, the 1980s witnessed further Whitehall decisions that reinforced Britain's dependency on Riyadh. The special British–Saudi relationship was given a brief jolt by bitter Saudi protests to the British government over the 1980 TV broadcast of *Death of a Princess*, a drama-documentary depicting the public beheading of a fictitious young princess, taken to be Saudi. But, as ever, economic interests prevailed, and by the early 1980s negotiations had resumed over major British arms exports. As the British–Saudi covert alliance was in full swing during the Afghan jihad, memoranda of understanding were signed in 1985 and 1988 to sell £15 billion worth of British military equipment to the Kingdom. The now controversial Al-Yamamah

(The Dove) deals involved British Aerospace (now renamed BAE Systems), supplying over 150 aircraft, including Tornado jets and Hawk trainers, along with entire air bases, missiles and much else. The agreements constituted not simply arms deals but an entire re-equipping of the Saudi military, at a stroke enabling Britain to overtake the US as the Kingdom's biggest arms supplier. Britain allegedly beat France's rival offer by outbidding the bribe paid to the Saudis.[33] Subsequently, BAE was accused of sending hundreds of millions of pounds to a Saudi prince involved in negotiating the contracts, with the authorisation of the Ministry of Defence.[34] If true, it is hard to believe that these deals were anything other than a means to enrich the Saudi buyers, since Riyadh has little possible use for the equipment, being entirely dependent on the US military in a crisis. These deals also meant that Britain was now even more beholden to the good will of the Saudi regime. In a 1987 interview, Margaret Thatcher stressed the 'excellent' relations between the two countries: the already minimal likelihood of Whitehall seriously distancing itself from the Saudis on any major issue now appeared to be ended.

ARMING THE AYATOLLAH

While both sets of Al-Yamamah arms negotiations were taking place with Saudi Arabia, Britain was covertly helping to arm the Saudis' main rival for supremacy in the Muslim world – this was revolutionary Iran, which was now vigorously instituting a brutal Shia theocracy under Ayatollah Khomeini. At the same time, in flagrant contravention of a UN embargo on supplying either side, Britain was also arming Saddam Hussein's Iraq, which had invaded Iran in September 1980; the ensuing eight-year long conflict would cost over a million lives. Whitehall was arming all sides against each other, another long-standing feature of policy in the region.

British policy towards the Iran–Iraq War may have been guided by the same reasoning as outlined in a 1984 US State Department memo, which noted that 'victory by either side would have far-reaching consequences' on the balance of power in the region – Britain, together with the US, aimed to hold that balance of power.[35] British officials proceeded to help bolster Saddam's regime by secretly relaxing the restrictive arms exports 'guidelines' announced in parliament and allowing the supply of a range of military equipment by some private companies, along with export credits. Following a familiar pattern, a private security firm also provided 'ex-SAS' members to train Saddam Hussein's bodyguard.[36]

Similarly, Britain used various means to arm the ayatollah's Iran. From the very first day of the Iran–Iraq War, Britain sent millions of pounds worth of tank barrels and tank engines to Iran, calling them 'non-lethal' equipment, which helped to maintain the 890 Chieftain tanks and 250 Scorpion tanks the British had delivered to the shah during the 1970s. Further exports of hundreds of Land Rovers and six air defence radars followed.[37] Other back channels were used. One scheme involved Whitehall's connivance with a company called Allivane International to secretly ship arms to Iran in the mid to late 1980s; another enabled the British company BMARC to export naval guns, spares and ammunition to Iran via Singapore in 1986.[38] Around the same time Royal Ordnance, a government-owned company, exported five shipments of tetryl chemicals, a compound used to make explosives, and explosive powder to Iran, in the process breaking both the UN embargo and Britain's own export guidelines.[39]

Moreover, London was a major centre through which Iran's multi-billion worldwide arms orders flowed. The Iranians used the offices of the National Iranian Oil Company (NIOC) as a front organisation for their arms procurement effort; it acted as a base to buy the spare parts for their British-supplied tanks and to take advantage of London's banking and shipping facilities. This arms procurement effort in London was an open secret; NIOC's offices were located on Victoria Street, a brief walk from the Department for Trade and Industry and Scotland Yard. Yet it was not until

September 1987, seven years into the Iran–Iraq War, that Britain announced its intention to close the NIOC down; even after this there was still no crackdown on British traders and companies selling weapons and equipment to Iran.[40]

Britain was also intimately involved in US covert operations towards Iran during a wave of hostage-taking in Lebanon in which dozens of foreigners, principally Americans, were seized in the course of the 1980s. These kidnappings were principally undertaken by groups with links to the pro-Iranian Hezbollah (Party of God) organisation, which was established in Lebanon in 1982 when Iranian Revolutionary Guards were deployed to the Beqaa Valley following the Israeli invasion of Lebanon that year. The kidnappings were, to an extent, Tehran's retaliation for Western support of Iraq in the war against Iran and US support of Israel in the invasion of Lebanon. The challenge to US power in the region was compounded when, in October 1983, a massive truck bomb at the barracks of US peacekeepers in Beirut killed 241 servicemen; the perpetrator was the Islamic Jihad Organisation, which was inspired by the Islamic revolution in Iran and also behind many kidnappings.

In the course of 1983, the CIA's station chief in Beirut, William Buckley, and the British agent Leslie Aspin, who was now working as an arms supplier to the Lebanese Christian militia, had several meetings to discuss options against terrorists operating in Lebanon. Buckley apparently wanted to form a special Lebanese mercenary unit to kidnap terrorists or their relatives until Hezbollah released its own hostages. But in March 1984, Buckley himself was kidnapped in Beirut, and Vice President George Bush and CIA Director William Casey called on the British for help in securing his release; by now, a familiar pattern of the US imploring the British for help in specialist covert action. The issue of paying a ransom was put on the table.[41]

The US and Britain had already taken to paying ransom for hostages – during the 1979–81 US embassy hostage crisis in Iran, for example, the Carter administration had secretly released funds frozen in the US at the outbreak of the Iranian Revolution and most of the $3.5 billion in property held by the shah in the US.[42] In 1980–81 the British also paid a ransom for the release of two Britons held by Hezbollah in Lebanon; Aspin arranged for machine guns to be shipped to the Iranians, who promptly released the British captives. The intermediary role was allegedly played by the Syrian arms trafficker, Monzer al-Kassar, who deposited the money from the Iranians into Aspin's account at the Bank of Credit and Commerce International (BCCI) – the bank that, it would be revealed in the 1990s, was being used by numerous drugs and arms traffickers around the world.[43] It was a deal that set the precedent for the Iran-Contra Affair that was to follow.

By mid-March 1984 the British were recommending that they try to pay a ransom for Buckley by offering arms to Iran, and Aspin was chosen to coordinate the deal.[44] Aspin later recounted his involvement in the affair in an affidavit submitted to his solicitors, stating that he had been contacted by William Casey in June 1984, and that Casey had asked him:

> to assist in the sale of [arms] to Iran in exchange for hostages. These hostages were being held in Lebanon, so in June 1984 I started [attending] a series of meetings in London, one of them being at the US embassy ... During these meetings, it was discussed as to how one could get the hostages released, ways of doing it, some of them improper, some proper.[45]

Iran's payments for the arms were controlled by Marine Colonel Oliver North, working at the US National Security Council, who used them to covertly fund the US-backed Contra guerrillas in Nicaragua, thus bypassing the US Congress.

Aspin obtained access to Downing Street, later claiming that Ian Gow, Margaret Thatcher's personal secretary, was his point of contact for the Iran ransom negotiations. Thatcher and her senior officials were in constant contact, by cable and in person, with the secret White House hostage team and there is evidence that they began facilitating Aspin's attempts to ransom Buckley in March 1984, a week after his capture. Later that month, Aspin placed a $40 million order for American cannon shells to be dispatched to Iran.[46] In May, Oliver North met secretly with Andrew Green, a British intelligence officer working as a counsellor in the Washington embassy (who would go on to become Ambassador to Syria and Saudi Arabia), to discuss the hostage rescue. North also got on with purchasing weapons from the Soviet bloc for onward shipment to Iran and the Contras.[47]

In the summer and winter of 1984, the arms procured by North were shipped to the Iranians. Further deals involving missiles and radars were made in 1985, followed by others between 1986 and 1 January 1988, when the last arms deal with Iran was signed. Aspin laundered the payments received – some $42 million – through a series of British and European banks.[48] The deals may have helped the Contras pursue their dirty war in Nicaragua but they did not secure the release of William Buckley, who was never released but hideously tortured and killed. One of the ironies of the British ransom and arms dealing efforts, Loftus and Aarons point out, was that while the purpose was to influence Tehran, as the assumed controllers of Hezbollah, it was actually the Syrian government that was paying the kidnappers' bills and controlled them, unbeknown to the US and British secret services.[49]

Some of the arms bound for Iran and the Contras were sourced by Monzer al-Kassar's network. In another remarkable twist, however, it turned out that although the British believed he was working for them, al-Kassar was actually a double agent also working for the Soviet Union. The British had been willing to put the Americans in contact with al-Kassar's network in return for information from the CIA on IRA fundraising in the US.[50] A decade later in the British parliament, MP Tam Dalyell asked Foreign Minister Douglas Hogg 'if it was with his authority that Monzer el-Kassar was authorised in June 1984 to ship arms to Iran.' Hogg replied emphatically no.[51]

While al-Kassar was being trusted by the British to act as their agent in this covert arms ring, he was also continuing to supply arms to a wide variety of terrorist operations, from assassinations in Spain to an attack in Paris's Jewish quarter, and the notorious hijacking of the *Achille Lauro* cruise ship in 1985 in which one man was murdered; according to Loftus and Aarons, it was al-Kassar who smuggled the killers to safety. For years, however, al-Kassar was able to travel in and out of Britain with impunity to report to his handlers at MI6.[52] Loftus and Aarons also note that MI6 'had known all about al-Kassar's role in terror bombing since 1981', thanks to Leslie Aspin, but he remained its 'top informant'. Al-Kassar was of vital importance to the British in convincing groups such as the PLO and the Palestinian Abu Nidal's terrorist organisation to keep their deposit accounts at the BCCI bank, which the British had infiltrated and were monitoring. Every time a sheikh deposited money there, the British could trace the distribution of funds through al-Kassar to terrorist groups in the Middle East. MI6 kept the fact of al-Kassar's recruitment unknown to Thatcher and even MI5.[53] Al-Kassar is currently the subject of a US court indictment for weapons trafficking and money laundering; no such action against him has ever been taken by the British government.[54]

The Abu Nidal organisation killed hundreds of people in over a dozen countries in the early 1970s and throughout the 1980s, its most notorious attacks being the indiscriminate killing of 18 people at Rome and Vienna airports in December 1985. Yet Nidal visited London in the mid-1980s, a fact which infuriated the Israelis whom Whitehall failed to inform.[55] Furthermore, the British discovered in 1986 that Nidal was holding accounts worth $50 million at BCCI, and in July the following year MI5 and MI6 approached a bank employee and persuaded him to pass on information about the accounts' activities.[56] The British decision to monitor rather than freeze these accounts was criticised by the US, but Britain insisted on not intervening. The monitoring enabled the British to retrospectively link Syria, where Nidal was then based, to an attempted terrorist bombing at Heathrow Airport in 1986, which involved a Nidal agent receiving funds from the BCCI bank account of a Syrian intelligence officer.[57] The British surveillance ended when Nidal's organisation got wind of it; it is not clear exactly when this was, but evidence indicates that it was not until the end of 1989.[58] During this period, Abu Nidal is believed to have been behind bomb attacks in Sudan, Cyprus and Greece, among others, but his most significant alleged role in a terrorist attack was on Pan Am flight 103 – the Lockerbie bomb which killed 270 people in December 1988. After Abu Nidal's death in 2002, one of his former aides stated that Nidal had told him that he had been behind the bombing, a theory that some other informed commentators have long held in the face of the trial verdict that found two Libyans guilty.[59]

The British secret service's willingness to monitor rather than curb such a terrorist as Nidal follows an historical pattern and is also instructive in light of the later apparent recruitment of Islamist militants, to which we come later. But Nidal may have served a purpose beyond enabling the British to monitor terrorist activities. A number of militant Palestinian groups were formed in the years following the Palestinians' expulsion from Jordan in 1970–1; Abu Nidal's group split from the Fatah faction of the PLO, led by Arafat, in 1974. These splits in the Palestinian movement, especially after its challenge to Jordan's pro-Western regime in the 1970 crisis, would have been welcomed by planners in London and Washington. Furthermore, Nidal's resort to grotesque acts of mass murder, as at Rome and Vienna, inflicted huge damage on the Palestinian cause generally, serving to conflate the Palestinian movement with terrorism in the eyes of the world's public. The role played by Abu Nidal's organisation fits with the long-standing British interest in keeping the Middle East divided and at war with itself; it can only be speculated whether this played a role in the British decision to allow Nidal to continue to operate.

The Aspin–al-Kassar networks were not the only ones used by MI6 to help arm revolutionary Iran. In the mid-1980s MI6 also worked with an Iranian-born arms dealer, Jamshed Hashemi, who had acted as a middle-man in the sale of missiles to Tehran in the Iran–Contra Affair. The purpose was to monitor Chinese arms shipments to Iran that might be used to threaten Western shipping in the Gulf during the Iran–Iraq War. MI6 funded Hashemi to arrange a false end-user certificate for the purchase of £350 million worth of Chinese Silkworm missiles destined for Iran. These were shipped in 1987, together with other deals for British-made armed motor boats and ammunition, also sanctioned by MI6, in violation of the government's guidelines banning weapons exports to Iran; the motor boats, exported via Greece, were used against civilian shipping in the Gulf.[60] Hashemi reported to MI6 on his involvement in these deals up until 1992; he also made several donations to the Conservative Party in the late 1980s and early 1990s and personally met Margaret Thatcher three times. During these meetings, he claimed that he passed on personal messages from Iranian President Hashemi Rafsanjani, a close relative, urging Britain to ease sanctions against Iran. In 1996, however, Hashemi was arrested by Britain's Serious Fraud Office after allegations by a US company that he had defrauded it over a contract to supply satellite telephones to the Iranian Ministry of Defence. Hashemi said he had been betrayed by the British government, having supplied information to it for years. He was released from prison in 1999, following a deal which prevented MI6 operations from being disclosed in court.[61]

Britain would continue its involvement in arming Iran into the 1990s. According to former MI6 officer, Richard Tomlinson, in 1995 MI6 became aware of a network involving the Israeli secret service that was organising a Chinese shipment of 60 tons of chemicals to Iran in order to help Israel secure the release of its pilot, Ron Arad, taken prisoner in Lebanon years before. Rather than try to halt the project, MI6 cooperated with it to gain intelligence on Iran's military network, even though it risked giving Tehran a chemical weapons capability.[62]

The policy of directly helping, and turning a blind eye to, the arming of the Islamic republic is especially instructive in light of the current demonisation of Iran over its apparent attempt to acquire nuclear weapons. What these episodes illustrate is not so much a double standard in British foreign policy, but expediency: the willingness to do whatever, with whomever, at the time to achieve short-term objectives irrespective of the long-terms costs and any moral calculation.

As well as conniving with the Iranian regime in the 1980s, the British and Americans also sought a more direct route to address the challenge posed by Iran and its allied forces in the region. After the October 1983 bombing of the US marine barracks in Beirut and the killing of William Buckley, the British, Americans and Saudis – the familiar grouping, already collaborating in Afghanistan – decided to eliminate the then leader of Hezbollah in Lebanon, Sheikh Sayyed Mohammad Fadlallah.[63] A joint covert plan was drawn up, the full details of which remain unclear, but which involved the CIA subcontracting the operation to Lebanese agents led by a former British SAS officer; the operation was funded by the Saudis to the tune of $3 million. On 8 March 1985 a car packed with explosives blew up 50 yards from Fadlallah's residence in Beirut, killing around 80 people, including women and children, and injuring over 200, but Fadlallah himself escaped.[64] In an effort to cover its tracks, the CIA tried to blame Israel for the bombing, which few believed; the Saudis ended up paying Fadlallah a $2 million bribe to stop attacking the Americans.[65]

The British could be helpful to the Americans in running and organising hit squads. One CIA officer involved in the Afghan War at the time, Gust Avrakotos, noted that Britain had few lawyers to contend with and 'a prime minister to the right of Attila the Hun'. On a visit to MI6 in the mid-1980s to help put it to work at the service of the Americans, especially in Afghanistan, Avrakotos observed that 'they had a willingness to do jobs I couldn't touch. They basically took care of the "How to kill people department"'.

Later, after more US funding to the Afghan War materialised, Avrakotos noted:

> The Brits were eventually able to buy things that we couldn't because it infringed on murder, assassination and indiscriminate bombings. They could issue guns with silencers. We couldn't do that because a silencer immediately implied assassination – and heaven forbid car bombs! No way I could even suggest it, but I could say to the Brits, 'Fadlallah in Beirut was really effective last week. They had a car bomb that killed three hundred people.' I gave MI6 stuff in good faith. What they did with it was always their business.[66]

The 1980s witnessed the unprecedented growth of the radical Islamist movement, thanks principally to the Afghan War, the Islamisation programme of Pakistan's General Zia, Saudi funding to Islamist causes around the world and Iranian sponsorship of a variety of Islamist groups – to all of which developments British policy had contributed in different ways. Gilles Kepel has noted that 1989 marks Islamism's peak of intensity as a political force. In that year Algeria's radical Islamist political party, the Islamic Salvation Front (FIS), was formed, becoming a fast-growing political force that soon captured half the votes in local and national elections, before a military coup prevented its taking political power. During the Palestinian uprising in the occupied territories, which had broken out in 1987, the hegemony of the secular PLO was for the first time challenged by a new Islamist force, the Islamist Resistance Movement, or Hamas.[67] Both the FIS and Hamas, among other Islamist movements, had a measure of popular support, having become the main political alternative to what were seen as failed secular nationalist movements.

The year 1989 also saw the Soviet army evacuating its last troops from Afghanistan, defeated by the Afghan rebels and the foreign mujahideen; while in Sudan, a military coup catapulted the Islamist ideologue, Hassan al-Turabi, into power at the head of the National Islamic Front Party, which sought to impose an Islamic state under sharia law.[68] The new Sudanese regime had strong ties to the Muslim Brotherhood, and in August 1989, six weeks after coming to power, al-Turabi attended a meeting of the International Muslim Brotherhood – in London. At this meeting al-Turabi, according to some sources, declared Sudan's willingness to act as a base from which Islamist terrorist groups could operate around the world.[69] Within three years, Osama Bin Laden had moved to Khartoum and established a new base for jihadist operations there. London was a fitting location for this meeting since it was, even more than Khartoum, to become a, and perhaps *the*, global centre for radical Islamist organising in the following decade.

CHAPTER 10

Nurturing al-Qaida

THE EARLY 1990s brought Islamist terrorism to both Europe and the US for the first time, with the first jihadist war in Europe – Bosnia after 1992; the bombing of the World Trade Center in New York in 1993; and the first attacks in Western Europe – the 1995 bombs on the Paris metro. Saudi Arabia also suffered its first major terrorist attacks in November 1995 – when a van bomb blew up an office housing a US military mission training the National Guard – and in June 1996 – when the Khobar Towers skyscraper housing US Air Force personnel was hit by a massive truck bomb, killing 20 people. Numerous other countries were also affected by terrorism. Algeria was plagued by a brutal civil war between government and Islamist forces which cost 100,000 lives after it broke out in 1992. In Afghanistan, mujahideen factions fell on each other after the fall of the Soviet-backed government in 1992, killing thousands and destroying the capital, Kabul; their vicious lawlessness prepared the way for the Taliban's later assumption of power. India and various Central Asian states also witnessed a surge in terrorism promoted by Pakistani groups seeking to 'liberate' Indian-controlled Kashmir and extend Islamist revolution.

These were the ugly products of a globalisation of terrorism, as militant jihadists, drawing on the war in Afghanistan in the 1980s and trained in Afghan and Pakistani camps, returned home to fight their own governments, trying to emulate their success against the Soviets. The jihadists' ideology had evolved into what the French analyst Gilles Kepel has described as jihadi–Salafist, demanding a return to the traditions of the devout ancestors (*Salafi* in Arabic) and an adherence to the sacred texts in their most literal sense.[1] This meant a commitment to violence and to challenging what was regarded as the moderation of groups such as the Muslim Brotherhood, which were criticised for participating in elections and giving false religious legitimacy to regimes that should be overthrown.[2] A further boost to this process was provided by ongoing Saudi patronage of some of these forces alongside a gradual reduction of Saudi funds to the Muslim Brotherhood. The latter incurred Saudi wrath by supporting Saddam Hussein's invasion of Kuwait in 1990, which also appeared to threaten Saudi Arabia. The Brotherhood's influence was being eclipsed by more violent groups now on the scene, and it was the jihadists that the Saudis needed to cultivate to propagate Wahhabi Islam and ensure the survival of the House of Saud.[3]

In the summer of 1993, amidst this growing militancy, British intelligence prepared a report for the Foreign Office entitled 'Islamic Fundamentalism in the Middle East'. It amounts to a neat summary of some of the beliefs that have led British officials to collaborate with radical Islamists. The report outlined MI6's view on the origins and impact of fundamentalism, noting that 'it breeds on failure to resolve economic and social problems, corruption in government and the bankruptcy of political ideologies – Communism, Nasserism, Baathism etc'. These were, of course, ideologies which the British had done their utmost to undermine, thus paving the way for the advance of fundamentalism. The report also showed that officials were aware that 'private Saudi and Gulf money donated for Islamic causes is a common factor in much of the region' – as they continued to deepen their support for these regimes.

Then the report recognised 'Islam's potential as a focus of opposition, offering a ready-made ideology emphasising social justice', and also, crucially, that 'fundamentalism is not necessarily synonymous with political radicalism or anti-Western policies' – a revealing comment and a key reason why Britain had been collaborating with these groups for so long. The report continued:

> The fundamentalist groups advocating violence and revolution are in a minority. Nevertheless, there is a strong anti-Western streak in all main political fundamentalist movements in the region. Western, particularly American, culture and materialism are seen as a threat to Islamic values. The fundamentalists' wider objectives are more or less incompatible with Western liberal principles – they are opposed to political pluralism, religious tolerance and women's rights.

This last point was surely correct, but these were also features of virtually every government that Britain had supported in the Middle East for decades, precisely to counter more pluralist governments more supportive of, say, women's rights.

The report also noted that fundamentalist groups 'are prepared to use the ballot box to gain power. But there is every doubt that these "parties of God" would subject their political authority, once achieved, to further the democratic process.' However, the conclusion read:

> Fundamentalism does not pose a coherent and monolithic threat to Western interests in the way that Communism once did. It is not supported by a superpower. Its appeal in Western countries is confined to Muslim minorities and the threat of subversion is, in the UK at least, minimal. Dealings with extreme fundamentalist regimes would be highly unpredictable but not necessarily unmanageable.[4]

The analysis that Britain could have manageable relations with fundamentalist regimes is highly revealing. The belief that fundamentalism does not pose a strategic threat to Western interests helps explain why Britain collaborated with these groups against forces that did pose such a threat, notably Nasserism. Meanwhile, the view that fundamentalism's appeal in Britain was small partly explains the authorities' toleration and protection of some of these groups during the rise of Londonistan in the 1990s. These, then, were the views of key British officials as Whitehall continued its policy of de facto support for radical Islam, or at least several strands of it, in the 1990s.

SAVING THE SAUDIS AND THEIR FINANCIAL EMPIRE

After Saddam Hussein invaded Kuwait in August 1990, the Saudi regime contributed over $50 billion to the US- and UK-led war which annihilated Iraq's army in February 1991. The conflict handed a massive boost to radical Sunni Islam. In meetings with the Saudi intelligence chief, Prince Turki, and Defence Minister Prince Sultan, Bin Laden offered the use of his battle-hardened Arab–Afghan forces in defence of the Kingdom, but the Saudis rejected these overtures, opting instead for the deployment of half a million infidel US forces in the Land of the Two Holy Places.[5] The reality was obvious: the Saudis were totally dependent on the US for their survival. The jihadist groups, committed to eradicating the Western presence from Saudi Arabia, now saw the Saudi rulers as having betrayed Islam and would more easily find recruits to their cause within Saudi Arabia, which was soon targeted for terrorist attacks.

Britain leapt to the defence of its fundamentalist ally and the Kuwaiti regime of Jaber al-Sabah, whose family had ruled the emirate, under British protection, since the mid-eighteeenth century. Al-Sabah was one of Whitehall's closest allies in the region, presiding over an oil-rich state investing billions of its revenue in the British economy. Britain sent the second-largest contingent in the allied force – over 40,000 troops – along with naval vessels and RAF squadrons which operated from Saudi bases. British covert forces also played a significant role: the SAS deployment was the largest since the Second World War, and involved working behind enemy lines to destroy Iraqi communications facilities and 'Scud' mobile anti-aircraft launchers in advance of the main US-led attack. A team of MI6 officers also helped organise the Kuwaiti resistance in liaison with the Saudis. A training camp for Kuwaiti volunteers was set up in eastern Saudi Arabia, alongside similar US programmes, while several members of the SAS were attached to these training teams, also providing weapons.[6] The long-standing US-British–Saudi covert alliance was again in evidence, and was really an extension of the operation that had only just ended in Afghanistan.

General Sir Peter de la Billiere, the former SAS officer appointed commander of British forces in the Gulf, later recollected:

> As we, the British, had backed the system of sheikhly rule ever since our own withdrawal from the Gulf in the early 1970s, and seen it prosper, we were keen that it should continue. Saudi Arabia was an old and proven friend of ours, and had deployed its immense oil wealth in a benign and thoughtful way, with the result that the standard of living had become very high. It was thus very much in our own interest that the country and its regime should remain stable after the war.[7]

The 'benign and thoughtful' way that the Saudis had used their oil wealth was, of course, sheer delusion, as we see below; the point was that these were our allies, and they could do what they wanted with their money as far as the British elite was concerned.

During the war, the US encouraged the Shias of southern Iraq to rise in revolt against Saddam, but once this duly began in March 1991 Washington allowed Iraqi forces to regroup and brutally crush the revolt, slaughtering thousands. US aircraft flew above Iraqi helicopters, in effect giving them protection while, at one point in the uprising, US troops stopped the Shia rebels from reaching an arms depot to obtain ammunition.[8] Washington preferred to keep Saddam in power than unleash forces that might be allied to its enemy, the Islamic Republic of Iran. So too with Britain, which had also initially encouraged the rebels; MI6, along with the CIA, had helped set up the Free Iraq radio station, which broadcast Anglo-American propaganda throughout the country. One British intelligence official, when asked about the earlier appeals for revolt, replied: 'We hadn't thought it through properly.'[9] This was nonsense: both London and Washington's urging of the Shias to revolt was classic policy – using Islamic forces to achieve specific short-term objectives, in this case to destabilise Saddam's regime and pave the way for Iraq's ouster from Kuwait. Once this objective had been achieved, these forces became expendable, by now a very familiar pattern in Anglo-American connivance with Islamic forces in the region.

With Saddam back in his box, his regime could still be useful. Britain and the US returned to recognising that Iraq's brutal but secular dictatorship could counter Shia Iran's bid for pre-eminence in the region – a policy that had begun when London and Washington had armed Iraq during its war with Iran that had begun a decade before. This support of a secular nationalist regime against radical Islamists was a reversal of traditional British and US policy in the region, showing the degree to which Shia Iran had become a strategic threat to the West. It was, however, only temporary: soon, as Saddam consolidated his hold on power under a strict international sanctions regime, British and US policy would revert to conniving with Islamist forces to overthrow him, as we see in Chapter 13.

As US troops were massacring Saddam's forces from their bases in Saudi Arabia, Bin Laden turned virtually overnight from being a supporter to an opponent of the Saudi regime. At the same time, he was continuing to recruit volunteers, many of them Saudi, for guerilla training in his camps in Afghanistan, in preparation for the upcoming jihad. Rather than expelling Bin Laden from Saudi Arabia, however, the Saudis reportedly tried in early 1991 to broker a deal with him, whereby Bin Laden would leave Saudi Arabia in return for the Saudis providing money to supply his Arab–Afghan forces and on condition that Saudi Arabia itself would not be targeted by terrorism.[10] While appearing to have been 'expelled' from Saudi Arabia, Bin Laden moved to Sudan in 1992, where Hassan al-Turabi's National Islamic Front regime offered him a new base. However, the Saudis never encouraged the Sudanese to take any action against him; rather, Bin Laden may have remained on their payroll.[11]

It was only in April 1994, after continual open criticisms of the House of Saud, that the Saudis revoked Bin Laden's citizenship. Even after this, however, they apparently kept trying to buy him off, some analysts claim.[12] Thus, in 1996 the Saudis, still fearful, presumably, of Bin Laden-inspired attacks in the Kingdom, reportedly gave their blessing to a secret deal Bin Laden struck with a Pakistani military officer with close links to the ISI, in which the latter would continue to supply al-Qaida with protection and arms.[13] It has also been alleged by some intelligence sources that in the same year a group of Saudi princes and business leaders met in Paris and agreed to continue aiding Bin Laden's terrorist network.[14] A 2002 report by French intelligence expert Jean-Charles Brisard noted that at least $300 million had flowed to al-Qaida and other jihadist groups in previous years, most from private Saudi donors and charities.[15]

US intelligence was reporting the Saudi funding of terrorism by the mid-1990s at least. A classified CIA report from 1996, revealed by the US media in 2003, stated that 'Islamic activists dominate the leadership of the largest charities' and that 'even high-ranking members of the collecting or monitoring agencies in Saudi Arabia, Kuwait and Pakistan – such as the Saudi High Commission – are involved in illegal activities, including support for terrorists.'[16] It is scarcely credible that the British weren't also aware of this alleged Saudi role.

Another major development for the Saudis was that the end of the Soviet system in 1989–91 presented Islamic finance with its greatest opportunity for growth since its revival in the mid–1970s. Major political obstacles to global financial deregulation, championed by Thatcher and Reagan's economic monetarism the previous decade, were now removed. Saudi money could now spread even further across the world and along with it came the preaching of Wahhabi mullahs, teaching inside newly-built mosques and religious schools, reaching Muslims from North Africa to Central Asia.[17] Saudi banks and charities led the charge, acting as the primary vehicles to finance the spread of Islamic fundamentalism.[18]

Much of the Saudi and other Arab money in the Islamic financial system was managed by American and European banks, while some terrorist groups also apparently used British banks to set up some of their accounts. The account of the Advice and Reformation Committee, Bin Laden's front organisation in London, received funds from banks in Sudan, Dubai and the United Arab Emirates. From London, the money was transferred to al-Qaida cells in Western cities, and to several Islamic centres and charities in locations including Bosnia, Kosovo and Albania.[19]

There was, however, little political will on either side of the Atlantic before 9/11 to monitor and control terrorist financing. There is no evidence that Britain ever tried to press the Saudis to close down avenues of funding for Islamist groups. Britain's economic dependence on the Saudis was now so great that Whitehall felt unable to challenge any significant policies of its favoured ally, a stance still apparent today. Rather, all the evidence points to Britain's continued toleration, and tacit support, of the Saudis' 'Islamic' foreign policy. It was the same for the US, which also failed to challenge Saudi support for 'charities' operating in other Muslim countries. When, in 2000, such pressure was finally mooted by the US State Department's counter-terrorism chief in a draft cable to various US embassies, other State Department officials overturned the cable's recommendations with the counter-argument that these charities performed numerous good works.[20]

Britain's dependency on the Saudis was largely the result of policy choices taken over previous decades, when Whitehall planners consistently chose to side with the reactionary regimes in the Middle East. One thing had changed, though. In the past, ministers had in private clearly recognised the repressive, mediaeval nature of the Saudi regime but were cautious in public about identifying too closely with it – for fear of inviting still more criticism from nationalist regimes in the region and losing even more British influence there. Now, however, British ministers under the Thatcher and Major governments took every public opportunity to exude praise for the Saudis, acting as apologists for their policies in order to win commercial and military contracts.

In January 1996, a Foreign Office minister, Jeremy Hanley, described Saudi Arabia as 'a country whose foreign policy has shared similar objectives to our own', one which has 'played a crucial role in the promotion of moderate and sensible policies', and which 'has been a bastion of stability and moderation in a region not always known for those qualities.'[21] A year earlier, Hanley had told parliament that 'Her Majesty's Government have no plans to link the UK's trade and defence policies with Saudi Arabia's performance in the area of respect for human rights … [or] with Saudi Arabia's performance in the area of respect for religious liberty.'[22] The Saudis could do whatever they liked and still rely on the protection of the British government and the monstrous self-deception that the Saudis were 'moderate and sensible'.

Meanwhile, Margaret Thatcher's love of tyrants did not end with her departure from office in 1990. In an extraordinary speech at London's Chatham House in October 1993, she asserted that Saudi Arabia was 'a leader of the wider Islamic family of nations' and 'a strong force for moderation and stability on the world stage', adding that 'I am a great admirer of Saudi Arabia and the leadership of King Fahd.' Britain was continuing its 'military training, advice and equipment' programmes, Thatcher said, since 'Saudi Arabia has never used its arms irresponsibly.' She added for good measure:

> But what about 'inside Saudi Arabia'? I have no intention of meddling in that country's internal affairs. It is one of my firmest beliefs that although there are certain basic standards and goals we should expect from every member of the international community, the precise pace and approach must reflect different societies' cultural, social, economic and historical backgrounds.

Thatcher concluded by saying that 'in spite of the threat which Islamic fundamentalism seems to pose in some countries, I have no doubt that Islam itself is one of the key forces for stability in modern Saudi Arabia. Another such stabilising force is the solid rock of a well established and respected monarchy.'[23]

This comment revealed Thatcher's inability to accept that it was precisely the Saudis who were actually among the chief propagators of Islamic fundamentalism.

As British arms continued to flow as part of the arms deals signed the previous decade, Whitehall also provided other military services, such as training the Saudi National Guard, still led by Crown Prince Abdullah. By so doing, the British may well have helped further train some former Saudi jihadists of the Afghan War, many of whom had now returned to the Kingdom and joined the National Guard.[24] Other al-Qaida sympathisers are known to have joined the National Guard and may also have benefited from this British training.

BIN LADEN'S LONDON BASE

While backing the Saudi royals, however, Britain also provided a hospitable base for those who had by now become their nemesis. In July 1994, Osama Bin Laden established an office in London, called the Advice and Reformation Committee (ARC), which sought to promote worldwide opposition to the Saudi regime – an immediate response to the Saudis revoking his citizenship, according to a declassified CIA report.[25] Run from a house in Wembley, north London, the ARC was equipped with a bank of fax machines and computers which churned out dozens of pamphlets and communiqués lambasting the lavishness of the House of Saud and its waywardness from promoting sharia law in the country, as well as calling for a break-up of the Saudi state. According to recent US court documents, the ARC was 'designed both to publicise Bin Laden's statements and to provide cover for activity in support for Al Qaeda's "military" activities, including the recruitment of trainees, the disbursement of funds and the procurement of equipment and services.' In addition, the London office served as a communication centre for reports on military, security and other matters from various al-Qaida cells to its leadership.[26]

A US Congressional research service report, released just after the September 11th attacks in 2001, noted that Bin Laden even visited London in 1994 and stayed for a few months in Wembley to form the ARC.[27] Other sources claim that he visited London in 1994 to meet members of the Algerian Armed Islamic Group (GIA), and even that he travelled regularly to London in 1995 and 1996 on his private jet.[28] Whatever the truth of these claims, Bin Laden's telephone billing records from 1996–8 show that nearly a fifth of his calls, 238 out of 1,100 – the largest single number – were made to London, showing the importance of this base.[29] It was the ARC that arranged a meeting between Bin Laden and a number of CNN journalists in March 1997.[30]

The ARC's staff included two members of Ayman al-Zawahiri's terrorist organisation, Egyptian Islamic Jihad (EIJ), Adel Abdel Bary and Ibrahim Eidarous, both of whom were later indicted in the US for involvement in the 1998 embassy bombings, when simultaneous explosions in Nairobi and Dar es Salaam killed over 200 people. Abdel Bary is alleged by the US to have managed al-Qaida training camps and guest houses before arriving in Britain, where he was granted asylum in 1993; two years later he was sentenced to death *in absentia* for his alleged involvement in the bombing of the Khan al-Khalili tourist landmark in Cairo. In May 1996 Abdel Bary is accused of being appointed by al-Zawahiri as leader of the London cell of the EIJ.[31] Eidarous is alleged to have begun organising the EIJ's cell in Azerbaijan in August 1995 before coming to London in September 1997 to become the leader of its London base.[32] While in Britain, where he was also granted political asylum, Eidarous is accused of maintaining satellite phone links with the al-Qaida leadership, and, with Abdel Bary, of providing forged passports for EIJ operatives in the Netherlands and Albania.[33] On the day of the East Africa bombings, both disseminated the claims of responsibility through faxes to the media; lawyers for the two men deny that they had advance knowledge of the bombings but an MI5 officer, later giving evidence to an immigration appeal, stated that the faxes were actually sent before the bombings took place.[34] The two men were detained by the Special Branch in September 1998 under the Prevention of Terrorism Act, on charges that they were associated with the 1998 bombings.[35]

The head of Bin Laden's ARC was the Saudi dissident Khaled al-Fawwaz, who was arrested by British police acting under a US extradition request in September 1998 for his alleged involvement in the East Africa bombings the previous month. Until this point the British authorities had allowed al-Fawwaz and the ARC to operate openly for four years. The US indictment against al-Fawwaz alleges that he provided Bin Laden with 'various means of communications', including a satellite telephone to speak to al-Qaida cells, and that he visited Nairobi in 1993 and established a residence there for Abu Ubaidah, one of al-Qaida's military commanders.[36] Al-Fawwaz has been held in Britain since 1998, and US attempts to have him extradited have been consistently blocked by the British courts after appeals by al-Fawwaz's lawyers claiming his human rights would be breached in US prisons.[37]

The evidence suggests that the ARC's activities were initially tolerated by the British, who may have seen them as a useful source of intelligence. Al-Fawwaz's lawyers have, for example, said that he was in regular contact with MI5 from the time he came to Britain in 1994 until his arrest four years later. His meetings often lasted for three or more hours while his phone was probably tapped and his correspondence intercepted.[38] 'Perhaps MI5 thought it was better to monitor al-Fawwaz ... for intelligence,' the *Guardian* has noted.[39]

After the terrorist massacre of tourists in Luxor, Egypt in November 1997, Egypt's President Mubarak blasted the British for hosting militants in London allegedly linked to this and other attacks, including Abdel Bary, and requested their extradition. It has been reported that the British government refused this request.[40] However, it appears that the government did indeed seek to deport the militants, following a request from the Egyptians, but was hindered by Egypt's rejecting a British request to ensure that they would get a fair trial and, if found guilty, would not be executed. Thus the deportation was prohibited by the European human rights convention, which forbids deportation of suspects who might be subject to torture or inhuman treatment.[41]

Another Saudi dissident in London was Saad al-Faqih, a former professor of surgery at King Saud University who had lent his medical expertise to the anti-Soviet jihad in Afghanistan. Al-Faqih fled Saudi Arabia in 1994 and set up another opposition group to the regime, the Movement for Islamic Reform in Arabia (MIRA), in London in 1996 and was given political asylum.[42] Al-Faqih has recently said that he maintains 'high-level contacts' with the British intelligence services and gives them advice about Saudi Arabia.[43] In 2004, the US government designated al-Faqih as a provider of financial and material support to al-Qaida since the mid-1990s, and accused him of being in contact with Bin Laden.[44] However, al-Faqih has been living openly in Britain for well over a decade and has not once been questioned by the British authorities.[45] His alleged involvement in terrorism has been questioned by several well-informed analysts, who point to the fact that no case has been brought against him, let alone proven, that MIRA is a legitimate opposition group to the Saudis and that his designation by the US as a terrorist is mainly about placating its Saudi client.[46]

But the British may have seen the ARC and other Saudi groups as providing more than just intelligence. The American journalist Steve Coll, citing interviews with British officials, offers a reason why Britain was reluctant to crack down on the centres of opposition to Saudi Arabia: 'It was an article of faith in Washington and London during the early 1990s that a little outside pressure, even if it came from Islamists, might help open up the Saudi kingdom to new voices, creating healthier and more stable politics in the long run.'[47] Coll's notion that British and US planners wanted to use an Islamist lever to influence the Saudi internal agenda is certainly credible and consistent with past policies in the region. However, his notion that this aimed at 'healthier' (rather than simply pro-Western) politics is less credible: London and Washington were more likely to have seen internal reform as a way of consolidating the House of Saud's rule.

Al-Faqih himself provides another explanation for the British government tolerating these groups. Asked in an interview in November 2003 about living in Britain, al-Faqih replied that the British 'have discovered that betting on strategic relations with the [Saudi] regime is dangerous. It is better to have relations with the people and I assume they know how much public support we have.'[48] Al-Faqih also recently said that 'the British are shrewd enough to know that the Saudi regime is doomed and they want to be in a position to deal with alternative leaders.'[49] Al-Faqih here exaggerates the support for MIRA in Saudi Arabia and it is nonsense to equate it with 'the people'. Yet the point that Britain was attempting to cultivate relations with future policy-makers in the country by tolerating these opposition groups is certainly credible. While Britain has long shored up the feudal rulers of Saudi Arabia, the long-term stability of the regime has equally long been questioned. Again, opposition groups could act as a kind of proxy force for Whitehall; to a certain extent, therefore, Britain may have been trying to play both sides.

The London base allowed Bin Laden to motivate his supporters around the world. The perpetrators of the 1995 bomb attacks in Saudi Arabia had read Bin Laden's writings after being faxed them from London.[50] It was also from London that various of Bin Laden's key fatwas were sent around the world. The ARC, for example, disseminated the English translation of Bin Laden's August 1996 declaration of jihad against the Americans 'occupying the Land of the Two Holy Places', calling for the US to be driven from Saudi Arabia, the overthrow of the House of Saud and Islamic revolution all over the world.[51] Two years later, in February 1998, the ARC publicised Bin Laden's creation of an 'International Front for Jihad against the Crusaders and the Jews', joining together a variety of terrorist groups. However, 'this caused little stir in Whitehall', *Times* journalists Sean O'Neill and Daniel McGrory note.[52]

Also instructive is that the British and US intelligence services repeatedly turned down the chance to acquire information on Bin Laden and al-Qaida in the 1990s. In early 1995, for example, the Sudanese government, then hosting Bin Laden, offered to extradite or interview him and other key operatives who had been arrested on charges of planning terrorist atrocities. The Sudanese proferred photographs and details on various Arab–Afghans, including Saudis, Yemenis and Egyptians who had fought in Afghanistan against the Soviets. 'We know them in detail,' said one Sudanese source. 'We know their leaders, how they implement their policies, how they plan for the future. We have tried to feed this information to American and British intelligence so they can learn how things can be tackled.' This Sudanese offer was rejected, reportedly due to the 'irrational hatred' the US felt for the Sudanese regime, as was a similar subsequent offer made specifically to MI6.[53] Three years later, Britain was also to ignore an arrest warrant for Bin Laden issued by Libya, as we see in Chapter 13.

So safe did Bin Laden's supporters feel in London that, in 1995, they sent overtures to the Home Office enquiring whether their leader could claim political asylum. The then home secretary, Michael Howard, later said that an investigation by his staff into Bin Laden resulted in a banning order being placed on him.[54] In January 1996, the Home Office sent a letter to Bin Laden stating that he be 'excluded from the United Kingdom on the grounds that your presence here would not be conducive to the public good.'[55] Presumably, giving asylum to Bin Laden would have been a step too far for the British in view of their need to be seen to be placating the Saudis.

The 1998 US embassy bombings were not the only terrorist outrages being planned by Bin Laden, or those close to him, during the period when the ARC was based in London. By late 1994, the CIA was designating Bin Laden as a terrorist threat, knowing that his inner circle were working closely with the Sudanese intelligence services which were, in turn, running terrorist and paramilitary operations in Egypt and elsewhere.[56] In June 1995, an al-Qaida team attacked Egyptian President Mubarak's presidential motorcade during a visit to the Ethiopian capital, Addis Ababa.[57] In 1996 a secret CIA analysis showed that the US was aware of Bin Laden's financing of Islamic extremists responsible for attempted bombings against one hundred US servicemen in Aden in December 1992, funneling money to Egyptian extremists to buy weapons and bankrolling 'at least three terrorist training camps in northern Sudan'.[58] After moving to Afghanistan in May 1996, Bin Laden set up terrorist training camps there under the protection of the Taliban. It beggars belief that British intelligence was also not aware of Bin Laden's activities during the period when it tolerated his London base.

In contrast to Britain's toleration of the ARC and MIRA, different treatment was meted out to the leader of another Saudi opposition group in London, Mohamed al-Masari, a refugee from Saudi Arabia who in 1994 established the Committee for the Defence of Legitimate Rights. By early 1995, the Saudi government was vigorously protesting to Whitehall about al-Masari's attempts to subvert the Saudi regime, and threatening to cancel arms deals if the government failed to take action against him. Given the high stakes involved, in April and May 1995, Foreign Secretary Douglas Hurd and Prime Minister John Major gave speeches apparently directed at al-Masari saying that Islamic dissidents were 'extremely unwelcome' in London.[59] The following December, Whitehall, prioritising arms exports to the Saudis, took the unprecedented step of ordering al-Masari's expulsion, and attempted to dispatch him to wherever local authorities could be persuaded, settling on the Caribbean island of Dominica, to whom British aid was quadrupled as a sweetener.[60] However, the British courts ruled that the expulsion would be illegal, the government having failed to show that al-Masari would not be in danger after his removal.[61] According to former CIA officer, Robert Baer, the Saudis were behind at least two assassination attempts against al-Masari; it is not clear whether these were in Britain or elsewhere.[62]

The *Guardian* interpreted the Major and Hurd speeches as a sign that the government's stance towards Islamic dissidents was hardening, prompted by Arab governments pressing Britain to clamp down on them. Yet government action was largely limited to al-Masari, clearly to appease the Saudis, while until September 1998 other dissidents, like Bin Laden's associates, were allowed to go about their business freely. They appeared to operate with the tacit consent of the British authorities, with the most likely reason being that, consistent with the historical record, they were seen as useful to the British.

CHAPTER 11

Pakistan's Surge into Central Asia

In the early 1990s it was not only Saudi Arabia that bolstered the rise of radical Islamist groups which emerged from the Afghanistan war. Neither did Pakistani covert operations end with the death of General Zia, who was killed in a mysterious plane crash in 1988, and the return of civilian governments in the form of Benazir Bhutto's Pakistan People's Party (1988–90 and 1993–6) and Nawaz Sharif's Muslim League (1990–93). Rather, Islamabad undertook a new wave of operations by using Pakistani, Afghan and other Sunni jihadists to promote its foreign policy goals, both in Kashmir and across Central Asia – a big push, the consequences of which are still with us.

Moreover, Britain armed and trained the Pakistani military at this time while deepening commercial relations. London not only turned a blind eye to the Pakistani push but conducted covert activities of its own, its eyes set on new oil and gas reserves in the Central Asia region. Just as Britain had sponsored Islamic radicals to destabilise the Soviet regime in the past, now Pakistan's backing of these forces was useful to Britain in countering communist governments that emerged after the collapse of the Soviet empire, and to reduce Russian influence in the region. Islamabad's surge in Central Asia coincided with a new jihad in Bosnia from 1992, backed by Pakistan, Saudi Arabia and Iran as well as Britain and the US, as we shall see. These concurrent episodes constituted a second wave in the development of global terrorism after the first wave in Afghanistan the previous decade.

KASHMIR AND THE BRITISH RESPONSE

Even after the Soviet withdrawal from Afghanistan in 1989, Muslim volunteers for jihad continued to flow into Pakistan and Afghanistan.[1] Throughout the early 1990s Pakistan's intelligence service, the ISI, trained around 20,000 militant volunteers at a special training school north of Peshawar, the city in northwest Pakistan near Afghanistan which became the home of countless Afghan refugees after war broke out in 1979, and was the mujahideen's primary organising centre. The school's founder was Abdul Sayyaf, the pro-Saudi mujahideen leader during the Afghan War, and its funders were mainly Saudi Arabia and Osama Bin Laden.[2] Pakistan's secret services also continued to run some of the Afghan training camps, and funded training by another mujahideen commander, Gulbuddin Hekmatyar, of militants from the Harkat-ul-Mujahideen (HUM), the Hizb-ul-Mujahideen (HM) and the Lashkar-e-Toiba (LET) groups. It was from this infrastructure of terrorism that the Taliban would soon emerge and which Bin Laden would draw on after arriving back in Afghanistan in 1996.

The ISI's mission was to bring under its control the Indian state of Jammu and Kashmir – which had a Muslim majority and had been the subject of dispute and war between the two nations since partition in 1948 – and unite it with Pakistani-controlled Kashmir (Azad Kashmir). Many of the ISI's arms supplied by the US in the 1980s had been stockpiled and were now distributed to the Kashmir insurgents, who, trained in their Afghan camps, started entering Indian Kashmir in 1991. By 1993, the ISI was said to be operating over 30 military camps for Kashmiri youths in Azad Kashmir, and had trained around 20,000 militants there.[3] Infiltration was stepped up during Benazir Bhutto's prime ministership and involved attacks on Indian military targets and a campaign of assassinations against

Kashmiri civil leaders opposed to the escalation of the jihad.[4] Some analysts suggest that, following the end of the Afghan War, the ISI also tried to use Bin Laden for its jihad in Kashmir.[5]

Benazir Bhutto later recalled ISI officers telling her at the time that they could not fight the clandestine war with Kashmiris alone, since they were not effective enough, and that they needed foreign jihadists.[6] By 1995, at least 10,000 foreign militants had also been trained by Pakistani–Afghan forces, in addition to the Pakistanis. According to one estimate, by the end of the decade the Pakistani military had helped train up to 60,000 militants to fight in Kashmir or Afghanistan.[7] A secret CIA report of 1996, later declassified, stated that the ISI was funding the HUM, which had now changed its name to Harkat-ul-Ansar (HUA), to the tune of $30–60,000 a month. It described the HUA as an 'Islamic extremist organisation that Pakistan supports in its proxy war against Indian forces in Kashmir', and was 'increasingly … using terrorist tactics against Westerners and random attacks on civilians.'[8]

Throughout the late 1980s and early 1990s, the constant refrain by British ministers was that relations between Britain and Pakistan were 'excellent' or 'close and friendly'.[9] A blind eye was turned towards Pakistani actions in both Kashmir and Afghanistan. In May 1989 Margaret Thatcher's foreign secretary, Sir Geoffrey Howe, told the House of Commons that Bhutto's government in Pakistan 'wish[es] nothing better than to see the establishment of conditions in Afghanistan that enable the millions of refugees to return to their own country. She and her country realise the importance of securing the establishment in Afghanistan of a broad-based government that is truly representative of the people of Afghanistan.'[10] This was at a time when Pakistan was transforming the Afghan terrorist camps into springboards for the jihadist surge into Kashmir.

Nothing changed under the grey John Major, who succeeded to the premiership after Thatcher's demise in November 1990. British officials continued to reject Indian claims of Pakistan's involvement in training militants bound for Kashmir. Foreign Office Minister

Mark Lennox-Boyd's summary of the situation in July 1991 was typical, as he rather distantly referred to 'Indian claims, and Pakistani denials, that Kashmiri extremists are receiving support from Pakistan with training and supply of weapons'.[11] However, when in June 1992 John Major himself discussed Kashmir with his Pakistani counterpart, Nawaz Sharif, he said that 'I made clear our concern about interference in Kashmir by militants in Pakistan'[12] – but this was as far as any statement went, still not mentioning official support for the militants. At the same time, London enhanced military and commercial relations with Islamabad.

The essential reason was that Pakistan was viewed by the late 1980s as a significant market for British goods, including arms. The Thatcher government signed a memorandum of understanding on arms exports with the Zia regime in 1988, covering the period from June 1988 to January 1993, the details of which were kept confidential. By 1994 Britain had sold Pakistan six naval frigates for an undisclosed sum, amidst discussions about the sale of Chieftain tanks.[13] Pakistani military officers were trained by the British either in Britain or Pakistan throughout the early 1990s and beyond – while these forces were stepping up their sponsorship of the Kashmir jihad. Pakistan was regarded more broadly as 'a particular target for our trade promotion efforts'; between 1989 and 1993 British trade with Pakistan rose by 10–12 per cent a year.[14] By the mid-1990s Britain was the second largest foreign investor in Pakistan, which received Britain's third largest aid programme in Asia.[15]

Whitehall's failure to confront Pakistan-sponsored terrorism, and its basic support of Islamabad, complete with arming and training its military, had major consequences in Kashmir and beyond. Thousands of Britons of Pakistani origin have joined the jihad in Kashmir since the early 1990s; by early 2001, security sources were saying that around 900 Britons were visiting Kashmir for military training *every year*.[16] Many of them, along with native Azad Kashmiris, have undergone military training in the camps of the HUA and the LET. One Briton, recruited by the HUA in 1994, was Birmingham-born student Mohammed Bilal, who, in December 2000, would become Britain's first suicide bomber when he rammed a bomb-laden car into the Indian army headquarters in the Indian Kashmir city of Srinagar, killing six soldiers.[17]

Another Briton involved in the jihad in Kashmir was Omar Saeed Sheikh, a former student at the London School of Economics, who was recruited by the HUA in 1993 and claims that later that year he undertook military training at the Khalid bin Waleed camp in Afghanistan, joining a special course from September–December run by the Pakistani army's Special Services Group. This course taught surveillance, disguise and interrogation techniques, as well as the use of assault rifles and rocket launchers. At the end of the course, the camp was visited by senior HUA fighters, including its leader Maulana Masood Azhar. When the latter was captured in Kashmir by Indian forces in 1994, HUA leaders approached Sheikh to help secure Azhar's release; Sheikh subsequently visited India and proceeded to kidnap four Britons and an American, demanding Azhar's release; however, he was captured by the police and spent the next five years in an Indian jail.[18]

Sheikh's story is of special significance since there have been accusations that while he was a student in London in 1992 he was recruited by MI6 as an agent in the Bosnian War, as we see in the following chapter.[19] If true, there were particular reasons why Britain would have ignored Sheikh's support of HUA operations in Kashmir. According to B. Raman, a former Indian intelligence officer, British intelligence generally turned a blind eye to Britons of Pakistani origin joining the jihad in Kashmir. 'British intelligence was aware of members of the Pakistani diaspora going to Pakistan for training but closed its eyes to it' since the targets would be Indian not British.[20] The intelligence services later followed a similar policy in monitoring the 7/7 bombers, with catastrophic consequences.

During the 1990s, some groups operating in Kashmir with ISI

support turned to terrorism in places such as Tajikistan, Bosnia, Chechnya and the Philippines.[21] The HUA expanded its focus from Afghanistan and Kashmir and participated in the Bosnian War from 1992, kidnapping US and British nationals in New Delhi in 1994, and was involved in kidnapping Westerners in Kashmir the following year.[22] The HUA also set up a network of activists in the US and began to raise funds from members of the Muslim community in Britain.[23]

By now, the Pakistani military and intelligence community also had its sights set on another target well beyond Kashmir – Central Asia.

VERY BRITISH COUPS

The Pakistani strategy to 'recover' Kashmir was part of a broader campaign to exert influence over the Central Asian Silk Road to China, which would benefit the country economically and enable it to act as a strategic power between Iran and China.[24] It soon involved covert operations in Tajikistan and Uzbekistan to Pakistan's north, and the Russian republic of Chechnya to its west. By 1994, the military under Benazir Bhutto's government was training hundreds of Chechens, Uzbeks and Tajiks at camps in Afghanistan in techniques of guerilla warfare, the aim being to export Islamist revolution in the region and reduce Russian influence.[25]

There is simply no British criticism of this Pakistani surge in the public record, in sharp contrast to regular condemnations of Ayatollah Rafsanjani's Iran, an official enemy, for its sponsorship of terrorism at this time. Islamabad's Islamist adventures were useful in hastening the break-up of the Soviet Union and countering its successors, both the communist governments that arose in the Commonwealth of Independent States, declared in December 1991, and Russia itself. The main prize being fought over was the huge oil and gas reserves of the region – notably in the Caspian Basin and its surrounding countries of Azerbaijan, Turkmenistan and Kazakhstan – which the British oil company BP later stated were on the scale of those in Britain's North Sea 'and thus of significant global interest'.[26] The area was seen by the regional powers, and Britain and the US, as a resource-rich new frontier ripe for exploitation by foreign companies. This great power competition was a re-run of the nineteenth-century Great Game and, from the British perspective, an extension of the Afghan War to counter Moscow's influence in the region. Islamist forces were, once again, useful as the shock troops to help secure the prize.[27]

Between 1993 and 1996 Britain opened six new embassies in Central Asia, which 'were there to promote British interests, helping British companies win new business and encouraging the development of stable, market based economies,' Foreign Office Minister Lord Chesham stated.[28] By the end of the decade, BP would have a major stake in big oil projects in Azerbaijan and Kazakhstan, while another British company, Monument, had a predominant position in Turkmenistan. BP would thank the Foreign Office for 'securing [its] commercial positions in these countries'.[29]

Pakistan's new push into Central Asia beyond Kashmir began in Tajikistan in late 1990. Cross-border raids from Afghanistan of the kind promoted by the CIA and MI6 in the mid-1980s were carried out by hundreds of Pakistani-trained mujahideen forces under Ahmed Shah Massoud and Gulbuddin Hekmatyar, both of whom continued to receive CIA aid up to 1992, along with money from Saudi Arabia.[30] Their principal aim was to promote unrest against the still communist government, the Tajik Supreme Soviet, in the dying days of the Soviet Union. After the Tajik regime proclaimed independence in 1991, and maintained itself in power following the collapse of the Soviet Union later that year, a civil war ensued between a coalition of Islamic and secular factions against the communist government; by the time a peace accord was signed in 1997, 20,000 people had been killed, 600,000 were displaced and the economy was wrecked.[31]

In the mid-1990s, Pakistan's ISI was also supporting Islamist insurgents in the Adolat (Justice) movement in Uzbekistan, which also received funds from Saudi Arabia and some Gulf states.[32] Adolat had been formed by Juma Namangani, a former Soviet paratrooper who returned from service in Afghanistan converted to Wahhabism. The party was banned by communist President Islam Karimov, who retained power through rigged elections and repression, and Namangani fled to Tajikistan.[33] In 1998, Namangani founded the Islamic Movement of Uzbekistan (IMU), which declared a jihad in the country and formed a network extending across several Central Asian republics. The IMU is said to have been backed militarily and financially by the ISI and bankrolled by Saudi Arabia and the Taliban, among others.[34] It began launching terrorist strikes in Uzbekistan in 1999 from bases in neighbouring Afghanistan and Tajikistan.[35]

Chechnya was another territory subject to Pakistani-sponsored attack. In 1994 al-Qaida had begun sending fighters into Chechnya from bases in Afghanistan.[36] In April of that year the ISI began training a young Chechen warlord, Shamil Basayev, and other Chechen militants, at a camp in Afghanistan run by Hekmatyar. After graduating, Basayev and the other Chechens were sent to another camp in Pakistan to undergo training in guerilla tactics, where Basayev met several ISI generals.[37] Basayev's jihad began in earnest in early 1995 when a battalion of Afghan mujahideen stationed in Pakistan were sent into combat in Chechnya. The ISI retained tactical control over these forces and helped turn what began in the early 1990s as an anti-Soviet struggle for self-determination into an Islamic jihad.[38] In 1996, the ISI and Bin Laden decided to fund and arm hundreds more militants to be sent to Chechnya. By 1998, several hundred Chechens were being trained in ISI-sponsored camps in Afghanistan, while others were being trained by the ISI in Pakistan in 'sophisticated terrorism and urban warfare'.[39]

Alongside these operations by Britain's key ally, there was one country in which Britain played a very direct destabilising role alongside Islamist forces: Azerbaijan, a country which was emerging from Soviet control and possessed much of the Caspian region's untapped oil and gas resources. British policy-makers set themselves the goal of getting a large slice of the cake. In the early 1990s, in order to curry Azeri government favour and secure a massive oil deal, the British government helped funnel arms to the Azeris and promoted two coups to establish a pro-Western business environment in the country.

From the evidence that has emerged, it was a group of Americans who began the covert operation in Azerbaijan, just as the Soviet republic was proclaiming its independence from the Soviet Union in late 1991. At this time a US company, run by three career air force officers with CIA links and a past record of involvement in covert operations, set up an office in the Azeri capital, Baku. The company, called Mega Oil, was approached by the Azeri government to recruit and train mercenaries to help fight its war in the disputed region of Nagorno-Karabakh in the western part of Azerbaijan. What was to become a two-year operation then began to recruit 2,000 Afghan jihadists and procure weapons for them; many were recruited in Peshawar, Pakistan, by being offered $2,000 dollars each. The weapons procurement programme was to amount to some $20 million worth, while training was provided by retired US special forces officers.[40]

In December 1991, a referendum held in Nagorno-Karabakh, a mainly Christian region, resulted in the majority Armenian population declaring independence from predominantly Muslim Azerbaijan; the majority also called for unity with neighbouring Armenia, which was backed by Russia. Full-scale war broke out in 1992 as Azerbaijan launched offensives to regain control of the territory, and both Azerbaijan and Armenia were subject to international arms embargoes. According to Russian intelligence, around 1,500 Afghan veterans entered Azerbaijan in the Autumn of 1993, their numbers rising to 2,500 the following year. Some of these militants had been recruited by Gulbuddin Hekmatyar, still an ally of Bin Laden, who in turn established an office in Baku around this time which acted as a base for jihadist operations in Dagestan and Chechnya.[41] The Afghan fighters in Nagorno-Karabakh took part in various battles against the Armenians, taking high casualties.[42] The war was, however, a catastrophe for Azerbaijan. By the time a ceasefire was imposed in mid-1994, Armenia had captured not just Nagorno Karabakh but other huge swathes of Azeri territory, while 30,000 people had been killed and over half a million people displaced from their homes. The Azeri mujahideen brigade was dissolved, and its remaining fighters took to sabotage and terrorism.[43]

The British government was also covertly helping to arm Azerbaijan. The *Independent* reported in January 1994 that London had 'given tacit support to an illegal scheme to supply Azerbaijan with military backing in its war with Armenia.' A British peer, Lord Erskine of Rerrick, who was reported to be an intelligence officer, was allegedly part of a British–Turkish business consortium secretly negotiating with the Azeris to provide arms, British mercenaries and military trainers to the government. The deal, reached in 1993, was worth £150 million annually, which the Azeris would pay mainly in the form of oil.[44]

When questions were asked in parliament about the *Independent* report, Foreign Office Minister Douglas Hogg first replied that he was unaware of any discussions with British companies about the supply of arms, contradicting Erskine's assertion that he had discussed this with the Foreign Office in 1993.[45] Yet two weeks later, in February 1994, Hogg told parliament that 'investigations to date suggest that there may be truth in the allegation that these attempts [to procure arms and mercenaries] have been made, but as yet we have no evidence that they have succeeded.' He added that 'if evidence of illegality is found the matter will be put in the hands of the customs or police.'[46] Two months later, Hogg reversed his stance, stating that officials have found 'no evidence to support the allegations of recruitment of United Kingdom mercenaries by the Azerbaijani government.'[47] No mention was made of arms at all. This was good enough for parliament, and nothing further was heard of the matter.

This was not the only covert British involvement in Azerbaijan. A further aspect of the story centres on the coup in June 1993 which overthrew Abulfaz Elchibey, Azerbaijan's first non-communist leader, who had been elected with 60 per cent of the vote in June 1992. Elchibey was faced with heavy military defeats in Nagorno-Karabakh which, along with poor management of the economy, provoked a military rebellion to break out in mid-1993. The June coup was led by a Moscow-backed warlord, following which a new president emerged in the person of Heidar Aliev, a former KGB chief who had served in the Politburo in the Brezhnev era. On what turned out to be the eve of the coup, Prime Minister John Major told parliament that 'there is no doubt that there are huge markets opening up in that part of the world [Azerbaijan] which I believe will be satisfactory for the United Kingdom, provided that we are prepared to take an interest in them at an early stage.'[48]

Indeed, there are allegations that MI6 played a role in the June 1993 coup 'to secure a more pro-Western, pro-business regime in the country', and also that its earlier plotting contributed to the May 1992 coup in which a communist government was overthrown by the military and Elchibey's Azerbaijan Popular Front Party, which led to the elections bringing Elchibey to power.[49] A Turkish intelligence report on the 1993 coup, later reported in the *Sunday Times*, stated that British and American oil companies were also 'behind the *coup d'état*' and that company representatives offered to supply the incoming government with military equipment in an arms-for-oil deal. BP denied any involvement but said that some other oil company representatives did discuss the supply of arms.[50]

British policy was, once again, based on pure political expediency, with London again finding itself on the same side as mujahideen forces – any regime was suitable, whether led by an anti-communist democratic figure such as Elchibey in 1992 or a former communist tyrant such as Aliev in 1993, as long as it promoted British business interests.

Soon after assuming power, Aliev instituted an autocratic regime that became a byword for corruption, as it suppressed political dissent. The regime also sought to encourage foreign investment and was increasingly keen on Western oil companies. By December 1993, British ministers were saying that relations with Azerbaijan were 'in very good order' and that the 'trade opportunities ... especially in the oil sector, are large and important to us'.[51] In September 1994, Aliev handed BP the lead role in a consortium of Western companies (including the US companies Amoco and Unocal) that would manage three giant oil fields in the country – a £5 billion deal. The British government had lobbied intensively for this outcome. Before the June 1993 coup, British officials were advocating 'relentlessly' for BP to win Azeri oil contracts and 'for months Britain's diplomatic mission to Azerbaijan had operated out of the BP offices'.[52] In April 1995, by which time the oil contract with BP had been signed, Douglas Hogg told parliament that 'we enjoy excellent relations with Azerbaijan'.[53]

Throughout the 1990s, further discussions took place on building a 1,700-kilometre-long new oil pipeline from Azerbaijan to the Turkish port of Ceyhan; a consortium led by BP would manage the project, which was agreed by the end of the decade. By 2009, the pipeline was pumping over 700,000 barrels of oil a day.

AIDING THE TALIBAN

Pakistani sponsorship of Islamic militants went furthest in Afghanistan, where, beginning in 1995, the ISI and Saudi intelligence funded and armed the Taliban movement. This backing enabled the Taliban to win a brutal civil war among mujahideen factions that followed the collapse of the pro-Soviet government in 1992, and eventually to take control of Kabul in 1996.

The first Taliban were mainly students of the Pakistani

madrassas, notably those run by the JUI.[54] General Pervez Musharraf later wrote in his autobiography that 'the Taliban were not a new, post-Soviet phenomenon. They were taught by the same teachers in the same seminaries that had produced the mujahideen.' He added that 'we had hoped that the Taliban, driven by religious zeal based on the true principles of Islam, would bring unity and peace to a devastated country.'[55] This was nonsense: the Taliban were the most extreme militants, consciously forged by Pakistan simply as its proxy force in Afghanistan.

Thousands of students of the Pakistani madrassas crossed into Afghanistan in 1995 and 1996, advised and armed by the Pakistani army as they gradually took control of Afghanistan's urban centres.[56] The fighters included cadres of various Pakistani terrorist groups such as the LET and the HUA, also encouraged by the ISI. The US embassy in Islamabad wrote that the HUA was operating camps in Afghanistan under the direction of the ISI.[57] The Saudis played their customary role of bankrollers of the enterprise, and are believed to have transferred hundreds of millions of dollars in direct payments and oil price subsidies to Pakistan's military during the mid-1990s, helping the ISI build up its proxy forces in both Afghanistan and Kashmir.[58]

The US also supported the Taliban in its rise to power, seeing it as a counter to Iran and a force that would sign lucrative deals with the US oil company, Unocal, the story of which has been told by other analysts and needs no repetition here.[59] A top secret CIA report written once the Taliban gained power in Kabul in September 1996 noted that the 'Taliban's leaders espouse a puritanical Islamic state' and have 'imposed Islamic law, including punishments such as stoning and amputation' and 'rigidly enforced the seclusion of women'. Yet it concluded that 'there is no evidence that a Taliban government would be systematically unfriendly to US interests', and that the belief of some Taliban officials that the US was funneling assistance to them 'could provide openings for a dialogue on regional issues'.[60] At the same time, the US State Department declared that it wanted to 'engage the new Taliban interim government at an early stage to: demonstrate USG [US government] willingness to deal with them as the new authorities in Kabul, seek information about their plans, programs and policies, and express USG views on areas of key concern to US stability, human rights, narcotics and terrorism.'[61]

Although the US provided no arms to the Taliban, it tacitly accepted its allies, Pakistan and Saudi Arabia, doing so. It was only after the Taliban had been in power for a year, in late 1997, that the US started to break with it, probably due to domestic pressure on the Clinton administration over the Taliban's appalling treatment of women, its eventual refusal to support the Unocal project and its harbouring of Bin Laden.[62] At this point, the CIA stepped up covert support for anti-Taliban fighters, notably the Afghan commander, Ahmed Shah Massoud.[63]

There is little information in the public domain as to Britain's stance towards the Taliban. However, what is clear is that London never raised public objections to Pakistan's sponsorship of these militants, acquiescing in Islamabad's surge in Afghanistan as surely as it had elsewhere in the region. While the Pakistani army was nurturing the Taliban in 1995–96, Britain was training its officers in Britain and describing the country as a 'great friend'.[64] Once the Taliban had assumed power, British government statements in parliament were striking in their lack of overt condemnation of the new regime. In October 1996, for example, the Home Office minister in the dying days of the Major government, Ann Widdecombe, was asked whether the Taliban's capture of Kabul meant a sufficient 'fundamental change' for the British government to accept more Afghan asylum seekers. Her reply was:

> We do not believe that the recent developments in Afghanistan constitute such a fundamental change in the circumstances so as to justify ... declaring that the country has undergone a major upheaval. Afghanistan has been in a

> state of upheaval for a number of years. The fall of Kabul to Taliban is part of this long-term continuing conflict.[65]

Thus the Taliban's assumption to power was no big deal; the Conservatives' desire to keep out Afghan asylum seekers was deemed more important than recognising the reality of the new rulers. It was true that, in Afghanistan, the Taliban were regarded by many as liberators when they took power, ending a vicious war which had driven hundreds of thousands of people from Kabul and killed tens of thousands. However, they immediately set about violently enforcing their strict Islamic code, closing girls' schools and imposing harsh punishments such as amputations, as noted in the CIA report referred to above, and all of which the British government was no doubt aware.

In February 1997, Foreign Office Minister Baroness Chalker was asked whether the Taliban government was violating human rights and replied that 'the Taliban in general appear still to be enforcing their restrictive regulations. We will continue to impress upon them the need to respect the principles of the UN charter and internationally agreed human rights standards.'[66] This was also an extraordinarily conciliatory statement, issued when it was obvious to all observers that the Taliban cared not one hoot about any human rights standards.

The election of the Blair government in May 1997 made little difference to British policy initially. The new international development secretary, Clare Short, told parliament that British policy was not to cut off aid to the Taliban-controlled areas of Afghanistan, but that 'all parties should recognise, protect and promote the equal rights and dignity of men and women'.[67] It was only, it appears, in late 1997 or even early 1998 that Britain decided to provide aid only on the condition that it would reach women as well as men.[68] This hardening of position coincided with stronger statements about the Taliban's abuse of women's human rights, and fits with the change in US policy at a similar time. The British stance towards the Taliban appears to have followed the US lead, initially regarding them, as did the US, as a force for stability in Afghanistan, protected as it was by its key ally, Pakistan.

British and US policy was to have catastrophic consequences. Not only did Pakistani and Saudi arms and money continue to flow to the Taliban, enabling it to conquer the north of the country in the autumn of 1998, but by now Bin Laden was firmly ensconced in the country, having arrived in Jalalabad, eastern Afghanistan, from Sudan in May 1996, just in time to see the Taliban take Kabul. He was initially protected by Yunis Khalis, one of the mujahideen commanders covertly backed by Britain a few years earlier.[69] It is believed that both Pakistan and Saudi Arabia then struck deals with Bin Laden. Soon after his arrival Bin Laden met representatives of the Pakistani military who encouraged him to back the Taliban in return for protection by the Pakistani government. The ISI then helped Bin Laden establish his headquarters in Nangarhar province and agreed to provide him with arms, a deal which was also blessed by the Saudis.[70] According to US intelligence reports, ISI officers at the level of colonel met Bin Laden or his representatives in the autumn of 1998 in order to coordinate access to training camps in Afghanistan for militants destined for Kashmir. The CIA suspected that Pakistan was providing funds or equipment to Bin Laden as part of the operating agreements at these camps. Meanwhile, Bin Laden got on with the task of building up his terrorist infrastructure in Afghanistan.[71] The US Defence Intelligence Agency later noted in a now declassified cable that 'Bin Laden's Al Qaeda network was able to expand under the safe sanctuary extended by Taliban following Pakistan directives.' It also noted that his camp in Afghanistan was built by Pakistani contractors funded by the ISI, which was 'the real host in that facility'.[72] The ISI is also believed to have tipped off Bin Laden about a series of US attempts on his life in the late 1990s in retaliation for the embassy bombings in East Africa.[73]

Meanwhile, that year, 1998, saw high levels of British military cooperation with Pakistan across all three services. Sixteen

Pakistani military officers were being trained in Britain, the RAF had an exchange team based in Pakistan, and the Royal Navy conducted exercises with the Pakistani navy in the Indian Ocean.[74] If Pakistan's support for terrorism was not sufficient to deter British support for its military, neither was its conduct of six nuclear tests in May 1998, which followed those by India. Foreign Secretary Robin Cook expressed his 'dismay' to the Pakistan government and lamely recalled the British ambassador in Islamabad for consultations; no further actions were taken.[75]

It has been alleged that in 1998 the Saudis also agreed not to ask the Taliban to extradite Bin Laden to the US in return for the Taliban ensuring that al-Qaida would not target Riyadh; Prince Turki is alleged to have also promised to continue to provide financial assistance to the Taliban.[76] However, this policy changed under US pressure to secure Bin Laden's extradition, and at a meeting in June 1998 between Turki and Taliban leader Mullah Omar, the latter secretly agreed to hand Bin Laden over to the Saudis for trial for treason. But this was halted by the August 1998 US cruise missile attacks on terrorist camps in Afghanistan in retaliation for the bombing of the US embassies in Africa. When Turki arrived back in Afghanistan following the attacks, Omar reneged on his promise and reportedly accused Turki of acting as an emissary of the Americans. Following this, the Saudis cut funds to the Taliban and suspended diplomatic relations.[77]

Overall, Pakistan's surge into Central Asia had produced decidedly mixed results for Britain. On the one hand, Islamabad had helped to destabilise some communist governments during and following the break-up of the Soviet Union, facilitating British access to the region's rich energy resources. To this extent, Pakistan was helpfully acting as a de facto foreign policy proxy in a region of the world where Britain had few agents or assets to promote its interests, due to the long blackout imposed by the Soviet Union. Yet, on the other hand, Pakistan had also helped consolidate the Taliban and aided the establishment of Bin Laden's camps in

Afghanistan which, especially after the 1998 embassy bombings, directly threatened Western interests. Neither the Taliban nor Bin Laden's camps could have existed without Pakistani or Saudi patronage. In this light, it is clear that 9/11 was itself a product of the Pakistani surge in Central Asia, and this, in turn, had benefited from Britain's backing of Pakistan. The deep roots of 9/11 can be traced to many causes; one of them was London's long-standing view of radical Islamists as useful to securing its foreign policy goals.

CHAPTER 12

A Covert War in Bosnia

In March 1992 the territory of Bosnia-Herzegovina declared independence from Yugoslavia, provoking an attack on its capital, Sarajevo, by Bosnian Serb militias allied to the regime of Slobodan Milosevic in Belgrade. The war that followed lasted for three years, killed 150,000 people and forced two million to flee their homes in what became widely known as a systematic programme of 'ethnic cleansing'. European governments, including the British government of John Major, were widely criticised for failing to halt the atrocities, which, while perpetrated by all sides, were principally conducted by Serb forces against Bosnia's Muslim community. Yet Britain played a significant, if limited, covert role in the war, supplying arms to Bosnian Muslim and Croat forces and turning a blind eye to US arms supplies to, and military training of, these forces. Most importantly, Britain also acquiesced in, and may have covertly assisted, the movement of some Islamist militants into Bosnia as up to 4,000 volunteers went there to fight the Serbs; the militants were funded by al-Qaida, the Saudis and various Islamic 'charities', amidst a wave of solidarity around the Muslim world with the plight of their co-religionists. As a new generation of jihadists gained combat experience and developed new networks, Whitehall thus played a role in fomenting the third wave in the globalisation of terrorism, following the Afghan War and Pakistan's surge into Central Asia.

JIHAD IN EUROPE

In April 1992, a month after the outbreak of the Bosnian War, Afghan resistance forces finally captured Kabul and overthrew its pro-Soviet regime. That same month a veteran of the Afghan War, Sheikh Abu Abdel Aziz, visited Bosnia, where he proclaimed himself the first amir of the Bosnian Arab–Afghans. Little is known of Aziz, except that he is believed to be a Saudi of Indian descent who had been inspired to fight in Afghanistan by Abdullah Azzam, the principal organiser and mentor of the Afghan jihadists who was killed in a bomb blast in 1989. Aziz established his first headquarters in the central Bosnian town of Travnik, 50 miles west of Sarajevo; other jihadist camps were set up at Mehurici, outside Travnik, and in the city of Zenica, also in central Bosnia. The camps were based on the Afghan model, providing intensive military and weapons training and religious indoctrination.[1]

The Bosnian jihadist volunteers largely comprised Afghan veterans of mainly Saudi but also Pakistani, Egyptian and Yemeni origin, and they were joined by a younger group of disaffected, often unemployed European-North African youths, mostly from Algeria and Tunisia. One was the Kuwaiti-born Khaled Sheikh Mohammed, who within a few years would be masterminding the 9/11 attacks.[2] Two Saudi volunteers, Nawaf al-Hazmi and Khaled al-Mindhar, journeyed to the Balkans in 1995; six years later they would hijack American Airlines flight 77 and crash it into the Pentagon.[3]

The Bosnian mujahideen were initially attached to and supplied by regular Bosnian military units, although they often operated as special units or as 'shock troops', or indeed independently of formal military control.[4] The mujahideen undertook their first major combat operations in the summer of 1992 in north-central Bosnia, fighting ethnic Serb forces who had initiated an offensive against Muslims in the region.[5] Ideological differences between the incoming jihadists and the local Bosnian soldiers led to the setting up in August 1993 of a separate mujahideen battalion consisting of non-Bosnians, led by Aziz, and attached to the Bosnian army's seventh battalion.[6] Although the mujahideen had an impact on the war's progress, and won some significant battlefield victories, their overall military contribution was limited.[7] Yet their value to the Sarajevo authorities went far beyond their direct impact on the battlefield: their presence in Bosnia had a symbolic value, Bosnian President Alija Izetbegovic seeing them as a political tool for obtaining funding and support for the war against Serbia from countries throughout the Muslim world.[8]

As Sarajevo was besieged and surrounded by Serb forces for three years from 1992, and with Bosnian Muslims suffering numerous atrocities elsewhere, humanitarian aid flowed from various Muslim and non-Muslim organisations. But the financing for Bosnian jihadist activities came principally from Gulf businessmen and Saudi 'charities', acting as major conduits for sending aid and weapons, in violation of the arms embargo imposed on all sides in the war. Over the course of the war, public and private aid from Saudi Arabia to Bosnia amounted to around $150 million.[9] Al-Qaida is also reported to have funded the mujahideen in Bosnia, and other al-Qaida operations in Eastern Europe, partly via the Advisory and Reformation Committee based in London.[10] Bin Laden appears to have visited Bosnia several times between 1994 and 1998, having been issued with a Bosnian passport by its embassy in Vienna in 1993; he also had men and arms flown in from bases in Afghanistan. It is believed that Ayman al-Zawahiri, the leader of Egyptian Islamic Jihad terrrorist group, was assigned by Bin Laden to coordinate al-Qaida's operations in Bosnia at this time.[11]

The Saudi government was also the largest donor to the Third World Relief Agency (TWRA), a private organisation managed by a member of the Sudanese National Islamic Front Party, which acted as a conduit for money and arms. Bin Laden is also believed to have provided funds to the TWRA, which, Western intelligence believed, used half of the $350 million it collected to purchase and transport weapons to the Bosnian mujahideen.[12] The Clinton administration knew of the TWRA's illicit activities but chose to turn a blind eye. In 1996, for example, a senior Western diplomat in Europe accused the US government of deliberately ignoring the TWRA's violations of the arms embargo, but was told not to interfere since 'Bosnia was trying to get weapons from anybody, and we [the Americans] weren't helping much. The least we could do is back off'.[13]

Iran was the first government to send covert arms supplies to Bosnia when, in September 1992, a Boeing 747 carrying small arms, ammunition, anti-tank rockets and communications equipment landed in the Croatian capital of Zagreb. This marked the beginning of the 'Croatian pipeline', a supply line to Bosnian forces in Sarajevo as well as to the Croatians. The Iranian arms shipments ran for around a year before being reduced in late 1993 due to increased conflict between the Bosnian Muslim and Croat forces. During this stage, the US turned a blind eye to the shipments.[14] In April 1994, however, President Clinton, in high-level meetings in Washington, explicitly gave a 'green light' to further Iranian supplies to bolster the Bosnian Muslim and Croat forces.[15] After this, senior Croatian and Bosnian Muslim ministers visited Iranian President Ali Akbar Rafsanjani in Tehran and drew up a tripartite agreement for arms supplies and humanitarian aid. The arms flow began again on 4 May 1994, and around eight flights a month subsequently took place that year, rising to around three a week by early 1995.[16] US government estimates of the amount of Iranian equipment supplied varied from 5,000 to 14,000 tons from May 1994 to January 1996. It was then that the clandestine supplies halted again, after US ground troops were stationed in the region following the Dayton Accords that ended the war.[17]

The US also directly supplied arms to Bosnian forces throughout the war.[18] In February 1995, there was great agitation within the UN Protection Force in Bosnia when secret C-130 transport aircraft were seen making night-time air drops at Tuzla air base in eastern Bosnia – the so-called 'black flights'. These were known to be covert

US arms deliveries, conducted in collaboration with the Bosnian intelligence service and, probably, Turkey. Supplies included anti-tank guided weapons, Stinger surface-to-air missiles and communications equipment.[19] Turkey proved to be the second most important arms supplier after Iran, playing a role in the Croatian pipeline from 1992. Pakistan also chipped in to arm Muslim forces, supplying sophisticated anti-tank guided missiles, airlifted by the ISI.[20]

The covert Western role in helping to arm the Muslim forces in Bosnia has been most comprehensively exposed in a report by Professor Cees Wiebes of the University of Amsterdam. Wiebes' analysis was part of an official Dutch enquiry into the 1995 Srebrenica massacre, in which 8,000 Bosnian Muslim men and boys were slaughtered by Bosnian Serb forces while in a UN-designated 'safe area'. The analysis involved years of information-gathering on the activities in Bosnia of various intelligence agencies. It showed that Whitehall decided to turn a blind eye to the US arms deliveries, the report noting that:

> The UK Defence Intelligence Staff (DIS) was ... aware of the American secret arms supplies to the ABiH [Bosnian forces]. According to the British intelligence official, the DIS never made an issue of them, so as not to further damage the sensitive relationship with the US services ... The DIS received a direct order from the British government not to investigate this affair. This was not permitted for the simple reason that the matter was too sensitive in the framework of American–British relations.[21]

This apparent British deference to the US is striking, once again confirming the degree to which Britain was now beholden to the US in covert operations. It is particularly noteworthy given the major disagreement, indeed animosity, between British and US planners over broad strategy during the Bosnian conflict, to the point where the Americans cut off some intelligence to the British. The US had a much more openly pro-Bosnian government position and was willing, in contrast to the British, to lift the international arms embargo to get more supplies to the Croats and Bosnians. Meanwhile, there was considerable US concern over the apparent sympathy of General Michael Rose, commander of the British forces in Bosnia, with the Bosnian Serb forces, whom he regarded as more interested in peace than the Bosnian government; Rose also regarded the conflict more as a simple 'civil war' than a case of aggression against an independent Bosnian state, and the US was secretly bugging his office, along with other UN commanders.[22]

However, deference to the US may not be the correct or only explanation for why Britain didn't challenge the US arms deliveries. There is evidence that Britain was itself covertly supplying arms to both the Muslims and Croats in the early 1990s. Operation Clover, a US intelligence-sponsored plan with a $5 million budget, involved at least one British covert operative.[23] Delivering weapons required a convoluted method, since Croatia and Bosnia were under an international arms embargo.[24] So, according to one source, Britain turned to Monzer al-Kassar, the arms dealer linked with terrorists who was a British agent involved in secret supplies to the Iranians in the 1980s. Al-Kassar was now being described as a 'Syrian drug trafficker, terrorist and arms trafficker' by a US Senate investigation into the financial scandal surrounding the Bank of Credit and Commerce International, in which al-Kassar was involved.[25] It is not known precisely what weapons the British agreed to provide to Croatia, but it has been reported that in early 1992, 27 containers of Polish arms and ammunition were secretly supplied by al-Kassar to Croatia, on a false end-user certificate which designated Yemen as the destination.[26] The operation in Croatia may have continued into the second half of the 1990s, alongside a similar one to arm the Bosnians, though no details on this have emerged.

The US also secretly arranged for regular Bosnian Muslim and Croatian forces to receive military training, in late 1994 contracting a private company, Military Professional Resources Incorporated, which was staffed by retired American generals and intelligence officers.[27] Moreover, one former Bosnian mujahid told the media that in the winter of 1993 14 Americans claiming to be former special forces helped train Arab and Bosnian fighters near the town of Tuzla; this involved at least eight Sudanese Islamic militants being trained in 'insurgency warfare'. The foreign mercenary team was led by Abu Abdullah, a former colonel in the US military.[28]

Whitehall also appears to have turned a blind eye to this training; it seems inconceivable that officials did not know of it.

According to Bosnian Muslim military intelligence sources, Britain was also one of the main channels through which foreign jihadists entered Bosnia, while London hosted several financers and recruiters for the cause.[29] Moreover, it appears that Britain, along with the US, actively encouraged foreign jihadists to go to Bosnia. Washington's secret alliance with Iran and the Bosnian Muslims meant that it allowed mujahideen fighters to be flown in; Richard Holbrooke, the US's chief peace negotiator in the Balkans, later noted that the Bosnian Muslims 'wouldn't have survived' without this help and called it a 'pact with the devil'.[30] Furthermore, former Indian intelligence officer B. Raman has noted that 'according to reliable estimates, about 200 Muslims of Pakistani origin living in the UK went to Pakistan, got trained in the camps of the HUA [Harkat ul-Ansar, the Pakistani terrorist group] and joined the HUA's contingent in Bosnia with the full knowledge and complicity of the British and American intelligence agencies.'[31] Raman notes that 'the CIA asked the ISI to divert part of the dregs' of the HUA to assist the Muslims, and that the first group of militants entered Bosnia in 1992.[32] The contingent was organised by the ISI, funded by Saudi intelligence and armed by Iranian intelligence, while leadership and motivation were provided by serving and retired officers of the ISI and Turkish intelligence.[33]

By this time the Arabs of Afghan vintage had already started creating mayhem around the world and so these intelligence agencies wanted to avoid the use of Arabs; for this reason, 'they turned to Pakistanis, particularly Pakistanis living in the UK and other countries of West Europe. Thus began the radicalisation of the Muslim youth of Pakistani origin living in West Europe.'[34] In late 1994 there were also reports that militants arriving from overseas were being accompanied into Bosnia by US special forces equipped with high-tech communications equipment and were intending to establish a command, control, communications and intelligence network to coordinate Bosnian Muslim offensives.[35]

One British citizen of Pakistani origin who joined the HUA during the Bosnian War was Omar Saeed Sheikh, the London School of Economics (LSE) student who, as outlined in the previous chapter, would later kidnap several foreigners to try to secure the release of HUA leader, Maulana Masood Azhar, and who would later be accused of complicity in 9/11. During Easter 1993, Sheikh took part in a humanitarian mission by an organisation called Convoy of Mercy, which delivered relief supplies to the beleaguered Muslim civilians in Bosnia but which also, according to Sheikh, provided clandestine support to the Muslim fighters. However, Sheikh himself never made it into Bosnia due to fatigue, instead meeting a HUA activist who persuaded him to join the group.[36]

Pakistani President Pervez Musharraf states in his autobiography: 'It is believed in some quarters that while Omar Sheikh was at the LSE he was recruited by the British intelligence agency MI6. It is said that MI6 persuaded him to take an active part in demonstrations against Serbian aggression in Bosnia and even sent him to Kosovo to join the jihad. At some point he probably became a rogue or double agent.'[37] Musharraf's accusation is clearly explosive but is severely undermined by the fact that Sheikh could only have joined the jihad in Kosovo very late in 1999 (when the war was over) since he was in jail in India from 1994 until December 1999 after being arrested for the kidnapping mentioned above. Whether Sheikh was recruited by MI6 remains unclear, yet there is evidence that

Sheikh became an agent of Pakistan's ISI, as discussed further in Chapter 15.[38]

Among the other Britons who volunteered for the Bosnian jihad was Abu Hamza, later the notorious imam at the Finsbury Park Mosque in north London. An Egyptian, Hamza had been granted citizenship in Britain in 1986, and had gone on the hajj to Mecca and met Abdullah Azzam in 1987. In 1990 he met wounded mujahideen from Afghanistan in London while volunteering to provide medical treatment to them, paid for by rich Saudis, and in 1991 he emigrated with his family to Afghanistan. It was there in 1993 that Hamza lost both hands and an eye in an explosion, while in 1994 he set up his own organisation in Britain, the Supporters of Sharia, with a view to 'supporting the Mujahideen' around the world and bringing sharia law 'to the whole of mankind'.[39] The following year, Hamza made three trips to Bosnia, using a false name, and worked as a relief worker with an aid convoy carrying food, clothes and medical supplies. Once inside Bosnia, Hamza left the relief workers and sought out the mujahideen, spending most of his time with the Algerian factions, advising them, he later claimed. Hamza returned to Britain in late 1995, one of the hundreds of Britons returning from the conflict who entered the country without any questioning from the British authorities.[40]

Another Briton who for two years went back and forth from Britain to Bosnia, carrying supplies for the cause, was Abu Mujajid al-Brittani, a recent university graduate. Al-Brittani first went to Bosnia in 1993, ostensibly to transport food and medicine to Muslims in central Bosnia, but this was a cover for support activities for the jihad. Al-Brittani travelled the length of Britain to raise money for the cause and increase awareness among Muslims, again with impunity from the authorities. He was killed in combat in 1995.[41]

Few details have emerged on Britain's covert involvement in the dispatch of jihadists to Bosnia. There was also little mention of the Bosnian mujahideen in the British parliament; when there was, the government downplayed any concern. In February 1994, for example, Foreign Office Minister Douglas Hogg was asked what information he had on the activities of the Bosnian Muslim seventh brigade and curtly replied: 'The brigade is believed to be near Vitez in central Bosnia. We understand that it mainly consists of Bosnians displaced by the war. There are foreign volunteers but it is not possible to give precise information about their countries of origin.'[42]

SUPPORTING BOTH SIDES?

British policy towards the Bosnian war is difficult to pin down precisely. In his academic dissection of British strategy, Brendan Simms of Cambridge University has noted that 'British mediators deferred to the Serbs, bullied the Bosnians and did all they could to sabotage US plans for military intervention.' He writes that Yugoslav leader Milosevic's claim that Lords Hurd, Carrington and Owen gave him a green light to prosecute the war, 'comes as no surprise'. More than any other country, according to Simms, Britain obstructed all international efforts to come to Bosnia's military aid and instead championed the international arms embargo, which mainly had the effect of penalising the government in Sarajevo. Simms also writes that although Bosnian government forces committed atrocities, 'these were essentially reactive and quantitatively and qualitatively distinct from the systematic campaign of ethnic cleansing waged by the Croatian and Bosnian Serbs.' Britain therefore bore considerable responsibility for a proportion of the tens of thousands of deaths.[43]

However, Simms' book says little about the mujahideen or Britain's covert policies. When these are factored in, a more confusing picture emerges. Although Britain was formally opposed to the lifting of the arms embargo on the Bosnian government, it acquiesced in Iranian–US supplies to it and covertly supplied some of its own arms, as we have seen. Although Britain acquiesced in British Muslims going to fight in Bosnia, the British army's detachment to the UN protection force, UNPROFOR, also had several confrontations with the jihadists. Along with the US, London exerted pressure on the Izetbegovic government to expel the mujahideen after the Dayton Accords of December 1995. Indeed, the SAS is then believed to have conducted raids on training camps in which many mujahideen were killed.[44]

There are many gaps in our understanding of this period, but the most likely explanation for these apparent contradictions is that different parts of the British state were pursuing different, and clashing, agendas, with the secret services involved in the covert arms supplies and the dispatch of the jihadists. One media report mentioning Britain's arming of the Croats and Muslims noted that 'the Conservative government was trying in vain to create a balance of power with Serbian forces.'[45] And according to Wiebes, the British view in the war was that 'there were no good guys and no bad guys'; MI6 had a non-interventionist view and its 'motto' was to 'stay out as long as possible'.[46] It seems likely that the mujahideen were seen as a proxy tool for parts of the British state to help create this 'balance of power'. If so, this is a policy with some historical precedents, notably the 1948 Arab–Israeli conflict in which Britain saw Arab forces as helping to create some kind of regional balance to serve ongoing British interests, as we saw in Chapter 2. As in that war, British policy in Bosnia was also incoherent, in effect supporting both and neither sides as such. It is also possible that the British intelligence services saw Bosnia-bound British Muslims as a source of intelligence on the war. MI6 was certainly active in recruiting agents during the conflict, and is known to have run operatives at various levels, including in Izetbegovic's Cabinet.[47]

To the extent that Britain helped promote the Bosnian jihad, its policy contributed to the profound consequences the war had on the development of global terrorism. For one thing, some of the money raised to ostensibly help the suffering Bosnian Muslims may have been diverted to help fund the attack on the World Trade Center in New York in 1993, among other terrorist targets: for example, Sheikh Omar Abdul Rahman, the blind sheikh involved in the bombing, had links with the TWRA, one of the jihad's principal funders.[48] Bosnia also further radicalised some in the Pakistani diaspora, a process begun under General Zia's military regime in the 1980s. Abu Abdel Aziz, the commander of the mujahideen forces in Bosnia, appears to have had links with the Pakistani Lashkar-e-Toiba (LET) group; Aziz may have attended, or at least sent recorded messages to, the annual LET convention in Pakistan to inspire jihadists, and he may also have been involved in assisting jihadists in Kashmir.[49] Also, after the war, Wahhabi missionaries from Saudi Arabia flooded into the Muslim areas of Sarajevo, building mosques and establishing a deeper presence.[50] A decade on, in late 2007, analysts were noting that Islamic militants in the country were involved in criminal activity, exerting a rising influence over young Bosnians who were gathering increasingly around the growing Wahhabi movement in the country.[51]

Most importantly, a new generation of jihadists had received military training and combat experience to take back to their home countries, notably terrorists of the Algerian Armed Islamic Group (GIA) who proceeded to conduct numerous unspeakable atrocities in a brutal civil war. After Bosnia, many mujahideen veterans showed up in leadership positions in jihadist groups from the US to Europe, North Africa to the Middle East, Chechnya to Kashmir. US journalist Evan Kohlmann notes that the deployment of Islamist militants in Bosnia occurred at an early stage of the al-Qaida movement, and that the experience had long-lasting effects on the group: the Bosnian jihad enabled militant cells from different countries to connect and draw together in a new continent – Europe. Bosnia's geographical position meant it was a good jumping-off point for the expansion of terrorism into Britain, Italy, France and Germany.[52] It was the metro bombings in Paris in July 1995, towards the end of the Bosnian War, which marked the beginning of Islamist terrorist attacks in Europe.

In addition, there were now 'numerous Islamist terrorist facilities' in Bosnia, ranging from schools to operational bases, that had been set up by the Bosnian government under the cover of humanitarian organisations.[53] Thus, by the summer of 1995, 'the Islamist infrastructure in Bosnia-Herzegovina had already constituted the core of a new training centre for European Muslims.' This included the first organised deployment of suicide bombers, involving at least a dozen Bosnian Muslims who had graduated from training camps in Pakistan and Afghanistan in the spring of 1995.[54] By the end of the war, the US was pressing the Bosnian government to expel the mujahideen prior to the arrival of NATO peacekeeping troops, as required of it by the Dayton Accords. To evade this, the Izetbegovic government simply issued thousands of Bosnian passports and other paperwork to members of the foreign battalion – up to 400 are believed to have settled in Bosnia, many of them marrying local women. With valid documentation, lingering groups of mujahideen were able to operate without significant interference from the UN, the US or NATO. Many of the most dangerous elements were also protected by religious and political hardliners at senior levels in the Bosnian government.[55]

However, there is another aspect of the Bosnian jihad, with links to the present-day and British foreign policy, which has been even less told, and which concerns Turkey.

TURKEY'S USE OF JIHADISTS

While Turkey was clandestinely shoring up fellow Muslim forces in Bosnia with US support, it was also stepping up its brutal war against the Kurds in the southeast of the country. Turkish forces were to destroy 3,500 Kurdish villages, make at least 1.5 million people homeless and kill thousands in the 1990s, to counter the PKK's (Kurdistan Workers Party) part-nationalist, part-Marxist movement for an independent Kurdistan. The abuses reached their peak in 1994–6, in which period the British government under John Major stepped up arms exports to Turkey: Britain delivered £68 millions worth of weapons to Turkey in 1994, the year Ankara began major offensive operations against the Kurds; exports trailed off the following year but reached a new peak of £107 million in 1996. London also provided export credits for arms and military equipment in this period, reaching £265 millions worth in 1995. British equipment used by Turkish forces for repression included armoured cars and the Akrep vehicle, produced locally in Turkey under licence from Land Rover, which was deployed by Turkish forces pursuing Kurds over the border into northern Iraq. Only eleven export licence applications for arms and military equipment to Turkey were refused between January 1994 and November 1997, spanning the end of the Conservative government and the beginning of New Labour.[56] Whitehall consistently supported Turkey against the PKK and referred to the latter simply as a terrorist organisation, fearful that Kurdish separatism in Turkey would destabilise not only its NATO ally, but encourage the Kurds in Iraq and elsewhere. At the same time, various apologias for Turkish policy were delivered. In 1998, for example, Britain's defence secretary in the Blair government, George Robertson – who later became NATO secretary-general – said that 'I hope that the Turkish government will use their discretion and wisdom when the world community is focussing on the iniquities of Saddam and will be as generous and humanitarian to the Kurds as they have been in the past.'[57]

Yet Britain was not the only ally of the Turks in crushing the Kurds. It was once again fighting the same cause of countering nationalism as the jihadists – by now a familiar combination. Starting in the winter of 1995, a few hundred jihadist veterans from the war in Bosnia – known as 'Balkans' – were transported to Turkey by the Turkish intelligence service, MIT, and the Refah (Welfare) Party, the country's main Islamist party. According to US terrorism expert Yossef Bodansky, they were then taken for advanced training at a base in northern Cyprus and subsequently deployed to eastern Turkey for action against the Kurds, as well as to Chechnya, Kashmir and Afghanistan.[58] Several western European governments expressed concern about Turkey's use of the 'Balkans' in 1996. 'In response, the Turks replied that Ankara would not have done any of this without the blessing of, and support from, the Clinton administration,' Bodansky notes, adding: 'if that is the case, and the Clinton administration even tacitly endorsed the Turkish "recycling" of the "Balkans", then this is even worse than the US record in Afghanistan' – since by now it was perfectly clear that jihadist forces had turned to terrorism, including against the US.[59]

By this time, the Turkish state was also actively using the Turkish Hezbollah organisation to help counter the PKK. Set up in 1983, Turkish Hezbollah was a Kurdish organisation inspired by the Iranian revolution and the writings of Said Hawwa, a spiritual leader of the Muslim Brotherhood, and aimed to establish an Islamic state in southeast Turkey, but had no formal links to the Lebanese Hezbollah. Its southeastern group emerged in 1991 under the leadership of Huseyin Velioglu, an Ankara University graduate.[60] Hezbollah proceeded to conduct numerous brutal murders of PKK sympathisers in the cities of the southeast, killing more than a thousand people between 1992 and 1995. In 1993 local officials in the southeast claimed that the Turkish military had provided training for Hezbollah, and this was confirmed in an April 1995 report of the Commission on Unsolved Murders of the Turkish Parliament, which revealed that in 1993 a Hezbollah training camp had been operating with military assistance.[61] A government minister in the early 1990s, Fikri Saglar, has said that the 'high command of the Armed Forces' was 'the founder, promoter and indeed user of Hizbullah [sic] in the southeast' and that 'Hizbullah was expanded and strengthened on the basis of a decision at the National Security Council in 1985, and some of them were even trained at security force headquarters.'[62] These were the very forces, of course, to whom Britain was providing arms and otherwise backing.

In 2000, the Turkish state began to seriously clamp down on Hezbollah by arresting hundreds of its members; by now, it had moved away from solely targeting PKK members for execution and was killing secularists, moderate Muslims and representatives of

Kurdish charities.[63] Then, in November 2003, two suicide bombers drove explosives-laden vans into the British consulate and the HSBC bank in Istanbul, killing the consul general, nine staff and over 30 others – one of the costliest attacks on British targets by Islamist terrorists. The attacks may have been timed to coincide with President Bush's meeting with Tony Blair in Britain. One of the bombers, Azad Ekinci, had been a member of Hezbollah in the late 1990s, and had made repeated visits to Afghanistan, Pakistan and Chechnya. He was from Bingol, north of Batman, where much of the heaviest state-sanctioned fighting between Hezbollah and the PKK had taken place several years previously.[64] But the story also returns to Bosnia, since Ekinci had connections with another Turkish terrorist group, the curiously-named Great Eastern Islamic Raiders Front (known as IBDA-C) which had sent a small contingent to the Bosnian jihad, jointly with the Pakistani terrorist group, the HUA.[65]

The Istanbul bombing was a case of blowback, partly the result of sponsorship of radical Islamic forces by the Turkish state, in turn backed by British governments concerned as ever with countering nationalist forces, their version of 'stability' in the Middle East, and selling arms to allies.

CHAPTER 13

Killing Qadafi, Overthrowing Saddam

THE SECOND HALF of the 1990s witnessed the stepping-up of al-Qaida's propaganda battle with the West and a series of spectacular, brutal terrorist attacks. In June 1996 Bin Laden issued a declaration of jihad against the Americans and, two years later, announced the creation of an International Front for Jihad against 'the Crusaders and the Jews', which united a set of terrorist groups behind an agenda to kill Americans and remove the US presence from Muslim countries. The Front included al-Qaida, along with the Pakistani groups Lashkar-e-Toiba and Harkat-ul-Mujahideen, the Egyptian groups Jamaat Islamiya and Islamic Jihad, and several others. The 1996 declaration coincided with the bombing of the Khobar Towers complex in Saudi Arabia, which housed a US Air Force team, killing 20 people, including 19 US service personnel. In November the following year, 63 people, mostly tourists, were massacred in Luxor, Egypt by members of Jamaat Islamiya. Then in August 1998, the US embassies in Kenya and Tanzania were bombed by al-Qaida supporters, killing 224 people, mainly Africans.

These embassy bombings, on the eighth anniversary of the US deployment in Saudi Arabia to eject Iraq from its occupation of Kuwait, were followed two weeks later by US cruise missile strikes against Sudan and Taliban-controlled Afghanistan, which were strongly backed by the Blair government. The attacks on Afghanistan hit a series of camps named Zhawar Kili al-Badr, located a few miles from the Pakistan border, which had been planned and designed by the CIA and Pakistan's ISI and constructed in 1985 by forces loyal to Jalaluddin Haqqani, the mujahideen commander of a faction that received significant British and US covert aid.[1] The US air strikes also hit a camp where the ISI had been training Kashmiri militants.[2] By now the State Department's counter-terrorism officials were pushing Secretary of State Madeleine Albright to designate Pakistan a state sponsor of terrorism, noting that the ISI continued 'activities in support of international terrorism' by promoting attacks on civilians in Kashmir. But this recommendation was opposed by other officials in the State Department, prompting Albright to reject such a designation, arguing that this would have eliminated any influence the US had over Pakistan.[3] The primary purpose of the US strikes may have been to convince the American public that the US was taking decisive action against international terrorism; in fact, they may well have convinced the al-Qaida leadership to strike the US homeland on 9/11.

Britain had by now a decidedly ambivalent view of radical Islam. On the one hand, it was clearly seen as a threat, notably to its Saudi ally after the 1996 attack and to its US ally after the 1998 embassy bombings. On the other hand, Britain continued to tolerate the phenomenon of Londonistan, including the presence of Bin Laden associates who publicised the al-Qaida declarations around the world. Indeed, London had by now become, along with Taliban-controlled Afghanistan which housed Bin Laden, the principal administrative centre for the global jihad, where the authorities were, at the very least, turning a blind eye to terrorist activities launched from their soil, as we see in Chapter 16. Whitehall also continued its strong backing for the two most significant sponsors of radical Islam: Pakistan, while it promoted the Taliban regime in Afghanistan, the terrorist cause in Kashmir and its surge in central

Asia; and Saudi Arabia, which remained the largest financier of the Islamist cause worldwide.

Moreover, Britain continued to collude directly with radical Islamists, principally in Libya and Kosovo, and to a limited degree in Iraq, as we see later. As it had done historically, militant Islam proved useful to British planners in countering nationalist regimes – Qadafi in Libya, Milosevic in Yugoslavia and Saddam in Iraq. This phase in Britain's collaboration with Islamist forces occurred while the terrorist threat rose to challenge overall Western interests, showing how pragmatic elites continued to be. At stake were key issues for British foreign policy – the installation of favoured regimes to rule over major oil resources in Libya and Iraq, and the desire to see a pro-Western government in the heart of Eastern Europe to aid the expansion of the European Union and NATO.

None of the regimes targeted by Britain was benign, but neither were the forces with whom Britain worked to topple them; these were decidedly dirty wars. As it had done countless times before, Whitehall seemed prepared to work to the adage that 'the enemy of my enemy is my friend', whatever their nature or the longer-term consequences. The transition to New Labour in the election of May 1997 made no noticeable difference to these priorities. The 'ethical' dimension to foreign policy announced by the new foreign secretary, Robin Cook, soon after taking office, was palpable propaganda, accompanied as it was by a list of policy priorities that were virtually identical to those of John Major's previous government.[4] This didn't stop the media, taken in by New Labour propagandists, from proclaiming the new government's 'ethical foreign policy', a phrase the government never used, since it never intended such a change in direction. Had it done so, it may have halted continuing collaboration with radical Islamic, indeed terrorist, forces, under Tony Blair.

But we turn first to covert British collusion with a radical Islamic group in the dying days of the Major government.

NORTH AFRICAN INTRIGUES

While Bin Laden was drafting his declaration of jihad in early 1996, British intelligence was plotting with al-Qaida-associated terrorists in Libya to assassinate Colonel Qadafi. Qadafi had long challenged British interests and Western hegemony in the Middle East and Africa. The revolution that brought him to power in September 1969, recognised as 'popular' by British planners, overthrew the regime of eighty-year-old pro-British King Idriss, which provided a quarter of Britain's oil and was home to £100 million worth of British oil investment. The 'security of oil supplies must be our greatest concern', one Foreign Office official noted a year after the revolution.[5] However, Qadafi set about removing long-standing US and British military bases, nationalising the oil import and distribution industries and demanding vastly increased revenues from the oil-producing companies. The regime later sealed its fate as a British and US bête noire by espousing an independent militant nationalism and sponsoring various anti-Western regimes, as well as terrorist groups such as the IRA.

Britain and the US have long been accused of involvement in plots to overthrow Qadafi. The most direct attempt was the US bombing of Libya in 1986, conducted ostensibly in response to Libyan sponsorship of a terrorist attack in Germany and believed to have targeted Qadafi personally, but instead killing his adopted daughter. Ten years later, another opportunity occurred when a Libyan military intelligence officer approached MI6 with a plan to overthrow Qadafi, according to former MI5 officer and whistle-blower David Shayler. The Libyan, codenamed 'Tunworth', proposed establishing links with the Libyan Islamic Fighting Group (LIFG), an organisation formed in Afghanistan in 1990 from around 500 Libyan jihadists then fighting the Soviet-backed government. One former senior member of the LIFG, Noman Benotman, who first went to Afghanistan as a twenty-two-year-old in 1989, later said in an interview that during the Afghan War his mujahideen commander was Jalalludin Haqqani, and that he and fellow militants had benefited from British training programmes:

> We trained in all types of guerrilla warfare. We trained on weapons, tactics, enemy engagement techniques and survival in hostile environments. All weapons training was with live ammunition, which was available everywhere. Indeed, there were a number of casualties during these training sessions. There were ex-military people amongst the Mujahideen, but no formal state forces participated. We were also trained by the elite units of the Mujahideen who had themselves been trained by Pakistani Special Forces, the CIA and the SAS … We had our own specially designed manuals, but we also made extensive use of manuals from the American and British military.[6]

After Afghanistan, the LIFG joined the armed struggle in Algeria, fighting alongside the Armed Islamic Group (GIA), with whom it had built up close relations in Afghanistan and Pakistan. The British Home Office later noted that the LIFG's 'aim had been to overthrow the Qadafi regime and replace it with an Islamic state'.[7] The US government later described the LIFG as an 'al-Qaeda affiliate known for engaging in terrorist activity in Libya and cooperating with al-Qaeda worldwide.'[8] It shared the same aspirations and ideology as al-Qaida, although it never formally joined the organisation, having a more nationalistic stance and preferring to focus on the 'near enemy', i.e., the Qadafi regime.[9]

Shayler asserts that he was told by David Watson, an MI6 officer, that at Christmas 1995 he had supplied Tunworth with $40,000 to buy weapons to carry out the assassination plot and that similar sums were handed over at two further meetings.[10] A secret MI6 cable dated December 1995 – leaked in 2000 and published on the internet – revealed MI6's knowledge of an attempt to overthrow Qadafi in a coup led by five Libyan colonels scheduled for February 1996. It provided a detailed schedule of events:

> The coup was scheduled to start at around the time of the next General People's Congress on 14 February 1996. It would begin with attacks on a number of military and security installations including the military installation at Tarhuna. There would also be orchestrated unrest in Benghazi, Misratah and Tripoli. The coup plotters would launch a direct attack on Qadafi and would either arrest him or kill him … The plotters would have cars similar to those in Qadafi's security entourage with fake security number plates. They would infiltrate themselves into the entourage in order to kill or arrest Qadafi.[11]

The cable also noted that one Libyan officer and twenty military personnel were being trained in the desert for their role in the attack, and that the plotters had already distributed 250 Webley pistols and 500 heavy machine guns among their sympathisers, who were said to number 1,275 people, including students, military personnel and teachers. Messages to these sympathisers 'were passed via schools and mosques' while the plotters also had 'some limited contact with the fundamentalists' who were 'a mix of Libya [sic] veterans who served in Afghanistan and Libyan students'. It continued:

> The coup plotters expected to establish control of Libya at the end of March 1996. They would form an interim government before discussions with tribal leaders. The group would want rapprochement with the West. They hoped to divide the country into smaller areas, each with a governor and a democratically elected parliament. There would be a federal system of national government.[12]

The plot went ahead in February 1996 in Sirte, Qadafi's home city, but a bomb was detonated under the wrong car. Six innocent bystanders were killed, and Qadafi escaped unscathed. Shayler recollected how:

> At a meeting shortly after, [David Watson] ventured to me in a note of triumph that Tunworth had been responsible for the attack. 'Yes, that was our man. We did it,' was how he put it. He regarded it, curiously, as a triumph even though the objective of the operation had not been met and reporting indicated that there had been civilian casualties. Despite that, I very much got the impression that this was regarded as a coup for MI6 because it was playing up the reputation that the real James Bonds wanted to have.[13]

Annie Machon, Shayler's partner and a former MI5 officer, writes that, by the time MI6 paid over the money to Tunworth, Osama Bin Laden's organisation was already known to be responsible for the 1993 World Trade Center bombing, and MI5 had set up G9C, 'a section dedicated to the task of defeating Bin Laden and his affiliates'.[14] This is significant in light of Britain's toleration of Bin Laden's London base – the Advice and Reformation Committee – which would not be closed down for another two and half years.

US intelligence sources later told the *Mail on Sunday* newspaper that MI6 had indeed been behind the assassination plot and had turned to the LIFG's leader, Abu Abdullah Sadiq, who was living in London.[15] The head of the assassination team was reported as being the Libya-based Abdal Muhaymeen, a veteran of the Afghan resistance and thus possibly trained by MI6 or the CIA.[16] A spattering of other media investigations confirmed the plot, while a BBC film documentary broadcast in August 1998 was told that the Conservative government ministers then in charge of MI6 gave no authorisation for the operation and that it was solely the work of MI6 officers.[17] All these reports contradicted the earlier claim by now Foreign Secretary Robin

Cook that MI6 involvement in the plot was 'pure fantasy'.[18] Equally, the government's denial of knowledge of the plot was decisively contradicted by the leaked cable, which showed that civil servants in the permanent secretary's department, GCHQ, MI5 and the MoD were all aware of the assassination attempt some two months before it was carried out.[19] It is inconceivable that none of them would have informed their ministers. At the same time, Shayler was persistently hounded and prosecuted, the British elite's usual treatment meted out to insiders divulging information incriminating it.

As the LIFG stepped up its confrontation with the Libyan regime in 1995, it issued calls for Qadafi's overthrow. One communiqué, written in October 1995, around the time the organisation was plotting with MI6, described the Qadafi government as 'an apostate regime that has blasphemed against the faith of God Almighty', and declared that its overthrow was 'the foremost duty after faith in God'.[20] These calls were mainly issued in London, where several prominent members of the LIFG were based after having been granted political asylum.[21] American political analyst Gary Gambill, a former editor of the *Middle East Intelligence Bulletin*, notes that Britain accepted the LIFG dissidents since British views of Qadafi were 'at fever pitch' over the regime's alleged involvement in the Lockerbie bombing in 1988; thus 'Britain allowed LIFG to develop a base of logistical support and fundraising on its soil.'[22] While the Libyan regime complained that Britain was hosting nationals intent on overthrowing it, Whitehall continued to offer de facto protection to the LIFG. Indeed, it was only in October 2005, after the London bombings on 7/7, that the British government designated the LIFG a terrorist group. This was after Libya's rapprochement with Britain and the West that began in 2003.

One LIFG member was Anas al-Liby. A computer expert based in Sudan in the mid-1990s, al-Liby had moved there from Afghanistan, where he trained al-Qaida members in surveillance techniques. In 1993 al-Liby travelled to Nairobi and used the apartment of an al-Qaida member to develop surveillance pictures of the US embassy.[23] This was the first step in the five-year plot that culminated in the embassy bombings of August 1998, following which al-Liby was indicted and became one of America's most wanted fugitives, with a $25 million reward for his capture or killing. In 1995 al-Liby came to Britain and applied for asylum. Soon after, the Egyptian authorities sent a detailed file on his terrorist credentials to Whitehall, including allegations of his involvement in a failed assassination attempt on President Mubarak in Addis Ababa in June 1995. But Cairo's request for his extradition was refused; British officials reportedly questioned whether he would get a fair trial and feared he could face the death penalty.[24] Yet there is also the strong suspicion that the British security services were protecting al-Liby, along with the LIFG, given that MI6 was collaborating with it to kill Qadafi. Al-Liby was allowed to live in Manchester until May 2000, when his home was raided on orders from the Home Office, acting on a request from the US; copies of jihad training manuals were discovered, but al-Liby had already fled. Other members of the LIFG included Abu Hafs al-Libi, who reputedly lived in Dublin from 1996 until going to Iraq in 2004, where he served as one of Abu Musab al-Zarqawi's lieutenants in the al-Qaida group there until his death the same year; and Ibn al-Shaykh al-Libi, a commander of Bin Laden's Khalden training camp in Afghanistan.[25]

Significantly, it was the Qadafi regime that in March 1998 urged Interpol to issue the first arrest warrant for Bin Laden. It did so in response to the LIFG's presumed murder of a German intelligence officer, Silvan Becker, and his wife in Libya in March 1994, some eighteen months before Britain began collaborating with the group. Interpol then issued a red notice on Bin Laden and three of his Libyan associates.[26] Yet, according to two French intelligence experts, Guillaume Dasquié and Jean-Charles Brisard, the British and US intelligence agencies buried the arrest warrant and played down the threat due to MI6's involvement in the Libyan coup plot.

This story was later reported in the *Observer* under the headline: 'MI6 "halted bid to arrest bin Laden"'.[27] It was five months after the issuance of the arrest warrant that the US embassies in East Africa were bombed; perhaps if governments, including Britain's, had acted then, the bombings could have been averted.

The episode is interesting in that it shows how Britain's secret collusion with radical Islamists has directly undermined its ability to curb and prosecute them – a leitmotif, in fact, of Britain's postwar foreign policy where Whitehall has often collaborated with the very groups to which it claims to be opposed. Indeed, the extent of this collaboration has been so extensive that many open public trials of the leading terrorist figures are likely to expose it, a fact which also applies to the Saudi, Pakistani and US governments. This partly explains London's and Washington's overt opposition to pursuing open legal processes for terrorist suspects – and, most notably, Camp Delta at Guantanamo Bay, where suspected militants have been incarcerated and interrogated behind closed doors.

ISLAMIST GROUPS IN IRAQ

The US and British destruction of Iraq's military and, to a large extent, civilian infrastructure in the 1991 Gulf War was followed by the imposition of international sanctions on Saddam's regime enforced mainly at British and US behest. These, and especially their effects on the country's health and other basic services, contributed to the deaths of hundreds of thousands of ordinary Iraqis throughout the 1990s, a fact well documented by human rights groups and the United Nations; thus the sanctions, and by implication Britain, caused more Iraqi deaths than the brutal Saddam regime itself.[28] London and Washington saw sanctions as a method for containing the regime, but in the 1990s Britain also engaged in efforts to overthrow it, which led it into contacts with a number of Islamist groups.

Soon after opposing the Shia uprising in Iraq in early 1991, President George Bush senior authorised a major covert action programme, costing over $40 million, to assist Iraqi opposition groups by funding and training their guerilla forces. Shia and Kurdish forces from Iraq were secretly flown to Saudi Arabia for training in tactics, communications and use of weapons, the latter purchased from the former Soviet Union.[29] London and Washington also helped to establish two umbrella opposition groupings. The first, the Iraqi National Accord (INA), had been created in December 1990, and brought MI6 and the CIA into collaboration with Prince Turki's Saudi intelligence service and the Jordanians – the familiar array of forces seen so often in postwar covert action in the Middle East. Scott Ritter, the former US weapons inspector in Iraq, described the INA as a 'creation of the British MI6', its goal being to carry out a 'quick, simple coup' in Iraq by favoured military officers. It largely comprised Iraqi Baathists and former military officers, including a former brigade commander in Saddam's special forces, General Adnan Nuri. Its leader was Iyad Allawi, who had ties with MI6 and would become a prime minister after the 2003 invasion.[30] The INA conducted some bombings in Iraq, once targeting a cinema in Baghdad, which killed several civilians. It also led a coup plot scheduled for June 1996, but this was uncovered by the Saddam regime, which promptly arrested 120 of the conspirators, executing most of them.[31]

The second group, the Iraqi National Congress (INC), was created in June 1992 as an umbrella for the vying opposition factions, with a base in London and funding from the CIA. The INC was led by Ahmed Chalabi, a secular Shia with close links to US Defence Secretary Richard Cheney, and its broad base included the two main Kurdish parties, the Patriotic Union of Kurdistan (PUK) and the Kurdish Democratic Party (KDP), and the two main Islamist groups calling for the establishment of an Islamic state in Iraq. The first of these was the Supreme Council for the Islamic Revolution in Iraq (SCIRI), the principal Iraqi Shia group based in and backed by Iran since its founding in 1982, which undertook various bombings and assassinations against the Saddam regime and formed a militia, the Badr Brigade, to conduct cross-border raids into Iraq. The other, smaller Islamist group was al-Dawa al-Islamiya (Islamic Call), which had established branches in Tehran and London following its proscription in Iraq in 1980. Al-Dawa's London branch was headed by Ibrahim al-Jaafari, who, after the 2003 invasion, would return to Iraq and briefly become another prime minister. Both SCIRI and al-Dawa initially sat on the INC council, but pulled out in the mid-1990s, in part over disputes with the Kurds who wanted Iraq to become a loose federation rather than a centralised state.[32] Indeed, disputes within the INC led to its near-collapse in the mid-1990s.

British Foreign Minister Douglas Hogg was reported in 1995 as having 'regular meetings' with SCIRI.[33] However, according to Scott Ritter, Britain persuaded the CIA in the mid-1990s to move away from providing the bulk of its support from the INC to the INA. The primary reason was the US and British fear of a popular insurgency, which might bring more representative, and pro-Iran, elements into power and challenge Western control over Iraq, as opposed to a 'simple' coup that would replace Saddam with a new pro-Western Iraqi elite.[34] This factor probably explains why British and US contacts with SCIRI were apparently tentative. Another factor was SCIRI's own reluctance to get too close to Washington and London. When eleven Iraqi opposition groups met in Windsor, outside London, in April 1999 – the first major INC meeting for three years – SCIRI was noticeable by its absence.[35]

However, there appears to have been some significant British cooperation with SCIRI at times. In November 1998, Labour's foreign minister, Derek Fatchett, said that he was continuing to conduct 'regular meetings', every two or three months, with over a dozen Iraq opposition groups, including SCIRI.[36] These meetings may have involved not just discussion about future plans for Saddam's overthrow, but actual military cooperation. It is possible, for example, that some of the Anglo–American military strikes against Iraq in the late 1990s were in effect coordinated with SCIRI forces on the ground. On 23 November 1998 Fatchett met representatives of over a dozen Iraqi opposition groups, including SCIRI[37]; three weeks later, in December, British and US aircraft conducted a four-day bombing campaign against military targets in Iraq. London and Washington then quietly stepped up their 'secret' war, increasing the frequency of their bombing missions in the 'no fly zones' in northern and southern Iraq, flying thousands of sorties and dropping hundreds of tons of bombs. Largely uncommented on by the mainstream media, this aerial campaign marked the true start of the war against Saddam's Iraq that culminated in the March 2003 invasion.[38] In March 1999, RAF Tornadoes and US F-16 Falcons were targeting Iraqi radar and communications sites southeast of Baghdad at the same time as SCIRI's 'Voice of Rebellious Iraq' radio was reporting popular uprisings in some southern cities. The respected intelligence website, Stratfor, noted that during and since the December 1998 bombings, the air strikes appeared to be coordinated with, or were at least paving the way for, opposition activities on the ground.[39]

After the US Congress passed the Iraq Liberation Act in late 1998, which called for regime change and the overt funding of opposition groups, the INC was granted a further $100 million for military equipment and training. In January 1999 the US designated seven Iraqi opposition groups as eligible to receive training and weapons – including SCIRI which, however, refused to accept such US assistance, presumably out of fear of collaborating too actively with Washington. The US funding would support 'a campaign of guerilla warfare' put forward by the INC to destabilise Saddam's regime, with SAS soldiers expected to instruct the Iraqi exiles; a further example of British forces acting as a de facto covert arm of the US government. A core group of 200–300 exiles would receive initial training in sabotage techniques and the use of weapons and would then serve as an unofficial officer corps helping to train a further 2,000–3,000 recruits. It is unclear what happened to this small army.[40]

As well as contacts with SCIRI and the Saudis to overthrow

Saddam, Whitehall officials also had some meetings with another Islamist force, the Islamic Movement of Iraqi Kurdistan (IMIK). Established in 1987, the IMIK brought together cadres who had fought in Afghanistan in the 1980s. By the mid-1990s it had become the third most significant political and military force in the Kurdish region of northern Iraq, after the main secular parties, the PUK and the KDP. The IMIK was one of the seven groups designated by the US in 1998 as eligible for covert funding, and that March Derek Fatchett publicly acknowledged having met representatives from the group.[41] One of IMIK's leaders, Ihsan Sheikh Addel Aziz, said in a later interview in London that around this time 'we established normal and good relations with European countries – particularly Britain – and the USA to explain our just cause and intensify efforts for a positive future change in Iraq'; though he also said that his organisation did not receive any US financial aid. Aziz claimed that the IMIK was completely opposed to al-Qaida's 'criminal operations' but was 'a jihad movement that abides by the Koran and the prophet's *sunnah* [path].'[42] In 2003 the group was reported to still have a liaison office in London.[43]

Little is known of these British contacts, which are also interesting since parts of IMIK would soon evolve into an al Qaida affiliate. Around the turn of the millennium the group splintered into several factions, some of which subsequently coalesced, in September 2001, into the Jund al-Islam (Soldiers of Islam) group, which promptly declared jihad against the PUK and KDP, and carried out various attacks against Kurdish civilians. In December 2001 the group renamed itself Ansar al-Islam (Supporters of Islam); its amir was a long time member of the IMIK, Najmuddin Faraj Ahmad, known as Mala Fateh Krekar.[44] Krekar, who once praised Bin Laden as the 'jewel in the crown of Islam', was arrested in the Netherlands in 2002 on suspicion of involvement in terrorism in Iraq and deported back to Norway, where he had gained citizenship, to face further deportation to Iraq.[45] With funding from Saudi Arabia and al-Qaida, Ansar al-Islam established a small safe haven in mountainous northern Iraq and may have harboured Abu Musab al-Zarqawi, al-Qaida's leader in Iraq. In the first days of the March 2003 invasion of Iraq, US forces were to pound suspected Ansar al-Islam training camps and facilities in northern Iraq.

But, to return to the late 1990s, even as the dust was settling on the two devastated embassies in East Africa, Britain and the US had by now again plunged into actively supporting al-Qaida allies, this time in Kosovo.

CHAPTER 14

Intrigues in the Southern Balkans

In British mainstream commentary, the 1999 NATO bombing campaign against Slobodan Milosevic's Yugoslavia is seen as a 'humanitarian intervention'. Tony Blair still receives much praise for coming to the defence of the ethnic Albanians in Kosovo, whose plight was surely serious as they were subject to increasingly brutal abuses by the Yugoslav army towards the end of 1998. Yet the NATO bombing that began in March 1999 had the effect of deepening, not preventing, the humanitarian disaster that Milosevic's forces inflicted on Kosovo. The bulk of the atrocities committed by Yugoslav forces took place after the NATO bombing campaign began. In fact, some NATO intelligence agencies, including Britain's, were predicting that any bombing might well precipitate the full-scale 'ethnic cleansing' which they used as the public pretext for conducting their campaign.[1]

However, there is another critical aspect to this war that undermines its supposed 'humanitarian' motives, involving British collusion with the rebel Kosovo Liberation Army (KLA), which fought alongside al-Qaida militants and essentially acted as NATO's ground forces in Kosovo. The big debate in government and mainstream media circles during the war was whether NATO should put troops on the ground or whether Yugoslav forces could be sufficiently pounded from the air to stop their atrocities in Kosovo. The British and American governments were reluctant to commit ground forces, mainly for fear of incurring high casualties and getting sucked into a more protracted conflict; instead they turned to finding local allies and used these forces as a tool in their foreign policy. It was in this context that Islamist militants, working alongside the British-supported KLA, essentially took on the role of Western proxies, carrying out some of the dirty work that NATO could not. This story is, as we have seen, by no means unfamiliar in the postwar world.

Much later, in October 2006, then Chancellor Gordon Brown said in a speech on 'meeting the terrorist challenge' to an audience at Chatham House: 'The threat from al-Qaida did not begin on September 11th – indeed the attacks on the twin towers were being planned as the United States was taking action with Europe to protect Muslims in the former Yugoslavia.'[2] Brown was right; in fact, the British were providing military training to forces working with the very people planning the 9/11 attacks.

THE NATURE OF THE KLA

The Kosovo Liberation Army comprised ethnic Albanians committed to securing independence for Kosovo and promoting a 'Greater Albania' in the sub-region. Consisting of a mix of radicalised youths and students, professionals such as teachers and doctors, members of influential families and local rogues, it took to armed struggle and made its military debut in early 1996 by bombing camps housing Serbian refugees from the wars in Croatia and Bosnia and by attacking Yugoslav government officials and police stations.[3] By mid-1998 the KLA controlled parts of Kosovo and had armed and organised around 30,000 fighters; it was thus a formidable force on the ground when, amidst a growing civil war, the Yugoslav army launched a brutal full-scale offensive in Kosovo in March 1999.

From its inception, the KLA also targeted Serbian and Albanian civilians, especially those considered collaborators with the authorities. The US and Britain clearly recognised it as a terrorist organisation. In February 1998, the Clinton administration's special envoy to Kosovo, Robert Gelbard, described the KLA as 'without any question a terrorist group'.[4] British ministers were equally unequivocal. Foreign Secretary Robin Cook told parliament in March 1998: 'We strongly condemn the use of violence for political objectives, including the terrorism of the self-styled Kosovo Liberation Army.'[5] That same month EU foreign ministers signed up to a Common Position condemning the 'violence and terrorism employed by the Kosovo Liberation Army'.[6] Indeed, in November 1998, and again in January 1999, Cook said that 'most of the killings' in Kosovo recently had been carried out by the KLA, whose activities against ordinary Kosovars were only serving to 'prolong their suffering'.[7] Parliamentary statements by British ministers make clear that they continued to regard the KLA as a terrorist organisation right up to the beginning of the bombing campaign in March.[8] The KLA was also widely known to be involved in heroin trafficking into Britain while MI6 was investigating its links to organised crime.[9]

Moreover, the KLA had also developed connections to al-Qaida. Bin Laden reportedly visited Albania and established an operation there in 1994.[10] In the years preceding the NATO bombing campaign, more al-Qaida militants moved into Kosovo to support the KLA, financed by sources in Saudi Arabia and the United Arab Emirates. By late 1998, the head of Albanian intelligence was saying that Bin Laden had sent units to fight in Kosovo while the media noted CIA and Albanian intelligence reports citing 'mujahideen units from at least half a dozen Middle East countries streaming across the border into Kosovo from safe bases in Albania'.[11] US intelligence reports were also noting that al-Qaida was sending funds and militants to join the KLA, while numerous KLA fighters had trained in al-Qaida camps in Afghanistan and Albania. One of the 'links' between Bin Laden and the KLA identified by US intelligence was 'a common staging area in Tropoje, Albania, a centre for Islamic terrorists.' The KLA was helping hundreds of foreign fighters to cross from Albania into Kosovo, including 'veterans of the militant group Islamic Jihad from Bosnia, Chechnya and Afghanistan', carrying forged passports.[12] One KLA unit was led by the brother of Ayman al-Zawahiri, Bin Laden's right-hand man, according to a senior Interpol official later giving evidence to the US Congress.[13] One Western military official was quoted as saying that the Islamist militants 'were mercenaries who were not running the show in Kosovo, but were used by the KLA to do their dirty work.'[14]

Asked in parliament in November 1998 about a media article stating that mujahideen fighters had been seen with KLA forces in Kosovo, Robin Cook stated: 'I read that report with concern.'[15] His deputy, Foreign Office Minister Baroness Symons claimed, however, that the government had 'no evidence' that Bin Laden was funding the KLA.[16] In March 1999, another Foreign Office minister, Tony Lloyd, told the House of Commons that the government was aware of media reports of contacts between Islamic terrorist groups and the KLA but 'we have no evidence of systematic involvement'; the use of the word 'systematic' was likely instructive, implying that the government did indeed have some knowledge.[17]

There is some evidence that the Islamist penetration of Kosovo and Albania had been long planned. US terrorism expert Yossef Bodansky noted in a 1996 analysis, a year after the Bosnian war had ended, that the Bosnian government in Sarajevo and its Islamist sponsors had, since the early 1990s, been 'actively preparing for the next round of assault on the Serbs: this time through Kosovo', and that the plan was to escalate an armed struggle against Belgrade from bases in Albania. In June 1993, the Saudi Arabian government had donated $1 million to fund the building of a Bosnian base for guerillas to be sent into Kosovo. According to Bodansky:

> These Bosnian operatives would be able to carry out a series of terrorist operations which could be attributed to a Kosovo Albanian organisation, thus instigating a fierce reaction by the Serb security forces, and, consequently, a cycle of

> violence. The ensuing widespread violence in Kosovo, Sarajevo believed, would then be used to induce Western military intervention against Yugoslavia itself.[18]

At an international meeting in Khartoum in April 1995, Bodansky notes that Islamist groups and sponsoring governments, led by Sudan and Iran, agreed to set up two new centres in Tehran and Karachi, the latter intended to escalate a terrorist campaign in Kosovo. In the autumn of 1995, just as the war in Bosnia was coming to a close amidst continued NATO bombing, the Bosnian government began to deploy experienced mujahideen to Albania. By early the following year, violence had erupted in Kosovo, perpetrated by the KLA, as we have seen, which was seized on by the Clinton administration 'as an excuse for a marked increase in US intervention in Kosovo on behalf of "oppressed Albanians"', Bodansky comments, three years before the actual NATO bombing campaign.[19]

THE COVERT WAR

At some point in 1996 British intelligence, along with the US and Swiss services, made its first known contact with a senior KLA official in Albania, likely to have been Shaban Shala, a commander who would not only fight in Kosovo in 1999 but also inside Serbia in 2000.[20] Formal contacts between the KLA and the US took place in July 1998 when Chris Hill, the US special envoy for Kosovo, met KLA officials; the following day a British diplomat also met KLA officials in their headquarters in the central Kosovan village of Klecka.[21] The British government later claimed that 'an initial meeting' between an official in the British embassy in Belgrade and KLA leaders was held on 30 July 1998.[22] If so, this came two days after Baroness Symons recognised in an answer to a parliamentary question that the KLA was a 'terrorist' organisation and that 'it was clear' that it had 'procured significant quantities of arms in Albania'.[23] By October, Robin Cook was making clear that Britain was opposed to the KLA's political objective of forging a greater Albania: 'There is no place on the international map for a greater Albania – any more than there is for a greater Serbia or a greater Croatia.'[24]

Yet it was around this time that Britain started to train the forces it recognised as terrorists, whose political agenda it was opposed to and which had documented links to al-Qaida: a level of expediency that would have impressed British officials collaborating with the Muslim Brotherhood or Ayatollah Kashani in the 1950s, for example.

At some point in late 1998, the US Defence Intelligence Agency approached MI6 with the task of arming and training the KLA, the *Scotsman* newspaper later reported. A senior British military source told the newspaper that: 'MI6 then subcontracted the operation to two British security companies, who in turn approached a number of former members of the (22 SAS) regiment. Lists were then drawn up of weapons and equipment needed by the KLA.' 'While these covert operations were continuing,' the paper noted, 'serving members of 22 SAS regiment, mostly from the unit's D squadron, were first deployed in Kosovo before the beginning of the bombing campaign in March.'[25]

A few weeks into the bombing campaign, the *Sunday Telegraph* reported that KLA fighters were receiving SAS training at two camps near the Albanian capital Tirana, and at another near the Kosovan border, most likely near the town of Bajram Curri.[26] This was the centre of the KLA's military operations, where a series of training camps were dotted in the hills and from where arms were collected and distributed.[27] Crucially, it was also where jihadist fighters had their 'centre' and common staging area with the KLA, as noted by the previous US intelligence reports. The British training involved instructing KLA officers in guerrilla tactics and weapons handling, demolition and ambush techniques, as well as conducting intelligence-gathering operations on Serbian positions.[28] The whole covert operation was funded by the CIA while the German secret service, the Bundesnachrichtendienst (BND), provided weapons and training.[29] The BND had been providing covert support and training to the KLA since the mid-1990s.[30]

British ministers consistently denied any knowledge of the KLA's sources of arms or training when asked in parliament. On 13 April, three weeks after the bombing campaign began, and just days before the *Telegraph* reported the British training, Tony Blair told parliament that 'our position on training and arming the KLA remains as it has been – we are not in favour of doing so ... We have no plans to change that.'[31] Sometimes ministers used revealing language. Baroness Symons stated on two occasions, in March and May 1999, that there was 'no firm evidence' and 'no reliable information' on the KLA's sources of weapons and training – the use of the words 'firm' and 'reliable' being usual ways in which officials feign ignorance of issues they are perfectly aware of.[32] One reason for secrecy was that such training was in violation of UN Security Council Resolution 1160, which forbade arming or training forces in all Yugoslavia.

James Bissett, a former Canadian ambassador to Yugoslavia and Albania, later noted that the US training of the KLA in 1998 involved 'sending them back into Kosovo to assassinate Serbian mayors, ambush Serbian policemen and intimidate hesitant Kosovo Albanians.'[33] 'The hope', he wrote, 'was that with Kosovo in flames NATO could intervene and in so doing, not only overthrow Milosevic the Serbian strongman, but, more importantly, provide the aging and increasingly irrelevant military organisation [NATO] with a reason for its continued existence.'[34] KLA leaders similarly explained that 'any armed action we undertook would bring retaliation against civilians [by Serbian forces]' and that 'the more civilians were killed, the chances of intervention became bigger.'[35] This was precisely the strategy that Yossef Bodansky had outlined three years before NATO's bombing campaign. It seems that the KLA's escalation of ethnic tensions was an integral part of London and Washington's strategy – a familiar theme of postwar covert action in relation to collusion with Islamist groups.

The KLA certainly proved useful to Anglo-American planners. Tony Blair stated a month into the bombing campaign that 'the KLA is having greater success on the ground in Kosovo and indeed has retaken certain parts of it'.[36] Described in media reports as NATO's 'eyes and ears' on the ground in Kosovo, the KLA was using satellite telephones to provide NATO with details of Serbian targets.[37] Some of this communications equipment had been secretly handed over to the KLA a week before the air strikes began by some US officers acting as 'ceasefire monitors' with the Organisation of Security and Cooperation in Europe (OSCE); they were in reality CIA agents. They also gave the KLA US military training manuals and field advice on fighting the Yugoslav army and police. It was reported that several KLA leaders had the mobile phone number of General Wesley Clark, the NATO commander.[38] Robin Cook, meanwhile, held a joint press conference with KLA representatives at the end of March and was in direct telephone contact with its commander in Kosovo, Hashim Thaqi; the latter would in February 2008 go on to become the first prime minister of post-independence Kosovo.[39]

By early April 1999, more than 500 Albanians living in Britain had volunteered to go to fight in Kosovo, according to KLA representatives in London, though they were likely exaggerating the numbers. Just as during the Bosnian War a few years earlier, Britain and the US allowed, and may have facilitated, British and other Muslims to travel to Kosovo volunteering for the jihad. B. Raman notes that Pakistani militants associated with the Harkat ul-Mujahideen (HUM) terrorist group who had fought in Bosnia were diverted to Kosovo by the CIA.[40] Following the 2005 London bombings, John Loftus, a former US Justice Department prosecutor and US intelligence officer, claimed that MI6 worked with the militant Islamist organisation al-Muhajiroun (The Emigrants) to send jihadists to Kosovo.[41] Al-Muhajiroun was founded in Saudi Arabia in 1983 by Omar Bakri Mohammed, who in 1986 fled to

Britain after Saudi Arabia banned the organisation, and set up its British branch in early 1986. By the mid-1990s Bakri was being described in the British media as the 'head of the political wing of the International Islamic Front', founded by Bin Laden in 1998, and openly supported Bin Laden's calls for jihad; he told the media he was raising funds for the KLA and supporting their struggle in Kosovo.[42] Loftus told a US television station that al-Muhajiroun leaders 'all worked for British intelligence in Kosovo' and that 'British intelligence actually hired some al-Qaida guys to help defend Muslim rights in Albania and in Kosovo.' He claimed the CIA was funding the operation while British intelligence 'was doing the hiring and recruiting'.[43] These claims were, Loftus said, based on an interview given by Bakri himself to *al-Sharq al-Awsat*, a London-based Arabic-language newspaper on 16 October 2001.[44] However, despite extensive research, I have not been able to locate this interview on this or any other date; Bakri also denies (not surprisingly) ever working alongside British intelligence.[45]

Loftus also claimed that one of the Britons recruited for Kosovo by al-Muhajiroun was Haroon Rashid Aswat, a British citizen of Indian origin who later became Abu Hamza's assistant at the Finsbury Park Mosque, and who would later crop up in the investigations surrounding the 2005 London bombings. According to Loftus, Aswat was a 'double agent', working both for the British in Kosovo and after, and for al-Qaida.[46] Soon after Loftus made the claim, a *Times* report on Aswat's possible connections to the London bombings of July 2005 noted that questions were being asked about whether he was a 'useful source of information' to British intelligence and noted that 'senior Whitehall officials ... deny "any knowledge" that he might be an agent of MI5 or MI6' – a cautious formulation that can only add to suspicions.[47]

One Briton who can be more definitively linked to the Kosovo camps was Omar Khan Sharif, who in 2003 would become notorious for his aborted attempt to blow himself up inside a Tel Aviv bar: he pulled out at the last minute, but his accomplice detonated a bomb, killing himself and three others. According to a BBC documentary, Sharif spent three weeks at a camp in Albania during the Kosovo jihad, but the film (predictably) failed to mention that covert British training was also taking place in Albania at the time. Sharif had attended al-Muhajiroun meetings in Britain and was an admirer of Abu Hamza, who became his mentor; he also met Mohamed Siddique Khan, the 7/7 bomber with whom he tried to recruit other jihadists in 2001.[48]

US covert support of the KLA guerrillas did not stop when NATO's Kosovo campaign was brought to an end in June 1999, or even with the fall of Milosevic in October 2000. After the Kosovo conflict, KLA forces launched new wars in southern Serbia and Macedonia to promote their aim of a greater Albania, both of which were initially supported by the US – but, not apparently, by Britain. The BBC reported in January 2001 that 'Western special forces were still training' the KLA as a result of decisions taken before the fall of Milosevic. Now the KLA was reported to have several hundred fighters in the 5-kilometre-deep military exclusion zone on the border between Kosovo and the rest of Serbia, and were fighting to promote the secession of certain municipalities from Serbia. Moreover, 'certain NATO-led' forces 'were not preventing the guerrillas taking mortars and other weapons into the exclusion zone', and guerrilla units had been able to hold military exercises there, despite the fact that NATO was patrolling the area.[49] Other media reports noted that European officials were 'furious that the Americans have allowed guerilla armies in its sector to train, smuggle arms and launch attacks across two international borders', and that the CIA's 'bastard army' had been allowed to 'run riot' in the region.[50]

Of interest from the perspective of British foreign policy is that when, in March 2001, the guerillas began another war, this time across the other nearby border with Macedonia, it was led by several commanders previously trained by British forces for the Kosovo campaign. Now fighting under the banner of the National

Liberation Army (NLA), formed in early 2001, two of the Kosovo-based commanders of this push into Macedonia had been instructed by the SAS and the Parachute Regiment at the camps in northern Albania in 1998 and 1999. One was organising the flow of arms and men into Macedonia, while the other was helping to coordinate the assault on the town of Tetevo in the north of the country.[51] Another NLA commander, Gezim Ostremi, had been previously trained by the SAS to head the UN-sponsored Kosovo Protection Corps, which was meant to replace the KLA.[52]

NLA forces were now being called 'terrorists' by Foreign Secretary Robin Cook and 'murderous thugs' by NATO Secretary-General Lord Robertson, just as they had been before the March 1999 bombing campaign, when, as the KLA, the British were cooperating with them.[53] The NLA's ambushes and assassinations in Macedonia were little different from those perpetrated as the KLA. It also, initially at least, continued to be covertly supported by the US, which in one operation evacuated 400 NLA fighters when they became surrounded by Macedonian forces, and whose arms supplies helped the guerillas take control of nearly a third of Macedonia's territory by August 2001; it was only after this that Washington, under pressure from its NATO allies, started to rein in its proxy force and throw its weight behind peace talks.[54]

The following month, al-Qaida struck New York and Washington.

CHAPTER 15

9/11 Connections

IN CARRYING OUT such spectacular attacks as those on 11 September 2001, al-Qaida certainly achieved its intention of grabbing world attention. However, as French author Gilles Kepel has pointed out, 9/11 also represented the failure of jihadist forces to build a genuine mass movement and to promote a successful uprising in a single Muslim state. Al-Qaida resorted to media theatrics in the hope that raw terrorism might inspire where armed struggle had had no major success in popular mobilisation. 9/11 was more a sign of the decline, not the rise, of the militant Islamist movement.[1]

The attacks were, however, too good to be true for the Bush administration, which declared a 'War on Terror', amounting to a battle for the future of civilisation itself; Washington was now presented with an ideal pretext for carrying out a new period of global military intervention based on plans already conceived by the neo-conservatives in or close to the administration.[2] The invasions of Afghanistan and Iraq soon followed, along with the establishment of numerous new military bases, notably in the key energy-rich region of Central Asia. Deepened alliances were also forged with many repressive states around the world – from Colombia to Uzbekistan – which professed their opposition to terrorism as designated by Washington. Terrorism had replaced the 'Soviet threat' as the key pretext for Western support of these regimes.

But 9/11 also marked a new period in US and British collusion with radical Islam, in sharply different form to that which preceded it. Instead of primarily seeing these forces as allies to achieve foreign policy objectives, as on numerous occasions in the past, London and Washington would now publicly present them as their number one global enemy, but to achieve the same principal goal: control of key energy-rich regions, notably the Middle East. This new form of collusion did not, however, herald the complete end of the old form: as we shall see, Britain would still collaborate with some radical Islamic forces, and those allied to them, after 9/11.

Britain under Tony Blair happily stood 'shoulder to shoulder' with Washington in implementing this strategy, not only to put it beyond doubt who was the US's number one ally (in the face of rivals such as Germany and Japan), but also for other reasons of pure self-interest: that terrorism would provide a rationale for a new phase in Britain's own military intervention around the world. Since the government conducted a Strategic Defence Review (SDR) in 1998, British military forces had been quietly reconfigured from an ostensibly defensive role to an overtly offensive one, with a new focus on 'expeditionary warfare' and 'power projection' overseas. 'In the post Cold War world, we must be prepared to go to the crisis, rather than have the crisis come to us,' the SDR noted, outlining a strategy of using 'pre-emptive' military force. It also noted the need for a 'new generation of military equipment', including attack helicopters, new aircraft carriers, submarines and escorts, the Eurofighter multi-role warplane and the development of a successor to the Tornado bomber. 'Long range air attack' would be important 'as an integral part of warfighting and as a coercive instrument to support political objectives', while 'all ten attack submarines will … be equipped to fire Tomahawk land attack missiles to increase their utility in force projection operations.'[3]

This was all before September 11th. After, terrorism became the supreme rationale for the same interventionary strategy. In a report published three months after 9/11, the all-party parliamentary

Defence Committee repeated the call for a strategy of 'pre-emptive military action' and stated that 'we must ... be free to deploy significant forces overseas rapidly', adding:

> The implications of an open-ended war on terrorism – particularly one that will address the problems of collapsing and failed states which create the political space for terror and crime networks to operate – suggest that operations in Central Asia, East Africa, perhaps the Indian subcontinent and elsewhere, will become necessary as part of an integrated political and military strategy to address terrorism and the basis on which it flourishes.[4]

Moreover, in December 2003, nine months after the invasion of Iraq, the government would produce a new military strategy in a White Paper stating that 'the threat from international terrorism now requires the capability to deliver a military response globally.' It committed Britain 'to extend our ability to project force further afield than the SDR envisaged', including in 'crises occurring across sub-Saharan Africa and South Asia'. The paper repeated the need for 'expeditionary operations' and for new equipment such as cruise missiles and aircraft carriers, also reiterating 'the need to confront international terrorism abroad rather than waiting for attacks within the UK'.[5] For Britain, therefore, the War on Terror was replacing 'humanitarian intervention' – supposedly the concept that had guided Blair's bombing of Yugoslavia in 1999 – as the primary rationale for conducting military interventions overseas.

What was especially extraordinary about the British and US ability to manufacture this strategy from 9/11 was who London and Washington designated as their allies. In particular, Saudi Arabia and Pakistan were hailed as key collaborators in the War on Terror. In reality, the objective case for bombing Saudi Arabia and Pakistan was perhaps as great as bombing Afghanistan, and incomparably greater than targeting Baghdad. 9/11 was to a large extent a product of long-standing Saudi and Pakistani sponsorship of radical Islamist groups. Saudi Arabia had, for nearly three decades since 1973, bankrolled a range of Islamist groups, including Bin Laden, during the whole of which period Riyadh enjoyed the constant favour of London and Washington. Pakistan, meanwhile, was the creator of Taliban-controlled Afghanistan, which produced the 9/11 attacks among other atrocities, and had since the late 1970s established an infrastructure of terrorist camps and networks for export to its region and beyond. Even the interim report of the official 9/11 Commission in the US, published in June 2004, which severely downplays Pakistan's role in international terrorism, still noted that 'Pakistan, not Iraq, was a patron of terrorism and had closer ties with Osama Bin Laden and al-Qaeda leading up to the September 11 attacks' and that the Taliban's hosting of Bin Laden in Afghanistan before 9/11 'was significantly facilitated by Pakistani support.'[6]

Pakistani President Musharraf's supposed break with the Taliban after 9/11 was enough to satisfy Washington and London that Islamabad was now an ally. The Saudis failed to repudiate any of their past policies. Neither Islamabad nor Riyadh have been sidelined by London and Washington, still less bombed, since there is not so much a War on Terror or on the infrastructure of global terrorism, which certainly does exist, so much as a war on specially designated targets chosen as enemies by Washington and London to achieve specific foreign policy objectives.

Pakistan's role in 9/11 also raises a British connection. After 9/11, the *Times of India* reported that Lieutenant General Mahmood Ahmad, the director of the Pakistani intelligence service, the ISI, and a strong supporter of the Taliban, had ordered the wiring of $100,000 to the leader of the 9/11 terrorist group, Mohammed Atta. Ahmad's contact in sending the funds was said to be Omar Saeed Sheikh, the Briton of Pakistani origin who had developed links to the HUA terrorist group and whom Musharraf later accused of being an MI6 agent.[7] Subsequently, various media reported that the FBI and Western intelligence sources believed that Sheikh had indeed transferred the money to Atta and that the FBI had tracked more than $100,000 from banks in Pakistan to two banks in Florida, where accounts were held by Atta, though it did not mention the ISI.[8] Ahmad stepped down as ISI chief less than a month after 9/11, some reports suggesting that this was due to the FBI's uncovering of credible links between him and Sheikh in the wake of 9/11.[9] Sheikh is reported to have told the then Pakistani army corps commander in Peshawar and later Director of the ISI, General Ehsanul Haq, that he had learned of plans for terrorist strikes in the US on a visit to Afghanistan before 9/11.[10] Furthermore, Sheikh later said he was an ISI agent who had been operating from Lahore since his release from prison in 1999; US police and intelligence officials have also said that Sheikh has been a 'protected asset' of the ISI.[11] There are suspicions that Sheikh had been recruited by the ISI as long ago as 1992 while he was a student in London.[12] In this light, it is barely credible that the ISI did not have foreknowledge of 9/11.

Omar Saeed Sheikh is the most intriguing possible British connection to 9/11. After being held for five years in an Indian jail for kidnapping four British and American tourists on behalf of the HUA in 1994, Sheikh was released in December 1999; the Indian government had agreed to a hostage deal whereby Sheikh and two other militants (one of them, HUA leader Maulana Masood Azhar) were freed in return for the release of 154 passengers on an Indian Airlines jet hijacked by the HUA. While in jail, Sheikh is reported to have had nine meetings with a British diplomat, with his lawyer present, to check on his 'living conditions and general welfare'.[13] Yet British intelligence also reportedly tried to do a deal with Sheikh. According to a report in the *Times*, while in jail Sheikh 'was secretly offered an amnesty by British officials in 1999 if he would betray his links with al-Qaeda.' British intelligence officials 'knew of his terrorist credentials but believed that he had crucial information about Western recruits to militant Islamic groups.'[14] Another report noted that Whitehall officials told

Sheikh that he could 'live in London a free man if he told them all he knew'.[15] The reports stated that Sheikh refused the offer but there is reason to question this. For one thing, two days after Sheikh's release in early January 2000, the Foreign Office issued an extraordinary statement:

> It is quite possible that Mr Sheikh will come back to this country where his family is. And as a full British national he has every right to return. He has not contacted us but obviously, if he was to contact us, and asked us for passport facilities, then provided he could prove who he was, we would issue him with a passport. He has not been convicted of any offences. He has not even been brought to trial.[16]

Sheikh is reported to have visited his family in London that month, and again in early 2001, without the British authorities charging him (for the 1994 kidnapping of the Britons) or the police launching an investigation.[17] The Foreign Office statement can be interpreted in one of two ways. Either it showed that the British had done a deal with Sheikh, revealing that Whitehall was prepared to secretly collaborate with a known Islamist terrorist. Or, if a deal was never done, it illustrates how tolerant the British authorities were towards terrorism even when the victims were British. It is easy to see how this stance would send a message to other British Islamist radicals that their activities abroad would also be tolerated, even if they were involved in kidnapping and aircraft hijacking.

The consequences of British policy were profound, given Sheikh's involvement in a variety of further acts of terrorism. He is reported to have soon visited Afghanistan, where he devised a secure, web-based communications system for al-Qaida, served as a guerilla warfare instructor at training camps and met Taliban leader, Mullah Omar, as well as Bin Laden.[18]

Then in August 2001, in a turnaround from the Foreign Office statement eighteen months earlier, British intelligence was reported to be asking their Indian counterparts to apprehend Sheikh for questioning.[19] Whether Sheikh had broken his deal with the British or whether they had simply become concerned about his activities remains unclear. It is also instructive that the British turned to India for information on Sheikh and not Pakistan, giving further credence to the view that the Pakistanis were protecting him.

At this point, Sheikh is alleged to have wired the money to the 9/11 group and, a few days after 9/11, to have travelled to Afghanistan to meet Bin Laden.[20] He also later claimed to have known the militants who bombed the Srinagar state assembly in Kashmir in October 2001, killing 38 people, and those who stormed the Indian parliament in Delhi in December.[21] Most prominently, in 2002, Sheikh was found guilty in Pakistan of orchestrating the gruesome beheading of Daniel Pearl, the *Wall Street Journal* reporter, in Karachi, a murder sometimes explained by Pearl's possible uncovering of links between the Pakistani intelligence establishment and al-Qaida.[22] Sheikh surrendered to a former official of the ISI in early 2002, and after his trial was sentenced to death, but remains alive in a Pakistani jail from where he has also been accused of masterminding the July 2005 bombings in London.

Whether Sheikh had been working for the British or not, there is strong evidence that, even after 9/11, he was an ISI agent as well as an activist for al-Qaida, and may have acted as an intermediary between the two.[23] Several media reports suggest that Sheikh knows too much about this ISI connection ever to be allowed to leave Pakistan. General Musharraf turned down US requests to extradite him and was reported to have told the then US ambassador to Pakistan, Wendy Chamberlain, that 'I would rather hang Sheikh myself than have him extradited'.[24]

The possibility that a British citizen played a role in 9/11 might be expected to strongly interest Whitehall; the 9/11 attacks, which killed sixty-seven Britons, were 'the worst terrorist attack on British citizens in my country's history', Tony Blair kept repeating.[25] Yet there is no evidence that the British authorities have sought to investigate Sheikh's alleged links to 9/11 or have his story publicised. The government shows as much interest in exposing Sheikh's past as Islamabad, perhaps for what he might reveal about his connection to the security services. All this has occurred alongside Whitehall's general sweeping under the carpet of the possible Pakistani and Saudi roles in 9/11.

It was becoming clear that there was one other major capital city that those serious about tackling global terrorism needed to investigate further, somewhat closer to home.

CHAPTER 16

Londonistan: A 'Green Light' to Terrorism

LONDON IN THE 1990S was one of the world's major centres for radical Islamic groups organising terrorism abroad. Organisations such as Algeria's Armed Islamic Group (GIA), the Libyan Islamic Fighting Group, Egyptian Islamic Jihad and al-Qaida itself (through its office, the Advice and Reformation Committee) all established bases in London. Al-Qaida considered London to be the 'nerve centre' of its operations in Europe, and many of Bin Laden's top lieutenants operated from there.[1] Millions of pounds were raised in Britain to fund terrorist causes and recruit militants to fight across the globe, from Afghanistan to Yemen.

Thousands of British-based individuals passed through al-Qaida training camps in the 1990s – by the time of the July 2005 London bombings, the number was around 3,000, according to Lord Stevens, the former Metropolitan police chief.[2] The Home Office's official enquiry into the bombings would later disingenuously state: 'During the 1990s, *it is now known* that there was a flow of young Muslims, from the UK and elsewhere, travelling to Pakistan and Afghanistan for indoctrination or jihad.'[3] In fact, this was known at the time, and not only tolerated but may have been actively championed by the British authorities, as we have seen with the participation of British jihadists in the Bosnia and Kosovo wars.

A key feature of Londonistan was the operation of a so-called 'covenant of security' between radical Islamists in Britain and the security services. Crispin Black, a former Cabinet Office intelligence analyst, described the covenant as 'the long-standing British habit of providing refuge and welfare to Islamist extremists on the unspoken assumption that if we give them a safe haven here they will not attack us on these shores.'[4] A Special Branch officer said that 'there was a deal with these guys. We told them that if you don't cause us any problems, then we won't bother you.'[5]

A variety of Islamist figures have spoken about the existence of such an agreement. Abu Hamza, the former imam at the Finsbury Park Mosque, said at his trial at the Old Bailey that he believed a deal operated whereby his activities would be tolerated as long as they targeted only foreign soil. He recalled how Scotland Yard's intelligence wing, the Special Branch, assured him that 'you don't have anything to worry about as long as we don't see blood on the streets'.[6] Khaled al-Fawwaz, the head of Bin Laden's London office in the mid-1990s, told Swiss journalist Richard Labeviere in April 1998 that 'London is our association's headquarters ... The authorities are very tolerant, as long as one does not interfere in questions of internal politics.'[7] In August of the same year Omar Bakri Mohammed, who had established the militant al-Muhajiroun organisation, described how 'I work here in accordance with the covenant of peace which I made with the British government when I got [political] asylum.' Nine months later, he said in a further interview that 'the British government knows who we are. MI5 has interrogated us many times. I think now we have something called public immunity.'[8]

The 'covenant' can only be interpreted as utterly extraordinary, amounting to a 'green light' from Whitehall for groups to undertake terrorist activities overseas. The deadliness of this policy was revealed from the late 1980s onwards, as British-based groups, notably the GIA, Egyptian Islamic Jihad and the ARC, began to be involved in atrocities around the world. It was only after 9/11 that the 'covenant' began to be put under strain as the Blair government began drafting stricter anti-terrorism legislation. In October 2001, al-Muhajiroun released a statement which explicitly mentioned the covenant and the dangers that faced it:

> For the moment, Muslims in the UK have a covenant of security which prevents them from attacking the lives and wealth of anyone here ... However ... the Blair regime is today sitting on a box of dynamite and have only themselves to blame if after attacking the Islamic movements and the Islamic scholars, it all blows up in their face.[9]

The following month the government introduced new legislation in the Terrorism Act. Several organisations were declared illegal and banks were empowered to freeze the assets and accounts of organisations suspected of terrorism. In the three years after 9/11, 700 suspects were taken into British custody under the anti-terrorism law, though only seventeen had been convicted by mid-2005.[10]

However, the covenant of security did not simply die with 9/11. For one thing, individual Islamic extremists such as Abu Hamza and (for a while at least) the Palestinian-born Jordanian cleric Abu Qatada, were allowed to continue their activities, to which we come further below. Moreover, Whitehall's 'green light' to terrorism overseas was not switched off either. In fact, it directly contributed to the London bombings over three years later. In 2004, for example, MI5 monitoring of some of the later London bombers discovered them 'talking about jihadi activity in Pakistan and support for the Taliban', but since they were not discussing terrorist attacks in Britain, MI5 left them alone; the standard policy that was a crucial part of the covenant.[11] Had MI5 decided to act against these overseas activities, it is possible that 7/7 could have been prevented. Indeed, it was as much the militants themselves who tore up the covenant of security, especially after the invasion of Iraq in 2003, when Britain became even more of a target for their operations.

A key question is why the British authorities allowed the phenomenon of Londonistan to develop and be sustained. My view is that one reason is directly linked to the theme of this book, that collusion with radical Islamists was seen as having advantages for the promotion of British foreign policy, a continuation of the role that these groups had regularly played for Britain in the postwar world. Closely linked to this was the fact that the British security services saw the covenant as encouraging certain individuals to act as informants on the activities of Islamist groups, which would be useful in monitoring them; thus they were protected from prosecution as they engaged in terrorism abroad.[12] The policy of recruiting individuals involved in terrorism has several precedents, as we have seen, for example, the apparent attempted British recruitment of Omar Saeed Sheikh in 1999; the recruitment in the 1980s of Leslie Aspin – the terrorist financier who continued his activities while on the payroll of MI6; and the British toleration of Abu Nidal, whose terrorist activities continued as Britain monitored his bank accounts.

Some other arguments put forward to explain Londonistan contain some truth, but do not, in my view, explain everything. These include the notions that British leaders and the police were worried about acting against religious leaders for fear of a backlash in the Muslim community; that the security services, configured to deal with Irish terrorism, failed to anticipate and understand the extent of the new threat from Islamic radicals; and that Britain's 'liberal' human rights laws made it difficult for the government to clamp down on those associated with terrorism.

The argument that the police were reluctant to take action for fear of the effect on community relations is weak in, for example, the case of Abu Hamza, where Muslim community leaders went to the police at least seven times to complain about the extremism practised at the Finsbury Park Mosque during Hamza's tenure there;

it was the police that decided to take no action despite these pleas.[13] Equally, it is barely believable that the British security services failed to understand the nature or extent of radical Islam during the 1990s, a period when bombs were going off around the world, with obvious links to groups based in London. Indeed, and as we have seen, the British government was bombarded with requests from foreign governments to take action against organisations based in Britain, including the extradition of leading terrorist suspects. In 1997–98, MI5 devoted nearly as many resources to countering international terrorism as Irish terrorism – 16 per cent of its budget as compared to 19 per cent.[14]

As to whether the British legal system was responsible, it is certainly true that some legal cases against terrorist suspects have either been dragged out by lawyers or that extradition has sometimes been prevented by the ban under European human rights law from deporting subjects to countries where they risked being tortured. But, again, these legalities do not explain everything. In the 1990s the British government already had sweeping powers to deport suspected terrorists, at least to countries where torture was not practised. Under the 1971 Immigration Act the government could deport subjects if the home secretary 'deems [their] deportation to be conducive to the public good'.[15] One case regularly cited as exemplifying how the extradition laws have benefited terrorists is that of Rachid Ramda, the Algerian involved in a bomb attack on the Paris underground in 1995 which killed eight people. Repeated French requests to have Ramda extradited from Britain, where he had earlier gained refugee status, were delayed and it took ten years before he was deported to France in December 2005. Ramda's lawyers certainly made full use of the law to delay the process, and it was sometimes held up by the British courts – but as one MP, John Maples, has pointed out, it was also the home secretary who took over two years, before 9/11, to decide whether or not to deport him. This compares to the case brought in Britain against the former Chilean dictator, General Pinochet, which in 1998–2000 was dealt with in 15 months, including three appeals, showing that legal processes could move more quickly when serious political pressure was brought to bear.[16] The government also failed to use the laws available to it after 9/11, when the Terrorism Act was passed into law, making it an offence to send someone abroad for terrorist training and instruction. As *Times* journalists Sean O'Neill and Daniel McGrory have written, 'even after the new laws were introduced, Abu Hamza's followers continued to disappear off to camps run by outlawed groups, and still nobody in authority laid a finger on him.'[17]

BRITISH AGENTS?

Islamist groups have long performed a variety of key functions for British foreign policy, as we have seen earlier in the postwar period, notably as shock troops to promote unrest or coups, proxy covert forces to eliminate enemy leaders or conservative forces to help prop up pro-Western regimes. The hosting of these groups in London likely provided further advantages to British policy.

One was that it enabled relations to be cultivated with possible future leaders. British officials have had few qualms about whom they court. For example, Foreign Office Minister Kim Howells told a parliamentary enquiry in March 2007 that:

> At dinners at embassies around the world I have suddenly discovered that somebody happens to be sitting next to me who is from the respectable end of a death squad from somewhere. The ambassador has, with the best will in the world, invited that person along because he thinks that, under the new democracy, they will become the new government.[18]

The hosting of Saudi opposition groups in Britain, such as the Movement for Islamic Reform in Arabia and, moreover, Bin Laden's Advice and Reformation Committee, is especially interesting in this respect. As noted in Chapter 10, the British may well have seen such hosting as providing an insurance policy for the fall of the House of Saud. Given the uncertain future of the regime, Whitehall has likely tried to play both it and the opposition.[19]

A second advantage of the presence of Islamist groups in London was that it could help influence the domestic or foreign policies of key countries. Mahan Abedin, the editor of Jamestown University's respected *Terrorism Monitor*, has noted that 'the presence of these groups [in Britain] enables British intelligence to spy on their activities and effectively gain some form of leverage over the internal politics of their home countries.'[20] In this view, these groups are a useful tool, even a bargaining chip, for the British elite to increase its influence over, or put pressure on, Arab states. As the American journalist Steve Coll explains, also noted in Chapter 10, Britain tolerated Bin Laden's office in London in the mid-1990s since it saw it as providing 'a little outside pressure' on the Saudi regime.[21]

But with the Saudis, Britain has a difficult balance to strike. The former Home Secretary David Blunkett, who presided over the introduction of the 2001 Terrorism Act, has said that 'the intelligence world did take the view that we should soft-pedal on these radicals in London because of our interests in the Arab world', in particular British commercial interests with Saudi Arabia.[22] This comment suggests that Britain needed to be placating the Saudis, who were promoting the extremist groups, to endear Whitehall even further to the fundamentalists in Riyadh and to protect Britain's massive oil and arms exports interests. Given the Saudis' role in the development of global terrorism, this point is surely highly significant. It is perfectly consistent with the long history of British support for the Saudis and their foreign policy.

There was, I believe, another major advantage of hosting radical Islamist groups in London, linked very closely to fundamental and current British foreign policy aims – the promotion of the policy of international divide and rule.

British support of Islamist forces has often aimed to foment unrest both within and between states. The policy of *domestic* divide and rule to maintain colonial power has been seen in, for example, the encouragement of Muslims against Hindu nationalists in India, and of Arabs or Jews against the other in Palestine under the British mandate. However, British policies have often gone further than nurturing tensions between communities, and have sometimes involved attempts to break up states – a strategy of Balkanisation. The clearest example is the Soviet Union, where Britain sought to promote unrest in the Muslim republics by supporting the Basmachi rebellion in the 1920s and the various mujahideen wars in the 1980s and 1990s. The covert operations in Indonesia in the late 1950s and in Kosovo in the late 1990s also sought to Balkanise states. It is not that Balkanisation has always been pursued by Britain: Whitehall's interest in breaking up states depends on who controls them, and if they are ruled by dependable allies London will tend to favour strong central control.[23]

But Britain has been very consistent about promoting division *between* states, at least in the Middle East. Whitehall has had a long-standing policy of keeping the Middle East divided, in separate states ideally under the control of pro-Western monarchs or dictators. The declassified British files are replete with these concerns, which were at the root of the policies carving up the Middle East during and after the First World War and have essentially remained so ever since. This book has documented some of the examples, from Lord Crewe's view in the 1920s that 'what we want is … a disunited Arabia split into principalities under our suzerainty' to the Foreign Office's priority in 1958 of 'maintaining the four principal oil producing areas [Saudi Arabia, Kuwait, Iran and Iraq] under separate political control'.[24] Tony Blair's proposal in 2006 for an 'alliance of moderation' (pro-Western states) against the 'arc of extremism' (official enemies) in the Middle East, to which we come later, and Bush's 'you are either with us or against us' view after 9/11, are recent forms of the same strategy of international divide and rule. The overriding reason for keeping the Middle East divided has been to ensure that no single power dominates the region's oil resources and so that a strong combination of powers cannot challenge Western hegemony.

Radical Islamic forces have come in useful not only in promoting domestic unrest to bring about internal change but in keeping the region divided and in stoking tensions between states. In the 1950s and '60s, for example, the Muslim Brotherhood, with Western support, undermined moves by the nationalist regimes in Egypt and Syria to forge a closer regional alliance and helped shore up the conservative regimes, such as Jordan and Saudi Arabia, against the rising force of secular nationalism across the region. When it came to the Arab–Israeli conflict, Britain was not only prepared to collude with Islamic forces against the Jews, but also with Israel against the Arabs, as when the then head of MI6, George Young, said that Israel in the 1950s had 'slipped into the role at one time played by British forces – that of armed watcher ready to strike – the best guarantee of Egyptian, Syrian and Jordanian conduct'.[25] Israel's attack on Lebanon in 2006 to counter Iran-backed Hezbollah – to which Britain gave de facto backing – suggests that this Israeli function has not disappeared.

Selling arms to both sides in conflicts – a long-standing British policy – is certainly likely to keep tensions going between states. Just to take the Blair years (1997–2007), billions of pounds worth of arms flowed to the Arab states, mainly Saudi Arabia, but Israel also received more than £110 million of military equipment, including a range of supplies critical for offensive operations, such as components for combat aircraft and combat helicopters, components for tanks and military utility helicopters and armoured all-wheel drive vehicles.[26] Both Pakistan and India, regional enemies who have recently come to the brink of all-out war, have been heavily armed by Britain – India to the tune of nearly £900 million worth in the Blair years, and Pakistan with over £150 million worth. British supplies continued to flow as the two countries were on the verge

Hassaine worked for MI5, gathering information on Abu Hamza.[34] He later recalled how: 'I told them [MI5] Hamza was brainwashing people and sending them to *al-Qaeda* terrorist training camps in Afghanistan, that he was preaching jihad and murder and that he was involved in the provision of false passports. I told them he was a chief terrorist'; however, Hassaine's MI5 handler did not appear unduly worried.[35] A stream of would-be jihadists continued to visit the mosque to hear Hamza preach, including Richard Reid, the 'shoe bomber', and Mohammed Siddique Khan, the 7/7 bomber, who went there in 2002.[36]

From the late 1990s, Hamza had also begun organising military training for members of his Supporters of Shariah organisation at country retreats in Kent in England, Wales and Scotland, where they were taught how to strip down AK-47s and handguns. The *Observer* reported that at one training session in Wales in 1998, around ten jihadists were trained by British ex-soldiers, some of whom had fought in Bosnia. 'But the British security services were either unconcerned or ignorant about Hamza's activities,' the paper noted.[37] O'Neill and McGrory write that this training was provided by British army veterans whom Hamza had recruited from the back pages of a combat magazine, and that some of these training sessions were also monitored by the British authorities. One of the teams being monitored was among those sent to Yemen in December 1998 to kidnap sixteen Western tourists, of whom three Britons and one Australian died during a Yemeni government rescue attempt.[38] Hamza was in contact with these kidnappers, but when the Yemeni government handed over their 137-page dossier on Hamza to the British government in early 1999 it was initially ignored.[39] The following March, Hamza was arrested and questioned about the Yemen kidnappings but then released without charge. Meanwhile, when the government was later questioned in parliament about the Scottish and Welsh training camps, the Home Office minister, John Denham, gave a short, noncommittal response: 'I understand that the police have made enquiries: they have advised me that there is no evidence to show that any criminal offences have been committed at either location.'[40]

This was two months after 9/11. It was only later that the authorities moved against Hamza. In September 2002, the police launched an investigation into terrorist fundraising linked to the Finsbury Park Mosque and raided it the following January. In April 2003 the Home Office ordered that Hamza be stripped of his British citizenship and in a hearing that began in April 2004 the government, for the first time, accused Hamza of involvement with terrorist groups; he was arrested the following month, following a US government extradition request. A senior official in the US Department of Justice told O'Neill and McGrory: 'We wondered to ourselves whether he was an MI5 informer, or was there some secret the British government were not trusting us with? He seemed untouchable.'[41] The British government, not wanting to be seen to be handing over a British citizen to the US without trying him in Britain, then cobbled together a case accusing him of incitement to murder and racial hatred; after a trial in February 2006, Hamza was sentenced to seven years in prison.[42] However, even then, Hamza got off very lightly – the US authorities wanted to put him on trial for recruiting, financing and directing terrorism, but British prosecutors had accused Hamza of much lesser offences, so the trial did not even probe his alleged connections to terrorist groups.[43]

Hamza's case shows that the British security services were prepared to allow their informant to continue activities supporting terrorism overseas while gaining information on extremist groups' activities inside the Finsbury Park Mosque. This policy involved protecting him from prosecution for years, not only for the period 1997–2000, when he met the security services, but also for a time after 9/11. It is possible that some kind of deal was done to prevent Hamza divulging more about his relationship with the security services.

There is also the case of apparent British protection of Abu Qatada, who has become known as 'al-Qaida's spiritual leader in Europe' and was described by the judge reviewing his immigration status in 2004 as a 'truly dangerous individual ... at the centre in the United Kingdom of terrorist activities associated with al-Qaida'.[44] Yet it has been reported that Qatada was 'a double agent working for MI5' and that Britain ignored warnings before 9/11 from half a dozen friendly governments about Qatada's links with terrorist groups, refusing to arrest him. Instead, it has been said that the intelligence services were intending 'to use the cleric as a key informer against Islamic militants in Britain.' Many militants are said to have visited him, including the shoe bomber Richard Reid.[45]

Qatada had been in Afghanistan in the late 1980s and early 1990s, where it is claimed that he had known Abu Musab al-Zarqawi, who later became al-Qaida's leader in Iraq.[46] Qatada came to Britain in 1993 on a forged United Arab Emirates passport, claimed asylum and in 1994 gained indefinite leave to remain in Britain until June 1998.[47] During this period, it is alleged that he agitated and recruited for, among others, Egyptian Islamic Jihad and the Algerian GIA, and had contacts with Abu Doha, an Algerian extremist whose followers later plotted to bomb Strasbourg Market.[48] Qatada has denied claims that he was al-Qaida's European ambassador and insists he never met Bin Laden.[49]

Qatada's lawyers have said that he was monitored by the security services from the mid-1990s and that 'his actions had a large degree of tacit approval'.[50] They claim that:

> He had not been led by the police to believe that any of the activities which he was carrying on up to 2001 were illegal, quite the reverse; he had carried them on openly ... the security service knew the sort of views which he was expressing and took no steps to stop or warn him, to prosecute him or to prevent his fundraising for groups which are regarded as terrorist groups, notably the former

> Khattab faction fighting in Chechnya, or for training in Afghanistan.[51]

It emerged in later legal proceedings to decide Qatada's immigration status that MI5 had three meetings with Abu Qatada, in June and December 1996 and in February 1997. In the first meeting, Qatada recorded 'his passionate exposition of jihad and the spread of Islam to take over the world.' He also claimed 'powerful, spiritual influence over the Algerian community in London' and, according to the MI5 witness in the proceedings, 'agreed to use his influence to minimise the risk of a violent response to the possible extradition of [Rachid] Ramda, the UK leader of the GIA'; MI5 'had been asking him to act as a restraint on the GIA, and more generally Algerian refugee activities in the UK.'[52] In the second meeting, the MI5 officer noted that Qatada 'came the closest he had to offering to assist me in any investigation of Islamic extremism.' By the third meeting the officer was saying that 'I fully expected him to use that influence, wherever he could, to control the hotheads and ensure terrorism remained off the streets of London and throughout the United Kingdom.'[53] The judge considering Qatada's immigration status concluded that during this time, 1996–97, 'he may well have regarded the United Kingdom as a safe haven and believed that it was far more useful to be able to operate here.'[54]

While Qatada appeared to pose as being able to prevent terrorist attacks and expose dangerous militants, all along he continued activities in support of extremists, which was surely known to MI5. In March 1995 Qatada had issued a fatwa justifying the killing of wives and children of 'apostates' in order to stop the oppression of Muslim women and 'brothers' in Algeria; it provided a religious justification for the slaughter by terrorists of women and children.[55] Yet MI5 later claimed that in 1997 it reached an assessment of Qatada to the effect that he was not a jihadist; it also claimed that his views towards global jihad 'hardened' in the years following his meetings with MI5.[56] This reasoning is now very convenient.

In 1998, Qatada was sentenced *in absentia* in Jordan for inciting a series of bomb attacks in the country, and his extradition was requested by Amman. His period of indefinite leave to remain in Britain came up for review that year, at the same time as Britain was being warned by several countries of Qatada's links with terrorism – but he was allowed to remain in the country and not arrested.[57] In 1999, Reda Hassaine, the Algerian spy for MI5 working inside the Finsbury Park Mosque, was instructed by his MI5 handler to meet Qatada twice a month. After this point, MI5 continued to be aware that Qatada was said to be raising money for terrorist activities abroad, since Hassaine told them so.[58]

In February 2001 anti-terrorism police officers did arrest Qatada for his suspected involvement in the planned attack in Strasbourg, but it was decided that there was insufficient evidence against him and no charges were brought. Following 9/11, he was identified by the US as a 'specially designated global terrorist'. The British authorities did not move against him, however, and in October 2001 he gave an interview to the *Observer* claiming that MI5 had approached him through intermediaries 'to offer him a passport and an Iranian visa so he could leave the country' and escape to Afghanistan.[59] The report noted that the authorities believed that 'there was not enough hard evidence to bring charges against him' while he could not be deported to Jordan since the country retains the death penalty. However, there is also the suspicion that MI5 sought to protect their informer and did not want Qatada to reveal details of his relationship with them. Qatada reportedly refused the offer.[60]

In December 2001, when parliament was about to pass new anti-terror legislation after 9/11, Qatada disappeared. 'French anti-terrorist officers in Paris believe that their British counterparts at MI5 colluded in his disappearance,' the *Telegraph* reported.[61] Another informer for MI5 close to Qatada, Bisher al-Rawi, an Iraqi who had lived in Britain for nineteen years, later told a US military panel at Guantanamo Bay that: 'I am positive the British intelligence knew where he was, because I told them.'[62] He said he visited Qatada numerous times in the summer of 2002 with MI5's knowledge.[63] It later transpired that for nearly a year Qatada was in 'hiding' in a flat in Bermondsey, south London, where he was regularly visited by his wife and children, and also by contacts from abroad. *Time* magazine reported senior European intelligence officials saying that 'Abu Qatada is tucked away in a safe house in the north of England, where he and his family are being lodged, fed and clothed by [the] British intelligence services.' The sources say that 'the deal is that Abu Qatada is deprived of contact with extremists in London and Europe but can't be arrested or expelled because no one officially knows where he is. The British win because the last thing they want is a hot potato they can't extradite for fear of al-Qaida reprisals but whose presence contradicts London's support of the War on Terror.'[64]

Qatada was finally 'found' in October 2002, after releasing a 10-page document justifying the 9/11 attacks. He was detained by the British authorities a few days later on suspicion of undertaking 'a range of support activities, including fundraising, on behalf of various international terrorist organisations' and of making 'public statements of support for the violent activities of these groups'.[65] Qatada was subsequently held without charge in Belmarsh high security prison until being released, subject to a control order, in March 2005, when the Law Lords struck down an emergency anti-terror law that allowed his indefinite detention without trial.[66] However, the authorities detained him again five months later, soon after Britain signed an extradition agreement with Jordan; but Qatada was again released from prison in June 2008, subject to strict bail conditions and a 22-hour curfew, after the High Court upheld his appeal against deportation to Jordan, on the grounds that he was likely to face a terrorism trial based on evidence from witnesses who had been tortured.[67] In February 2009, however, the Law Lords ruled that Qatada could be deported to Jordan, since when he has been fighting extradition from prison in Britain.

MI5 recruited other people close to Qatada, such as Bisher al-Rawi, who was contacted soon after the 9/11 attacks to act as a go-between with MI5 and Qatada and to inform on the latter.[68] However, in 2002 MI5 passed on information to the CIA to the effect that al-Rawi was an Islamist terrorist – a completely false accusation, according to his lawyers. The US promptly seized him in the Gambia and locked him up in Guantanamo Bay for five years, where he claims he was constantly subjected to abuse and psychological torture; he was released in early 2007.[69]

Finally, there is the case of Sheikh Omar Bakri Mohammed, the Syrian-born head of al-Muhajiroun. Bakri's case is especially interesting in light of his possible cooperation with British intelligence in sending jihadists to Kosovo in the late 1990s, alongside MI6's covert operation to help train Kosovo Liberation Army fighters in secret camps in Albania. At this time, Bakri was being described in the British media as the 'head of the political wing of the International Islamic Front' founded by Osama Bin Laden.[70] It is also interesting given al-Muhajiroun's connections to the July 2005 London bombings.

Bakri had fled Syria after joining the Muslim Brotherhood in the revolt against the Assad regime, which brutally crushed the organisation in 1982. He went first to Saudi Arabia, but was expelled in 1985 and arrived in Britain in January 1986, where he was later given indefinite leave to remain. Bakri was arrested in 1991 after saying that Prime Minister John Major was a legitimate target for assassination due to Britain's involvement in the Gulf War against Iraq. He became leader of the first British branch of the Hizb-ut-Tahrir, but split with its international leaders and formed his own organisation, al-Muhajiroun, in January 1996.[71] In an interview with the London-based Arabic newspaper, *al-Sharq al-Awsat*, Bakri boasted that, in the late 1990s–early 2000s, he was sending 300–400 militants a year on military training and guerrilla warfare courses in Michigan and the Missouri desert in the US, some of whom went on to fight in Kashmir, Chechnya and Kosovo.[72] Russia was by then calling on the British government to close down al-Muhajiroun, saying that it was one of a number of organisations in Britain which had sent several dozen fighters to Chechnya.[73] A memo written by an FBI agent just prior to 9/11 also noted a connection between Bakri and several suspects attending US flight training schools, including one that was used by one of the hijackers.[74] But it was only in July 2003 that Britain's terrorism legislation was enforced against al-Muhajiroun. After its website appeared to contain an overt threat of terrorist attacks against government targets, al-Muhajiroun's offices were raided and Bakri was taken into custody and questioned, before being released without charge.[75]

It remains unclear whether Bakri was collaborating with the security services after the end of the Kosovo War in June 1999; his interviews noted earlier in this chapter suggest he believed he had 'public immunity' until at least mid-1999. The possibility of his collusion with the authorities was apparently picked up by some in the jihadist community. In November 2001, for example, the London-based Azzam publications, known for its support of Bin Laden, posted a notice appearing to warn jihadists away from Bakri and al-Muhajiroun, saying: 'As part of a plan to reinforce the "sincerity" of the leader [Bakri] of this organisation [al-Muhajiroun] in the eyes of British Muslims, we expect the British authorities to arrest him in the near future, but for him to be subsequently released.'[76] Bakri was indeed questioned many times by the police or security services – 'on at least sixteen occasions', he said himself – but always escaped arrest.[77]

Most intriguingly, after the 2005 London bombings, Bakri was not even interrogated by the security services as a possible suspect; instead he was allowed to leave the country. A month after 7/7, Bakri voluntarily left Britain for Lebanon, and a year later, in July 2006, the home secretary, Charles Clarke, announced that Bakri would not be permitted to return to Britain since 'his presence is not conducive to the public good'.[78] These decisions raise further suspicions about Whitehall's relationship with Bakri, given the jihadist activities he had been involved in, and also the well-publicised connections between the 7/7 bombers, and other would-be British bombers, and the al-Muhajiroun organisation. For example, Mohammed Babar – an American who pleaded guilty to a series of terrorist plots and who gave evidence against a group of other British bomb plotters – was a former member of al-Muharijoun, and liaised with their members in London during terrorist plotting in the two years after 9/11.[79] Babar personally met Bakri and later communicated with him by email and telephone, while setting up an al-Muhajiroun office in Peshawar, Pakistan.[80] Also, Omar Khyam, the leader of the 'fertiliser bomb plot' gang convicted in April 2007, had also attended al-Muhajiroun meetings.[81] Omar Khan Sharif, the would-be bomber of the Tel Aviv bar in 2003, also had links with al-Muhajiroun and was a follower of Bakri.[82] By the time Bakri travelled to Lebanon, al-Muhajiroun had formed 81 separate front organisations in six countries, according to a New York police investigation, and had 600–1,500 members in Britain.[83] It would have perhaps been rather useful for the security services to have questioned Bakri about his connections. Perhaps the British offered the same deal to Bakri as to Qatada, to leave the country and escape being brought to trial, given what this might reveal about his relationship to the intelligence services.[84]

In conclusion, it is possible that the covenant of security deterred Islamist attacks from occurring in Britain in the 1990s, but at the huge cost of the 'green light' to terrorism overseas. In the years after 9/11, however, both before and after the invasion of Iraq, a number of bomb plots in Britain began to be planned. The recruitment of Islamic radicals may have produced some intelligence on their overseas activities, but it is impossible to judge how useful this was or how much the British authorities tipped off their foreign counterparts. It is possible that the security services were just naïve in believing that their informants could control the 'hotheads'. But it is also possible that parts of the British security establishment were motivated not only by gaining information and restraining extremists but also by the perceived advantages to British foreign policy of hosting these individuals in London. This assertion is not proven, since further evidence is lacking, but is consistent with Britain's long-standing use of Islamists for foreign policy purposes. British policies had clearly become downright dangerous to the British and world public.

CHAPTER 17

7/7 and the London–Islamabad Axis

After 9/11, Pakistan appeared to withdraw its support for the Taliban in Afghanistan, and instead backed the Anglo-American war which destroyed the regime along with the al-Qaida bases in the country. General Pervez Musharraf's military regime, which had taken power in a coup in October 1999, was now seen in London and Washington as the frontline in the War on Terror. British leaders proceeded to shower praise on Musharraf for his 'strong position' on international terrorism and for being a 'staunch ally' and 'key partner'.[1] The Blair government's backing of Pakistan in the face of the Taliban enemy recalled the Thatcher government's alliance with another Pakistani military ruler, General Zia ul-Haq, in their covert war in Afghanistan in the 1980s. Both Blair and Thatcher accepted at face value Zia's and Musharraf's pledges to return Pakistan to democracy while they merely kept themselves in power. And both Blair and Thatcher saw the Pakistani military rulers as pro-Western forces of stability in their region, claiming they were the opponents of terrorism.

The reality was that Musharraf's regime, which lasted until the general finally resigned in August 2008 under threat of impeachment, largely empowered the radical Islamic forces in Pakistan while undermining the secular, nationalist parties – a repeat of Zia's rule. Although the regime tried to fight foreign al-Qaida militants in the Pakistan–Afghanistan border areas at

US behest, it backed or tolerated the domestic Pakistani terrorist groups in order to promote Islamabad's long-standing goal of 'liberating' Indian Kashmir. Neither did Musharraf really end Pakistan's support for the Taliban, as we see later. London's backing of Musharraf showed again how Whitehall was prepared, in the post 9/11 world, to collude with forces promoting radical Islam. Britain's Pakistan policy had severe consequences, contributing to the London bombings in July 2005 and to the threat of terrorism currently faced by Britain.

FROM OCTOBER 1999 TO 7/7

In the first few months following Musharraf's coup ousting elected Prime Minister Nawaz Sharif, British ministers were sometimes critical of the new military regime, but soon reverted to type. Foreign Secretary Robin Cook said within a month of the takeover that 'we cannot do business as normal with a military regime' and that it was 'important … that the international community does not provide any signal that it is willing to condone the military overthrow of a constitutional government.'[2] The British served notice to Pakistan that arms exports were being reviewed on a 'case by case basis', and for a while no exports were approved to Pakistan, although no formal arms embargo was put in place. This policy lasted for precisely eight months: in June 2000 the Labour government started approving arms exports to Islamabad again, engaging in business as normal with the military regime.[3]

The government saw Pakistan under Musharraf partly as an important market for arms exports, a policy that would not have been hindered by Musharraf's long-standing relationship with Britain, including his two spells of military training in Britain before he became head of the army – evidence of the British policy of cultivating future leaders.[4] By the end of 2000, Britain had issued 88 arms export licences to Pakistan worth £6 million.[5] British military training continued as normal during the eight-month arms export review: government figures show that there were 36 Pakistani military officers undergoing training in Britain in 2000 and 49 in 2001.[6] The *Guardian* reported that an SAS unit had been training in the mountains of Pakistan for several years.[7] This was all before 9/11, and before Musharraf's public declaration of support for the War on Terror, at a time when Pakistan was still the major provider of arms and other support to the Taliban regime in Afghanistan.

After 9/11, military relations deepened. By February 2002, Defence Secretary Geoff Hoon was saying that Britain was 'taking appropriate steps to restore our defence relationship' with Pakistan, which involved all three armed services conducting 'military visits, Pakistani access to United Kingdom military training opportunities, participation in bilateral exercises and visits by senior military and civilian defence officials.'[8] When tension mounted between Pakistan and India in early 2002 over Kashmir, raising international fears of a nuclear confrontation, British arms continued to flow to both Pakistan and India. In the eight months up to May 2002, Britain issued 125 arms export licences to Pakistan, while approving nearly 500 to India.[9]

When Jack Straw, who had succeeded Robin Cook as foreign secretary, was cursorily challenged about British arms sales in parliament, he replied that: 'Some of the supplies that I have approved in the past, such as de-mining equipment, have been extremely benign, albeit that they are classified as arms sales.'[10] This was highly misleading – the government's own reports show that Britain was providing a range of equipment that could have aided Pakistani offensive operations, including small arms ammunition and components for both combat aircraft and combat helicopters.[11] Straw also said at this time that 'to the best of my recollection ... I have neither seen nor approved any arms control licence in respect of India or Pakistan in the past two months.'[12] Straw's memory was clearly deficient: government figures released to parliament showed that twenty-three arms export licences had been approved to Pakistan in April and May 2002.[13] By 2007,

Britain had sold around £130 million worth of arms to Pakistan since the military coup.

British and US support of Musharraf's regime was supposedly based on its willingness to confront terrorism. The Foreign Office stated: 'The dilemma for President Musharraf is how to tackle terrorism and extremism whilst at the same time preventing alienation of his wider domestic constituency.'[14] Yet Musharraf took only very limited steps to curb the extremist groups in Pakistan, largely cultivating them, and was dependent on their support for countering his major enemies, who were the more liberal, secular, nationalist parties – a strategy typical of regimes lacking popular support backed by Britain in the Middle East, as we have seen.[15] For example, in the October 2002 general elections, 11 per cent of the vote and 20 per cent of the seats in parliament were won by a six-party alliance of Pakistan's religious parties, which included the Jamaat-i-Islami (JI) and the Jamiat Ulema-e-Islam (JUI), the organisations behind the growth of the madrassa network and the Afghan jihad in the 1980s. Their rise in 2002 owed much to Musharraf's attempt to de-legitimise the more popular liberal parties, such as the Pakistan Peoples Party (PPP), led by Benazir Bhutto before her assassination in December 2007, and the Pakistan Muslim League (PML), led by Nawaz Sharif. Both Bhutto and Sharif were personally blocked from contesting the 2002 elections and their parties portrayed by the regime as corrupt and incompetent to run the affairs of the country, paving the way for the religious parties.[16] The PPP and PML were, and are, far from angelic, having been widely accused of corruption and having presided over Pakistan's surge into Central Asia in the early 1990s; indeed, Pakistan's initial patronage of the Taliban, in 1994–96, occurred under Bhutto's rule. Yet these parties command the overwhelming share of the Pakistani popular vote; as Human Rights Watch pointed out in 2007, 'radical Islam would not win the day if Musharraf were coaxed into retirement' since 'Islamists have never polled more than 12% of the vote in national elections'. However, the leaders of the moderate parties were 'hounded into exile' and 'political activists have been harassed and jailed for not accepting Musharraf's supremacy.'[17] Far from confronting the Islamists, the International Crisis Group noted in an April 2005 report that in Pakistan's history, 'the mullahs have never been as powerful as now', and that:

> Instead of empowering liberal, democratic voices, the government has co-opted the religious right and continues to rely on it to counter civilian opposition. By depriving democratic forces of an even playing field and continuing to ignore the need for state policies that would encourage and indeed reflect the country's religious diversity, the government has allowed religious extremist organisations and jihadi groups to flourish.[18]

Musharraf's priority, like General Zia's in the 1980s, was to consolidate his own grip on power, and to do so he played a double game when it came to dealing with the Pakistani terrorist groups. In January 2002, for example, Musharraf delivered a major speech, pledging to clamp down on terrorism, and saying that Kashmir should now be considered a bilateral issue between Pakistan and India, thus appearing to sideline the Pakistani jihadists fighting there. This stance, together with public support for the US' War on Terror, was enough to make the regime a direct target of the Pakistani jihadists.[19] Yet three years later the jihadist media was still flourishing while leaders of ostensibly banned groups such as the Lashkar-e-Toiba (LET) and Jaish-e-Mohammed (JEM) appeared 'to enjoy virtual immunity from the law' and were 'free to preach their jihadist ideologies'.[20] The LET, Pakistan's best-organised and most powerful militant organisation, was proscribed by Musharraf in 2002, but 'no step has ever been taken to dismantle or even disarm' it.[21]

Moreover, the Pakistani state directly sponsored these groups. The LET was, as we saw in Chapter 9, created in 1990 with the help of the Pakistani intelligence service, the ISI, which has supported its operations in Kashmir where Pakistan has managed an extensive infrastructure of training camps for militants since the early 1990s.[22] The JEM, established in 2000, is also widely regarded as having been created by the ISI as a counterweight to the LET, which was viewed as having become too powerful in Kashmir.[23] Meanwhile, another militant group, the Harkat ul-Mujahideen (HUM), worked alongside the regular Pakistani army, then headed by General Musharraf, to seize the strategic mountain positions in the Kargil region of Indian-held Kashmir in May 1999. Although the Pakistani government formally banned the HUM in September 2001, its leaders continued to openly visit mosques and madrassas in Pakistan while reports suggested they were being protected by the ISI in safe houses.[24]

The Blair government was perfectly aware of Pakistan's support for terrorism in Kashmir before 7/7. Foreign Office Minister Peter Hain said in December 2000 that 'there is still far too much evidence ... over the past year to 18 months ... that cross-border terrorism is actively encouraged and, indeed, at times sponsored by agencies and elements closely aligned with the Pakistani authorities.'[25] The timescale mentioned by Hain is interesting, since this was the period in which Britain decided to start re-arming Pakistan. By May 2002, Trade Minister Baroness Symons publicly noted Pakistan's 'support for terrorism in Kashmir', telling parliament that Musharraf must stop this, as well as 'bringing an end to cross-border infiltration and taking action to dismantle training camps in Pakistani-controlled territory'.[26] The following month Foreign Secretary Jack Straw went even further, telling parliament that:

> A number of terrorist organisations – including Laskhar-e-Toiba, Jaish-e-Mohammed and Harkat Mujahideen ... have been at the forefront of violent activity in the region [Kashmir] ... Her Majesty's government accept that there is a clear link between the ISID [ISI] and those groups ... The

> fact cannot be avoided that over a period of years, successive governments of Pakistan have, through their Inter-Services Intelligence Directorate, encouraged and funded terrorists – otherwise known as freedom fighters – to make incursions across the line of control as outsiders in that dispute, and to engage in mayhem and terrorism.[27]

Straw urged Musharraf to 'stop supplies to militant groups' and 'close the militant training camps on Pakistan's side of the line of control'.[28] The following year, MI5 drew up a list of 100 terrorist suspects in Britain that included 40 Britons of Pakistani origin involved in the jihad in Kashmir.[29]

Yet Pakistan's sponsorship of this terrorist infrastructure in Kashmir did not stop, as we see later, and Whitehall applied no real pressure for it to do so – rather, it continued to arm, train and trade with Pakistan. It was Pakistan's policies towards Kashmir and the domestic Islamist groups that combined with the invasion of Iraq in 2003 to help produce the events in London on 7 July 2005.

THE LONDON BOMBINGS

The four coordinated London bombings constituted the worst single terrorist atrocity ever in Britain, killing 52 people and injuring 700. They were the first 'successful' Islamist terrorist attacks in the country and were conducted by four British-born Muslims, three of them of Pakistani origin living in Yorkshire, one of Jamaican origin living in Buckinghamshire. The bombings came two years after the invasion of Iraq and followed concerns voiced by some security officials that the country was likely to be attacked by 'home-grown' terrorists.[30]

That the invasion of Iraq in March 2003 would inspire British Islamists to target Britain was recognised by British planners. Three months before the London bombings, the Joint Intelligence Committee stated in a classified report, leaked the following year, that:

> There is a clear consensus within the UK extremist community that Iraq is a legitimate jihad and should be supported. Iraq has re-energised and refocused a wide range of networks in the UK ... The conflict in Iraq has exacerbated the threat from international terrorism and will continue to have an impact in the long term. It has reinforced the determination of terrorists who were already committed to attacking the West and motivated others who were not.[31]

This report followed a joint Home Office–Foreign Office analysis in 2004 – called 'Young Muslims and Extremism' – which was leaked in 2005. This stated that:

> A particularly strong cause of disillusionment amongst Muslims ... is a perceived 'double standard' in the foreign policy of Western governments (and often those of Muslim governments), in particular Britain and the US ... This perception seems to have become more acute post 9/11. The perception is that passive 'oppression', as demonstrated in British foreign policy, e.g. non-action on Kashmir and Chechnya, has given way to 'active oppression' – the War on Terror, and in Iraq and Afghanistan are all seen by a section of British Muslims as having been acts against Islam.[32]

This 'double standard' had been pointed out by Osama Bin Laden in a speech five years before 7/7, in 2000. He had said:

> The British are responsible for destroying the caliphate system. They are the ones who created the Palestinian problem. They are the ones who created the Kashmiri problem. They are the ones who put the arms embargo on the Muslims of Bosnia so that 2 million Muslims were killed. They are the ones who are starving the Iraqi children. And they are continuously dropping bombs on these innocent Iraqi children.[33]

Bin Laden's views had a degree of accuracy about them, far more so than the justifications for the London bombings put forward by the ringleader of the gang, Mohammed Siddique Khan. A few months after 7/7, the TV station, al-Jazeera, broadcast a video made by Khan on the eve of the attacks. He claimed that they had been timed to coincide with the anniversary of Britain ignoring a truce offer from Bin Laden to withdraw troops from Iraq or else face a terror campaign.[34] But Khan also made the argument that ordinary Londoners were a legitimate target since 'your democratically elected governments continuously perpetuate atrocities against my people all over the world. And your support of them makes you directly responsible.'[35] Khan's view was nonsense. Rather than being 'responsible' for the actions of their government, most Britons were against the invasion of Iraq – 58 per cent were opposed on the eve of the invasion, according to one poll, while Air Marshal Brian Burridge, commander of the British forces, noted that 'we went into this campaign with 33 per cent public support'.[36] Then there was Khan's contention that the British government was opposing 'my people' (i.e., Muslims), part of the current refrain of jihadist recruiters that Britain is 'at war with Islam'. In fact, and despite this perception, it is plainly untrue that Britain has been at war with 'Islam', notably in light of its alliances with Saudi Arabia and Pakistan and, moreover, its regular collusion with 'Islam's' most extreme adherents – indeed those like Khan.

This was the dirty secret at the heart of 7/7. The bombings were, to a large extent, a product of British foreign policy, not mainly since they were perpetrated by opponents of the war in Iraq, but because they derived from a terrorism infrastructure established by a Pakistani state long backed by Whitehall and involving Pakistani terrorist groups which had benefited from past British covert action.

The trail of the 7/7 bombers clearly goes back to Pakistan. Khan was trained in northern Pakistan in July 2003, learning how to fire assault rifles at a camp reportedly set up soon after Britain invaded

Iraq.[37] Three of the four 7/7 bombers – Khan, along with Shehzad Tanweer and Hasib Hussain – visited Pakistan between November 2004 and January 2005, while two of them, Khan and Tanweer, visited madrassas in Lahore and Faisalabad where they learned how to make explosives.[38] The 7/7 group may also have received 'advice or direction' from individuals in Pakistan between April and July 2005, and it was shortly after their return from Pakistan in February 2005 that they began planning the attacks, according to official reports on the London bombings.[39] Muktar Said Ibrahim, the ringleader of the 21 July 2005 bombing plot – the failed attempt by five British Islamists to attack London's transport system – had been in Pakistan at a similar time as Khan and Tanweer, between December 2004 and March 2005, and had also attended a training camp there.[40]

Moreover, it is possible that the 7/7 bombers and other would-be British terrorists were trained by the ISI. For example, Omar Khyam, a twenty-five-year old from Surrey, was the leader of a group of five men found guilty in April 2007 of a plot in Britain to explode bombs made of fertilizer. In 2000, he trained at a camp near Muzaffarabad – the capital of Pakistan-occupied Kashmir – where, he said, he saw the ISI instructing recruits in handling explosives. Khyam's family had a history of serving in the Pakistani military and the ISI and it was by 'using military connections' that he was found in Pakistan and brought back to Britain.[41] Similarly, Dhiren Barot, a British convert to Islam who was given a forty-year jail sentence in 2006 for plotting various bomb blasts in Britain and the US, reportedly underwent 'lengthy training in Pakistan near the disputed region of Kashmir in 1995', learning how to use an AK-47, grenades and chemicals.[42] These techniques might have been used in his subsequent planned terrorist activities, which included setting off a radioactive 'dirty bomb' and gassing the Heathrow Express train.[43] It is possible that Barot was trained by the ISI, given its control over camps sending jihadists into Kashmir.

There are also connections to past British policies. A camp

run by the HUM terrorist group in Mansehra, a remote area in the Northwest Frontier province near the Kashmir border, had for years taken British volunteers from the Finsbury Park Mosque for training, principally to fight in Kashmir. Khan reportedly visited this camp in July 2001 while Tanweer was trained there in handling explosives and arms.[44] The first batch of HUM volunteers who went to Afghanistan in the 1980s was trained in camps run by Jalaluddin Haqqani, of the Younis Khalis faction of the Hezb-e-Islami group to whom Britain provided military training and Blowpipe missiles; HUM cadres were also provided with Stinger missiles by the CIA, who also trained them in their use.[45] Britain appears to have again connived with the HUM, now renamed the HUA, during the Bosnian and Kosovan jihads, by helping to send militants to fight against Yugoslav forces.

A Pakistani state-sponsored offshoot of the HUM is the JEM, another militant group with whom some British bombers reportedly had contacts when visiting Pakistan. Tanweer is believed to have trained with JEM militants at the Mansehra camp mentioned above.[46] One JEM militant told the Pakistani authorities that he had met Tanweer in Faisalabad, southwest of Lahore, in 2003.[47] Rashid Rauf, a Briton of Kashmiri descent who was allegedly involved in the August 2006 plot to bomb Heathrow Airport, was also a member of the JEM.[48] Another JEM militant of British origin was Mohammed Bilal, a twenty-four-year-old from Birmingham, who in December 2000 drove a car full of explosives into an Indian army base at Srinagar, killing nine people. The JEM is known to recruit in Britain among men of Kashmiri and Punjabi descent.

Then there is the LET, also a part-ISI creation in whose camps in Pakistan hundreds of young British jihadists have also received guerilla training.[49] Some of the 7/7 bombers reportedly had contacts with the LET when visiting Pakistan. Tanweer is said to have spent up to four months at a madrassa in Lahore run by the Markaz Dawa al Irshad (MDI), the mother organisation of the LET, and may have been recruited for the London bombings there.[50] He also spent a few days at the sprawling MDI complex at Muridke, just outside Lahore.[51]

The nexus of terrorist links emanating from the London bombers very clearly points both to Islamabad and to current and past British foreign policy; indeed, 7/7 was partly a case of 'blowback'.

AFTER 7/7

Since the London bombings most of the known terrorist plots against British targets have also involved Britons of Pakistani origin with links to Pakistan-based groups. British ministers now say that 70 per cent of the terrorism affecting the UK has links to Pakistan.[52] Extremists in Britain continue to be in contact with terrorists based in Pakistan's border areas, from where they get guidance and in some cases training for operations, just like Khan and Tanweer.[53] Yet the British government continued to place great public faith in the Musharraf regime's willingness to confront terrorism right up to its demise, despite the fact that Pakistan had been sponsoring jihadist groups for the past three decades and despite those groups' links with the 7/7 bombers. 'The government of Pakistan is a key ally in the efforts we are making to combat extremism, radicalisation and terrorism, both in the UK and overseas,' Foreign Office Minister Ian Pearson said a fortnight after the London bombings.[54] London's adulation for Musharraf's Pakistan was more than matched by US Defence Secretary Donald Rumsfeld, who said in mid-2006 that 'President Musharraf has done an excellent job in a difficult country in a difficult environment, and is clearly dedicated to defeating terror … he has shown terrific leadership, courageous leadership', as the US pumped more than $10 billion in aid to Pakistan in the six years after 9/11, much of which was military aid.[55]

However, by early 2006 the Musharraf regime had become more than just a key ally to London. Defence Minister Adam Ingram explained that: 'Pakistan is critical to achieving many of HMG's [Her Majesty's Government's] international objectives, including counter-terrorism, counter-narcotics, counter-proliferation, regional stability, managed migration, human rights and engagement with the Islamic world.'[56] If this was the case, then the Pakistani regime was seen as a pillar of the British position in the world. Thus Britain was continuing its long-standing reliance on autocratic forces opposed to secular nationalism and allied to radical Islam to achieve its foreign policy goals – a continuation of decades of policy in the Middle East and Central Asia.

In fact, Pakistan's sponsorship of terrorism in Kashmir continued after 7/7. *Time* correspondent Mark Kukis wrote in 2006 that 'at worst, the Pakistani military is actively involved in the training of men like Tanweer and Khan. At the very least, the military rulers in Islamabad allow militants to carry on terrorist training in territories they control.'[57] Human Rights Watch noted in September that year that 'virtually all independent commentators' agreed that 'there was continuing militant infiltration' from Pakistan-occupied Kashmir into Indian Kashmir to conduct terrorism, and that 'there have been no indications that the Pakistani military or militant groups had decided to abandon infiltration as policy.' Indeed, 'all aspects of political life' in Pakistan-occupied Kashmir were strictly controlled by the Pakistani army and ISI, and the government in Islamabad. The 'closest allies' of the Pakistani military in the region were the militant groups, including the LET and the HUM, which 'have had free rein' to operate in Kashmir.[58]

Other reports noted that hundreds of militants were being trained in Kashmir by groups such as the LET, the HUM and the JEM, and that the Pakistani establishment still saw them as useful in its Kashmir policy.[59] Indian intelligence claimed in mid-2005 that there were 55 camps in Pakistan training terrorists – 29 of these were in Kashmir, while others were spread around the country, from the Northwest Frontier province to the southern province of Sindh.[60] Some of these camps were said to be run by the ISI; the others could only be run with its complicity. By late 2007, it was the same story: the International Crisis Group was noting that 'despite

Musharraf's pledges to end all terrorist activity from Pakistani soil, the infrastructure of groups such as Lashkar-e-Tayyaba and Jaish-e-Mohammed remains intact.'[61]

As before, it was not that Britain was unaware of Pakistan's support for terrorism. A report written by a naval commander at the Defence Academy, a think tank for the Ministry of Defence, and leaked to the media in October 2006, stated that 'the [Pakistani] army's dual role in combating terrorism and at the same time promoting the MMA [the coalition of religious parties] and so indirectly supporting the Taliban through the ISI, is coming under closer and closer international scrutiny ... Indirectly, Pakistan, through the ISI, has been supporting terrorism and extremism.'[62] It was, therefore, perhaps not surprising that media reports over a year after 7/7 suggested that Scotland Yard was 'frustrated by the assistance that the Pakistani intelligence organisation, ISI, has provided in the hunt for those who assisted the 7/7 bombers.'[63]

This was not enough, however, for British ministers to halt their effusive praise for Musharraf's supposed efforts to combat terrorism. In December 2006, for example, Blair met Musharraf 'to share a common agenda to promote enlightened moderation and to combat the forces of extremism,' Foreign Minister Kim Howells explained.[64] At their joint press conference in Lahore, Blair delivered a public paean to Musharraf, saying that 'relations with Pakistan are really at their highest point I think than they have been for many, many years', and offering Britain's 'support for the programme of enlightened moderation that President Musharraf' was supposedly promoting. Blair also said: 'I would like to pay tribute to his courage and his leadership in taking Pakistan on this journey of change and modernisation, but also in so doing symbolising I think the future for Muslim countries the world over.'[65]

The phrase constantly bandied about by the British government, 'enlightened moderation', seemed curiously nebulous. Yet Human Rights Watch Pakistan specialist Ali Dayan Hasan wrote that it was anything but:

> 'Enlightened moderation' is a hoax perpetrated by Musharraf for international consumption. What is known in Pakistan as the 'mullah-military alliance' remains deeply rooted, and the Pakistani military and Musharraf continue to view 'moderate' and 'liberal' forces in politics and society as their principal adversaries. The reason is simple: democracy, human rights and meaningful civil liberties are anathema to a hypermilitarised state. Pakistan's voters consistently vote overwhelmingly for moderate, secular-oriented parties and reject religious extremists, so the military must rely in the most retrogressive elements on society to preserve its hold on power.[66]

In 2007, British ministers continued to proclaim Musharraf's 'determination to combat terrorism' while noting that 'the bilateral relationship between Pakistan and this country is as close as it has ever been.' Foreign Minister Geoff Hoon also continued to tell parliament about 'Musharraf's commitment to promoting "enlightened moderation"'.[67] At the same time, independent groups continued to report that 'Musharraf's reliance on the mullahs to counter the moderate regional and national-level parties has empowered the religious parties and their affiliated madrassa unions, effectively stalling any movement towards tangible reform.'[68]

Just how enlightened Musharraf was, was further revealed a few months later, when in May 2007 riots broke out in Karachi leaving over 40 people dead. They had been instigated by the Muttahidi Quami Movement (MQM), which is headed by Altaf Hussein in London; Hussein had been granted British citizenship during the Blair years, but is prevented from returning to Pakistan since he faces criminal charges there. When asked why Hussein was not deported before being given citizenship, a British diplomat said that 'he has not committed a crime on British soil' – a refrain consistent with the policies of Londonistan.[69]

Set up in 1984 by General Zia to act as a counter to the Pakistan Peoples Party, the MQM was seen by Musharraf as playing a similar role and was now a partner in a coalition government in Sindh province.[70] The riots broke out when MQM supporters tried to block the exit from Karachi airport of Iftikhar Chaudhry, the chief justice suspended by Musharraf for failing to be sufficiently pliant to the dictator's needs. According to one eyewitness account, 'many of the 15,000 police and security forces deployed in the city stood idly by as armed activists' from the MQM blocked Chaudhry's exit. Indeed, 'with plumes of smoke billowing over the city ... there were extraordinary scenes as gunmen on motorbikes pumped bullets into crowds demonstrating against Pakistan's Pervez Musharraf, while police stood idly by and watched.' The report also noted that Hussein 'coordinated opposition to Mr Chaudhry's arrival and addressed crowds gathered on the streets of Karachi in a mobile phone call relayed by loudspeakers.'[71] Yet the riots only received one cursory mention in the British parliament, when Foreign Office Minister Geoff Hoon was questioned by George Galloway about Hussein's role in fomenting these riots – in reply, the minister failed even to mention the subject, which quickly slipped into oblivion.[72]

It was instructive that David Miliband, the new foreign secretary in Gordon Brown's government which succeeded Blair in June 2007, visited Pakistan on his first trip outside Europe the following month. He told a press conference in Pakistan that the two countries had 'shared commitments to global issues, ranging from terrorism to climate change' and sought to 'build a greater stability around the world'. In answer to one question, Miliband delivered an apologia for Musharraf, claiming that he had 'a global commitment to peace and to stability' and had 'reiterated to me very strongly' his commitment to 'tackle terrorism at its source'.[73]

Four months later, Musharraf imposed martial law in Pakistan, suspending the constitution and arresting human rights activists and lawyers. The British government reacted by publicly imploring a return to civilian and democratic rule –

the usual mantra – but Whitehall threatened no cut-off in aid or military support to the regime. As the International Crisis Group noted, Britain, along with the US and the EU, 'signalled they wish to continue cooperation with President Musharraf and his government, particularly on counter-terrorism. The focus has been on the need to remove his uniform and conduct elections – not on the necessity of restoring the constitutional order and the rule of law.'[74] Britain, along with the US, was reported as acting as an intermediary at this time to secure a deal with Musharraf to allow PPP leader, Benazir Bhutto, to return to Pakistan after nearly a decade in exile.[75] Shortly after her return, Bhutto was assassinated in Rawalpindi in December 2007. The following day, Gordon Brown continued to praise Pakistan as 'a major ally in the global effort to combat' terrorism.[76] Elections were held in February 2008 in which the PPP and the PML won most of the seats and the PPP led the new coalition government, but with Musharraf remaining as president until, under much pressure from the two main parties, he was forced to resign in August.

In conclusion, it is certainly ironic that jihadists target Britain for its alleged 'war on Islam' when it has long connived with Islamist forces and their Pakistani state sponsors. To a large extent, the 7/7 and other would-be British bombers and British foreign policy have come out of the same stable.[77] It is the Pakistani terrorist groups that were – on 7/7, and continue to be – the major terrorist threats to Britain and many other countries. The Western media is focused on Bin Laden, yet the Pakistani groups owe little or nothing to al-Qaida, and have arisen largely separately from it, thanks considerably to the support from the Pakistani state.[78] Britain's long-time support for Islamabad has increased the likelihood of terrorism in Britain – indeed, this policy is arguably more responsible for threatening Britain than the invasion of Iraq. While appearing to be confronting radical Islam in Pakistan, Britain has again been working in effect with forces allied to it, a policy which has helped marginalise secular, nationalist and democratic forces within the country – a long-standing priority based on Whitehall's fear of genuine democracy and consistent with the historical record outlined in previous chapters.

CHAPTER 18

Alliances of Moderation

By the last years of the New Labour government, the challenge to the British and US position in the Middle East was unprecedented in the postwar world. In Iraq, the occupation turned into a disaster for Anglo-American planners, while in Afghanistan a resurgent Taliban bogged down British forces and inflicted increasing casualties. Iran and, to an extent, Syria remained independent regimes unwilling to follow Western policies, with Tehran threatening to acquire nuclear weapons to challenge Israel's nuclear monopoly in the region. In Israeli-occupied Palestine, the democratic election in January 2006 of the rising force of the Sunni Islamist group Hamas – the West's 'bad Palestinians' – challenged Israel and the secular Fatah Palestinian faction – now the 'good Palestinians'. In Lebanon, Hezbollah militias backed by Iran inflicted a military defeat on Israel following the latter's invasion in July 2006 and continued to confront the pro-Western government there.

These developments challenged overall Western hegemony in the Middle East, which remained of primary importance for its oil and gas reserves. Of the three major oil-producing states, Iran was an official enemy, Iraq was out of control and Saudi Arabia's future was (as ever) uncertain. Only the fourth producer, tiny Kuwait, was run, as ever, by a dependable pro-Western regime. A rising Iran, and specifically the overthrow of Sunni dominance in

Iraq – amounting to the first Shia take-over of an Arab country – threatened to topple the order imposed in the region by the British after the First World War, an order characterised by the dominance of Sunni, monarchical regimes on which Britain and the US have long relied to promote their interests in the region.

Confronted with these challenges, Britain under Tony Blair and then Gordon Brown pursued two key policies. First was to follow US policy to a greater degree than at any time in the postwar world, notably in invading Iraq in 2003 and by supporting Israel – a reliance on Washington that reflected British weakness in securing the large interests at stake. But second, Britain also tried to deepen alliances with key Sunni forces, principally, as ever, the Saudis – who were engaged in an intensifying battle for regional and religious pre-eminence with their Shia rivals in Tehran – but also the Muslim Brotherhood, an old Sunni Islamist collaborator that was the major opposition to the regime in Egypt. The policy recalled British collusion with the Brotherhood in the 1950s, when Britain also faced major challenges to its interests in the Middle East but lacked allies to promote them. However, British policy could not be simply reduced to a Sunni versus Shia strategy: some enemies – notably Syria and Hamas – were not Shia forces, while in Iraq Britain, as we see later, worked through Shia Islamist forces to try to promote its interests.

Compounding the problems for Britain was, and remains, an increasing dependence on imported oil and gas. The most important government document on the subject of Britain's 'energy security', almost entirely passed over by the mainstream media, was produced in February 2003, just as ministers were denying that the anticipated invasion of Iraq had anything to do with oil.

Department of Trade and Industry White Paper concluded that Britain was set to become a net importer of gas by 2006 and of oil by around 2010. By this time Britain would very likely be importing around three-quarters of its primary energy needs while half the world's gas and oil would be coming from countries that are currently perceived as unstable. The paper stated that 'we need to give greater prominence to strategic energy issues in foreign policy' across the government and that 'our aims are to maintain strong relations with exporting countries' while 'in promoting diversity we will also work to minimise the risk of disruption to supplies from regional disputes.'1 Essentially, the paper was calling for the political status quo to be maintained in many repressive countries and implied that Britain might go to war to keep supplies flowing, which duly happened a few weeks later.

Five years later, in March 2008, the government produced another key document, the 'National Security Strategy of the United Kingdom'. It noted that competition for energy supplies was increasing and that global energy demand would be 50 per cent higher in 2030 than today. Critically, it added: 'the premium attached to energy security and the rising risk of energy shortages will increase the potential for disputes and conflict. Countries including China and Russia are already making control of energy supply a foreign policy priority.' In response to this threat, Britain must 'guard against the re-emergence of a state-led threat through maintaining strong national capabilities', including intelligence, military forces and nuclear weapons; Britain already had the second highest military budget in the world in cash terms, the report noted.2 The message was that China, albeit also a trading 'partner', posed a potential military threat to British interests, along with Russia, while it was obvious where these conflicts were most likely to be played out – Central Asia and the Middle East. Thus a new factor in British foreign policy planning towards the Middle East in the twenty-first century was keeping China, as well as a resurgent Russia, out of Britain's traditional client region.

The report was not an isolated analysis. New Labour ministers delivered numerous speeches on the issue of 'energy security' in their last years in government. In Gordon Brown's November 2007 Mansion House speech – in which his notion of 'hard-headed internationalism' was widely commented upon – he also stated that 'as energy supplies are under pressure there is a new global competition for natural resources'. He noted a need to 'strengthen' the British military and reiterated that the US was 'our most important bilateral relationship', inferring that British protection of these resources was intimately bound up with its military capabilities and the alliance with Washington.[3] Indeed, in 2009 the government's former chief scientific adviser, Sir David King, described the Iraq War as 'the first of the resource wars'.[4]

The most direct threat to British interests was, and remains, from the regime in Iran under President Ahmedinejad, elected in August 2005, which has consolidated Iran's independent foreign policy, raising the challenge to Israeli and US policy in the region, and forged closer relations with states such as Russia and Syria. Thus Iran's large oil resources remain outside Western control, but the challenge posed by Iran is also bound up with British fears of Russia and China. Foreign Office Minister Kim Howells said: 'We want it [Iran] to be much more engaged, because Western Europe needs Iranian gas very badly. We need to break the Russian monopoly on supplies of gas to Western Europe. That is a pretty controversial statement to make but the Russians need rivals.'[5] Thus the issue was that Iran's oil, which could offer an alternative to Russia, was controlled by an unfriendly regime. Howells also evoked the fear of Chinese expansion into the Iranian market, telling a parliamentary committee in November 2007 that 'there are 68 million people in Iran, and it is a market that the Chinese are positively slavering at. I do not think that any of us want to isolate Iran.'[6] Again, the fear was that the Iranian regime would turn further away from the West and develop closer relations, perhaps even a strategic partnership, with a China keen to break into Middle Eastern oil markets.

As for the prospect of Iran acquiring nuclear weapons, Howells revealingly told the same parliamentary committee that 'my greatest fear is that the Iranians believe that by developing a bomb they will add to their cachet in international circles in the same way that, at the end of the Second World War, many countries felt that if they had an atomic bomb they would become a big power in the world.'[7] Thus the danger was that Iran would match what Britain did sixty years ago and achieve an equality of power in a region which London and Washington seek to control over local and global rivals.

Britain may have engaged in extensive covert operations against Iran at this time, together with the US, although no evidence has emerged of Whitehall's role. It was widely reported that Washington was covertly providing militant Iranian opposition groups with money and finance.[8] Most notable was US backing of Jundullah ('Soldiers of Islam', but which calls itself the People's Resistance Movement of Iran), a radical Sunni group fighting from Pakistan's Baluchistan province, which conducted bomb attacks and suicide bombings against both Iranian military targets and civilians in Iran's province of Sistan-Balochistan. Jundullah was described in a House of Commons research paper as an al-Qaida 'affiliate' and its leaders previously fought with the Taliban.[9] ABC News reported in 2007 that the US had been encouraging and advising Jundullah since 2005.[10]

Iran accused Britain as well as the US of supporting Jundullah and also of backing militant groups fighting in another Iranian province, Khuzestan, bordering Iraq's Basra province, as well as supporting the huge demonstrations against the Ahmedinejad regime in late 2009. There were reports that British-made weapons were used in attacks in Iran.[11] Moreover, there were suggestions that the kidnapping of computer expert Peter Moore in Iraq in 2007 was carried out by Iran's Revolutionary Guards in retaliation for Tehran's belief that Britain was behind bomb attacks in Khuzestan.[12]

In 2007, the Bush administration gave the CIA approval to conduct 'black' operations to achieve regime change in Iran, involving a propaganda and disinformation campaign and a strategy to stop Iran's nuclear programme.[13] MI6 appears to have been engaged in this campaign, which may have involved passing on to Iran equipment containing viruses and modifications to sabotage its nuclear programme. According to Israeli journalist, Ronen Bergman, in 2006–07 at least three planes crashed in Iran belonging to Revolutionary Guards carrying personnel connected with the nuclear programme.[14] Britain also collaborated with Israel's secret service, Mossad, to counter Iran. In May 2008, the then head of MI6, Sir John Scarlett, visited Israel to promote what Israeli officials described as a 'strategic dialogue' with Mossad.[15] The following year, in further talks between the two, Scarlett was reportedly told by Mossad chief, Meir Dagan, that Saudi Arabia had given Israel permission to use its airspace to bomb Iran.[16]

To counter Iran, and the broader challenges to Britain's energy security, Britain also resorted to constructing what then Prime Minister Tony Blair called an 'alliance of moderation', in reality part of London's increasing reliance on Sunni forces in the region.

ENGAGING 'MODERATE' ISLAM

In August 2006 Blair delivered what was billed by Downing Street as a major speech on the Middle East to the World Affairs Council in Los Angeles. He noted that:

> There is an arc of extremism now stretching across the Middle East and touching, with increasing definition, countries far outside that region. To defeat it will need an alliance of moderation that paints a different future in which Muslim, Jew and Christian, Arab and Western, wealthy and developing nations can make progress in peace and harmony with each other.

Blair said that in the Middle East there was 'an elemental struggle about the values that will shape our future' between 'reactionary Islam' and 'moderate, mainstream Islam'. In the moderate camp were the Palestinian 'leadership' (that is, President Mahmoud Abbas, of the Fatah faction), the feudal sheikhdoms of the United Arab Emirates, Bahrain, Kuwait and Qatar, as well as Turkey; also mentioned was Israel, which was viewed as simply defending itself against Hamas and Hezbollah. Saudi Arabia was not mentioned but could be assumed to be regarded as one of the 'moderates' (i.e., pro-Western forces). In the 'reactionary' camp were al-Qaida, Hamas, Hezbollah and the Taliban, along with the regimes in Syria and Iran. The latter two were a 'constant source of destabilisation and reaction' – Damascus, for allowing al-Qaida militants to enter Iraq, Tehran, for supporting 'extremist Shia' there. For them, 'there is a choice: come in to the international community and play by the same rules as the rest of us; or be confronted.'[17] What the British prime minister meant was obviously that Iran and Syria should follow Western orders, or else.

However, the most important part of Blair's speech – missed by the media – was his articulation of how Britain's support for 'moderate' Islam was bound up with its broader foreign policy goals. Blair said Britain and the US should set about 'empowering' moderate Islam and that 'a victory for the moderates means an Islam that is open: open to globalisation.' However, 'there is a risk that the world, after the Cold War, goes back to a global policy based on spheres of influence', and that China will 'surely be the world's other superpower' in 20–30 years, along with a more powerful India and Russia. In this situation:

> The stronger and more appealing our world-view is, the more it is seen as based not just on power but on justice, the easier it will be for us to shape the future in which Europe and the US will no longer, economically or politically, be transcendent. Long before then, we want moderate, mainstream Islam to triumph over reactionary Islam.[18]

Blair seemed to be saying that the survival of Western

hegemony in the world was partly dependent on the triumph of 'moderate' Islam, which was seen as an ally of the West in the face of the rise of China and other emerging powers. Blair's comment was in reality reiterating long-standing British policy – that Islamic (indeed Islamist, in the case of the Saudis) forces would continue to be used to support fundamental British priorities.

After Blair left office, the Foreign Office distanced itself from the 'arc of extremism' concept, noting that 'inappropriate language can be counter-productive'.[19] The British Council told a parliamentary enquiry that using rhetoric such as 'extremism' could be 'seen as reviving colonial approaches and dividing the region on the basis of religious sects'[20] – a reference to the traditional British divide and rule policy which Blair was again articulating. But it was noteworthy that Gordon Brown's foreign secretary, David Miliband, was still using the term 'forces of moderation' in late 2007, and the policy was surely being retained.[21] The British division of the Middle East was essentially the same as Bush's 'you're either with us or against us' rhetoric after 9/11, and perhaps not unlike that of the Taliban, for whom the globe was divided into Dar al-Kufr (the lands of infidels, or non-Muslim states), Dar al-Munafiqin (hypocritical, religious states like Iran and Turkey) and Dar al-Islam (good Muslim states, such as Pakistan and Saudi Arabia).[22]

The preparation for Britain's new phase of empowering 'moderate Islam' was seen in a series of government documents from 2004–06 leaked to the New Statesman in early 2006. The documents were linked by a common theme: that in the Muslim world there existed often powerful opposition forces with whom Britain should work, notably the Muslim Brotherhood. One of the leaked documents, a joint Home and Foreign Office memo of July 2004 on the subject of 'working with the Muslim community' in Britain noted that 'the reformist movement can be traced to the Muslim Brotherhood (Hassan Al Banna) and Jamaati Islam (Maulana Maududi) which was orthodox but pragmatic' – a reference to two key Islamist organisations with whom Britain had covertly collaborated in the past.[23] But the Brotherhood was also understood as a 'political movement which sees Islam as the model for social and political organisation with sharia (Islamic law) being the basis for legislation.'[24] The author of this memo was Angus McKee, of the Foreign Office's Middle East and North Africa Department, who was one of the architects of this British policy of engagement with Islamist groups. McKee had earlier written a memo describing a conference in Paris where British and other European officials and academics discussed Islamist movements in the Arab world. He noted that most Islamist movements 'are wary of Western motives but ready to engage' and that in many countries in the Middle East and North Africa they 'form the principal structured opposition and are well organised.' McKee even noted that: 'Given that Islamist groups are often less corrupt than the generality of the societies in which they operate, consideration might be given to channeling aid resources through them, so long as sufficient transparency is achieved.'[25]

At around the same time, a specially commissioned paper was circulating in Whitehall. Written by Basil Eastwood, a former British ambassador to Syria, and Richard Murphy, the US assistant secretary of state in the Reagan administration, it was entitled 'We Must Talk to Political Islamists in the Middle East – and Not Just in Iraq'. The paper stated bluntly that 'in the Arab Middle East the awkward truth is that the most significant movements which enjoy popular support are those associated with political Islam':

> For a year now we have been engaged in a dialogue with a small group of people familiar with some of the different national branches of the Muslim Brotherhood, with Hamas and with Hizbullah. They do not formally represent these movements, but we believe that they do speak with authority. Some of them have been imprisoned for their beliefs and they

describe movements which are arguably more democratic than the Arab governments concerned (who habitually rig elections to ensure that such movements do not win).

Eastwood and Murphy then noted the differences between the political Islamists 'who seek change but who do not advocate violence to overthrow regimes, and the Jihadists, the Islamic extremists who do.' They concluded by stating that 'G8 governments must now, perhaps indirectly, get into dialogue with such movements and involve them in the civil society track of the broader Middle East Initiative' – the US programme to supposedly promote democratic reform in the region.[26]

One dissenter in this proposed strategy was the British ambassador to Egypt, Sir Derek Plumbly. He noted that 'obviously it is desirable to talk to Islamists if we can' and that 'we will continue to look for opportunities to talk to Islamists here.' However: 'I ... detect a tendency for us to be drawn towards engagement for its own sake: to confuse "engaging with the Islamic world" with "engaging with Islamism", and to play down the very real downsides for us in terms of the Islamists' likely foreign and social policies, should they actually achieve power in countries such as Egypt.'[27] Plumbly here was saying that there were forces other than the Islamists with whom Britain should be engaging. He was also repeating the views expressed by officials in the 1950s that the Muslim Brotherhood was essentially an anti-Western force. Yet this didn't stop British collusion with the Brotherhood then, and nor did it later.

The burgeoning influence of the Muslim Brotherhood as a political force in Egypt was confirmed five months after these memos were circulated. In the November 2005 parliamentary elections, Brotherhood candidates, running as independents (since the party was formally banned) won 88 seats and 19 per cent of the vote, making it the strongest single opposition group to President Hosni Mubarak's regime, which had been in power since 1981. Shortly thereafter, the British government apparently overrode Plumbly's objections and decided to step up engagement with the Brotherhood.

Julie McGregor, of the Foreign Office's Arab–Israel North Africa Group, wrote to the foreign secretary in January 2006 recommending that Britain 'increase the frequency of working-level contacts with Muslim Brotherhood parliamentarians (who do not advocate violence) particularly those who are members of parliamentary committees.' Interestingly, she noted that until 2002 the Foreign Office had had 'infrequent working-level (Second Secretary) contact' with Brotherhood MPs but these contacts were reduced after pressure from the Mubarak regime. Since 2002 Britain had 'only occasional contacts with MB members including one or two contacts with parliamentarians and random unplanned encounters.' The spiritual head of the Egyptian Muslim Brotherhood from 2002 until his death in January 2004 was Maamoun al-Hodeibi, father of Hassan al-Hodeibi, with whom Britain had collaborated in the 1950s; whether British officials had any contacts with Maamoun is unclear. McGregor also wrote that 'the US are reviewing their position on contacts with the MB, having previously refused any contact', signifying that the changed stance may have been coordinated with Washington. She also recognised that 'the presentation of any change in the way we deal with the Muslim Brotherhood will have to be carefully handled, in order to safeguard our bilateral relations with Egypt', whose government viewed it as a terrorist organisation.[28]

McGregor's note resulted in an apparent flurry of new British contact-making with the Brotherhood. In March 2006, the Foreign Office-funded Westminster Foundation for Democracy organised a 'consultation workshop' in Cairo which brought together various Egyptian political activists, 'including MPs from the government, opposition parties and those associated with the Muslim Brotherhood'.[29] In May, Foreign Office Minister Kim Howells told parliament that British officials in Egypt had had 'occasional contact with members of the Muslim Brotherhood since September 2001', and that other officials had met Brotherhood representatives in Jordan, Kuwait and Lebanon, and had 'limited contact' with members of the Syrian Brotherhood, 'whose leadership is in exile in London'.[30] Howells also said in response to another parliamentary question on the Muslim Brotherhood:

> We should be extremely careful not to paint all Islamists as violent because they most certainly are not and we are ready to engage with organisations and individuals who uphold the values of democracy and use peaceful means to achieve their objectives, challenging their views as necessary. Some of those have been elected, for example to the Egyptian parliament, as independents, but are clearly associated with the Muslim Brotherhood. Our diplomats have met such people on occasion. We do not go out of our way to engage in such meetings but when they occur we argue the case for a non-violent approach. We argue against terrorism and we seek cooperation.[31]

Howells added in a response to a further question by Conservative MP Keith Simpson on whether the Brotherhood was engaged in terrorism, that he had 'no information on that' and that 'the honourable gentleman will recall, of course, that this parliament has some history of engaging in secret talks with terrorist organisations, such as the IRA.'[32] This was an interesting response showing, first, that the government was continuing its long-standing policy of regarding Islamist forces as possible collaborators and, second, implying that the government was perfectly aware of the Brotherhood's links to terrorism.

The policy of engagement clearly continued beyond these leaked memos. In October 2007, for example, the Foreign Office was stating that 'we have a long-standing policy of engaging with Egyptian parliamentarians from all backgrounds, including those affiliated with the Muslim Brotherhood. We will continue to follow this policy.'[33]

British policy appeared to dovetail with the US, which, although having only limited known contacts with the Egyptian Brotherhood, had recently stepped up contacts with the Syrian Brotherhood.[34]

THE BROTHERHOOD'S UTILITY

New Labour's policy of engaging with the Muslim Brotherhood provoked criticism from right-wing writers like Melanie Phillips and the Conservative MP Michael Gove, as well as liberal journalists like Nick Cohen and Martin Bright, to whom the Foreign Office memos were leaked. The latter attacked the government for prioritising relations with the Islamist right at the expense of other voices in the Muslim community, and also for involving themselves with some individuals who condoned suicide bombings.[35] Some commentators blasted 'the Left' generally in noting then Mayor of London, Ken Livingstone's invitation to Yusuf Qaradawi, the spiritual leader of the international Muslim Brotherhood, to visit London, and the Stop the War Coalition's campaigning on Iraq and Palestine with the Muslim Association of Britain (MAB), the British wing of the Muslim Brotherhood. Martin Bright remarked that 'it is depressing that so few on the Left have been prepared to engage with the issue of the Foreign Office appeasement of radical Islam except to minimise its significance.'[36] I think Bright was right on this point, but the policy was not so much one of appeasement as rooted in Britain's ongoing collaboration with the Islamist right to achieve key British foreign policy goals.

Some of the leaked memos explicitly showed why Britain wanted to collaborate with the Brotherhood. Ambassador Plumbly suggested in his June 2005 memo that talking to the Islamists could be beneficial since 'we might gain useful information' – a policy consistent with the British strategy of recruiting extremists as informers, as we have seen. But Plumbly also wrote that the British interest in Egypt was to press the Mubarak regime to promote political reform and that 'the road that takes us there may well be bumpy, and it will certainly include a good deal more pressure from the Muslim Brothers on the streets'. Thus Plumbly clearly saw the Brotherhood as a lever to bring about internal change, a policy which, I have argued above, was also one of the perceived benefits of hosting extremist groups in Londonistan. The ambassador did not propose that Britain directly 'encourage the Brothers' or press the Mubarak regime to legalise it, since this would jeopardise London's relations with Cairo; however, if the Brotherhood were to be 'repressed aggressively, we will need to respond'.[37] Similarly, Angus McKee had recognised that the Brotherhood 'remain the largest and most effective opposition grouping in Egypt. Its ability to mobilise support and its critique of the current system are far more effective than those of the licensed opposition parties.'[38]

Foreign Office official Julie McGregor's arguments for increasing contacts were that it would 'help in discouraging radicalisation' and 'to influence these groups, who often have significant reach with the "grass roots"' as well as giving Britain 'the opportunity to challenge their perception of the West, including of the UK, and on their prescriptions for solving the challenges facing Egypt and the region.'[39] McGregor's first point about 'discouraging radicalisation' was that engagement with those less extreme than the jihadists might help stave off more violent change, perhaps the perennial Western fear of an Iran-style revolution. Yet it was just as likely that the Brotherhood would be a stepping stone towards precisely a more extreme regime.

What Britain was also doing by engaging the Brotherhood was insuring itself for a possible change of regime in Egypt, which duly occurred in February 2011, as we discuss in the final chapter. Egypt's future after Mubarak was long uncertain and the Brotherhood was seen as likely to play an important role in any new government or in a transition. The stakes were high in that Egypt was the leading Arab state, with wide political and intellectual influence in the region, and Britain was the largest foreign investor in the country, amounting to around $20 billion.[40] British elites wanted to be in a better position than after the fall of the shah of Iran in 1979, and cultivating the Islamists was in all likelihood regarded as critical. Given the challenges to British power, and oil interests, elsewhere in the Middle East, a regime in Cairo that remained outside Britain's sphere of influence would clearly be a disaster for Whitehall planners.

We can certainly dispense with the notion that British engagement with the Brotherhood was due to Whitehall's supposed support for democracy in the Middle East. London had long been opposed to popular governments and movements in the region, largely since they tended to be more 'anti-Western' than the authoritarian pro-Western regimes. Britain likely saw the Brotherhood – as it did from the 1950s to the 1970s – as a counter to the secular, nationalist forces opposition in Egypt and the region, notably the Kifaya (Enough) grassroots movement of secular nationalists and leftists, which emerged in 2004 as posing a popular challenge to the Mubarak regime. Thus Britain's engagement with the Islamists came at the expense of support for more liberal groups, as the comment by Ambassador Plumbly, noted above, implied. The Brotherhood might well also have been seen as keeping a lid on more popular nationalist change in Egypt and the Middle East. As the Palestinian analyst Yasir Ai-Zuatran noted: 'Some politicians and ordinary people in different Arab countries criticise and even laugh at members of the Muslim Brotherhood because of their conciliatory position toward ruling regimes, even becoming a tool in hands of governments to calm and domesticate the Arab street, which is ready for revolution and revolt.'[41]

With Syria, run by the regime of Bashar Assad, a former member of George Bush's Axis of Evil, British policy under Blair and Brown was different, but Islamists were again useful. Britain and the US most likely cultivated contacts with the London-based Syrian Brotherhood as a tool to pressure and destabilise the regime as well as to bolster the likelihood of a successor regime and make contacts with key figures in it. The US is known to have collaborated with the Syrian Brotherhood to destabilise the regime of Bashar's father, Hafez Assad, who ruled Syria until his death in 2000.[42] In August 2002, the Syrian Brotherhood, trying to position itself as the leader of the opposition, held a conference in London under the slogan 'Syria for all its people', and called for a new, 'pluralist' political system.[43] In June 2006, the National Salvation Front, a coalition grouping that included the Muslim Brotherhood (until it withdrew in 2009) and secular forces, held another opposition conference in London, involving 50 Syrian exiles, calling for regime change.[44] Opposition activities in Syria were clearly mounted from London and were apparently tolerated by the British authorities. Then Syrian Brotherhood leader Ali Sadreddine Bayanouni, who moved to London in 2000 after spending twenty years in Jordan, said in 2005 that 'We have members in Syria, but we avoid giving these activities any identifiable structure.'[45]

By late 2008, however, Britain, together with the US, changed tack in relations with Syria and began to try to court the regime, probably mainly to further isolate Iran. British ministers visited Damascus in 2008 and 2009, and Syrian Foreign Minister Walid al-Mualem visited London in July 2009. David Miliband now saw the Syrian regime as a source of 'stability' in the Middle East, but particularly striking was his view that 'it's very important that we continue to engage countries like Syria, which wants to be a secular state at the heart of a stable Middle East'.[46] Thus Syria could act as a 'secular' counter to Islamists in the region, although it remained unclear the extent to which London was also continuing to cultivate the Muslim Brotherhood opposition.

Given the Brotherhood's utility to British officials, who have a long history of working with virtually anyone who will help them achieve specific objectives, the organisation's links to terrorism could be largely overlooked by Whitehall, except to the degree that collaboration was bad for public relations and for relations with the Mubarak regime. Although some of the leaked British memos on the Brotherhood referred to its moderation and reformism, others showed British officials' awareness of its links to terrorism, consistent with Kim Howells' comments noted above. The Foreign Office's Angus McKee also wrote:

> Egyptian Muslim Brotherhood is a religio-political movement. Historic links to terrorism – assassinations in 1940s/50s and ideologue Sayyid Qutb modernised the concept of jihad. Since then, Islamic terrorist groups in Egypt have had only circumstantial links to the Brotherhood (e.g. attracting disaffected members) … There is no evidence that the Egyptian MB itself is now engaged in any terrorist activity. But it is possible that the MB forwards charitable donations to Palestine, perhaps even Hamas itself, as do many Egyptians and others, Muslims and non-Muslims. However, the intellectual, political and geographical milieux which the MB inhabits means there will always be members who move on to more violent activity, even terrorism, in other organisations.[47]

A few months later, Foreign Secretary Jack Straw claimed that 'I have seen no credible evidence that the current leadership of the Egyptian Muslim Brotherhood supports terrorist organisations in the Middle East.'[48] These words seemed carefully chosen to obscure all the nuances noted by McKee. In February 2009, Communities Secretary Hazel Blears was more forthright, saying that 'the Muslim Brotherhood is not a terrorist organisation but it supports terrorist organisations such as Hamas in Gaza.'[49]

Similarly, Britain's contacts with the Syrian Brotherhood were interesting in light of Tony Blair's comment about the organisation in February 2003, shortly before the invasion of Iraq. Blair then told parliament that: 'Iraq has a long record of support for terrorism; this includes support for radical Islamic groups such as the Syrian Muslim Brotherhood'; the term 'radical

Islamic' was noteworthy as was the belief that it was involved in terrorism.[50] Meanwhile, Blair, the architect of the strategy of support for 'moderate' against 'reactionary' Islam, noted in an earlier speech on the rise of 'religious radicalism' in March 2006:

> The extremism may have started through religious doctrine and thought. But soon, in offshoots of the Muslim Brotherhood, supported by Wahhabi extremists and taught in some of the madrassas of the Middle East and Asia, an ideology was born and exported around the world ... Today, in well over 30 or 40 countries terrorists are plotting action loosely linked with this ideology. My point is this: the roots of this are not superficial, therefore, they are deep, embedded now in the culture of many nations and capable of an eruption at any time.[51]

The trio of actors whom Blair identified as the chief proponents of terrorism were all groups the British government had helped cultivate since the late 1940s: the Muslim Brotherhood (albeit 'offshoots'), with whom the Foreign Office had just stepped up contacts; 'Wahhabi extremists' in Saudi Arabia with whom Blair and his predecessors had dealt happily for years; and the Pakistani madrassas nurtured by various Pakistani leaders consistently supported by Britain. Despite Blair's articulation of the need to empower the 'moderates', the reality was that Britain had long been colluding with the extremists.

All these comments suggested that British officials and ministers believed that the Muslim Brotherhood and its offshoots were not purely 'moderate' or reformist, and in this attitude they were similar to their predecessors in the 1950s, who recognised that they were collaborating with terrorists. Of course the Muslim Brotherhood was by now a very different organisation than in the 1950s; it was clearly much more complex and diverse, a network with branches in around seventy countries and contained a wide variety of political views. Many Brotherhood figures had renounced violence in favour of participation in electoral processes, and the organisation stood out from al-Qaida, which had long opposed it precisely for its lack of militancy. Yet the Brotherhood, as recognised by British officials, still strove for the establishment of Islamic states and the imposition of sharia law and had some documented links to terrorism. It could also be seen as a stepping stone for some individuals to turn to more violent groups.[52]

In the 1950s British collusion with the Brotherhood in Egypt and Syria was undertaken to overthrow nationalist regimes, notably Whitehall's bête noire, Nasser. Several decades after helping to defeat Arab nationalism, London and Washington were again in a somewhat desperate position in the Middle East, their strategy challenged on most fronts, and were looking for all the allies they could find. New Labour's engagement with the Muslim Brotherhood continued Whitehall's use of the Islamist right as a tool in its foreign policy. The policy should not be seen in isolation but as part of a broader search in the Middle East for allies to counter various current foes.

THE EVER-TURNING LONDON–RIYADH AXIS

The British government continued to see Saudi Arabia not only as a supplier of oil and buyer of British weapons but also as a Sunni counter to a resurgent Shia Iran – part, indeed, of the supposed 'alliance of moderation'. This continuing support for Riyadh was instructive in light of what the Saudis were actually up to.

A summer 2002 UN report on the financing of al-Qaida asserted that $16 million was sent to Bin Laden's organisation from sources in Saudi Arabia after the September 2001 attacks.[53] Nearly a year after 9/11, the CIA was stating that there is 'incontrovertible evidence that there is support for these terrorists within the Saudi government.'[54] In the immediate aftermath of the attacks, the Saudis continued their long-standing policy of trying to accommodate the most radical sheikhs in the Kingdom. This policy was only dashed in May 2003 when, during a visit by US Secretary of State Colin Powell, three coordinated suicide attacks on housing compounds in Riyadh killed 35 people. Mass arrests followed, as did the introduction of (very limited) steps by then Crown Prince, and now King Abdullah to allow some sectors of civil society a role in political decision-making.[55] From then on, it appears, the Saudis started taking some steps to clamp down on terrorism in the country and to control 'private' donations to al-Qaida. Some new laws were announced to regulate charitable donations, while the Saudi security services attempted to hunt down al-Qaida members in the Kingdom.

However, not all the new laws have been implemented and few punitive actions have been taken against individuals financing terrorism. Moreover, while some efforts have been made to clamp down on domestic extremists, little has been done to stop their export, while Saudi money has continued to flow around the world in support of Islamist causes. A US estimate from 2005 was that the Saudis were sending between $300–600 million around the world every year to fund radical religious organisations.[56] A report sponsored by the Council on Foreign Relations in the US noted that 'this massive spending is helping to create the next generation of terrorists'.[57] One Washington think tank estimated that the decades-long Saudi campaign to promote Wahhabism around the world had spent a massive $50 billion, and was the 'largest worldwide propaganda campaign ever mounted'; it has involved the building of 1,500 mosques, 2,200 colleges and schools and 210 Islamic centres, some of which have acted as support networks for the jihad movements.[58] By early 2008, five years after the Saudis began limited action against terrorist financing and activities in the country, the Bush administration's top treasury counterterrorism official, Stuart Levy, told a senate committee that Saudi Arabia remained the world's leading source of money for al-Qaida and other extremists.[59]

Many officials in the Saudi security services have been suspected of being al-Qaida supporters. Mabaheth, the Saudi body responsible for countering al-Qaida, is believed to have been penetrated by it – its staff was 80 per cent sympathetic to the Islamic insurgents, according to a source with first-hand knowledge of the unit speaking in 2004.[60] There have also been claims that some of the bomb attacks inside Saudi Arabia in recent years would not have been possible without the collusion of the National Guard or other security organisations.[61] Abdel Bari Atwan, the editor of the London-based newspaper, al-Quds al-Arabi, has argued that al-Qaida was party to official intelligence information about some assassinations in 2003 and 2004.[62]

The official enemy, Iran, has been constantly accused by London and Washington of helping the insurgents in Iraq, which has been equally constantly reported by the media. Yet Saudi Arabia has provided the bulk of foreign jihadists fighting there. The US military estimated in mid-2007 that 45 per cent of the foreign fighters in Iraq were Saudis and that they had carried out more suicide bombings than those of any nationality; indeed, half of all Saudis reportedly went to Iraq as suicide bombers.[63] Two years into the war it was estimated that over 2,000 Saudis had volunteered to go to Iraq, of whom 350 had already been killed.[64] By late 2006, Saudi citizens were providing millions of dollars in funding to Sunni insurgents in Iraq, much of it used to buy weapons.[65]

Furthermore, it appears that some Saudi militants have gone to Iraq with the complicity of the Saudi authorities. Soon after the invasion of Iraq, amidst rising militant anger inside the kingdom, Saudi Arabia showed signs of re-running the policy it adopted towards Afghanistan in the 1990s, when domestic radicalism at home was encouraged to find an outlet outside the Gulf. Militant clerics were allowed to use television and the media to urge angry youths to take the jihad to Iraq. The Saudi authorities were happy to try and stem the spread of influence in Iraq by its arch-rival,

Iran.[66] According to a US government consultant quoted by investigative journalist Seymour Hersh, the Saudis assured the White House that this time 'they will keep a very close eye on the religious fundamentalists' in Iraq and that if they are going to 'throw bombs' it will be at Hezbollah, Iran and the Syrians, and not at US forces.[67] Such Saudi involvement in the Iraqi insurgency amounts to a tacit proxy war against Iran in which the US and Britain at least acquiesced.

Britain's relationship with Saudi Arabia under New Labour, the product of decades of careful nurturing by Whitehall, remained very deep. For example, the Foreign Office's 'Engaging with the Islamic World' programme, which promotes outreach to the Muslim Brotherhood and other organisations, also includes a little-noticed project called 'Two Kingdoms: Friendship and Partnership'. Launched in 2005, the project aims 'to enhance UK relations with Saudi Arabia around a shared reform agenda' including discussions on subjects ranging from national security and terrorism to employment and education. 'The symbolism of the two kingdoms of the UK and Saudi Arabia sharing the same challenges is powerful in these times of misunderstanding,' the Foreign Office has noted.[68]

When King Fahd died in August 2005, Tony Blair praised the Saudi ruler as 'a man of great vision and leadership who inspired his countrymen for a quarter of a century as King.' Fahd was also 'a good friend of the United Kingdom' with whom 'we have developed extremely close political, commercial and defence links.'[69] Fahd was succeeded by his half-brother, Abdullah, with whom Britain had dealt since the early 1960s in supporting the Saudi Arabian National Guard, which Abdullah still personally commands. *The Daily Telegraph* noted that Prince Turki, the former intelligence chief with whom MI6 worked from 1977 until he left the post in 2001, had 'good connections to MI6', while the British and Saudi secret services were believed to remain very close – the Saudi royal family reportedly relied on a flow of intelligence from MI6 on the Shia regime in Iran, for example. More generally, Saudi intelligence was known to have employed a number of former MI5 and MI6 officers.[70] Prince Charles was also friendly with Prince Turki and had long-standing close relations to other members of the House of Saud.[71]

Labour ministers delivered a stream of extraordinary speeches on Saudi Arabia, involving routine apologias for the Kingdom's domestic and foreign policies, ignoring its role in nurturing global terrorism and supporting its foreign policy in the Middle East. In January 2006, then Foreign Secretary Jack Straw praised the Kingdom for its 'striking counter-terrorism successes over the last two years' and for 'winning the hearts and minds and the mobilisation of Saudi society against the extremists'; he went so far as to praise the Wahhabi fundamentalists for 'their leadership in the Muslim world' and for having 'faced down the perversion of religion which is the seedbed of terrorism'.[72] Three months later, Straw was in Riyadh, calling Britain 'Saudi Arabia's oldest friend and ally' and urging the two states to deepen the 'defence' relationship.[73] Earlier, in February 2005, Straw had told a 'UK–Saudi Arabia Conference' in London that 'our two kingdoms are working together to spread security in the Middle East – a region in which Saudi Arabia has such a clear and vital role to play.'[74]

Under Gordon Brown's premiership, the accolades continued. In his speech at the 'Two Kingdoms Dialogue' in London in October 2007, Foreign Office Minister Kim Howells went so far as to say that the two countries' relationship was 'a model for open and productive relations between European and Islamic governments', also convincing himself that 'we both want peace, security and prosperity' in the Middle East.[75] Foreign Secretary David Miliband joined the chorus by saying at a press conference in Saudi Arabia that 'the site of the two holy places makes Saudi Arabia a very important country in the modern world and the message that is sent out from here has repercussions right around the world.'[76] The foreign secretary was simply echoing British planners nearly a century before who saw a British-backed Saudi Arabia's control of Mecca and Medina as useful for British imperial purposes. By November 2008, Miliband was reiterating that Saudi Arabia was a 'key partner for the UK and projects significant influence across the Middle East.'[77] The following year, Defence Secretary Bob Ainsworth, visiting Saudi Arabia to promote military sales and cooperation, said that 'the relationship between our two kingdoms is better today than ever.'[78]

Apologias for the Saudis reached right across the mainstream political spectrum. In 2006, for example, the all-party Foreign Affairs Committee conducted an inquiry into the 'foreign policy aspects of the war against terrorism'. The group of MPs failed to notice that Britain's Saudi ally had been the major sponsor, for approximately three decades, of the terrorism it was meant to be investigating. Instead, the committee concluded that Saudi Arabia was 'taking very seriously the causes of terrorism and process of extremist recruitment' and was 'pursuing crucial long-term policies to tackle the causes of terrorism'. Indeed, Britain 'could usefully learn from Saudi Arabia's experience in this field, highlighting the two-way nature of cooperation with the Kingdom.'[79]

Britain continued to sign stupendous arms agreements with the Kingdom, notably the al-Yamamah 3 deal in December 2005 to supply Typhoon aircraft and other equipment worth an initial £8 billion, but possibly up to £40 billion. At the same time, allegations continued to surface concerning bribes from Britain's largest arms company, BAE Systems, to the Saudi regime, prompting an investigation by the Serious Fraud Office (SFO), which was extraordinarily stopped by Tony Blair in late 2006.[80] Blair argued that proceeding with the enquiry 'would have been devastating for our relationship with an important country with whom we cooperate closely on terrorism, on security, on the Middle East peace process.'[81]

Britain had around £15 billion worth of investments and joint ventures in Saudi Arabia, which was by far Britain's largest trading partner in the Middle East and its largest market for exports outside of OECD countries.[82] However, British ministers, notably Gordon Brown, as chancellor in Blair's government, led a push to deepen still further the financial interdependence between Britain and the Saudis and the wider Islamic world – a direct continuation of the policies decided on by Brown's Conservative predecessors in 1973. In 2006 and 2007 Brown and his then deputy at the treasury, Ed Balls, delivered half a dozen speeches all on the same theme – how to make the City of London the favoured destination for 'Islamic finance'. Brown noted in June 2006, for example, that following his recent visit to Saudi Arabia he 'saw how the City is becoming the investment location of choice for the Middle East and Muslim countries all over the world.'[83]

That same month, Britain hosted an Islamic Finance and Trade Conference organised by the Muslim Council of Britain. It was supported not only by the Foreign Office and the Department for Trade and Industry, but also by two Jeddah-based organisations, the Organisation of the Islamic Conference and the Islamic Development Bank, both well-established instruments of Saudi foreign policy. As the keynote speaker, Brown told the conference of his desire 'for making Britain the gateway to Islamic trade, to make Britain the global centre for Islamic finance.' 'Today', Brown said, 'British banks are pioneering Islamic banking', with London housing more banks supplying services under Islamic principles than any other Western financial centre. The chancellor also thanked the Muslim Council of Britain and others who had 'worked with the government through our tax and regulatory reform to support the development of Sharia compliant finance.'[84]

Ed Balls noted in 2007 that there were £250 billion worth of funds in the Islamic finance system, which was forecast to grow 15 per cent annually, and that 'we want to see more of this business coming to London'.[85] Britain was, Balls said, the largest European investor in Oman, the largest non-Arab investor in Egypt and the second largest investor in Saudi Arabia and Pakistan, with thirty-five trade offices in Muslim countries around the world.[86]

At the same time, the City of London was seeking to showcase itself to Gulf investors amid a financial boom that was sweeping the Middle East before the global financial crisis struck in 2008. Awash with cash from record oil prices, the six countries of the Gulf Cooperation Council (Saudi Arabia, Kuwait, the UAE, Bahrain, Qatar and Oman) had launched massive public and private investment drives to raise oil and gas output and develop sectors such as tourism and financial services. Western banks and companies 'have been rushing to the region to capitalise on the business opportunities', the *Financial Times* reported.[87] Oil-rich Middle East investment funds now have $1.5 trillion under their management, while the City has become the world's central petrodollar recycling plant, where oil dollars are invested, lent or traded and pumped back into the global economy. These petrodollars have emerged as one of the key drivers of the international equity markets, as well as a main source of liquidity and financing for hedge funds, private equity, currency traders and governments.[88]

Saudi Arabia's importance to Britain also involved its 'commitment to keeping the oil market well supplied and, as far as possible, price stable.'[89] When the oil price shot up in early 2008 to over $100 a barrel, sparking major fuel price rises in Britain and worldwide, Gordon Brown did as his predecessors in the Conservative and Labour governments of 1973–75; he not only visited Saudi Arabia to persuade the Saudis to increase oil supply and reduce prices, he also offered Britain as a location for the Saudis and other oil producers to invest their 'very substantial revenues'.[90]

These policies ensured that the British economy was set to become ever more intertwined with the Islamic financial system, in turn deepening British dependence on the state champions of extremist Islam, the Saudis, and Britain's other traditional allies in the region, the Gulf sheikhdoms. The whole strategy depended, however, on Middle Eastern regimes and companies being willing to invest in Britain; which in turn depended on British ministers being sufficiently sycophantic towards their feudal clients and on those rulers maintaining their power, and thus on preserving the traditional political and economic order in the Middle East. The new prize for the City was only attainable with the cooperation of the leading forces in the Islamic world. It is hard not to view the outreach to the Muslim Brotherhood, and indeed the policies that contributed to Londonistan, as part of the same broad strategy.

Severely muddying the waters, however, were Iraq and Afghanistan, where British policy was being further challenged, and which again reveals the resort to working with Islamist forces to achieve objectives.

CHAPTER 19

Allied to the Enemy: Iraq and Afghanistan

ANGLO-AMERICAN ATTEMPTS TO shape the Middle East in accordance with their interests have largely failed in Iraq and Afghanistan. In Iraq, planners have been unable to impose their will on the country following the March 2003 invasion and US strategy, with Britain in tow, has continually, and often desperately, shifted. The impact of the occupation has been devastating - the number of deaths has been fiercely contested but is likely to be in the hundreds of thousands, and possibly over a million.[1]

Initially, the Bush administration believed it would simply install favoured pro-US Iraqi exiles in power in Baghdad. When it became clear these figures were unpopular and incapable, the US resorted to direct rule to try to install a neo-conservative state. When this dream largely evaporated, Washington gave in to the demand for free elections, which it initially opposed, and which mainly empowered the Shias in the centre and south of the country and the Kurds in the north.[2] Faced with a rising resistance movement among both Sunnis and Shias, Washington then embarked on a 'surge' in the number of US forces and an attempt to incorporate Sunni groups into its military strategy, reversing the original policy of 'de-Baathification' which had purged Iraqi institutions of personnel from Saddam's ruling party. In 2008, the US announced that its combat troops would withdraw from Iraqi cities in 2009 and from the whole country by the end of 2011, a decision later implemented by Bush's successor, Barack Obama. Despite holding several elections, Iraq has been far from having a truly representative, accountable government able to provide security and basic services to the population. Rather, the elected Iraqi governments, notably those under Shia prime minister Nouri al-Maliki after 2006, have become increasingly authoritarian while the country has become increasingly divided along sectarian lines.

In invading, Britain and the US sought to maintain overall control over Iraq's oil by ensuring a strong, pro-Western government in Baghdad, to establish bases in the country to police the region and to further resist the spread of Iranian influence. Their strategy has been confronted by various strands of resistance to the occupation, including Sunni nationalist groups in the centre of the country, Shia militias in Baghdad and terrorists linked to al-Qaida who have conducted numerous suicide bombings. Al-Qaida was initially handed a massive boost by the occupation, seeing the war as a further opportunity for recruiting jihadists, though its importance as a strategic actor in Iraq has declined since the death of its leader in Iraq, Abu Musab al-Zarqawi, in 2006. Washington and London have also had to contend with regional states competing to promote their interests in post-Saddam Iraq. Iran has been supporting Shia groups, trying to prevent a return to a Sunni-run dictatorship. Syria has wanted to see a pro-Damascus regime in Baghdad and has been backing some of the Sunni insurgents. Turkey is opposed to an independent or more powerful Kurdistan in the north, for fear of the effects on its own Kurdish minority.

The important aspect of the invasion and occupation of Iraq related to the story in this book is how Britain – following the US lead – worked through Islamist groups to try and achieve its goals, or, rather, to mitigate its failure in Iraq. In predominantly Shia southern Iraq, where Britain led the occupying forces until its withdrawal of combat troops in 2009, it relied on some, while opposing other, Shia militias to enforce 'order' and, eventually, its own exit. In the centre of the country, a similarly sectarian strategy was supported by Britain, in backing US attempts to arm and empower Sunni groups, some of whom had links to al-Qaida, to counter the insurgency.

ISLAMISING SOUTHERN IRAQ

The lead for working with certain Shia forces in Iraq was set by Washington. In the 1990s, the Clinton, Major and Blair governments had regular contacts with the principal Shia opposition force in Iraq, the Supreme Council for the Islamic Revolution in Iraq (SCIRI), based in and supported by Tehran, as discussed in Chapter 13. The Shias, who made up the majority of the population, had been brutally suppressed under Saddam's rule, and Sunnis had dominated Iraq ever since Britain had created the country and put King Faisal on the throne in 1921. In August 2002, in the run-up to the invasion, the US invited SCIRI to an opposition gathering in Washington, along with five other groups. SCIRI also played a prominent part in pre-invasion opposition conferences in London in December 2002 and in Iraqi Kurdistan in February 2003.[3] British officials were in regular contact with SCIRI both in London and Tehran at the time of the invasion.[4]

US planning for post-invasion Iraq was partly based on empowering SCIRI and other Shia leaders who were promised key roles in the country's future, while SCIRI's paramilitary arm, the Badr Corps, remained armed with US acquiescence after the invasion. Washington may have sought to establish a new centre of Shi'ism in Iraq to counter that in Iran – perhaps seeing Najaf, the Iraqi shrine city that is the holiest place in Shia Islam, replacing Qom, the clerical centre in Iran.[5] For its part, SCIRI opted to accept key positions inside US-established institutions to benefit from US protection while moving the political process forward in its favour.[6]

Washington has since regarded SCIRI – which removed the

word 'revolution' from its name in 2007 to become the Islamic Supreme Council of Iraq (ISCI) – as its 'privileged instrument' with which it is in a 'cosy relationship', according to the International Crisis Group.[7]

ISCI's former leader, Abdul Aziz al-Hakim, who was succeeded by his son, Ammar, on his death in 2009, was cast as a moderate by the US and Britain, meeting President George Bush at the White House in 2004 and in 2006. Then Foreign Secretary Jack Straw described having 'good relations' with al-Hakim in March 2006, while in January 2007 then Defence Secretary Des Browne met al-Hakim in Baghdad, describing him as 'a very devout man'.[8] When al-Hakim visited London in December 2006, Browne described him as 'a very significant player in Iraqi politics' due to his position as head of the United Iraqi Alliance, a coalition of mainly Shia-based political parties. His family had suffered violence at the hands of the Saddam regime and he 'personally has made a significant contribution to freedom in his country'; Browne added that he 'had views to which we should listen'.[9]

While some ISCI ministers have served in the Iraqi government, its politics are hard to pinpoint precisely, sometimes projecting itself as a theocratic force supportive of Iran and sometimes as a more independent Iraqi nationalist force appealing to Shia moderates; overall, the organisation is pragmatic, wanting to lead the Shia community in Iraq.[10] As seen from London and Washington, the main utility of ISCI and its Badr army, which was then believed to have around 10,000 fighters, was as a counter to the forces of the 'extremist' Shia cleric Moqtada al-Sadr and his Jaish al-Mahdi (Mahdi army), a militia force centred in Baghdad which conducted numerous attacks on British and US forces. Yet as regards the imposition of Islamic law, ISCI may well be no more moderate than the Sadrists; although there are differences on which aspects of Islamic law should be enforced, there is a consensus among both groups on the idea of a sharia law-based society and the monopoly of the higher clergy in interpreting Islamic traditions.[11] ISCI is a more conservative, elitist Islamist force, based in the shrine cities of Najaf and Karbala, representing the Shia middle class and with little popularity in the country. The Sadrists, by contrast, are a mass-based movement centred in Baghdad and with a base in many of the poorer Shia districts of the country. All militias have indulged in atrocities in Iraq; Anglo–American connivance with ISCI developed while the latter established secret detention centres, practicing torture on its enemies and sending out death squads to assassinate opponents.[12]

The province of Basra in the south of the country, the site of the country's main oil fields, underwent a rapid Islamisation under the British occupation. Almost immediately after the fall of Saddam's regime, Shia militias established a presence in the universities and hospitals which they gradually took over through intimidation and violence.[13] The local power apparatus soon fragmented into partisan fiefdoms under the control of the three main Shia militia groups: ISCI, which was influential in the intelligence service; the Sadrists, who dominated the local police force; and Fadhila, an offshoot of the Sadrists, who controlled the Oil Protection Force (the unit responsible for safeguarding the oil wells).[14] Though the situation was complex and involved shifting tactics on the ground, Britain's initial policy, as per the American, was essentially to rely on and side with ISCI to counter the other two militias, in particular the Mahdi army.

A study by the Washington Institute for Near East Policy noted that ISCI met the British military on a daily basis throughout the early summer of 2003, after which 'it became a favoured partner of the British on interim advisory councils across the south'. ISCI was given provincial governorships, council seats and police chief appointments as these institutions were established. At the same time, groups and individuals associated with ISCI 'used police supplied intelligence to undertake targeted killings of Sunnis and Shiites accused of Baath-era crimes'. Although the British were aware of these actions, 'the movement's careful courting of the coalition ... shielded it from further scrutiny.'[15]

Subsequently, British policy towards the Shia militias varied incongruously from trying to counter them to turning a blind eye to their brutal activities, through to direct support for them. The failure of the British forces to provide adequate security for the population after the collapse of the state meant that the vacuum was filled by the militias. Indeed, the British were widely accused in Basra province of 'handing off power to militia elements and afterward turning a blind eye to the wholesale intimidation and murder practiced by Islamist militias to preserve a permissive environment for its troops.' Even more incriminating, one British general was quoted as referring to his 'pragmatic use of the militias', with the occupation force headquarters in the south paying bribes to key tribes north of Basra in barely concealed protection rackets.[16] Other British commanders confirmed that Britain doled out cash to some insurgents, though no details emerged on the recipients.[17] At other times, the British mounted attempts to eliminate the Shia militias, such as Operation Sinbad, which ran from September 2006 to March 2007 and sought to root out local militias and hand over security to vetted Iraqi security forces. But these attempts were periodic only, and often had the effect of accelerating the militias' penetration of the police and army.[18]

In December 2007, the British government announced the 'handover' of its 'security responsibility' for Basra province to the Iraqi authorities. This was faithfully reported by the British media as a transfer of security to the Iraqi army and police, and also as a 'withdrawal'. In reality, the handover was essentially to the Shia militias who had long controlled Basra province. The International Crisis Group had already reported in 2007 that Basra was controlled by militias and that whatever semblance of order existed there was due to a balance of power between them; security forces acted only as bystanders, at worst as one or another side's accomplice.[19] Another US study noted that the south had become a '"kleptocracy" where well-armed political–criminal Mafiosi have locked both the central government and the people out of power.'[20]

Retired US general, Jack Keane, said that Britain was helping to turn Basra into a city of 'gangland warfare'.[21]

Shia militias' control of the province was evident in the fact that British intelligence made an apparent deal with them not to attack Britain's retreating forces. British officers released 26 Mahdi army prisoners, including some 'grade A terrorists', in the run-up to withdrawing from their base at Saddam Hussein's former palace in September 2007, for example. This was intended to 'help the British leave Basra without having to conduct a fighting withdrawal,' the *Guardian* reported.[22] The government denied that a deal had been made but conceded that it had been talking to Mahdi army officials from the summer of 2007 through to the end of the year.[23] The Ministry of Defence stated that 'we will work with any groups wishing to reduce violence and join the democratic process working towards a safer and prosperous Iraq', a comment showing that (unintended) humour remains a feature of government public relations operations.[24] A senior British official was reported as saying that 'our leaving basically means that the extremist militias have less excuse to engage in lawlessness and violence.'[25]

Another part of this apparent deal was a restriction on British forces' movements into Basra city. When the Iraqi government under Prime Minister Nouri al-Maliki launched a surprise assault on the Shia militias in Basra in March 2008 – known as Operation Charge of the Knights – bitter street battles killed dozens of militiamen, but 4,000 British troops 'watched from the sidelines for six days' and no British soldier was able to enter Basra without the approval of then Defence Secretary Des Browne.[26] The Ministry of Defence denied that a deal had been done, while Air Chief Marshall Sir Jock Stirrup, chief of the defence staff, later claimed that the operation was the 'crowning success' of the British policy of training Iraqi forces to deal with security; he added that 'we drew up plans to confront the militias but the Iraqi government did not want us to implement them'.[27]

As for the 'withdrawal', in October 2007 the government

announced that the British army would 'protect the border and supply routes' and 'come to the assistance of the Iraqi security forces when called upon', and then would move to an 'overwatch' function which would retain a 're-intervention capability'.[28] In December 2008, Gordon Brown announced that most of Britain's 4,100 troops would withdraw by July 2009, but that 300 would remain to train the Iraqi navy to patrol the waters around the southern port of Umm Qasr, near most of Iraq's oil fields. When, on 30 April 2009, the British declared an end to combat operations, and began to hand over 'military authority' in Basra, ostensibly to a US force, Brown said that 'we hope to sign an agreement with the Iraqi government about the future role that we can play in training and in protecting the oil supplies of Iraq.'[29] Some British military personnel would also remain at US military headquarters in Basra.[30]

'The great majority of people in Basra were glad to see the British go,' wrote the *Independent*'s Patrick Cockburn from the city. A BBC poll conducted in Basra found that 2 per cent of people believed the British presence had had a positive impact on the province since 2003, while 86 per cent said the impact had been negative.[31] The increasing power and influence of the Shia militias in southern Iraq ensured that secular forces were eclipsed. In the early summer of 2003, southern Iraq might have avoided being handed over to the militias, when various nationalist and socialist politicians and professionals were offering an alternative to the Islamists; yet 'the moment passed and was never to come again'.[32] The Islamist takeover ensured that women, liberal progressives and secularists such as university lecturers and human rights campaigners disappeared from the provincial and municipal councils, and from public life. The region divided along ethnic, tribal and political lines while British and US support of one side, ISCI, helped to polarise the Shia community further, exacerbating the conditions for endemic intra-Shia conflict.[33]

The irony is that London and Washington were backing the

main force, ISCI, also seen by Tehran as its primary ally and vehicle in Iraq; Iran was widely believed to be providing the organisation's Badr army with weapons and training. As the Norwegian expert on Iraq, Reidar Visser, noted, 'US forces are working round the clock to weaken Tehran's traditional arch-enemy in Iraq's Shiite heartland – the Sadrists – while Iran's preferred and privileged partner since the 1980s, ISCI, keeps strengthening its influence everywhere.'[34] The various warnings within US policy-making circles that Iran would become the main beneficiary of the US strategy were apparently brushed aside. One reason is that the hawks likely believed that the Shias they were promoting were uninterested in replicating an Iran-style theocracy in Iraq.[35] But the major, more pragmatic, reason for backing ISCI is that London and Washington viewed the Sadrists' Mahdi army as their greater opponent and the Shia militias as the major power-brokers in the south.

In the centre of the country, the situation was different in that the occupation forces were dealing with a predominantly Sunni insurgency, concerning which the US performed a spectacular U-turn in 2006 by attempting to bring Sunnis more directly into the political process. The previous policy of de-Baathification was abandoned and personnel previously loyal to Saddam were encouraged to return to their jobs and senior Sunni generals encouraged to rejoin the army.[36] Lacking other key partners, the US began to cultivate Sunni tribal chiefs and local sheikhs to lure them away from the insurgency. Moreover, in June 2007 the US risked exacerbating the developing civil war by beginning to arm some of the Sunni insurgent groups, some of whom were 'suspected of involvement in past attacks on American troops or of having links to such groups,' the *New York Times* reported. Many members of these groups, known as the wakening Councils or the Sons of Iraq, also had connections with al-Qaida in Mesopotamia, a terrorist organisation which President Bush accused of having links to al-Qaida's central leadership.[37] In return for receiving US weapons the Sunni groups agreed to focus their attacks on al-Qaida and not on US troops. Washington's strategy was intended to drive a wedge between two wings of the Sunni insurgency – Baathists loyal to Saddam and Islamist militants linked to al-Qaida – which had often previously worked in alliance; the policy 'could amount to the American's arming both sides in a future civil war,' the *New York Times* pointed out.[38] By the end of 2007, the Awakening Councils numbered over 100,000 personnel, on whom the US had spent $17 million, including paying their salaries. They were credited with chasing pro-al-Qaida jihadists out of al-Anbar province but also accused of corruption, extortion and brutal tactics.[39] The Iraqi government announced the disbandment of these Sunni militias in April 2009. By this time, the militias were being accused of conducting a surge of violence, including car bombings, across Baghdad.[40]

The then US commander in Iraq, General David Petraeus, gave explicit credit for this empowerment of Sunni militias to British commanders. British forces were 'hugely useful' in strengthening the coalition 'with diplomatic skills and experience learnt in Northern Ireland,' he said.[41] When Gordon Brown was asked in a press conference in October 2007 about the US strategy, he replied: 'On this issue of training people or arming people, look, we are building up security forces in Iraq in a way that hasn't happened as quickly as it should have but it is happening now … So yes, it is right that the Americans train up security forces.'[42]

Overall, British expediency, of working with whatever forces to promote their interests, in a situation of political weakness and widespread local opposition to the British presence, was again in evidence during the occupation of Iraq. In particular, British policies reinforced sectarian and factional fault-lines, an outcome typical of the colonial strategy of divide and rule, with grave mmediate, and uncertain long-term, consequences for the people of Iraq and the wider region.

AFGHANISTAN: THE NEW GREAT GAME

Britain's current war in Afghanistan is relevant to the story in this book in two main respects. First, because Britain is now fighting Islamist forces it previously covertly supported, a fact which continues to go largely unnoticed in the mainstream media. Second, because Whitehall is again in effect colluding with Islamist actors to salvage what it can from Afghanistan and achieve fundamental foreign policy objectives. This entails, on the one hand, dealing with elements within the Taliban to promote a familiar divide and rule strategy in the country and, on the other, collaborating with Pakistan when it is in reality extending a second round of support to Afghan insurgents following that in the 1990s, when Islamabad largely created the Taliban to rule Afghanistan.

The war in the southern Afghan province of Helmand, bordering Pakistan, has gradually escalated since the initial British deployment, formally part of NATO's International Security Assistance Force (ISAF), in May 2006. The original British force of 3,300 troops was increased to 5,500 in the autumn of 2006, to 7,800 by the summer of 2007, and to 8,100 in summer 2008, while in December 2009 Gordon Brown announced a still further increase to bring the total combat troops to around 10,000, including 500 special forces. British arms have included Harrier attack aircraft, Apache helicopters and 'enhanced blast' thermobaric weapons, which ignite a fine mist of fuel creating massive explosions.[43] The US has similarly increased its forces – President Obama announced an extra 17,000 troops for southern Afghanistan in February 2009 and a further 30,000 in December 2009. Faced with the prospect of military defeat and an increasingly unpopular war in Britain, David Cameron announced soon after becoming prime minister in May 2010 that all British combat troops would withdraw from Afghanistan by 2015, though some forces for training purposes could remain.[44]

Defence Secretary in Gordon Brown's Labour government, Des Browne, said that the Taliban 'were bound to oppose improved security and, indeed, the Taliban overtly said that this is what they would do as we and others ... entered the south of the country.'[45]

Thus Whitehall was fully expecting to provoke a full-scale war. When Afghan President Hamid Karzai criticised the British deployment in January 2008, telling a press conference that 'when they came in, the Taliban came', he was simply repeating what British officials already knew, though this didn't stop them reacting with fury at Karzai's comment.[46] An academic paper by two members of the UN mission in Afghanistan, UNAMA, similarly notes that ISAF's military operations since 2001 have 'pushed' anti-government elements 'towards active insurgency'.[47]

Thus the British fear – that the withdrawal of NATO forces would mean a Taliban takeover of the country – has become a self-fulfilling prophecy. A confidential August 2009 report by General Stanley McChrystal, the US military commander in Afghanistan, stated that 'the overall situation is deteriorating' and that NATO faced a 'resilient and growing insurgency'.[48] By late 2009, the Taliban had 'shadow governors' in thirty-three out of thirty-four Afghan provinces, up from twenty in 2006, and a permanent presence in 80 per cent of the country, compared to 54 per cent at the end of 2007.[49] Meanwhile, the war has gradually intensified. In 2009, for example, there were over 7,000 attacks using roadside bombs, a threefold increase over 2007.[50] Lieutenant General David Richards, the former Commander of British Forces in Afghanistan who became chief of the general staff, described the fighting as 'probably as intense as anything the British army has seen since Korea'.[51] This was well before 2009, a year when British casualties rose to their highest level since the Falklands War, to over 100 during the year. By the end of 2011, nearly 400 British troops had been killed and over 1,800 wounded in action in Afghanistan.[52]

During 2001–05, some analysis suggests that the Afghan population largely supported the government, but in 2006–07, public opinion began to shift in favour of anti-government elements in unstable areas and by late 2008 the population was voluntarily providing support to the insurgents.[53] British policy is likely a bigger recruiting sergeant for the Taliban than al-Qaida. ISAF's Director of Intelligence, Major General Michael Flynn, provided a briefing in December 2009 that outlined information given by militants to ISAF. It stated that they 'view Al Qaeda as a handicap', and that they were motivated by the government being seen as corrupt and ineffective, by crime and corruption being pervasive among the security forces and because promised infrastructure projects have been ineffective.[54] Despite billions of dollars in aid allocated to Afghanistan in recent years, development is meagre as a third of the population goes hungry and 73 per cent have no access to safe drinking water.[55] Human rights, notably for women, are deteriorating again, after an improvement following the fall of the Taliban in 2001, while the Afghan government, although elected, is as corrupt as ever and unwilling or unable to satisfy peoples' basic needs.

Reports also suggest that many Afghans have turned towards the Taliban due to the high civilian casualties inflicted on the population, notably by the policy of bombing villages sheltering Taliban fighters – traditional British imperial practice in the Middle East since the 1920s but now carried out by the US. Civilian casualties from the fighting have risen every year since 2001, and the number of deaths was estimated by the UN to be nearly 9,000 up to the end of 2010.[56] Roughly a third of these are attributable to coalition or government forces.[57] Of course, British forces realise the need to keep civilian casualties to a minimum: as Lieutenant General Nick Houghton, the MoD's chief of joint operations, has explained: 'we recognise that the kinetic eradication of the Taliban is not a sensible option and would act to alienate both the public locally and internationally.'[58] But while British and US leaders stress that all steps are taken to minimise civilian casualties, Human Rights Watch said in January 2010 that 'the US and NATO have a poor track record in holding their forces accountable for attacks in violation of the laws of war that cause civilian deaths and injury.'[59] Equally, ISAF's own confidential report of August 2009 concedes that its military strategy was causing 'unnecessary collateral damage'.[60] While British and US leaders publicly stress that their military actions are proportionate, US Lieutenant Colonel David Kilcullen said in 2009 that US aerial attacks in the Afghan–Pakistan border area have killed 14 al-Qaida leaders at the expense of 700 civilian lives.[61]

David Cameron's government came into office saying that Afghanistan was its 'top foreign policy priority' and that the war was 'vital to our national security'.[62] However, British objectives had by now been severely downgraded. Foreign Minister Alastair Burt bluntly said in November 2010 that 'there was never any question that Afghanistan was going to be some form of military victory'.[63] Foreign Secretary William Hague said that the objective in Afghanistan was to help the country 'maintain its own security and prevent al-Qaida from returning' and to 'assist the government of Afghanistan in exercising its authority and influence across the country, paving the way for reconstruction and effective governance'.[64] Yet a parliamentary enquiry report of February 2011 noted that the recent US military surge 'has created more insecurity' and that security in the country 'was worse than at any point in the past thirty years'. Many independent witnesses to the enquiry gave evidence to the effect that the large-scale presence of troops in southern Afghanistan 'is one of the main causes of the conflict and that it specifically impedes Afghan peacemaking efforts', because it reduces the pressure on the Afghan elite to make peace, because the Afghan government cannot deliver on any peace deal for as long as military strategy is outside its control and because the Taliban are less likely to make peace with a government under foreign domination.[65]

The military leaders of the Afghan insurgency inflicting casualties on the British are a roll call of those supported by Whitehall in the 1980s. The past is again returning to haunt British policy in Afghanistan, and British soldiers, along with Afghan civilians, are paying the highest price for this blowback. One major insurgent leader is Jalalludin Haqqani, whose 'Haqqani network', a group of militants which includes his son, Sirajuddin, is spearheading the war against NATO and government forces.[66] Now in his seventies, Jalalludin Haqqani was a military leader in the US-backed Younis Khalis faction of the Hezb-e-Islami group in the 1980s, and worked with the US and ISI to train and deploy volunteer mujahideen fighters to fight the Soviets.[67] Britain also supported the Khalis faction in the 1980s, providing training and missiles to one of Haqqani's commanders, Hadji Abdul Haq. One of Khalis' junior commanders in the 1980s was Mohammed Omar, now Mullah Omar, the present overall leader of the Taliban whose closest aide is now Haqqani.

The Haqqani network has been provided with huge stockpiles of arms and ammunition by Mullah Omar and been charged with coordinating suicide attacks throughout the country. It is believed to have been behind the deadly July 2008 attack on the Indian embassy in Kabul which killed 58 people.[68] Haqqani is also suspected of running much of the insurgency in Kabul and eastern Afghanistan, carrying out car bombings and kidnappings, including spectacular attacks on US military installations. Sirajuddin Haqqani is reported as being based in North Waziristan in Pakistan, where he controls military operations spanning al-Qaida, Pakistani and Afghan fighters.[69]

Another military commander in Afghanistan is Gulbuddin Hekmatyar, whose faction of the Hezb-e-Islami has organised various bombings of government and foreign forces, such as one attack in August 2008 that killed 10 French soldiers. Hekmatyar said in a rare interview that his fighters helped Bin Laden escape from the US offensive in the Tora Bora mountains of Afghanistan after 9/11.[70] Now in his early sixties, Whitehall officials met Hekmatyar at least twice during the 1980s and provided covert aid and training to this ruthless killer to enable his forces to fight the Soviets.[71]

Furthermore, both Haqqani and Hekmatyar are reportedly being protected by Pakistan's ISI, and covertly supported by its

S wing, which directs operations outside Pakistan. The Haqqani network is considered a 'strategic asset to Pakistan', according to US and Pakistani officials consulted by the *New York Times*. The ISI provides fuel, ammunition and new recruits from Pakistani madrassas to the militant groups, and also tips them off when the US plans military missions against them.[72] Hekmatyar maintains several bases not only in Afghanistan but also in Afghan refugee camps in Khyber Pakhtunkhwa province of northern Pakistan, running madrassas and a weekly journal.[73] It is thus difficult to square British support for Islamabad with confronting the Taliban in Afghanistan.

Furthermore, Britain is again in effect colluding with Afghan Islamist forces, albeit in a very different way than in the past. Knowing that a purely military conflict with the Taliban is unwinnable, and with flagging domestic political support as British casualties rise, Britain has been forced to pursue a political end to the war by promoting negotiations with the Taliban. A rather desperate Whitehall is now dependent on cultivating relations, and reaching agreement, with radical Islamist elements to secure its exit from Afghanistan.

The Brown government's analysis, which appears to be shared by its Conservative/Liberal Democrat successor, was that there is 'no single authoritative leadership of the insurgency in either Afghanistan or Pakistan', and that the 'Taliban' consists of at least six main factions: the insurgency in the south, including Helmand, which has the largest number of fighters and is led by Mullah Omar; the Haqqani and Hekmatyar groups in the east; and three groups in Waziristan in Pakistan belonging to tribes with 'different motivations'. In this situation, British strategy is to 'fragment the various elements of the insurgency' and 'separate the hard-line ideologues ... from those who can be drawn into domestic political processes'.[74] The Foreign Office's analysis is that 'the UK's interest is in exploiting existing, and creating future, vulnerabilities in the insurgency in order to allow the Afghan government to split and coopt significant elements.' Those who cannot be reconciled will be 'isolated' and 'will need to be defeated militarily'.[75]

Britain is prepared to deal with any elements, including hard-line Islamists, provided they have a domestic focus rather than a global one. Thus British strategy is one of 'separating those who want Islamic rule locally from those committed to violent jihad globally'; the former can be part of an 'inclusive political settlement'.[76] 'The truth is that a lot of those who are fighting under the Taliban label are not global jihadists,' Gordon Brown's foreign secretary, David Miliband noted.[77] Britain's other conditions for talks are that fighters should abide by the constitution, renounce violence and have no 'close operational links' to al-Qaida – the word 'close' being noticeable.[78] When the British army released a new counter-insurgency manual in November 2009, advocating talks with the enemy, Major-General Paul Newton, launching the document, said that 'there's no point talking to people who don't have blood on their hands'.[79]

That Britain has a purely pragmatic, expedient stance in dealing with extremist forces was confirmed by Britain's then ambassador to Afghanistan, Mark Sedwill, who said that it is wrong to describe the government as talking to 'moderate' Taliban, as the media has reported, 'because it suggests there is a spectrum of ideology and ... this isn't the way in which we expect to go'. It 'isn't a question of moderation or not moderation; it isn't really about their beliefs. It's about their affiliations and the reasons they drifted into the insurgency in the first place.'[80]

Whitehall has supported Saudi Arabia's hosting of a meeting between the Afghan government, 'former Taleban insurgents' and a representative of Gulbuddin Hekmatyar, in September 2008, and subsequent other initiatives aimed at negotiating an end to the conflict.[81] But the British government has also reportedly had direct contacts with the Taliban.[82] By mid-2009, the mainstream media was reporting new British efforts to talk to the Taliban and that the British had been instigating contacts with Taliban commanders for more than a year.[83] In fact, such efforts go back much further. Even before the 2006 British deployment in Helmand, Britain was promoting secret negotiations with Taliban leaders to achieve a political solution to the conflict. As long ago as March 2004, for example, a little-known meeting took place between then Foreign Secretary Jack Straw and Maulana Fazlur Rahman, a pro-Taliban 'firebrand cleric' who is president of the Jamiat Ulema-e-Islam (JUI) Party in Pakistan which ran and sponsored the madrassa network out of which the Taliban developed.[84] The JUI was the driving force in the coalition of six religious parties in the Pakistani National Assembly and is also politically aligned to the HUM terrorist group.[85] At their meeting, which was organised in Pakistan by the British High Commissioner, Straw reportedly asked Rahman to mediate in talks with the Taliban. Rahman told a local journalist: 'The British authorities are working on behalf of the United States. This indirect process has been chosen to avoid any ill-effects ahead of the forthcoming presidential elections in America ... Britain is holding indirect talks with the Taliban militia to seek an honourable American exit from Afghanistan.' Rahman also said that, following the meeting, 'I was invited to different institutions which work under the British Foreign Office', and on a visit to London in March 2004 he held a further meeting with Foreign Office minister, Mike O'Brien.[86] A Foreign Office minute of March 2004, obtained by the author under a Freedom of Information Act request, notes that the Foreign Office regarded Rahman as 'a significant figure in Pakistani politics with whom we are keen to engage'.[87] Thus Britain was again negotiating with a leading extremist Islamist group, in order to help the Americans, and was apparently open to working further with it. In August 2009, Rahman met US negotiators in Islamabad, as part of President Obama's policy of 'reaching out to some of Pakistan's most fervent Islamist and anti-American parties', Pakistan's reputed *Dawn* newspaper commented.[88]

The strategy of sowing divisions in the insurgency is being

coordinated with the US, and is similar to that pursued in Iraq. Indeed, the US recruited British Lieutenant-General, Sir Graeme Lamb, to help divide the Afghan insurgency and separate fighters from their leaders; Lamb was also involved in the US strategy in Iraq, working with Sunni tribes to break with the insurgency and al-Qaida.[89] The strategy has included an innocent-sounding US plan called the Community Defence Initiative, entailing US special forces embedding themselves with anti-Taliban militias which are provided with training, support and development aid for their communities.[90]

Simple bribes have been another aspect of the British divide and rule strategy, a policy familiar to students of British history. British intelligence officers have for years spent money on Afghan warlords to keep them onside.[91] 'The judicious use of money can help persuade both individuals and groups to accept the authority and legitimacy of the host government,' the army counter-insurgency field manual states. It adds that money 'can be a substitute for force', offering 'a cost-effective means for pulling community support away from the insurgents.'[92] This policy again appears to be coordinated with the US. In November 2009, the Obama administration announced a $5 billion civilian aid package to Afghanistan, including funds to woo low- and mid-level commanders away from the insurgency, providing 'quick cash to locals for construction or security needs'.[93]

The war in Afghanistan amounts to a new period of competition over resources and great power rivalry in Central Asia. General Sir Richard Dannatt, then chief of the general staff, said in a speech to the International Institute for Strategic Studies in London in late 2007 that Britain 'is well into a new and deadly Great Game in Afghanistan – only this time with a different adversary.'[94] The new Great Game is motivated by several factors other than the ostensible one of defeating terrorism, which have been clearly spelt out by ministers and military leaders but have largely passed unmentioned in the British media. The key issue is the ongoing British and US desire to control the crucial Middle East and Central Asia regions, in the face of the immense challenges to their position there. 'The entire region in which Afghanistan sits is of vital strategic importance to the United Kingdom,' then Defence Secretary Bob Ainsworth said at Chatham House in London in July 2009.[95] In the next decade, two of the key challenges faced by Britain are 'competition for resources' and 'the rising economic and political power of Asia', Ainsworth noted in a speech on Afghanistan two months later.[96] But the war in Afghanistan is intimately bound up with Britain's very ability to conduct military intervention overseas. 'Failure in Afghanistan', Ainsworth has said, 'would embolden those who preach extremist violence' and also 'leave the UK and our armed forces with diminished support for action in the future and a tarnished reputation.'[97] This view was echoed by General Dannatt's successor as chief of the general staff, General David Richards, who told another Chatham House audience in September 2009 that 'success in Afghanistan is truly a grand strategic issue for our nation'. Key was the 'grand strategic impact on the UK's authority and reputation in the world of the defeat of the British armed forces and its impact on public sentiment in the UK.' Not only could Afghanistan become a base for exporting terrorism but the 'hugely intoxicating impact on extremists worldwide of the perceived defeat of the USA and NATO' might inspire still bigger threats.[98]

The British and Americans see a defeat for NATO in Afghanistan as challenging their global power, similar to the concerns articulated during the war in Kosovo in 1999. Thus the Foreign Office notes that Afghanistan is a 'test for the international community', especially the UN and NATO, and that 'failure for the international community would have far-reaching effects not only for regional security but also for the authority and credibility of those key multilateral institutions that underpin the UK's security and support for the international rule of law.'[99]

An additional factor in Afghanistan is the need for the British to uphold themselves to the US. General Dannatt said in May 2009 that Britain's 'military reputation and credibility' has been called into question 'in the eyes of our most important ally' due to 'some aspects of the Iraq campaign'. Therefore, 'taking steps to restore this credibility will be pivotal – and Afghanistan provides an opportunity.'[100]

These statements show that Afghanistan is not regarded by the British elite as an ordinary war but that fundamental foreign policy interests are at stake. Moreover, securing these increasingly depends not only on the application of military force but on the willingness of elements in the Taliban to play ball. Britain is now reliant on Islamist actors to secure what it would like to regard as an honourable exit from Afghanistan.

PAKISTAN: FRIEND OR FOE?

Britain continues to work closely with Pakistan in its Afghanistan policy, but numerous reports suggest that Islamabad is aiding the Taliban beyond the policy noted above of supporting Haqqani and Hekmatyar. Wikileaks files have revealed the US Ambassador in Islamabad, Anne Paterson, noting in September 2009 that Pakistan is covertly sponsoring four major militant groups, including the Afghan Taliban and Lashkar-e-Toiba.[101] The US media has reported that the ISI regularly holds strategy meetings with the Taliban, to discuss 'whether to intensify or scale-back violence' in Afghanistan.[102] Barnett Rubin, a former UN adviser on Afghanistan, has written that intelligence collected during Western military offensives as long ago as mid-2006 'confirmed' that the ISI was 'continuing to actively support the Taliban leadership, which is now working out of Quetta', the principal city in Pakistan's Baluchistan province. He added that 'the argument that poverty and underdevelopment, rather than Pakistani support, are responsible for the insurgency does not stand up to scrutiny.'[103] Pakistan has given the Taliban a free hand to operate from Quetta amidst Islamabad's huge military presence there. One reason is that Islamabad welcomes the Taliban's role in suppressing Balochi nationalist forces which threaten Pakistan's territorial integrity.[104]

British leaders have long been perfectly aware of Pakistan's role. In September 2006, for example, a confidential Ministry of Defence document leaked to the media 'suggested Pakistan's ISI intelligence agency was supporting the Taliban'. The leak coincided with then President Musharraf's state visit to Britain, and an embarrassed Downing Street issued the preposterous statement that the document 'did not reflect the views of the government'.[105] The British government has reportedly sent several dispatches to Islamabad asking that the ISI use its meetings with the Taliban to persuade the latter's commanders to reduce their attacks on Western forces, but the civilian government under President Asif Ali Zaradari has either been unable or unwilling to break the ties that bind the ISI to the militants.[106] Indeed, British military commanders in Afghanistan have long been reported as 'seething with anger at the ISI's support to the Taliban'.[107] Then Foreign Secretary David Miliband said in November 2009 that 'sometimes, they [the Taliban] take orders from a Taliban central command in Peshawar or Quetta.'[108] Colonel Chris Vernon, then the chief of staff for southern Afghanistan, has described how the Taliban's headquarters in Quetta has coordinated 'about 25' mid-level commanders across the Afghan south.[109]

The claim by some commentators that it is only renegade or former ISI officers who are supporting the Taliban appears false, and 'in truth the ISI are a disciplined force tightly controlled for the most part by the Pakistan military'.[110] The ISI has provided vital components to the Taliban for using Stinger missiles which have been fired at British and US pilots in Afghanistan.[111] According to a CIA assessment, elements in the ISI also worked with the Taliban to bomb the Indian embassy in Kabul in July 2008.[112] Similarly, a report by the Rand Corporation claimed that officers in Pakistan's Frontier Corps, which patrols the border areas with Afghanistan, even sometimes join the Taliban in attacking NATO and Afghan army forces.[113] This evidence is especially noteworthy in that the Frontier Corps is a key force in the Pakistani army that Britain is supporting as part of a £10 million aid package to Pakistan, announced in 2008 as 'the most comprehensive anti-terrorist programme Britain has signed with any country'.[114] Britain is building a training camp for the Corps in Baluchistan and will attach twenty-four military advisers to train its soldiers in a three-year programme that was to begin in late 2010.[115] The Pakistan army and ISI used elements of the Frontier Corps to help train and equip the mujahideen to fight the Soviets in the 1980s. One result of this policy was strong links between Corps soldiers and militants that persist to this day. Analysts suggest that a number of those who have enlisted for service in the Corps have been educated in Pakistani madrassas and are sympathetic to the militants.[116]

Crucially, Pakistan's present support for the Taliban is related to past British policy. Thus Adam Thomson, the Foreign Office's director of South Asia and Afghanistan, told a parliamentary enquiry that 'historically – at our behest, in part – the ISI developed relations with Islamic groups [in Afghanistan] ... It has not proved that easy for it, as an institution, to turn that off and to turn it around quickly.'[117] In submitting evidence to the same parliamentary enquiry, General Richards referred to Pakistan's 'twenty years of helping the Taliban, which is what they did historically, for understandable reasons at the time.'[118] Richards didn't elaborate why this was 'understandable' but he appeared to infer that Britain had little problem with it – a view that is certainly consistent with the historical evidence.

Pakistan continues to regard Afghanistan as part of its sphere of influence, the reason Islamabad cultivated the Taliban and ensured its takeover of the country between 1996 and 1998. Professor Shaun Gregory of the University of Bradford argues that Pakistan continued supporting the Taliban after 9/11, despite its public stance, since it regarded the Taliban as its best instrument for achieving its objectives in Afghanistan, notably an end to the NATO presence and Indian influence in the country.[119]

It is now hardly a secret that Islamabad has been playing a distinctly double game when it comes to tackling the pro-Taliban militant groups based in the northwest of Pakistan, notably the remote, mountainous Federally Administered Tribal Areas (FATA) region bordering Afghanistan. Around 500 foreign jihadists from Afghanistan, mostly Arabs, Uzbeks and Chechens, sought refuge there in late 2001, following the Anglo–American bombing campaign, with Bin Laden possibly among them.[120] It is from there that various militant Pakistani factions, as well as al-Qaida fighters, have planned and trained for numerous acts of terrorism in Pakistan and indeed in Britain, and also from there that cross-border attacks into Afghanistan have been launched, targeting British and NATO forces.[121] Pakistan has tried at different times to either appease or attack these militant groups. It first signed peace deals with some of them, as in 2004 and 2006, but then, faced with rising terrorist attacks in Pakistani cities, launched an all-out offensive operation, in the South Waziristan agency of FATA province, in late 2009, involving 30,000 troops.[122] Yet in both scenarios, the Afghan Taliban has been let off the hook. The peace deals provided de facto Pakistani permission for the Taliban to continue cross-border attacks against British forces in Afghanistan, provided that Pakistan itself was not targeted.[123] Similarly, the 2009 military offensive was aimed principally at just one faction of the Pakistani Taliban – that linked to the Mehsud tribe, the Tehrik-i-Taliban, which has battered Pakistan with around 80 per cent of the recent suicide attacks in the country. To conduct this offensive, the Pakistani army made deals with two other militant commanders, Maulvi Nazir and Hafiz Gul Bahadur, whose forces are fighting NATO troops in Afghanistan; the two groups promised to stay neutral during the fighting in return for which the Pakistani military would not attack them.[124]

Defying reality, present Conservative ministers have continued to deliver various speeches and statements praising Pakistan for helping to 'stabilise' Afghanistan. One rare exception came in July 2010, however, when, during his visit to India, David Cameron went furthest in publicising what British ministers have long known, accusing Pakistan of promoting 'the export of terror'.[125] Yet normal service was soon resumed. In April 2011, Cameron told a joint press conference with Pakistani prime minister Yousaf Gillani that 'we both have an interest in a peaceful, stable, democratic Afghanistan'.[126] The following month, he remarked that 'Pakistan has suffered more from terrorism than any other country in the world. Their enemy is our enemy. So far from walking away, we've got to work even more closely with them.'[127]

There are probably two key reasons for the conciliatory British stance towards Pakistan. First, as then prime minister Tony Blair reportedly insisted to the then commander of British forces in Afghanistan, General David Richards, Britain should 'go softly on Pakistan because of the ISI's cooperation with MI5 in catching Britain's domestic terrorists'.[128] This is a largely absurd position given the ISI's links with many of the terrorist groups connected to the same would-be British bombers the ISI is supposed to be investigating. Second, and more credible, as explained by then Defence Minister Adam Ingram, the British and NATO force in Afghanistan 'is dependent on Pakistani support for the provision of a logistical line of communication from Karachi, as well as permission for RAF overflights.'[129]

Thus the British war in Afghanistan has, if anything, reduced Whitehall's ability to influence Pakistan's sponsorship of terrorism. Indeed, the situation is truly absurd: in order to defeat the forces of the Taliban, Britain is dependent on their main ally. Britain's position is so weak that it has to rely on pro-Islamist forces to support the projection of British power, even when the strategy is self-defeating.

CHAPTER 20

Good and Bad Revolutions: The Arab Spring

The Conservative/Liberal Democrat coalition government under Prime Minister David Cameron took office in May 2010 at a time when Britain and its US ally not only faced a global financial crisis but also numerous political challenges in the Middle East. Although Britain had by now extricated its forces from Iraq, it was still fighting an unwinnable war in Afghanistan and was confronting an Iranian regime challenging several Western policies in the region. Elsewhere, instability threatened to cause chaos in nuclear-armed Pakistan, Israel's brutal blockade of Hamas-controlled Gaza threatened to spark further wars with the Palestinians while Somalia tottered on the brink of an Islamist takeover. Only the pro-Western regimes in North Africa and the Gulf appeared relatively stable.

But even this soon proved illusory as a period of revolutionary upheaval, not seen since the 1950s, rocked the Middle East in 2011. This witnessed the fall of longstanding dictatorships first in Tunisia in January, then in Egypt in February and finally in Libya in August, where Muammar Qadafi's regime was overthrown with the aid of British and French air strikes lasting seven months. By the end of 2011, Yemen's leader, Abdullah Ali Saleh had been forced to relinquish power to his deputy and Syria's dictator, Bashar Assad, was just clinging to power after months of protests bordering on civil war in which the regime killed over 5,000 people. At the same time, national elections saw Islamist parties voted into office in Tunisia and Morocco while in Egypt's parliamentary elections the Muslim Brotherhood secured more votes than any other party. During the regional turmoil, in May 2011, US forces conducted a raid on a 'safe house' in Pakistan finally killing Osama bin Laden. Indeed, by this time, the US, more often with British backing, was at war with virtually the entire Middle East, executing strikes from unmanned aerial vehicles – drones – in half a dozen countries in the region but mainly against Taliban militants in Pakistan and Afghanistan.

During the 'Arab Spring', British ministers, largely parrotted by the mainstream media, have consistently professed that their aims are to spread democracy and human rights throughout the region. Yet, what has rather been in evidence is Britain's exertion of military force to secure its oil and gas interests and its ongoing opposition to democracy, especially in the Gulf states. Both these policies contain elements of ongoing British collusion with radical Islamic actors.

REMAINING 'A MAJOR PLAYER IN THE WORLD'

The new government's key foreign policy priorities emerged soon after taking office. The overarching aim, as Cameron outlined in a speech at the Lord Mayor's Banquet in November 2010, was for Britain 'to remain a major player in the world'. Now, with the world's fourth largest 'defence' budget, Britain will 'remain one of only a handful of countries with the military, technological and logistical means to deploy serious military force around the world', Cameron said. He highlighted Britain's Joint Strike Fighter and Typhoon aircraft, a new aircraft carrier, seven new nuclear-powered hunter-killer submarines and Trident nuclear weapons, the latter described as 'our ultimate insurance policy in an age of uncertainty'.[1] The new government's *National Security Strategy*, released the previous month, similarly highlighted the need to 'project power … well beyond our shores'.[2]

Yet the task of maintaining Britain's power in the world is

being increasingly challenged by China and India, 'the world's two emerging superpowers', in the words of Cameron's Foreign Secretary William Hague, together with the broader shift in economic power 'to the countries of the South and the East', which also include Brazil, Turkey, Mexico and Indonesia.[3] This shift has been the focus of numerous speeches by British ministers, who clearly see it as a major new feature of international relations impacting on Britain's position in the world. Europe Minister David Lidington said in a speech in April 2011 that by 2050 only two European countries will be among the world's top ten economies. He argued: 'We cannot resist this shift, nor should we seek to'; rather, 'the question is how best we manage it. The challenge for us is to work out how we can best serve our national interests against this changing backdrop ... The world is shifting beneath our feet'.[4]

Ministers have outlined several ways, beyond the ability to deploy military force, to preserve British influence in this changed global context. One relates to Britain's commitment to increase its aid and reach the international target of 0.7 per cent of the national budget; aid is described by Cameron as 'the most visible example of Britain's global reach' and 'a powerful instrument of our foreign policy'.[5] Another is the policy of 'ramping up our support to British business', William Hague noted in May 2011 when he launched a 'Foreign Office Business Charter'. Hague told an audience at Ernst & Young that 'the Foreign Office must support British commerce more than ever before' and that 'commercial diplomacy will be central to all Foreign Office activities', also repeating that economic might was shifting towards the emerging powers and that Britain had to build stronger links with them.[6] The third priority is to remain 'the closest ally of the United States', as Hague informed Georgetown University in Washington in November 2010, reiterating Britain's 'first-rate' military intervention capabilities and noting 'five major military campaigns' that the US and Britain had fought together in recent years.[7] The special relationship is also sealed by British firms having invested nearly half a trillion dollars in the US economy.[8]

In the Middle East, the task of preserving British power and influence is harder than ever, and the two key challenges to policy-makers - in addition to the threat to British prestige posed by the Taliban's prospective defeat of British forces in Afghanistan - remain Iran and oil. The threat of Iran being a nuclear power able to extend its influence in the region has led to British ministers consistently holding out the prospect of military intervention against Tehran, largely in support of the US and Israel. William Hague told Parliament in September 2010 that 'the option of military action should not be withdrawn from the table' and the following month he said in a media interview: 'I'm certainly not calling for a military intervention but none of us in, among the NATO countries have ever taken off the table the prospect of a possibility of military action'.[9]

Indeed, in November 2011, media reports suggested that the British military was stepping up contingency planning for potential action against Iran amidst ongoing concerns about Tehran's nuclear enrichment programme. Military planners were reportedly examining where best to deploy Royal Navy ships and submarines equipped with Tomahawk cruise missiles as part of what would be an air and sea campaign.[10] The US under the Obama administration, meanwhile, has continued to issue directives authorizing covert action in Iran, notably to fund Iranian dissident groups through the US Agency for International Development, while Secretary of State Hillary Clinton has said that the US is 'doing a lot' to support the opposition in Iran.[11]

Continuing to ensure Western access to, and control over, Middle Eastern energy resources is now more complex than in the earlier postwar period and bound up with the emergence of the new global powers. Largely unnoticed by the mainstream media, British ministers in the coalition government have given speech after speech reiterating that 'access to existing and untapped [energy] resources is becoming more difficult' and that Britain is increasingly dependent on imported oil and gas: as production from the North Sea declines, imports of gas are expected to rise from

30 to 50 per cent of Britain's energy needs by 2020, for example.[12] In a speech in February 2011, Foreign Office Minister Lord David Howell said that 'we want to secure [energy] prices that are both predictable and affordable' but noted that they have recently been anything but, with oil prices reaching a record $147 per barrel in summer 2008 and then crashing to less than $40 six months later.[13]

As world energy consumption is predicted to double in the next 25 years, the fundamental challenge is that 'global competition for resources is rising' and leading to higher oil prices in an era when Western economies are already undergoing a financial crisis.[14] The British analysis is that its problems concerning oil and gas are principally caused by 'the pressures being exerted on world energy markets by the rapid growth of China and other emerging economies who are hungry for abundant and affordable energy'.[15] Howell notes that China recently overtook the US as the world's largest energy consumer and that 93 per cent of the increase in energy demand between now and 2030 will come from non-OECD countries.[16]

What ministers have been saying, with only a slight reading between the lines of these numerous speeches, is a repetition of the constant postwar mantra that who controls oil supplies will control the future of the world economy. In February 2011, Lord Howell told a conference in Japan on the subject of the 'future energy challenge' that:

> This new energy landscape requires a different, more agile diplomacy than in the past, to guarantee both our energy security and our wider safety. Energy issues are clearly both drivers of, and driven by, geopolitics. It is therefore right that energy policy is a high priority for our Foreign & Commonwealth Office. We recognise that the UK needs to work bilaterally and multilaterally to address the opportunities and challenges that the international environment poses. The present Middle East political turmoil presents an acutely vivid picture of the dangers to conventional energy patterns. Like

> Europe, Japan draws substantial oil supplies from that region. We must do all we can to ensure that legitimate aspirations for democracy and freedom are balanced with orderly political evolution in the countries and societies of the Middle East region, and to allow the peoples of the Arab world to work out their future in a context of stability.[17]

Howell's assertion that Britain's interest lay in 'stability' and an 'orderly political evolution' in the Middle East was instructive; it was issued 11 days after the fall of Hosni Mubarak in Egypt and as a popular uprising was gathering force against Qadafi in Libya, a major oil producer. Howell was clearly referring to the need to ensure that pro-Western governments emerge from the revolutionary upheavals. His and other ministers' concern with 'geopolitics' essentially means that China must not be allowed to gain a significant foothold over Middle Eastern oil. William Hague touched on the same issue in a parliamentary debate on the day in February 2011 that Mubarak was forced to resign, saying:

> There is an eastern dimension to the whole of what is happening in the Middle East. Chinese influence and investment are everywhere. Chinese warships are in the Mediterranean for the first time in several hundred years. The influence of the rising powers of Asia on the Middle East is heavy and growing. Exports from the Middle East -we are looking immediately more at the oil-producing countries to the east of the region -are increasingly going to the east. Sixty-six per cent of all oil production from Saudi Arabia goes eastwards. A large proportion of China's fossil fuel imports come from this region. This cannot be brushed aside; it is a decisive element in the unfolding pattern of Middle East reform. As far as we are concerned, there are some energy implications, to which we should not be blind. Egypt itself is not a major energy producer but it has some oil and quite a

> lot of gas, which it exports through the Arab peace pipeline to Jordan, Syria and Israel. Extraordinarily - perhaps this is often overlooked - Israel relies on Egypt for between 30 per cent and 40 per cent of its daily gas supplies. The continuation of that pipeline is an extremely important element in the situation. All over the region new gas pipelines are being developed, such as the so-called Islamic gas pipeline between Iran, Iraq and Syria. We have to understand that a new pattern of energy transportation and production is emerging in the area.[18]

The need to counter Chinese influence and ensure continued control over Middle Eastern energy sources has been paramount during the Arab Spring. 'We look today at unfolding events in Egypt, Gaza, Israel, Jordan, Syria and Iraq and they will all have an effect on energy security', Lord Howell said in February 2011.[19] In parliament a week later, he outlined British interests in the Middle East as including 'countering radicalisation, securing energy supplies and ensuring open and accessible markets. It also includes working to promote an environment in which trade and investment can flourish through shared standards and a level playing field for business, and encouraging participation by all members of society'.[20] Europe Minister David Lidington later put it more bluntly, telling an Atlantic Council meeting in the US that the Western interest in the Arab Spring should be 'the spread of capitalist democracy'.[21]

Indeed, British policy towards each of the recent upheavals in the Middle East has been shaped by its energy interests, in the context of this increasing rivalry with China and declining British influence. Once again, the promotion of basic British policy has witnessed a role for Islamist actors.

TAKING OUT INSURANCE: RE-ENGAGING THE MUSLIM BROTHERHOOD

The popular revolution that overthrew Mubarak in Egypt on 11 February 2011 occurred after 18 days of demonstrations spearheaded by young, secular protestors that united most sections of Egyptian society fed up with three decades of repressive, corrupt rule. Britain had, along with the US, consistently supported Mubarak since he took over from Anwar Sadat in 1981, and continued to back him right up until his demise. Just three months before Mubarak fell, in November 2010, William Hague made his first visit to Cairo as foreign secretary, proclaiming that 'Egypt is a key regional and international partner'.[22] Five months earlier, a new British ambassador to Egypt, James Watt, said that 'Egypt's role is critical for the future stability and success of much of the region' and that 'Britain has strong shared interests with Egypt, and I intend us to continue being an engaged and active partner, drawing on all the resources we have to offer'.[23] Indeed, Britain had been a significant arms supplier to the Mubarak regime. In 2010, deliveries had included components for all-wheel drive vehicles with ballistic protection, military communications equipment, surveillance equipment and components for armoured personnel carriers and submachine guns.[24]

Four days after major protests erupted in Egypt on 25 January, and with tens of thousands of demonstrators occupying Tahrir Square in central Cairo calling for Mubarak to be removed, a joint British-French-German statement referred to 'the moderating role President Mubarak has played over many years in the Middle East' and simply called on him to implement political and economic reforms 'to meet the aspirations of the Egyptian people'.[25] On 31 January, Lord Howell reminded parliament that Britain was the biggest foreign investor in Egypt, with investments of more than £13 billion. He said that 'it is not for us to decide who governs Egypt' and urged Mubarak 'to appoint a broad-based Government' to ensure 'an orderly transition to a more democratic system, including through holding free and fair elections'.[26] Indeed, Howell epitomised decades of British expediency in the Middle East by telling parliament:

> We have to take the situation as it is and, at the moment, the leadership and the power remain in the hands of Mr

> Mubarak. It is perfectly true... that tens of thousands of people are calling for his removal, but others are equally determined that he should not be removed. We will have to see how this works out.[27]

Howell's comments were echoed by another Foreign Office Minister, Alastair Burt, who told the House of Commons at the same time Howell was informing the House of Lords, that 'whatever government emerges in Egypt, and whether the president continues or something else happens in due course, our strategic interests remain the same'.[28] It was at this point, on 1 February, that former Prime Minister Tony Blair spoke up in favour of supporting the beleaguered Egyptian dictator, describing him as 'immensely courageous and a force for good', and warning against a rush to elections that could bring the Muslim Brotherhood to power.[29] A few days later, on 6 February, William Hague, asked by the media whether it was time for Britain to call for Mubarak to resign, was still saying that 'I don't think that is for us in another country to say'.[30]

A further five days on, Field Marshal Mohammed Hussein Tantawi, Mubarak's minister of defence and head of the supreme council of the armed forces, assumed power when Mubarak stood down; a sign that, while the head of the regime had fallen, many other key figures in it remained in place. Indeed, within six months of Mubarak's overthrow, thousands of protesters re-occupied Tahrir Square, demonstrating against the military's failure to make a speedy transition to civilian rule; they were met by a brutal display of force that killed 35 people in November and signifying that Egyptian state repression would continue.

Whitehall's policy of continuing to support the Mubarak regime but also waiting to see how things worked out in order to quickly change loyalties, was reminiscent of policy towards the shah of Iran in 1978, when Britain continued to back the shah right up to the point that it recognised he could not survive, as documented in chapter 7. It is not known if Britain set about increasing its contacts with the Muslim Brotherhood, the largest organised opposition party in Egypt, as Mubarak tottered on the brink of removal, but this may be unlikely simply due to the speed of events. Soon after Mubarak fell, however, Britain certainly did make new contacts with the Brotherhood. Details remain murky, however, and Freedom of Information requests by the author have been rejected by the Foreign Office on the grounds of being contrary to the 'public interest'. What is known is that Britain has had consistent contacts with the Muslim Brotherhood in recent years, following the Blair government's stepped-up engagement with the organisation in 2005-06, outlined in chapter 18. Foreign Secretary William Hague informed parliament just after the fall of Mubarak that the Brotherhood was 'an important part of Egypt's national political mosaic' and that 'we retain, as the previous Government did, certain contacts with the Muslim Brotherhood – in particular with those who were elected Members of Parliament in the 2005 elections. There has been normal contact with them, and that contact continues'.[31]

Soon after Mubarak was removed, in early March 2011, Foreign Office Minister Alastair Burt was reported by the Muslim Brotherhood's website to be conducting a two day visit to Egypt in which he would meet senior politicians and key opposition figures such as the Brotherhood, although it is unclear whether meetings with the Brotherhood went ahead.[32] The following month, however, the British Consul-General in Alexandria, Marie-Louise Archer, and another Foreign Office official, Martin Hetringen, visited Muslim Brotherhood officials at the latter's new headquarters in Alexandria which had recently been opened by Mohamed Badie, the Brotherhood's leader in Egypt.[33] The meeting, hosted by Hamdi Hassan, assistant secretary-general of the Muslim Brotherhood's parliamentary bloc, was not reported in the mainstream British media and is not mentioned on the Foreign Office website. Archer was, however, quoted in the *Jerusalem Post* as saying that the meeting was part of 'British efforts to increase cooperation and accepting cultural differences with Egypt's political and intellectual trends after the January 25 revolt' while the Foreign Office told the paper that 'we will continue to have contact with those members of the Muslim Brotherhood who are a part of, or are likely to become a part of, the current dialogue'.[34] The Muslim Brotherhood's official website reported that Hetringen expressed the British government's 'desire to open the door for direct political dialogue with the Brothers', and noted that Foreign Office delegations had previously been keen to hold meetings and contacts with the group's leaders and members, 'despite obstacles placed in their way'.[35]

The April and, possibly, March, contacts with the Brotherhood are interesting in light of David Cameron's earlier, one day visit to Egypt's new military rulers on 21 February. Then, Cameron and his advisers made a point of telling the media that the British prime minister would meet other opposition figures in Egypt but not members of the Muslim Brotherhood.[36] The reason, according to the *Daily Telegraph*, was that 'Cameron said he had deliberately chosen to meet non-Brotherhood members of the opposition in order to bolster them and their role in post-Mubarak Egypt'.[37] Clearly, such concerns about bolstering the Brotherhood did not prevent subsequent British contacts, albeit at lower than prime ministerial level. Indeed, in June 2011, the British ambassador to Egypt, James Watt, told journalists at the British Embassy in Cairo that there was no threat to stability in Egypt from the Muslim Brotherhood and, according to an Arabic news report, that Britain was applying 'no conditions on Britain's support during this transitional period'. At the same time, Watt reportedly noted that BP had decided to invest a massive $11 billion in Egypt.[38]

British policy is not to overtly support the Muslim Brotherhood or to want to see Islamist policies predominate in the future Egyptian government. Ministers have openly opposed the prospect of this and have welcomed the secular nature of the opposition to Mubarak, and there is no evidence to doubt that this is the British position. In a media interview in February 2011, William Hague said that there was a 'danger' of a Muslim Brotherhood takeover in Egypt and that if an election were held other opposition parties might not be strong enough to win.[39] Rather, meeting the Brotherhood is clearly a way of insuring Britain – protecting its strategic and commercial interests – in the likely event that the organisation plays a key, even dominant, role in the political transition or future government. Indeed, in the first post-Mubarak elections for the lower house of parliament, held in December 2011, the Muslim Brotherhood's Freedom and Justice Party (FJP) won a startling 37 per cent of the vote. A few days after the election, ambassador Watt paid a visit to the Chair of the FJP, Mohamed Morsy, congratulating him on his party's victory. 'Watt told Morsy that Britain will deal with any elected Egyptian government so a long as it represents the will of the people', one Egyptian news website noted.[40]

British re-engagement with the Brotherhood has been mirrored by US policy: the media has reported that the Obama administration has 'reassessed' its relationship with the Brotherhood, resumed formal contacts with it and that is 'ready to cooperate' with it so long as the Brotherhood respects the rule of democracy, minorities' rights and human rights.[41] The latter concerns are mainly for public relations purposes since the priority in Washington and London is to ensure a pro-Western political transition in Egypt that protects Western financial investments. Also important to the US is that Egypt maintains its peace treaty with, and acquiescent approach to, Israel and the latter's policies in the West Bank and Gaza. British planners can be assumed to be little concerned about the Muslim Brotherhood's domestic political agenda; its 2011 election manifesto professed to help build democracy in Egypt but also called for the application of sharia law and was noticeably discriminatory against women, stating, for example, that 'the FJP has the greatest respect, appreciation and support for women's role as wives, mothers and makers of men; and aims to better prepare them for this role'.[42] Other concerns are also likely to be ignored, such as those expressed by the former head of MI6, Sir Richard Dearlove, who recently told an audience at foreign affairs think tank Chatham House: 'I, for one, have absolutely no illusions about what the Muslim Brotherhood is, or can be. It can be a social organisation. It can be a political organisation. But it is at heart, in my view, a terrorist organisation.'[43] Similarly, US policy-makers are unlikely to be deterred from their re-engagement with the Brotherhood on the grounds that, as wikileaks files have shown, US authorities include the Brotherhood among a list of 36 terrorist organisations.[44]

British officials can be expected to deepen their arch-pragmatic stance towards the Muslim Brotherhood, especially in the light of the latter's election gains. Thus according to Lord Howell, Britain 'should have a calibrated attitude' to the Brotherhood, recognizing that it 'should not be judged as just one lump, or one group of people with more extreme views'. Rather, 'we have to try and disengage slightly from the historical record of the Muslim Brotherhood in Cairo, which at times was extreme' since 'today's Muslim Brotherhood is obviously of a different pattern and the senior people in it have a position that should be understood and discussed.'[45]

LIBYA – ISLAMIST BOOTS ON THE GROUND

Britain's continued willingness to work with Islamist forces has also been evident in the very different context of Libya, where it took a brutal civil war between armed opposition forces and remnants of the regime to eventually overthrow Libyan ruler, Muammar Qadafi, who was killed in October 2011. Massive NATO air strikes, mainly by Britain and France, were conducted during March-October in support of the rebel forces and significantly contributed to the rebel victory. What concerns the story here is not a review of the whole intervention but the extent to which it involved an Islamist element being supported by Britain in furtherance of its objectives in the Middle East. The Islamist forces were only part of the military opposition that overthrew Qadafi, but were an important element, especially in the east of the country which was where the uprising began and which provided the centre of opposition to Qadafi. The episode, to some extent, echoes past British interventions where Islamist actors have acted as among the foot-soldiers in British policy to secure energy interests. That the British military intervention to overthrow Qadafi was primarily motivated by such interests seems clear – in the absence of access to government files – to which we briefly turn later. Such oil and gas interests in Libya, however, has been downplayed by ministers and largely ignored by the media, in favour of notions of Britain being motivated by the need to support the human rights of the Libyan people and promote democracy: concerns completely absent when it came to defending the rights of other Middle Easterners being abused at precisely the same time, notably Bahrainis, to which we turn in the next section.

Britain provided a range of support to the rebel Libyan leadership, which was grouped in the National Transitional Council (NTC), an initially 33-member self-selected body of mainly former Qadafi ministers and other opposition forces, formed in Benghazi in February 2011 to provide an alternative government. UN Security Council Resolution 1973 was passed on 17 March, imposing a no fly zone over Libya and authorizing 'all necessary measures ... to protect civilians' under threat of attack. In an echo of Kosovo in 1999, it was certainly questionable whether civilians in Libya were under the extent of attack described by British ministers as justification for their military intervention, such as David Cameron's claim that 'we averted a massacre'.[46] Subsequently, British policy went well beyond the narrow strictures of the UN resolution, clearly seeking to target Qadafi personally and overthrow the regime. British air strikes and cruise missile attacks began on 19 March and within the first month of what became a seven-month bombing campaign NATO had flown 2,800 sorties, destroying a third of Qadafi's military assets, according to NATO.[47] The RAF eventually flew over 3,000 sorties over Libya, damaging or destroying 1,000 targets, while Britain also sent teams of regular army, SAS and MI6 officers to advise the NTC on 'military organizational structures, communications and logistics'. Britain also assisted NATO airstrikes by deploying SAS troops to act as ground spotters and supplied military communications equipment and body armour. Whitehall also aided the NTC's 'media and broadcasting operations' and invited the NTC to establish an office in London.[48] Military operations were coordinated with France while the US, which played no overt part in the military intervention, authorised $25 million in covert aid to the rebels in April.[49] British ministers denied that they provided arms and military training to the NTC (given that an international arms embargo was applied to Libya) but media reports suggested that the US gave a green light for the new Egyptian regime to supply arms and also asked Saudi Arabia to covertly do so.[50]

The NTC's military forces were led by various former Libyan army officers, such as Colonel Khalifa Haftar who had set up the 'Libyan National Army' in 1988 with support from the CIA and Saudis and who had been living for the past 20 years near Langley, Virginia, home of the CIA, which also provided him with a training camp.[51] But Islamist elements were also prominent. Two former mujahideen who had fought in Afghanistan led the military campaign against Qadafi's forces in Darnah, to the east of Benghazi, for example. Abdel Hakim al-Hasady, an influential Islamic preacher who spent five years at a jihadist training camp in eastern Afghanistan, oversaw the recruitment, training and deployment in the conflict of around 300 rebel fighters from Darnah. Both al-Hasady and his field commander on the front lines, Salah al-Barrani, were former members of the Libyan Islamic Fighting Group (LIFG), the Islamist force that had long targeted Qadafi, and which Britain covertly funded to kill Qadafi in 1996. It was also reported that Sufyan Ben Qumu, a Libyan army veteran who worked for Osama bin Laden's holding company in Sudan and later for an al-Qaida-linked charity in Afghanistan, ran the training of many of Darnah's rebel recruits. Qumu spent six years at Guantanamo Bay before he was turned over to Libyan custody in 2007; he was released, along with al-Hasady, from a Libyan prison in 2008 as part of Libya's reconciliation with the LIFG.[52] Al-Hasady, who had fought against the US in Afghanistan in 2001, had been arrested in Pakistan in 2002 and turned over to the US, imprisoned probably at the US base at Bagram, Afghanistan, and then mysteriously released. The US Deputy Secretary of State, James Steinberg, told Congressmen he would speak of al-Hasady's career only in a closed session.[53]

In an interview with an Italian newspaper in late March 2011, al-Hasady said he had previously recruited 'around 25' men from the Darnah area to fight against coalition troops in Iraq. Some of them, he said, were 'today are on the front lines in Adjabiya', a coastal city in north-central Libya which saw some of the heaviest fighting against Qadafi's forces.[54] Wikileaks cables obtained by the British media revealed US files highlighting supporters of Islamist causes among the opposition to Qadafi's regime, particularly in the towns of Benghazi and Darnah, and that the latter area was a breeding ground for fighters destined for Afghanistan and Iraq.55 Captured al-Qaida documents that fell into American hands in 2007 showed that Libya provided more foreign fighters to Iraq in per capita terms than any other country and that most of the volunteers were from the country's northeast, notably Benghazi and Darnah. Former CIA operations officer Brian Fairchild wrote that since 'the epicentre of the revolt [in Libya] is rife with anti-American and pro-jihad sentiment, and with al-Qaida's explicit support for the revolt, it is appropriate to ask our policy makers how American military intervention in support of this revolt in any way serves vital US strategic interests'.[56]

Other commentators recognised the Islamist nature of some of the rebels. Noman Benotman, a former member of the LIFG who had fought the Soviets in Afghanistan, estimated that there were 1,000 jihadists fighting in Libya.[57] Sir Richard Dearlove observed that the rebel stronghold of Benghazi was 'rather fundamentalist in character' and Admiral James Stavridis, NATO's Supreme Allied

Commander in Europe, said that US intelligence had picked up 'flickers' of terrorist activity among the rebel groups; this was described by senior British government figures 'very alarming'.[58] Shadow foreign secretary Douglas Alexander said in parliament that since there was evidence of the presence of al-Qaida-linked forces among the rebels, Britain should 'proceed with very real caution' in arming them. In response, William Hague downplayed the concern, saying that 'of course we want to know about any links with al-Qaida, as we do about links with any organisations anywhere in the world, but given what we have seen of the interim transitional national council in Libya, I think it would be right to put the emphasis on the positive side'.[59] Following a Freedom of Information request by the author to the Ministry of Defence, asking for the latter's assessment of the presence of al-Qaida forces or their sympathisers in the Libyan rebel forces, the MoD replied that it did not even want to disclose whether it held such information because this would be contrary to the 'public interest'.[60]

The extent to which these Islamist and al-Qaida-linked elements may have received weapons or military support from the British, French, Egyptians or Saudi Arabians is not yet known, but officials in Chad and Algeria repeatedly expressed concerns that the al-Qaida in the Islamic Maghreb organisation might have acquired heavy weapons, thanks to the arms supply.[61] What is known is that the state of Qatar was a major financial backer of the Libyan rebels, providing them with a massive $400 million worth of support, much of which was provided to the Islamist radicals. Moreover, Qatar also sent hundreds of troops to fight on the frontline and to provide infantry training to Libyan fighters in the western Nafusa mountains and in eastern Libya. Much of Qatar's support went to the so-called 17 February Martyrs Brigade, one of the most influential rebel formations led by Abdel-Hakim Belhaj, a leading member of the LIFG who became the rebel military commander in Tripoli.[62]

Qatar's support for the Islamists in Libya was surely known to British ministers, as they consistently supported Qatar's prominent role in the campaign against Qadafi, alongside deepening military and commercial cooperation, as we see in the next section. Indeed, Qatar's chief-of-staff, Major-General Hamad bin Ali al-Atiya, later said: 'We acted as the link between the rebels and Nato forces'.[63] Qatar also played a key role alongside Britain in the 'Libya contact group' that coordinated policy against the Qadafi regime; the first meeting of the group, in April 2011, for example, was convened by Qatar and co-chaired by Britain in Doha. After Qadafi was overthrown, Libya's new oil minister, Ali Tarhouni, issued a rebuke to Qatar saying that 'anyone who wishes to come to our house should knock on the front door first'; this was described by the *Economist* as 'a thinly-veiled warning to Qatar to stop favouring ambitious Islamists at the expense of the shaky central government'.[64]

What is especially intriguing about this episode relates to the past British support for the LIFG to overthrow Qadafi and whether the British still saw LIFG fighters and other Libyan Islamists as, in effect, their boots on the ground, similar to the way the British saw the Kosovo Liberation Army, then working alongside al-Qaida, in the Kosovo war of 1999. This is surely likely but again the details are murky. Certainly, there were plenty of LIFG fighters available to challenge Qadafi both in Britain and Libya, helped by a reconciliation process between the regime and the LIFG begun in 2007 and presided over by Saif al-Islam al-Qadafi, the son of the ruler. This process resulted in 2009 in dozens of LIFG members being freed from jail in Libya in return for giving up their war against the regime. In July 2009, 30 LIFG members living in Britain, some of them senior figures in the group, signed on to the reconciliation process. British Home Office Control Orders imposed on them, having been regarded as posing a danger to UK national security, were, in some cases at least, dropped.[65] Many of the released LIFG fighters are likely to have taken part in the uprising against Qadafi alongside those who had never been captured by the regime. A series of documentaries shown on the al-Jazeera news channel followed a group of Libyan exiles in London return to Libya to take part in the overthrow of Qadafi.[66]

In mid-March 2011, when the Qadafi regime was still clinging to power in Tripoli, Libyan authorities paraded in front of the world's media a British citizen captured in Libya and branded an Islamic terrorist. Salah Mohammed Ali Aboaoba said he was a member of the LIFG and had moved from Yemen to Britain in 2005, where he stayed until 2010, having been granted asylum, living with his family in Manchester and raising funds for the LIFG.[67] There is no evidence that the British authorities facilitated the despatch of LIFG fighters from Britain to Libya, which may have been a re-run of the Kosovo conflict. Yet there is the suspicion that the Libyan reconciliation process could have enabled the British, and US, to maintain contacts with the LIFG and to regard them as potential future collaborators to remove Qadafi.

At the very least, Britain in 2011 once again found that its interests – mainly concerning oil – coincided with those of Islamist forces in Libya. By now, however, the British relationship with the LIFG was clearly quite complex. Blair's government had been so keen to curry favour with Qadafi that in 2004 MI6 was involved in the seizure of LIFG leader Abdel-Hakim Belhaj and his deputy Sami al-Saadi. Belhaj was captured at Bangkok airport and claims he was handed over to the CIA, who he alleges tortured him and injected him with truth serum before flying him back to Tripoli for interrogation. Belhaj subsequently spent six years in solitary confinement at Tripoli's notorious Abu Selim jail, and claims that he was questioned by three British agents, who ignored his complaints about mistreatment. MI5 sent a delegation to Tripoli in 2005, apparently to cement relations with the Qadafi regime at a time when the British were concerned with the potential threat posed to British security by other dissident members of LIFG living in the UK, whom they believed were increasingly inspired by al-Qaida. MI5 also gave the Libyan regime the names, personal details and addresses of 50 LIFG members living in the UK.

Once again, the episode highlights how expedient British policy towards the LIFG was – covertly supporting the organisation in the mid-1990s and acquiescing in its presence in London as a counter to the Libyan regime, then taking action against it at the behest of Qadafi, while later finding itself on the same side again and working alongside those, such as Qatar, providing significant military and financial support to it.

The events of 2011 in Libya also revealed Britain's pragmatic approach to dealing with a dictator: attempts to overthrow Qadafi in the 1980s (notably in the 1986 bombing of Libya) and in the 1990s (in the 1996 British-backed attempted coup) morphed in the early 2000s into a reconciliation process between Britain and Libya; promoted by the Blair government, this culminated in the lifting of international sanctions against the regime in 2003. It was only when domestic forces rose up in opposition to Qadafi in early 2011, that Britain again switched allegiance back to anti-regime forces. The British concerns all along have mainly been commercial, linked to energy interests. It was oil interests that inspired the Blair government to start dealing with Qadafi after 2003. Anglo/Dutch oil company Shell signed a deal with Libya's state-owned energy group in March 2004 covering the establishment of a 'long-term strategic partnership' and British ministers and senior civil servants met Shell to discuss the company's oil interests in Libya on at least 11 occasions and perhaps as many as 26 times in the subsequent four years.[69] BP, meanwhile, announced an agreement to explore for oil and gas, potentially worth up to £15 billion, in May 2007.[70]

Britain was so beholden to the trade opportunities offered by Qadafi that Blair's successor, Gordon Brown, refused to put pressure on the Libyan regime to pay compensation for 200 victims of the IRA's lorry bomb that exploded in London's Docklands in February 1996 – the Semtex explosive for which is suspected of having been supplied by Libya. Letters sent by Brown and Foreign Office ministers to those seeking compensation made it clear that the government was unwilling to put any pressure on the Libyans that might jeopardise British trading and commercial interests: 'Libya has genuinely become an important international partner for the UK on many levels', then Foreign Office Minister Bill Rammell wrote in November 2008 to one of those injured in the lorry bombing.[71] By the time the Libyan uprising was unfolding in early 2011, hundreds of British companies, including some of the biggest names in the country, were pursuing lucrative business opportunities and contracts with Qadafi's regime, scrabbling to secure their part of the estimated £1.5 billion bilateral trade between Libya and Britain and to take a share of the £102 billion in infrastructure investment that Libya had committed to spend over the next two years.[72]

So keen was Britain to support Qadafi at this time that considerable military equipment was exported. Around £61 million worth of arms exports to the regime were approved during 2009-10, including sniper rifles, components for combat aircraft and ammunition. Licences were also granted for crowd control equipment such as anti-riot/ballistic shields, smoke canisters and stun grenades right up to the end of 2010.[73] These sales followed those of water cannon and armoured personnel carriers in 2007, the latter which were used against protesters in Libya in February 2011. One British company was allowed by the government to supply riot control training to the Libyan police while Whitehall also secured an £85 million deal for a communications system for Libyan tanks. These tanks were subsequently bombed by NATO in 2011.[74]

However, in the months preceding the 2011 uprising, there were also signs that the Qadafi regime's conciliatory stance towards the West was again changing, In particular, in late 2010 the state-owned Libyan National Oil Company announced that it was not expecting to issue any new oil concession licences in 2011.[75] This was a sign of the growing 'resource nationalism' in Libya identified in a November 2007 memo by the US embassy in Tripoli, later revealed by wikileaks. The memo argued that the Libyan regime was 'in the process of reworking long-standing oil concessions with several different IOCs' (international oil companies) and was promoting a 'resurgence of measures designed to increase the GOL's [government of Libya] control over and share of revenue from hydrocarbon resources'. It added that 'those who dominate Libya's political and economic leadership are pursuing increasingly nationalistic policies in the energy sector that could jeopardize efficient exploitation of Libya's extensive oil and gas reserves.'[76] These concerns reinforce the notion that Britain and its allies viewed the opportunity to remove the regime that presented itself in early 2011 as too good to be missed, and Islamist forces helped them to do this.

SAUDI ARABIA AND THE UTILITY OF INTERVENTION

Whitehall's long-standing special relationship with the theocratic rulers in Riyadh has been enhanced by the new coalition government at a time when evidence continues to emerge on the extent of Saudi funding of terrorism and when the Saudis have taken drastic measures to clamp down on democracy in Arabia. Britain's alliance with the House of Saud has also taken on new importance with the coalition government's announcement of deepened relations with the Gulf states. The new government's Gulf initiative, aiming to enhance trade and investment with countries such as Qatar, Kuwait, the United Arab Emirates and Oman, has resulted in a string of meetings with the region's autocratic rulers and constant apologias for their rejection of democracy, but have been ignored by the mainstream media.

As noted in chapter 18, Saudi Arabia has long been the most significant source of funds for radical Islamic and terrorist causes around the world. A secret cable written by US Secretary of State, Hillary Clinton, in December 2009, revealed in late 2010 by wikileaks, noted that 'donors in Saudi Arabia constitute the most significant source of funding to Sunni terrorist groups worldwide' and that 'Saudi Arabia remains a critical financial support base for al-Qaida, the Taliban, LeT [Laskhar-e-Toiba], and other terrorist groups, including Hamas, which probably raise millions of dollars annually from Saudi sources'. The cable added that 'it has been an ongoing challenge to persuade Saudi officials to treat terrorist financing emanating from Saudi Arabia as a strategic priority' and that 'Riyadh has taken only limited action' to interrupt the flow of money to terrorist groups which have launched attacks in Afghanistan, Pakistan and India.[77]

Yet not only Saudi Arabia, but also other Gulf states were recognised in the cable as being the source of terrorist funding. The Kuwaiti regime of Emir Sabah al-Sabah 'has demonstrated a willingness to take action [against terrorist financing] when attacks target Kuwait', the cable noted, but 'has been less inclined to take action against Kuwait-based financiers and facilitators plotting attacks outside of Kuwait'. Thus 'al-Qaida and other groups continue to exploit Kuwait both as a source of funds and as a key transit point'. Donors in the United Arab Emirates, meanwhile, 'have provided financial support to a variety of terrorist groups, including al-Qaida, the Taliban, LeT and other terrorist groups, including Hamas'. The cable added that 'the UAE's role as a growing global financial centre, coupled with weak regulatory oversight, makes it vulnerable to abuse by terrorist financiers and facilitation networks'.[78]

Finally, Qatar 'has adopted a largely passive approach to cooperating with the US against terrorist financing' and its overall level of counter-terrorism cooperation with the US 'is considered the worst in the region'. Terrorist groups were said to exploit Qatar as a fundraising locale and 'although Qatar's security services have the capability to deal with direct threats and occasionally have put that capability to use, they have been hesitant to act against known terrorists out of concern for appearing to be aligned with the US and provoking reprisals.'[79] A US Congressional Research Service report has noted 'possible support for al-Qaida by some Qatari citizens.[80]

The states listed in Clinton's cable are those with which the British coalition government has recently announced a significant deepening of relations. In October 2010, for example, the Queen welcomed the Emir of Qatar, Sheikh al-Thani, to Windsor Castle.[81] During the visit, a joint statement by Cameron and al-Thani noted that Qatar and Britain 'enjoy a special defence relationship' underpinned by a Defence Cooperation Arrangement signed in 2006, involving British military training of the Qatari armed forces in Qatar and Britain. It also noted that Qatar has a diverse range of investments in Britain and is a major supplier of energy, providing 11 per cent of Britain's gas demand.[82] As regards Kuwait, David Cameron announced in February 2011 the creation of a UK-Kuwait Trade and Investment Task Force, a commitment to double trade to $4 billion a year by 2015, and the signature of a memorandum of understanding on trade and technical cooperation.[83] The Kuwait Investment Authority has its overseas headquarters in London and has invested some £150 billion over the last fifty years, the majority of it in Britain.[84] The Gulf states including Saudi Arabia now account for around half of all British arms sales and the government estimates that they will spend around $100 billion on 'defence and security' technology over the next five years.[85]

Along with these contacts have come extreme British apologias for the Gulf regimes' political orientations. Governments which Britain opposes are simply told by Ministers to adopt democracy. When it comes to allied regimes, however, notably those in the Gulf, a large amount of latitude is allowed. A standard formula, as outlined by David Cameron in a speech to the Kuwait National Assembly in February 2011, runs as follows:

> It is not for me, or for governments outside the region, to pontificate about how each country meets the aspirations of its people. It is not for us to tell you how to do it, or precisely what shape your future should take. There is no single formula for success, and there are many ways to ensure greater, popular participation in Government. We respect your right to take your own decisions, while offering our goodwill and support.[86]

These words can be expected to be received gratefully by Gulf leaders keen to stave off the threat of democracy. At other times,

British ministers have convinced themselves that Kuwait – run by the al-Sabah family since the mid-eighteenth century - is already a democratic society. For example, during his visit in February 2011, Cameron referred in a press conference with the Kuwaiti prime minister to 'small and democratic countries like Kuwait'.[87] He also mentioned the 'gradual development of a liberal democratic society that you are overseeing, the vital steps you're taking on your own journey to democracy'.[88] In fact, although Kuwait allows elections to its National Assembly, real power lies in the hands of the Emir and the prime minister, who is appointed by the Emir and not accountable to parliament, which has extremely limited powers.

Sultan Qaboos of Oman, meanwhile, has been in power since a British coup installed him in 1970, and became the world's longest serving ruler once Qadafi was overthrown, a fact not advertised by Whitehall. Qaboos' regime, a major British ally, was described as 'enlightened and effective' by then International Development Minister Alan Duncan in October 2010.[89] In reality, Oman is an absolute monarchy with almost all power concentrated in the hands of the Sultan, who serves as chief of state and head of government, supreme commander of the armed forces, prime minister, and minister of defence, foreign affairs and finance, in addition to personally appointing all other ministers.

But Saudi Arabia remains the biggest prize for British patronage and is by far Britain's largest export market outside the OECD, while the UK is world's second largest foreign investor in the country.[90] A further Freedom of Information Act request by the author, this time asking the Foreign Office for its assessment of terrorist funding emanating from Saudi Arabia, was met with the response that such 'disclosure of information is likely to prejudice relations between the UK and Saudi Arabia'.[91] Whitehall's knowledge of Saudi sponsorship of terrorism can be taken for granted, however. The real concern was described by Foreign Office Minister Lord Howell, who told an audience in Riyadh that 'Saudi Arabia is the heart of world oil production that underpins global markets', located in 'a region which contains the planet's largest oil reserves'.[92] Thus, in the words of the Foreign Office website, 'Saudi Arabia and the United Kingdom have long been close allies, and the breadth and depth of Britain's relationship with the Kingdom continues to increase'.[93]

The website adds that the two countries have 'a shared interest in ensuring regional stability'.[94] 'Stability' here is understood as ongoing British/Saudi opposition to democracy in the region and the long-standing British backing – documented in previous chapters – of Saudi Arabia's role of superpower on the Arabian peninsula to ward off threats to continued feudal rule. One case in point is the Saudi intervention in Yemen in November 2009, when its air force bombarded the north-western Yemeni region of Sa'dah to counter the Shia Houthi insurgent group; the action was undertaken in support of Yemeni government forces which had earlier launched a military offensive against the Houthis called 'scorched earth'. The Saudis used British-supplied Tornado fighter-bombers, damaging or destroying civilian buildings such as market places, mosques, petrol stations, small businesses, a primary school, a power plant, a health centre and dozens of houses and residential buildings. Amnesty International commented that the Saudis 'carried out indiscriminate attacks and other violations of international humanitarian law' that resulted in hundreds and possibly thousands of civilian deaths.[95]

But the Saudi role as regional policeman and counter to democracy is principally evidenced in its intervention in Bahrain in March 2011. Then, 1,000 Saudi troops with armoured support crossed the narrow causeway into Bahrain in support of the Bahraini King's call to help put down pro-democracy demonstrations. Beginning in mid-February, thousands of Bahrainis had set up a camp city at the Pearl Roundabout in the capital, Manama, mirroring the protests in Cairo's Tahrir Square. They had, however, more limited demands than their Egyptian counterparts, calling for greater political participation essentially under a constitutional monarchy, a legitimate parliament, free and fair elections, an end to corruption and equality for the long-repressed Shia majority in Bahrain.

The Saudi intervention in Bahrain was backed by Britain at the same time as ministers were claiming, with regard to their campaign in Libya, that 'it is for the people of Libya to choose their own government'.[96] Moreover, it is likely that the British gave the Saudis and Bahrainis a green light for the intervention. Only five days before, on 9 March, as protests were growing in the country, David Cameron's National Security Adviser, Peter Ricketts, and Chief of Defence Staff General David Richards, met King Hamid al-Khalifa in Bahrain.[97] 'Ricketts paid tribute to Bahrain's major and remarkable strides on the path of reform and modernization thanks to the royal reform project initiated by HM the King', one Bahraini news report noted.[98] The British meeting was followed by one by US Defence Secretary Robert Gates, on 11 March.[99] Evidence has also emerged from two diplomatic sources at the UN that the Saudis were given a green light to intervene in Bahrain by US Secretary of State Hillary Clinton, in exchange for a 'yes' vote by the Arab League for the no-fly zone over Libya.[100]

Saudi forces entered Bahrain in a convoy of British-made armoured personnel carriers known as Tacticas, which were manufactured by the British company, BAE Systems.[101] Saudi Arabia's National Guard, trained by Britain since 1964 to ensure the defence of the House of Saud, was part of the Saudi force and British training in internal security over many years would no doubt have helped develop tactics to suppress the popular uprising in Bahrain.[102] Other British-supplied equipment available to the Bahrainis included tear gas and crowd control ammunition, equipment for the use of aircraft cannons, assault rifles, shotguns, sniper rifles and sub-machine guns, all of which had been supplied in 2010.[103]

Following the intervention, Amnesty International noted that 'the Bahraini government launched a clearly planned and orchestrated crackdown using excessive force to suppress protests calling for political change and reform', while 'security forces used shotguns, rubber bullets, tear gas and, in some cases, live ammunition, sometimes at very close range, and in circumstances where the use of weapons ... could not be justified'.[104] Over 600 civilians were detained without charge in unknown conditions, including doctors, lawyers, human rights workers, academics and youth bloggers. At the same time, some 2,000 Shia workers who stayed away from work during the unrest were sacked without any unemployment insurance while teachers and students were expelled from schools and universities.[105] Two months after the intervention, Amnesty was still documenting the government's 'relentless crackdown on human rights', as emergency powers were used to arrest people without judicial warrant and detain incommunicado protesters and political activists, while some detainees had been tortured or ill-treated following arrest. Amnesty also noted 'suspicions that the whole of the majority Shia population of Bahrain is being punished for the February-March protests'.[106]

British acquiescence in the intervention was entirely predictable given that the coalition government had announced its intention to back the Bahraini regime soon after it won the election in May 2010. 'We began, from our first day in office, a major, long-term effort to intensify Britain's links with the countries of the Middle East, North Africa and the Gulf – in diplomacy, trade, education, health and civil society – as part of a distinctive British policy towards the region', William Hague said later, in February 2011; he added that 'I reaffirmed last week to leaders in Bahrain and the UAE that we are committed to intensifying our engagement on foreign policy.'[107] In July 2010, the King of Bahrain visited David Cameron at Number 10 Downing Street and the two leaders 'agreed to expand existing co-operation between their countries across the board including on culture, education, defence and security, trade and investment and foreign policy'.[108] Five months later, in December 2010, the Foreign Secretary welcomed the Crown Prince of Bahrain to

London, 'underlining the coalition government's commitment to building its relationship with Bahrain', the Foreign Office stated. The latter's report of the meeting added that Hague 'noted concerns raised ahead of the elections, regarding implementation of the electoral law and allegations of restrictions on campaigning, and welcomed the positive response of the Bahraini Government and their assurances that they would continue progress on political reform'.[109]

In the early hours of 17 February 2011, the Bahraini police moved into the Pearl Roundabout area of Manama to clear the encampment of protesters and in a brutal crackdown left five dead and over 200 injured. Foreign Secretary Hague said that he conveyed the 'concern' of the British government to Bahrain and 'urge[d] all sides to avoid violence and the police to exercise restraint' while praising the regime for recent 'important political reforms' and 'the long friendship between Bahrain and the UK'.[110] On the same day, the British government announced it was reviewing its 'recent licensing decisions' concerning military exports to Bahrain. Two days after the Saudi intervention in March the Prime Minister's website stated that David Cameron personally telephoned the King of Bahrain calling on him to end the violent suppression of street protests and to 'respect the right to peaceful protest and respond to the legitimate concerns of the Bahraini people'.[111] Yet British policy explained by William Hague was decidedly more conciliatory. Hague told the Foreign Affairs Committee that he spoke to Saudi Foreign Minister Prince Saud on 14 March and that:

> 'He assured me that these [Saudi forces in Bahrain] were for the defence of installations and the external defence of Bahrain, while it would be the Bahraini forces and police that tried to restore order in their own country. So that is where we are on Saudi Arabia.'

Hague added that he had been assured by Bahraini Foreign Minister,

Sheikh Khalid al-Khalifa, that the Bahraini government 'remained absolutely determined to continue that process of dialogue' and repeated the mantra that 'there are casualties on both sides'.[112] Other statements by Hague did condemn the Bahraini use of force but were always qualified by urging restraint on 'all sides' or praise for the regime's supposed offer of dialogue with opposition groups.[113]

Faced with massive international criticism of his government's brutal crushing of protest, the King of Bahrain instituted a commission of enquiry into the events of February and March. Released in November 2011, the report concluded that the security forces had used 'excessive force' and had tortured detainees and killed 35 people.[114] In early December, however, David Cameron once again met King al-Khalifa in Downing Street. According to the prime minister's office, Cameron 'emphasised the importance of strengthening respect for human rights in Bahrain' and 'urged the King to deliver swiftly on the commitments he has made to implement the recommendations from the Inquiry'. At the same time, however, 'the leaders also discussed how they could boost trade co-operation between the two countries and the opportunities for British business to invest in Bahrain, particularly in the infrastructure sector'.[115] While Cameron was hosting al-Khalifa, hundreds of people wrongfully detained or convicted following unfair trials were still languishing in Bahraini jails while those dismissed from the posts had received no signs of being reinstated.[116]

THE RECKONING

Current British policy in the Middle East is as expedient as it has been over the last century. The reliance on making deals with the Taliban and on their supporters in Islamabad, together with pragmatic engagement with the Muslim Brotherhood, are policies that previous generations of British planners would recognise, while the alliance with the arch-fundamentalists in Saudi Arabia has been a major constant. The primary threats to British interests in the Middle East have changed over the decades from Russian expansion to Arab nationalism to – presently – a resurgent Iran, with an omniscient fear being that of independent development. But the fundamental predicament has been declining influence in a region where Britain retains critical interests: ensuring overall Western control of oil, and the resources flowing from oil, to the greatest extent possible by maintaining favoured regimes in power. Having declined from the supreme architect of the region that imposed its country borders and rulers to a second-rank power that clings to Washington's coat-tails, Britain is now in a weaker position in the region than ever, overwhelmingly reliant on the US. British elites have had few qualms or illusions about those with whom they have collaborated to achieve their goals, and their policy has been based on short-term calculations of maximising influence. The fact that collaboration with Islamists or terrorists has been pursued with little heed paid to the longer-term consequences is a sign of the weak position in which the British have constantly found themselves.

British influence in the Middle East in recent decades should not be exaggerated but there is no doubt that it has contributed to the rise of radical Islam and the undermining of secular, more liberal forces which the British public is told by their governments (and media) are Britain's allies around the world. The policy has promoted violence and wars, the overthrow of often popular governments, the bolstering of the most reactionary domestic forces, as well as tensions between states and sectarian divisions within them. Government policies are widely believed to be pursued in the 'national interest', but this is a myth: Britain's foreign policy-making system is far removed from promoting the public interest. Rather, Whitehall's secret affairs with radical Islam have increased the terrorist threat to Britain and the world; a distinctly immoral aspect of foreign policy has made Britain, the Middle East and much of the rest of the world more insecure.

Notes

INTRODUCTION

1. Prime Minister, *A Strong Britain in an Age of Uncertainty: The National Security Strategy*, October 2010, p.18
2. House of Commons, Intelligence and Security Committee, *Could 7/7 have been prevented?: Review of the Intelligence on the London Terrorist Attacks on 7 July 2005*, May 2009, paras 214-16; Gordon Brown, Speech, 17 June 2008, www.pm.gov.uk
3. Rosie Cowan and Richard Norton-Taylor, 'Britain now No 1 al-Qaida target – anti-terror chiefs', *Guardian*, 19 October 2006; David Leppard, 'Police expect Mumbai-style terror attack on City of London', Times, 20 December 2009
4. 'Ex-MI5 boss: "Govt exploits terrorism fear"', Sky News, 17 February 2009
5. General Sir Richard Dannatt, Speech, 15 May 2009, www.mod.uk
6. See, for example, Melanie Phillips, *Londonistan: How Britain is Creating a Terror State Within* (Gibson Square, London 2006); Michael Gove, *Celsius 7/7* (Weidenfeld & Nicholson, London, 2006)
7. See Sean O'Neill and Daniel McGrory, *The Suicide Factory: Abu Hamza and the Finsbury Park Mosque* (Harper Collins, London, 2006)
8. David Leppard, 'Iraq terror backlash in UK "for years"', *Times*, 2 April 2006
9. Home Office and Foreign Office, 'Young Muslims and extremism', April 2004, pp.4-5, leaked on *Times* online website, www.timesonline.co.uk
10. See especially Robert Dreyfus, *Devil's Game: How the United States Helped Unleash Fundamentalist Islam* (Metropolitan, New York, 2005)
11. See Olivier Roy, 'Islamic radicalism in Afghanistan and Pakistan', *Writenet Paper No.6*, UNHCR, 2001

CHAPTER 1: IMPERIAL DIVIDE AND RULE

1. Francis Robinson, 'The British Empire and the Muslim World', undated, University of London, Royal Holloway College, http://eprints.rhul.ac.uk
2. Cited in Martin Gilbert, *Churchill and the Jews* (Pocket Books: London, 2007), p. 35
3. Ibid., pp. 53–4, 115, 120
4. Robinson, ibid.
5. John Hunwick, 'African and Islamic Revival: Historical and Contemporary Perspectives', www.uga.edu/islam/hunwick.html
6. Robinson, ibid.
7. Ibid.
8. Cited in 'The Two-Nation Theory and Partition: A Historical Overview', South Asian History, http://india_resource.tripod.com

9. Robinson, ibid.
10. Cited in B. Pande, 'History in the Service of Imperialism', www.cyberistan.org
11. Ibid.
12. Cited in 'Indian Partition and Neo-Colonialism', *Coalition to Oppose the Arms Trade* magazine, Issue 47, www.coat.ncf.ca
13. Patrick French, *Liberty or Death: India's Journey to Independence and Division* (Flamingo: London, 1998), p. 45
14. Robinson, ibid.
15. Cited in Ferruh Demirmen, 'Oil in Iraq: The Byzantine Beginnings', 25 April 2003, www.globalpolicy.org
16. Janet Wallach, *Desert Queen: The Extraordinary Life of Gertrude Bell* (Weidenfeld & Nicolson: London, 2006), p. 244
17. Efraim Karsh, *Islamic Imperialism: A History* (Yale University Press, 2007), pp. 99–107
18. 'An Official Proclamation from the Government of Great Britain to the Natives of Arabia and the Arab Provinces', 4 December 1914, Public Record Office (PRO), FO141/710/9
19. PRO, FO141/710/9, 'Proclamation to the People of Arabia', 27 May 1915
20. PRO, FO141/710/9, Government letter to Sherif of Mecca, November 1914
21. 'The McMahon Letter', 24 October 1915, www.domino.un.org
22. Cited in David Fromkin, *A Peace to End all Peace: Creating the Modern Middle East, 1914–1922* (Penguin: London, 1989), p. 145
23. Fromkin, pp. 96–7
24. Cited in Wallach, p. 182
25. Wali Hassan, 'Lawrence, T. E', *Oxford Encyclopedia of British Literature* (OUP: Oxford, 2005)
26. Cited in Charles Allen, *God's Terrorists: The Wahhabi Cult and the Hidden Roots of Modern Jihad* (Little Brown: London, 2006), pp. 246–7
27. Cited in Fromkin, p. 106
28. Ibid., p. 424
29. Captain Bray, 'A Note on the Mohammedan Question', March 1917, in J. Priestland (ed.), *Islam: Political Impact, 1908–1972, British Documentary Sources,* Vol.2
30. Said Aburish, *The Rise, Corruption and Coming Fall of the House of Saud* (Bloomsbury: London, 1994), pp. 9–41
31. Fromkin, p. 506
32. Cited in Gilbert, p. 67
33. Cited in William Roger Louis, *The British Empire in the Middle East* (OUP: Oxford, 1998), p. 174
34. John Loftus and Mark Aarons write that Philby was sent to Ibn Saud to bring the latter into line, but ended up betraying the British policy of supporting Sherif Hussein by instead working with Ibn Saud to ensure his victory in Arabia. For Philby's duplicitous role see Loftus and Aarons, *The Secret War Against the Jews: How Western Espionage Betrayed the Jewish People* (St Martin's Press: New York, 1994), chapter 1
35. Hassan Hamdan al-Alkim, *The GCC States in an Unstable World* (Saqi: London, 1994), p. 37

36. Gilles Kepel, *The War for Muslim Minds: Islam and the West* (Harvard University Press, 2004), p. 160
37. Allen, Preface
38. Cited in Jan Morris, *Farewell the Trumpets: An Imperial Retreat* (Penguin: London, 1978), p. 265
39. See Fromkin, pp. 465–74
40. Cited in Michael Sargent, 'British Military Involvement in Transcapia (1918–1919)', Conflict Studies Research Centre, April 2004, p. 6
41. Suhnaz Yilmaz, 'An Ottoman Warrior Abroad: Enver Pasa as Expatriate', *Middle Eastern Studies*, October 1999, p. 59
42. Fromkin, pp. 485–8
43. Ahmed Rashid, *Taliban: Islam, Oil and the New Great Game in Central Asia* (IB Tauris: London, 2002), pp. 147–7
44. Meir Litvak, 'A Failed Manipulation: The British, the Oudh Bequest and the Shia Ulama of Najaf and Karbala', *British Journal of Middle Eastern Studies*, Vol.27, No.1, p. 69
45. Ibid.
46. Ibid.
47. See Wallach, passim
48. Peter Sluglett, *Britain in Iraq: Contriving King and Country* (IB Tauris: London, 2007), p. 57; Fromkin, p. 508
49. Naomi Shepherd, *Ploughing Sand: British Rule in Palestine, 1917–1948* (John Murray: London, 1999), p. 7
50. Barbara Tuchman, *Bible and Sword: England and Palestine from the Bronze Age to Balfour* (Phoenix: New York, 1984), pp. 335–6
51. Shepherd, pp. 7–8
52. Cited in Tom Segev, *One Palestine Complete: Jews and Arabs Under the British Mandate* (Abacus: London, 2000), p. 9
53. Gilbert, pp. 55, 149, 231
54. Ibid.
55. Ibid., p. 75
56. Ibid., pp. 53–4, 115, 120
57. It has long been claimed that some British officers incited the Easter riots. Most famously, there are the claims of Richard Meinertzhagen, a pro-Zionist political officer of General Allenby, the British commander in Palestine, that several pro-Arab British officers in the military administration had incited the Easter riots to prove there was no chance of creating a Jewish home. Meinertzhagen accused Colonel Bertie Waters-Taylor, Allenby's chief of staff, of giving instructions to al-Husseini on how to 'show the world' that Palestinian Arabs would not stand for Jewish rule. According to Meinertzhagen, 'Waters-Taylor explained that freedom could only be attained through violence', and he also informed al-Husseini that the Jews intended to assassinate him. Meinertzhagen had earlier recorded in his diary that 'there are already signs of serious anti-semitism in Whitehall and efforts to stultify the Balfour Declaration'. During the riots he wrote to the Foreign Office, stating that 'the officers of the administration are, almost without exception, anti-Zionist in their views and are encouraging the Arabs ... The Arabs are encouraged and imagine that by acts of violence they can sabotage Zionism.' As Tom Segev argues in his analysis, however,

Meinertzhagen is a very doubtful source for such a serious charge, and very little other evidence has emerged. The more likely explanation for the riots was British unpreparedness, amounting to criminal negligence on the part of the mandatory authorities. See Segev, pp. 140–1; see also Joseph Norland, 'In Memoriam: Col Richard Meinertzhagen', *The Israel Report*, May/June 2004; Jacqueline Shields, 'Arabs Riots of the 1920s', www.jewishvirtuallibrary.org. In a similar vein, the authors John Loftus and Mark Aarons claim in their book on covert operations against Israel that the British secret service helped organise and incite terrorist acts against Jews in Palestine in the 1920s, in order to curb Jewish immigration into Palestine. 'According to several of our sources', they write, 'Great Britain was the first modern country to use its intelligence service to organise terrorist attacks against the Jews.' British intelligence agents 'sponsored waves of Arab terrorism, protests and propaganda that began to wear down the Foreign Office's resolve towards the Jews.' The authors state that this was organised from British staging areas in Transjordan and was partly directed by secret service agent, Harry Philby. Loftus and Aarons, pp. 33–4

58. Shepherd, pp. 40, 60
59. Segev, p. 186
60. Ibid., pp. 314–16
61. Robert Dreyfus, p. 61
62. John Newsinger, *The Blood Never Dried: A People's History of the British Empire* (Bookmarks: London, 2006), p. 138
63. Susan Carruthers, *Winning Hearts and Minds: British Governments, the Media and Colonial Counter-Insurgency, 1944–1960* (Leicester University Press, 1995), p. 57
64. Cited in Gilbert, p. 157
65. Review of Joseph Schechtman, 'The Mufti and the Fuehrer', originally published in 1965, http:www.dangoor.com
66. Elliott Green, 'Arabs and Nazis – Can it be True?', *Free Republic*, January/February 2005; Matthias Kuentzel, 'National Socialism and Anti-Semitism in the Arab World', *Jewish Political Studies Review*, spring 1915, www.matthiaskuentzel.de; Carl Savich, 'Islam under the Swastika: The Grand Mufti and the Nazi Protectorate of Bosnia-Herzegovina, 1941–1945', 2005, www.rastko.org.yu
67. Said Aburish, *A Brutal Friendship: The West and the Arab Elite* (Indigo: London, 1997), p. 162
68. Richard Mitchell, *The Society of the Muslim Brothers* (OUP: Oxford, 1993), p. 56
69. Stephen Dorril, *MI6* (Simon & Schuster: London, 2002), pp. 537–8.
70. The Brotherhood's principal anti-Jewish text, written by one of its leading thinkers, Sayyid Qutb, and published in 1950, was entitled 'Our Struggle with the Jews' and claimed that Jews were behind worldwide moral and sexual decline: 'Behind the doctrine of atheistic materialism was a Jew; behind the doctrine of animalistic sexuality was a Jew; and behind the destruction of the family and the shattering of sacred relationships in society was a Jew,' Qutb wrote. Cited in Matthias Kuentzel, 'National Socialism and Anti-Semitism in the Arab World'. Elements in the British elite also, of course, supported Hitler, partly based on their own anti-

semitism; sections of the aristocracy were openly calling for an alliance with Hitler against the godless Bolsheviks. Notable was Edward Windsor, the former king, who 'acted as a willing tool of Nazi intelligence and a key player in the efforts to bring about an Anglo–Nazi pact against the Soviets', Loftus and Aarons comment, based on numerous personal sources. Loftus and Aarons, pp. 47–55, 87–91, 104–6

71. Political Intelligence Committee, 'The Ikhwani el Muslimeen', 25 February 1944, WO201/2647
72. GHQ, Middle East Forces, 'The Ikhwani el Muslimeen Reconsidered', 10 December 1942, PRO, FO141/838
73. Brynjar Lia, *The Society of the Muslim Brothers in Egypt: The Rise of an Islamic Mass Movement, 1928–1942* (Uthaca: Reading, 1998), p. 41
74. Cited in Lia, p. 181
75. Mitchell, pp. 28–9
76. British embassy, Cairo, 'First Fortnightly Meeting with Amin Osman Pacha', 18 May 1942, FO141/838
77. Ibid.
78. Ibid.
79. Sir Miles Lampson to A. Eden, 24 December 1942; GHQ, Middle East Forces, 'The Ikhwani el Muslimeen Reconsidered', 10 December 1942, PRO, FO141/838
80. Political Intelligence Committee, 'The Ikhwani el Muslimeen', 25 February 1944, WO201/2647

CHAPTER 2: PARTITION IN INDIA AND PALESTINE

1. See my *Web of Deceit: Britain's Real Role in the World* (Vintage: London, 2003), pp. 234–5
2. Ibid., pp. 235–6
3. Robinson, 'The British Empire and Muslim Identity in South Asia', University of London, Royal Holloway College, http://eprints.rhul.ac.uk; French, p. 43
4. Cited in 'Indian Partition and Neo-Colonialism', *Coalition to Oppose the Arms Trade* magazine, Issue 47, www.coat.ncf.ca
5. V. N. Datta, 'Pangs of the Partition: How Pakistan Came into Being', *The Tribune* (Chandigarh, India), 21 January 2001, wwwtribuneindia.com
6. Patrick French, *Liberty or Death: India's Journey to Independence and Division* (Flamingo: London, 1998), p. 126
7. Narendra Singh Sarila, 'Creation of Pakistan', *Times of India*, 17 March 2000. The Lahore resolution was amibivalent in calling for 'independent states' – in the plural – for areas in which Muslims were in the majority. The resolution was only clarified in April 1946 in the Delhi Resolution which proposed that 'Pakistan zones, where the Muslims are in a dominant majority, be constituted into a sovereign independent state.' This meant that the administration of East Pakistan would be controlled from West Pakistan, which later led to the bloody creation of Bangladesh out of East Pakistan in 1971. See French, p. 124
8. Narendra Singh Sarila, *The Shadow of the Great Game: The Untold Story of India's Partition* (Constable: London, 2006), pp. 9–12

9. Ibid., pp. 177, 183, 191
10. Ibid., pp. 192, 208
11. Ibid., pp. 27–8
12. Ibid., p. 27–9
13. French, p. 222
14. Sarila, chapters 12 and 13
15. Ibid., pp. 336, 383
16. Cited in Sahrif Al Mujahid, 'Freedom Struggle: A Synoptic History', *Dawn* (Pakistan), 30 December 2006
17. Cited in Sarila, *The Shadow of the Great Game*, p. 196
18. Francis Robinson, 'Islam and the West: Clash of Civilisation?', undated, http://eprints.rhul.ac.uk
19. Sarila, p. 11
20. Chapman Pincher, *Inside Story: A Documentary of the Pursuit of Power* (Sidgwick & Jackson: London, 1978), p. 198; Richard Aldrich, *The Hidden Hand: Britain, America and Cold War Secret Intelligence*, (John Murray: London, 2008), p. 263
21. Shepherd, p. 222
22. Cited in Ilan Pappe, *The Making of the Arab-Israeli Conflict, 1947–1951* (IB Tauris: London, 2001), p. 14
23. Ilan Pappe, *The Ethnic Cleansing of Palestine* (One World: Oxford, 2007), p. 31
24. Joshua Landis, 'Syria and the 1948 War in Palestine', www.hamrablues.com
25. Pappe, *The Ethnic Cleansing of Palestine*, pp, xii, 40
26. Pappe, *The Making of the Arab-Israeli Conflict, 1947–1951*, p. 153
27. Pappe, *The Ethnic Cleansing of Palestine*, pp. 119–21
28. Ibid., p. 120
29. Pappe, *The Making of the Arab-Israeli Conflict, 1947–1951*, p. 139
30. Ibid., p. 262
31. Jon and David Kimche, *Both Sides of the Hill: Britain and the Palestine War* (Secker and Warburg: London, 1960), p. 86
32. Pappe, *The Ethnic Cleansing of Palestine*, pp. 92–6, 99, 124–5
33. Ibid., p. 125
34. Lorenzo Vidino, 'The Muslim Brotherhood's Conquest of Europe', *Middle East Quarterly*, Winter 2005
35. Kimche and Kimche, p. 89
36. Mitchell, pp. 56–8
37. 'The British Record on Partition as Revealed in British Military Intelligence and Other Official Sources: A Memorandum Submitted to the Special Session of the General Assembly of the United Nations', April 1948, found at http://emperor.vwh.net/history/pris.htm
38. Loftus and Aarons, *The Secret War Against the Jews*, pp. 186, 200; Kimche and Kimche, pp. 117–8, 126
39. Pappe, *The Making of the Arab-Israeli Conflict*, p. 100
40. Kimche and Kimche, p. 86
41. Pappe, *The Making of the Arab-Israeli Conflict*, p. 84
42. Ibid., p. 100
43. Pappe, *The Ethnic Cleansing of Palestine*, p. 44

44. Said Aburish, *A Brutal Friendship: The West and the Arab Elite* (Indigo: London, 1997), pp. 95, 320
45. Ibid., pp. 95, 320
46. Aldrich, p. 267
47. Pappe, *The Ethnic Cleansing of Palestine*, pp, xiii
48. Kimche and Kimche, p. 38
49. Aburish, *A Brutal Friendship*, pp. 95, 320
50. Sir A. Kirkbride to E. Bevin, 20 May 1947, PRO, FO371/62231
51. Foreign Office (signature illegible) to J. Troutbeck, 14 October 1949, PRO, FO371/75120
52. J. Troutbeck to Foreign Office, 13 September 1949, PRO, FO371/75120
53. J. Troutbeck to Foreign Office, 4 October 1949, PRO, FO371/75120
54. E. Bevin to British Embassy, Cairo, 22 September 1949, PRO, FO371/75120

CHAPTER 3: SHOCK TROOPS IN IRAN AND EGYPT

1. For the Kenya, Malaya and British Guiana interventions, see my *Web of Deceit*
2. 'The Problem of Nationalism', in W. Strang to T. Lloyd, 21 June 1952, in *British Documents on the End of Empire*, Series A, Vol.3, part 1, pp. 13–19
3. Foreign Office brief for E. Shuckburgh, 7 January 1956, PRO, FO371/118861
4. C. Rose, minute, 8 February 1952, PRO, FO371/98328
5. J. Watson to H. Trevelyan, 15 May 1956, PRO, FO371/118862
6. D. Fergusson to R. Stokes, 3 October 1951, PRO, FO371/919599
7. F. Shepherd to O. Franks, 2 October 1951, PRO, FO371/91464
8. Cited in Brian Lapping, *End of Empire* (Paladin: London, 1985), p. 266
9. Embassy, Tehran to Foreign Office, 26 January 1952, PRO, FO371/98684; 'Sir F. Shepherd's Analysis of the Persian Situation', 28 January 1952, PRO, FO371/98684
10. F. Shepherd to H. Morrison, 15 March 1951 PRO, FO371/91454; Memoranda by S. Falle, 2 August 1952 and 4 August 1952, PRO, FO248/1531
11. Memorandum by S. Falle, 4 August 1952, PRO, FO 248/1531
12. See my *Web of Deceit:* pp. 312–3
13. A Foreign Office file in March 1953 notes that it is unclear if Kashani had broke with the Fadayan by the time of Razmara's assassination but states that 'he later broke with them and could not use them for intimidation'. Foreign Office, 'Assessment of the Position and Potentialities of Kashani', March 1953, PRO, FO371/104566
14. US Department of State, Office of Intelligence Research, 'Iran: Potential Character of a Kashani-Dominated Government', 31 March 1953, PRO, FO371/104565
15. Dorril, p. 585
16. Ibid., p. 582
17. Foreign Office, 'Assessment of the Position and Potentialities of Kashani', March 1953, PRO, FO371/104566
18. C. M. Woodhouse, *Something Ventured* (Granada: London, 1982), p. 118
19. Dorril, p. 571
20. Ibid. p. 593

21. *Clandestine Service History, Overthrow of Premier Mossadeq of Iran, November 1952–August 1953*, at http://cryptome.org/cia-iran-all.htm
22. Ibid.
23. A. Rothnie, Foreign Office, minute, 25 March 1953, PRO, FO371/104566
24. Foreign Office, 'Assessment of the Position and Potentialities of Kashani', March 1953, PRO, FO371/104566
25. Foreign Office, official name illegible, 27 March 1953, PRO, FO371/104566
26. Dreyfus, p. 115; Dorril, p. 593; Mark Gasiorowski, 'The 1953 Coup d'Etat in Iran', Louisiana State University, http://iran.sa.utoronto.ca
27. Gasiorowski, 'The 1953 coup d'Etat in Iran'
28. Dreyfus, p. 110
29. Masoud Kazemzadeh, 'The Day Democracy Died: The 50th Anniversary of the CIA Coup in Iran', October 2003, www.ghandchi.com; Baqer Moin, *Khomeini: Life of the Ayatollah* (St Martin's Press: New York, 2000), p. 224
30. 'Account of a Conversation', 1 September 1953, PRO, FO371/104571, cited in Masoud Kazemzadeh, 'The Day Democracy Died'
31. Dreyfus, p. 119
32. Ibid., p. 112
33. Ibid.
34. Mitchell, p. 39
35. Ibid., p. 77
36. P. Adams, 'Egypt: the Dawn of Democracy?', 28 July 1975, PRO, FCO93/625
37. R. Campbell to E. Bevin, 23 February 1949, PRO, FO371/73463
38. R. Campbell to Foreign Office, 2 March 1949, PRO, FO371/73463
39. R. Bowker, Foreign Office, minute, 30 October 1951, PRO, FO371/90117; R.Stevenson, British embassy, Cairo, to A. Eden, 6 December 1951, PRO, FO371/90121
40. D. Stewart, Foreign Office, minute, 4 December 1951 and 11 December 1951, PRO, FO141/1450
41. D. Stewart, Foreign Office, minute, 4 December 1951, PRO, FO141/1450
42. R. Beaumont to A. Parsons, 11 June 1971, PRO, FO39/970
43. Mitchell, pp. 113–4
44. R. Stevenson to W. Churchill, 27 May 1953, PRO, FO371/102704
45. Chancery, British Embassy, Cairo to Foreign Office, 19 February 1954, PRO, FO371/108373
46. Mitchell, p. 138
47. W. Churchill to Nasser, 27 October 1954, PRO, FO371/108318
48. R. Stevenson to H. Macmillan, 11 July 1955, PRO, FO371/113579
49. Ibid.
50. Scott Lucas, *Divided We Stand: Britain,the United States and the Suez Crisis* (Sceptre: London, 1991), pp. 93–5
51. J. Watson to H. Trevelyan, 22 March 1956, PRO, FO371/118862; Anthony Nutting, *No End of a Lesson: The Story of Suez* (Constable: London, 1967), pp. 34–5
52. Anthony Eden, *Full Circle* (Cassell: London, 1960), p. 426
53. I. Kirkpatrick to Foreign Secretary, 12 September 1956, PRO, FO371/118832
54. Dorril, pp. 610, 629–34
55. Ibid., p. 629
56. Dreyfus, p. 107

57. I. Kirkpatrick to Foreign Secretary, 12 September 1956, PRO, FO371/118832
58. Said Aburish, *Nasser: The Last Arab* (Duckworth: London, 2004), p. 88
59. Dreyfus, pp. 101–2
60. Dorril, p. 632
61. British Embassy, Paris to Foreign Office, 20 December 1956; T. Garvey, Foreign Office, minute, 14 December 1956, PRO, FO371/118836
62. Foreign Office, minute, 'Some Developments in the Internal Situation of Egypt and Nasser's Position', 30 December 1956, PRO, FO371/125416
63. T. Evans, 11 March 1957, Foreign Office minute, undated [July 1957], PRO, FO371/125444

CHAPTER 4: ISLAM VERSUS NATIONALISM

1. Cabinet Office, 'Study of Future Policy 1960–1970', note by the Joint Secretaries, 26 October 1959, PRO, CAB21/3844
2. Ibid.
3. D. Riches, minute, 8 August 1958, PRO, FO371/132545
4. Selwyn Lloyd, 'International Status of Kuwait', 26 January 1959, PRO, CAB134/2230
5. 'Future of the UK in World Affairs: Note of a Meeting Held in Sir Roger Makins' Room on Thursday 5 December 1957', PRO, T234/768
6. John Loftus, 'The Muslim Brotherhood, Nazis and Al-Qaeda', Jewish Community News, 4 October 2004
7. Richard Labeviere, *Dollars for Terror: The United States and Islam* (Algora: New York, 2000), p. 49
8. Cited in Dreyfus, *Devil's Game*, p. 126–7
9. Aburish, *House of Saud*, pp. 50, 161; Dreyfus, p. 121
10. W. Morris to A. Stirling, 18 September 1968, FCO8/812
11. Cited in David Holden and Richard Johns, *The House of Saud* (Pan Books: London, 1982), pp. 192, 197; Lucas, *Divided We Stand*, p. 113
12. C. Crowe to Earl Home, 30 June 1963, PRO, FO371/168869
13. Eden, *Full Circle*, p. 334
14. Cited in Lucas, p. 117
15. Aburish, *A Brutal Friendship*, p. 238; Aburish, *Nasser*, pp. 157–60; Dreyfus, p. 124
16. M. Weir to P. Blaker, 3 February 1962, PRO, FO371/163009
17. Foreign Office, Levant Dept minute, 24 February 1956, FO371/121858
18. Ibid.
19. J. Watson to H. Trevelyan, 22 March 1956, PRO, FO371/118862; M. Wright to Foreign Office, 19 March 1956, PRO, FO371/121858
20. Cited in Jonathan Bloch and Patrick Fitzgerald, *British Intelligence and Covert Action* (Junction: London, 1983), p. 120
21. S. Lloyd to prime minister, 15 March 1956, PRO, FO371/121858
22. Dorril, p. 622; Lucas, p. 130; Matthew Jones, 'The "Preferred Plan": The Anglo-American Working Group Report on Covert Action in Syria, 1957', *Intelligence and National Security*, Vol.19, No.3, Autumn 2004, p. 403
23. J. Gardener to A. Eden, 9 December 1954, PRO, FO371/110840
24. Jones, p. 403

25. Ben Fenton, 'Macmillan backed Syria assassination plot', *Guardian*, 27 September 2003; Jones, p. 403
26. Ibid.; Jones, p. 407
27. Fenton; Jones, p. 409
28. Dorril, pp. 614–5, 622, 636–7, 642, 655–6; Lucas, p. 218; Fenton; Jones, p. 410
29. Aburish, *A Brutal Friendship*, pp. 127–30
30. Aburish, *Nasser*, p. 130
31. C. Johnston to S. Lloyd, 14 May 1957, PRO, FO371/127880
32. C. Johnston to M. Rose, 23 October 1957, PRO, FO371/127882
33. Schmuel Bar, 'The Muslim Brotherhood in Jordan', Moshe Dayan Centre, undated, p. 27, www.tau.ac.il/dayancenter
34. C. Johnston to M. Rose, 23 October 1957, PRO, FO371/127882
35. C. Johnston to S. Lloyd, 3 July 1957, PRO, FO371/127880
36. C. Johnston to S. Lloyd, 8 May 1957, PRO, FO371/127880
37. Eden, p. 353
38. H. Mason to M. Hadow, 23 January 1957, PRO, FO371/127878
39. C. Johnston to Foreign Office, 15 February 1957, PRO, FO371/127878
40. C. Johnston to M. Rose, 23 October 1957, PRO, FO371/127882
41. Foreign Secretary to British Embassy, Washington, 15 July 1958, PRO, FO371/134009
42. Chiefs of Staff Committee, 'Redeployment of Forces in the Middle East for the Next Twelve Months', 5 September 1958, PRO, DEFE4/111
43. Bar, 'The Muslim Brotherhood in Jordan'
44. F. Tomlinson, 'Indonesia', 11 March 1958, FO371/135849
45. Audrey and George Kahin, *Subversion as Foreign Policy: The Secret Eisenhower and Dulles Debacle in Indonesia* (New Press: New York, 1995), p. 12ff
46. R. Scott to Foreign Office, 12 December 1957, FO371/129531
47. Foreign Office, 'Notes for Discussion of Indonesia in Cabinet', 5 February 1958, FO371/135847
48. Audrey and George Kahin, ibid.
49. H. Caccia to Foreign Office, 14 May 1958, PRO, PREM 11/2730
50. The major Islamic force in Indonesia at the time was the Masyumi (the Indonesian Muslim Consultative Council), which had been formed by the Japanese occupation forces in 1943 to co-opt Islam in Indonesia and was now a loose federation of modernist Islamic social and educational organisations. The CIA had provided financial support to Masyumi's election coffers in Indonesia's first general election in 1955 in which it won 21 per cent of the vote, becoming the second largest party overall and the largest party outside Java; following the election, Masyumi supplied the country's prime minister, Berhanuddin Harahap, in late 1955 and early 1956. However, Masyumi leaders later withdrew from the government, opposing Sukarno's plans to include communists in the Cabinet and his plans for 'guided democracy', which appeared to demonstrate a willingness to replace parliamentary democracy with one-party rule; Masyumi also publicly opposed the Sukarno regime's take-over of Dutch companies in early December 1957, arguing that the impact on the economy would be disastrous. Masyumi now began plotting with other right-wing elements to bring about a replacement government. The US was in contact with Masyumi leaders at this point and appears to

have given their plan encouragement though not serious backing. When the colonels held a conference in West Sumatra in January 1958 to discuss forming a counter-government, several prominent Masyumi leaders attended and played key roles, including Harahap, Mohammad Natsir – another former prime minister and Masyumi's chair – and also Sjafruddin Prawiranegara, a former governor of the Bank of Indonesia; Prawiranegara was appointed the rebel republic's first prime minister in February 1958. Masyumi was dissolved in 1962 and its leaders imprisoned. On their release in 1967, some former leaders set up a new Islamist organisation, the Dewan Dakwah Islamiyah Indonesia (DDII). The DDII would forge close relations with the Islamic World League – established by Saudi Arabia in 1962 – and became the Saudis' preferred counterpart when they began using their oil wealth to finance the spread of conservative, puritan brands of Islamic teaching in Indonesia. Robert Lucius, 'A House Divided: The Decline and Fall of Masyumi (1950–1956)', Naval Postgraduate School, Monterey, California, September 2003, p. 204; Kahin and Kahin, pp. 112, 117–18, 140; Martin van Bruinessen, 'Genealogies of Islamic Radicalism in Post-Suharto Indonesia', Utrecht University, www.let.uu.nl

51. Kahin and Kahin, p. 88
52. International Crisis Group, *Recycling Militants in Indonesia: Darul Islam and the Australian Embassy Bombing*, 22 February 2005, p. 2
53. Kahin and Kahin, p. 78
54. Ibid., p. 202
55. Washington Embassy to Foreign Office, 15 May 1958, PREM 11/2730
56. Kahin and Kahin, pp. 175–85
57. Ibid., p. 205
58. Ibid., pp. 214–16
59. Martin van Bruinessen, an expert on Islamic groups in Indonesia, notes that 'the roots of the present Muslim radical groups in Indonesia can be traced to two relatively "indigenous" Muslim political movements, the Darul Islam movement and the Masyumi party'; See 'Genealogies of Islamic Radicalism in Post-Suharto Indonesia', op. cit
60. International Crisis Group, p. 1

CHAPTER 5: THE GLOBAL ISLAMIC MISSION

1. PUS Steering Committee, 'Foreign Policy', 8 March 1968, PRO, FCO49/167
2. Foreign Office, 'The British Interest in Oil', March 1967, PRO, FCO54/77
3. See my *Unpeople: Britain's Secret Human Rights Abuses* (Vintage: London, 2004), pp. 301–3
4. Ibid., pp. 303–9
5. W. Morris to M. Stewart, 'British Policy Towards Saudi Arabia', 16 April 1969, PRO, FCO8/1181
6. See my *Web of Deceit*, chapter 12
7. Lord Privy Seal, memo, 2 October 1961, PRO, CAB 129/C(61)140
8. Minute by Moberly, 18 December 1957, PRO, FO371/126905, cited in Simon Smith, *Kuwait, 1950–1965: Britain, the al-Sabah and Oil* (OUP: Oxford, 1999), p. 80
9. Dreyfus, *Devil's Game*, p. 132; Lorenzo Vidino, 'Aims and Methods of

Europe's Muslim Brotherhood', *Current Trends in Islamist Ideology Vol.4*, 1 November 2006
10. Cited in Aburish, *House of Saud*, p. 130
11. M. Man to Foreign Office, 2 November 1964, PRO, FO371/174671
12. C. Crowe to F. Brenchley, 18 March 1964, PRO, FO371/174671
13. F. Brenchley to Earl Home, 18 April 63, PRO, FO 371 /168868
14. C. Crowe to Foreign Office, 31 March 1964, PRO, FO371/174671
15. C. Crowe, to R. Butler, 16 April 1964, PRO, FO371/174671
16. Dreyfus, p. 136
17. Lorenzo Vidino, 'The Muslim Brotherhood's Conquest of Europe', *Middle East Quarterly*, Winter 2005
18. Ibid., pp. 156–7, 172–4
19. Ibid., pp. 156–7
20. Aburish, *Nasser*, p. 303
21. Sylvain Besson, *Le temps*, 26 October 2004, cited in Dreyfus, p. 79
22. Ian Johnson, 'The beachhead', *Wall Street Journal*, 12 July 2005. The article also notes that in 1959 Ramadan organised a European Muslim Congress in Munich, which was co-financed by a CIA front organisation, Amcomlib (the American Committee for Liberation from Bolshevism). Then in May 1961 a CIA agent in Munich reportedly met Ramadan to propose a joint propaganda effort against the Soviet Union
23. Aburish, *Nasser*, pp. 256–7
24. Abdel-Bari Atwan, *The Secret History of Al-Qaida* (Saqi: London, 2006), p. 69
25. Cited in Efraim Karsh, *Islamic Imperialism: A History* (Yale University Press, 2007), p. 217
26. P. Unwin, minute, 31 August 1966; H. Fletcher to P. Unwin, 8 September 1966, PRO, FO371/190187
27. D. Speares to J. Richmond, 12 January 1967, PRO, FO371/190189
28. P. Unwin, minute, 20 September 1966, PRO, FO371/190188
29. Foreign Office, 'The Limits of the Middle East', 6 November 1964, PRO, FO371/175547
30. Foreign Office brief, 'Anglo/UAR Relations and British Interests in the Arab world', 1 November 1964, PRO, FO371/178597
31. Foreign Office brief for George Thomson, September 1965, PRO, FO371/183911
32. Cited in Aburish, *House of Saud*, p. 131
33. Dreyfus, p. 145
34. Foreign Office, 'Possible Change of Regime in Saudi Arabia', February 1964, PRO, FO371/174671
35. 'Record of a Conversation Between President Kennedy and the PM', 15 November 1962, PRO, PREM11/3878
36. See my *Unpeople*, chapter 16
37. Joint Intelligence Committee, 'The Implications of the Yemeni Revolt', 30 November 1992, PRO, CAB158/47
38. See *Unpeople*, chapter 16
39. M. Man to M. Stewart, 15 March 1965, PRO, FO371/179878
40. M. Man to F. Brenchley, 23 June 1965, PRO, FO371/179880
41. Foreign Office to Jeddah, 20 February 1966, PRO, FO371/185517

42. C. Brant, minute, 24 March 1966, PRO, FO371/190211
43. W. Morris, memorandum, 'Saudi Foreign Policy', 3 April 1969, PRO, FCO8/1172
44. C. Crowe to Earl Home, 30 June 1963, PRO, FO371/168869
45. Foreign Office, 'Possible Change of Regime in Saudi Arabia', February 1964, PRO, FO371/174671
46. C. Crowe to Earl Home, 31 August 1963, PRO, FO371/168869
47. C. Crowe's valedictory despatch, 14 October 1964, PRO, FO371/174676
48. Mark Phythian, *The Politics of British Arms Sales Since 1964* (Manchester University Press, 2000), pp. 207–10
49. Foreign Office to Jeddah, 27 February 1966, PRO, FO371/185484
50. Denis Allen to various FCO posts, 16 August 1968, PRO, FCO49/168
51. FCO Planning Staff, 'Non-Military Means of Influence in the Persian Gulf, SE Asia and Australasia', August 1968, FCO49/19
52. FCO, 'Position Papers on Current Issues of United Kingdom Foreign Policy', June 1970, PRO, FCO49/305
53. PUS Steering Committee, 'Foreign Policy', 8 March 1968, PRO, FCO49/167
54. FCO brief, 'Saudi Arabia', May 1968, FCO49/167
55. D. McCarthy to M. Weir, 8 July 1965, PRO, FO371/179880
56. *Web of Deceit*, chapter 20
57. Van Bruinessen, 'Genealogies of Islamic Radicalism in Post-Suharto Indonesia', p. 3
58. *Web of Deceit*, p. 396
59. Van Bruinessen, op. cit.
60. The Jemaah Islamiya (JI) militant group, one of Indonesia's most brutal organisations, has its roots in the Darul Islam movement. Many JI members draw ideological inspiration from past DI struggles and are the children of DI members, while many current members of DI have cooperated in JI activities. The JI was founded in the early 1990s as an ideological hybrid of Darul Islam and Saudi Wahhabism, and inspired by Hassan al-Banna and Sayyid Qutb, the Egyptian Muslim Brothers who espoused doctrines legitimising militant jihad against non-Islamic regimes. Abu Bakar Bashir, the spiritual head of the JI, also has a long-standing relationship with the Indonesian military. In the late 1970s, he had been involved in a violent underground movement known as Komando Jihad, which sought to establish an Islamic state in Indonesia and carried out a number of bombings of cinemas, night clubs and churches. Some analysts suggest that Komando Jihad was, to a considerable degree, controlled by General Ali Murtopo, the head of the Indonesian intelligence service, BAKIN, which saw its activities as legitimising clampdowns on less radical Muslim politicians. The movement also consisted of activists from Darul Islam. After serving its purpose, Komando Jihad was 'uncovered' by the authorities, and Bashir was actually jailed in 1978 for his activities with it. It was after his release in 1982 that Bashir began recruiting for the Afghan jihad. Martin van Bruinessen, 'The Violent Fringes of Indonesia's Radical Islam', and 'Islamic State or State Islam?: Fifty Years of State-Islam Relations in Indonesia', University of Utrecht, www.let.uu.nl; Marc Erikson, 'The Osama Bin Laden and al-Qaeda of Southeast Asia', *Asia Times*, 6 February

2002; David Jenkins, 'Military Secret Returns to Haunt', *The Age*, 14 October 2001, www.theage.com.au
61. Hilal Khashan, 'The New World Order and the Tempo of Militant Islam', *British Journal of Middle Eastern Studies*, Vol.24, No.1, May 1997, pp. 5–11
62. W. Morris, 'Annual Review for 1971', 5 January 1972, PRO, FCO8/1905
63. P. Adams to A. Douglas-Home, 7 September 1973, PRO, FCO93/42; P. Adams, 'Egypt: The Dawn of Democracy?', 28 July 1975, PRO, FCO93/625
64. Beverly Milton-Edwards, *Islamic Fundamentalism Since 1945* (Routledge: London, 2005), pp. 54, 58

CHAPTER 6: 'HANDY WEAPONS' IN JORDAN AND EGYPT

1. FCO, 'Potential Problems in British Foreign Policy', January 1974, PRO, FCO 49/499
2. Gilles Kepel, *Jihad: The Trail of Political Islam* (IB Tauris: London, 2003), p. 61
3. Mshari Al-Zaydi, 'History of the Jordanian Muslim Brotherhood', 27 December 2005, www.awsat.com
4. Schmuel Bar, 'The Muslim Brotherhood in Jordan', Moshe Dayan Centre, undated, p. 6, www.taw.ac.il/dayancenter
5. Al-Zaydi, 'History of the Jordanian Muslim Brotherhood'; Kepel, *Jihad*, p. 335; Dreyfus, *Devil's Game*, p. 200
6. FCO, 'Country Assessment Sheet: Jordan', 1 September 1970, PRO, FCO17/1067
7. S. Egerton to Private Secretary, 3 November 1970, PRO, FCO17/1075; James Lunt, *Hussein of Jordan* (Macmillan: London, 1989), p. 149
8. Billy McLean to A. Douglas-Home, 3 November 1970, PRO, FCO17/1067
9. British Embassy, Kuwait to FCO, 5 October 1970, PRO, FCO17/1067
10. MoD, 'Training of Jordanian Special Forces in Jordan by SAS', March 1971, PRO, FCO17/1427
11. P. Laver to Pooley, 26 October 1971; J. Champion to R. Evans, 21 September 1971, PRO, FCO17/1427
12. P. Laver to Evans, 3 March 1971, PRO, FCO17/1427
13. Leslie Aspin, *The Kovacks Contract* (Everest: London, 1975), p. 102
14. Loftus and Aarons, *The Secret War Against the Jews*, pp. 378–83, 385–6; Aspin, p. 106
15. Aspin, pp. 13, 105
16. Ibid., pp. 107, 124–126
17. Ibid., pp. 180–1
18. Loftus and Aarons, pp. 381–6
19. Kepel, *Jihad*, p. 65
20. Dreyfus, *Devil's Game*, pp. 147–8
21. P. Adams, 'Egypt: the Dawn of Democracy?', 28 July 1975 PRO, FCO93 / 625
22. Kepel, *Jihad*, p. 83
23. Ibid., pp. 66–7
24. Jason Burke, *Al-Qaeda: Casting a Shadow of Terror* (IB Tauris: London, 2003), p. 137; Kepel, *Jihad*, p. 65
25. Dreyfus, *Devil's Game*, p. 153; Joel Beinin, 'Political Islam and the New Global Economy: The Political Economy of Islamist Social Movements in

Egypt and Turkey', Stanford University, Department of History, September 2004, p. 10
26. Kepel, *The Roots of Radical Islam* (Saqi: London, pp. 108), 132
27. Kepel, *Jihad*, p. 83
28. Dreyfus, *Devil's Game*, p. 162–3
29. Beinin, 'Political Islam and the New Global Economy', p. 7
30. M. Holding, 'Moslem Brotherhood in Egypt', 24 June 1971, and a handwritten note by a Mr Kay, PRO, FO39/970
31. Ibid.
32. Kepel, *The Roots of Radical Islam*, p. 108
33. Milton-Edwards, *Islamic Fundamentalism Since 1945*, p. 63
34. Beinin, p. 11
35. Kepel, *The War for Muslim Minds*, pp. 85–6

CHAPTER 7: THE SAUDI AND IRANIAN REVOLUTIONS

1. J. Craig to C. Le Quesne, 27 September 1973, PRO, FCO93/42
2. H. Walker, 'Saudi Arabia: Annual Review for 1974', 2 January 1975, PRO, FCO8/2570; P. Wright to A. Rothnie, 25 February 1974, PRO, FCO8/2332
3. FCO, 'Britain in an Altered World: The Outlook for Foreign Policy', 26 February 1974, PRO, FCO49/507
4. Edward Heath, *The Course of my Life* (Hodder & Stoughton: London), pp. 502–6
5. Aburish, *A Brutal Friendship*, p. 85
6. Edward Heath writes of the oil supplies from Abu Dhabi in his autobiography, p. 502; the declassified files highlight Saudi oil supplies though are short on details. See various files in PRO, T317/2142
7. E. Heath to King Faisal, 15 November 1973, PRO, FCO8/2105
8. Aburish, *A Brutal Friendship*, p. 86
9. A. Rothnie to Foreign Secretary, 2 July 1975, PRO, FCO8/2570
10. Kepel, *Jihad*, pp. 70–5
11. Greg Palast and David Pallister, 'FBI claims Bin Laden inquiry was frustrated', *Guardian*, 7 November 2001
12. P. Wright to A. Rothnie, 18 January 1973, PRO, FCO8/2104
13. FCO, Brief for the prime minister, 21 February 1973, PRO, FCO8/2123; A. Rothnie, 'Saudi Arabia: Annual Review for 1973', 22 January 1974, PRO, FCO8/2332
14. FCO, Brief for the prime minister, 21 February 1973, PRO, FCO8/2123
15. P. Walker to Prime Minister, 13 December 1973, PRO, PREM15/2184
16. A. Rothnie, 'Saudi Arabia: Annual Review for 1973', 22 January 1974, PRO, FCO8/2332
17. FCO, 'Saudi Arabia: Summary Note of a Meeting with HM Ambassador on 24 January', 31 January 1973, PRO, FCO8/2107
18. Treasury brief for Chancellor, 27 November 1974, PRO, T317/1945
19. F. Barratt to S. Cambridge, 14 October 1974, PRO, FCO8/2342
20. Treasury, 'Chancellor's Visit to Saudi Arabia', December 1974, PRO, T277/2880
21. S. Cambridge to A. Rothnie, 26 April 1974, PRO, FCO8/2342
22. Treasury, 'Chancellor's Visit to Saudi Arabia', December 1974,

PRO, T277/2880; D. Mitchell, 'Chancellor's Visit to Saudi Arabia', 5 December 1974, PRO, FCO59/1185

23. A. Rothnie to J. Callaghan, 29 November 1975, PRO, FCO8/2572
24. Ibid.
25. Treasury, 'Chancellor's Visit to Saudi Arabia', December 1974, PRO, T277/2880
26. C. Chivers, 'Saudi Investment Policy', 2 January 1975, PRO, T317/142
27. Brief by HM Treasury, 'Visit by Crown Prince Fahd of Saudi Arabia', 15 October 1975, PRO, FCO8/2605
28. 'Crown Prince Fahd's Visit', speaking note for PM, 17 October 1975, PRO, FCO8/2603
29. FCO brief, 'Chancellor's Visit to Saudi Arabia: Political Brief', November 1974, PRO, FCO59/1185
30. D. Allen to A. Parsons, 4 February 1972, PRO, FCO8/2124
31. Record of a conversation between Secretary of State for Foreign and Commonwealth Affairs and HRH Prince Saud bin Faisal, 22 October 1975, PRO, FCO8/2603
32. FCO steering brief, 'Visit of Crown Prince Fahd of Saudi Arabia, 20–23 October 1975', PRO, FCO8/2602
33. Aburish, *The Rise, Corruption and Coming Fall of the House of Saud*, pp. 134–5
34. US State Department to US Embassy, Jeddah, 4 May 1974, PRO, FCO8/2344
35. A. Rothnie to Ministry of Defence, undated [March 1974], FCO8/2343
36. Brigadier Donaldson, 'Fifth Report', 16 December 1970, PRO, FCO8/1755
37. FCO, 'Visit of Prince Abdullah bin Adul Aziz: Defence Relations', 2 July 1973, PRO, FCO8/2125; Holden and Johns, p. 436
38. FCO brief, 'Chancellor's Visit to Saudi Arabia: Political Brief', November 1974, PRO, FCO59/1185
39. Holden and Johns, p. 361
40. H. Walker to T. Clark, 8 February 1975, containing a translation of a Saudi press statement, PRO, FCO8/2590
41. Cited in Campaign Against the Arms Trade 'UK arms sales to Saudi founded on bribery: MoD misleading of Parliament exposed', www.caat.org.uk
42. FO brief for HM Queen, 'Visit of Crown Prince Fahd of Saudi Arabia, 20–23 October 1975', PRO, FCO8/2603
43. D. Tatham to FCO, 10 September 1973, PRO, FCO8/2105
44. Steve Coll, *Ghost Wars: The Secret History of the CIA, Afghanistan and Bin Laden from the Soviet Invasion to September 10, 2001* (Penguin: London, 2004), p. 80
45. John Cooley, *Unholy Wars: Afghanistan, America and International Terrorism* (Pluto Press: London, 1999), p. 225; 'Prince Turki bin Faisal ibn Abdul Aziz al Saud', www.globalsecurity.org; Coll, pp. 87–8
46. 'Speech to the Irano-British Chamber of Commerce', 29 April 1978, www.margaretthatcher.org
47. Sir John Hunt to Prime Minister, 13 November 1978, PRO, PREM16/1720
48. David Owen, *Time to Declare* (Penguin: London, 1992), p. 395
49. Owen, pp. 397–8; Anthony Parsons, Britain's ambassador to Iran, writes in his memoirs that during his meeting with the shah on 16 September 1978,

the shah asked him 'if we could influence the moderate mullahs into a more tractable frame of mind'. Parsons says he replied that 'I and my immediate predecessors had avoided all contact with the religious classes' and it was no use expecting the British to do this now. *The Pride and the Fall: Iran 1974 to 1979* (Jonathan Cape: London, 1984), p. 71. As for the US government, it remains unclear to what degree it had official contacts with the Iranian revolutionaries as the rebellion against the shah was gathering pace in the late 1970s. Richard Cottam, a former CIA officer involved in installing the shah in power in 1953, and who had retained contacts with Iranian dissidents, repeatedly tried to open a dialogue between Khomeini's circle and the US government, but his efforts were rebuffed. (Dreyfus, pp. 226–8, 231–5) On the other hand, the deputy commander-in-chief of NATO forces, US General Huyser, was dispatched by Washington to Iran in January 1979 to negotiate the neutrality of the Iranian armed forces during the upheaval, and is believed to have had some contacts with Khomeini's representatives. Alexandre de Marenches, the head of the French secret service, later wrote: 'The Carter administration, in its idiotic desire to change Iran's political system, had put pressure on the shah, who, weakened, ordered his armed forces not to respond. Better yet, the unspeakable Carter dispatched General Huyser to Iran, who, while making the rounds, told the Iranian armed forces, entirely outfitted with American materiel, that they would not see any more spare parts if they chose to respond; thus, they put Khomeini in power and started the Shiite revolution.' (Alexandre de Marenches, cited in Labeviere, *Dollars for Terror*, p. 213) De Marenches' last point seems exaggerated; so too was the view of some in Iran who saw the Carter administration's (limited) criticism of the shah's human rights record as de facto support to the opposition. If it was indeed the US plan to cultivate the Islamists, it appears very cautious, from the evidence available; it certainly exploded in November with the hostage crisis.

50. Owen, *Time to Declare*, p. 398
51. A. Parsons to FCO, 11 October 1978, PRO, PREM16/1719
52. B. Cartledge to W. Prendergast, FCO, 30 October 1978,PRO, PREM16/1719
53. Cabinet conclusion of meeting, 9 November 1979, PRO, CAB 128/64
54. See files in PRO, PREM16/1720
55. A. Parsons to FCO, 4 December 1978, PRO, PREM16/1720
56. Owen, p. 400
57. Ibid.
58. The writer William Engdahl claims that the British helped organise the Khomeini takeover to enable BP to conclude an oil deal. This section in Engdahl's book is substantially without footnotes or other corroboration, and remains unconvincing to me. See Engdahl, *A Century of War: Anglo-American Oil Politics and the New World Order* (Pluto Press: London, 2004), pp. 171–3
59. Owen, p. 402
60. Cited in 'Britain sought to discourage shah', BBC news, 30 December 2009
61. House of Commons, *Hansard*, 13 February 1979, Col.956.
62. House of Commons, *Hansard*, 15 February 1979, Col.312; see also 8 February 1979, Col.574
63. Sir John Hunt to Prime Minister, 20 March 1979, PRO, PREM 16/2130
64. 'Britain sought to discourage shah', BBC news, 30 December 2009

65. Ibid.
66. House of Commons, *Hansard*, 20 November 1979, Col.203
67. Owen, pp. 401–2
68. 'Press Conference for British Press in Washington', 18 December 1979, www.margaretthatcher.org; House of Commons, *Hansard*, 14 April 1980, Col.790
69. House of Commons, *Hansard*, 17 January 1980, Col.1867; 14 April 1980, Col.797. According to Stephen Dorril, when six officials of the US embassy managed to escape being taken hostage and asked for sanctuary in the British embassy, they were turned away, much to the dismay of the CIA – an act presumably intended to disassociate Britain from the US in the eyes of the new regime. Dorril, *The Silent Conspiracy: Inside the Intelligence Services in the 1990s* (Mandarin: London, 1993), p. 390
70. 'East–West Relations', 28 January 1980, www.margaretthatcher.org
71. House of Commons, *Hansard*, 22 April 1980, Col.121; 29 April 1980, Col.1144
72. Dreyfus, pp. 240–1
73. Ibid., pp. 240–1
74. Ibid., p. 241
75. Michael Evans, 'When Reagan first helped Khomeini', *Times*, 21 November 1986; Fisk, p. 149; John Simpson, *Behind Iranian Lines* (Fontana: London), 1988, p. 99

CHAPTER 8: TRAINING IN TERRORISM: THE AFGHAN JIHAD

1. House of Commons, *Hansard*, 28 January 1980, Cols.935–40
2. For example, in April 1981, Margaret Thatcher told a press conference in Delhi that 'I am not recommending military intervention in Afghanistan. We are trying to do everything we can through diplomatic channels.' 'Press Conference Leaving New Delhi', 17 April 1981, www.margaretthatcher.org
3. Cooley, *Unholy Wars*, p. 93
4. Burke, *Al-Qaeda: Casting a Shadow of Terror*, p. 72
5. Husain Haqqani, 'Afghanistan's Islamist Groups', *Current Trends in Islamist Ideology*, Vol.5, 2007; Burke, p. 64
6. J. Drinkall to J. Callaghan, 25 October 1975, PRO, FCO37/1551
7. J. Drinkall to R. O'Neill, 8 December 1975, PRO, FCO37/1551
8. K. Himsworth to D. Lieven, 24 June 1975, PRO, FCO37/1551
9. D. Slater, minute, 2 February 1973, PRO, FCO37/1215
10. Ibid.
11. J. Drinkall, 'Afghanistan: Annual Review for 1974', 2 January 1975, PRO, FCO37/1550
12. Cited in Anthony Davis, 'A brotherly vendetta', *Asia Week*, 6 December 1996, www.asiaweek.com
13. Burke, p. 64
14. Dreyfus, *Devil's Game*, p. 263
15. Ibid., pp. 250
16. Ibid., pp. 264–5
17. Memo from Z. Brzezinski to President Carter, 26 December 1979, http://edition.cnn.com

18. 'SCC Meeting on Afghanistan (CIA appreciation of Soviet Intentions)', 17 December 1979, at www.margaretthatcher.org
19. Margaret Thatcher, speech to the Foreign Policy Association, 18 December 1979, www.margaretthatcher.org
20. House of Commons, *Hansard*, 28 January 1980, Cols.935–40
21. 'Speech at Refugee Camp on Pakistan's Afghan Border', 8 October 1981, www.margaretthatcher.org
22. Atwan, p. 35
23. 'Prince Turki bin Faisal ibn Abdul Aziz al Saud', www.globalsecurity.org; Adam Robinson, *Bin Laden: Behind the Mask of the Terrorist* (Mainstream: Edinburgh, 2001), p. 97; Peter Bergen, *Holy War: Inside the Secret World of Osama Bin Laden* (Phoenix: London, 2002), p. 58; Atwan, *The Secret History of al-Qaeda*, p. 155; Kepel, *Jihad*, p. 144
24. Cooley, *Unholy Wars*, p. 226
25. Simon Reeve, *The New Jackals: Ramzi Yousef, Osama Bin Laden and the Future of Terrorism* (André Deutsch: London, 1999), p. 167
26. Burke, *Al-Qaeda*, p. 73
27. Omid Marzban, 'Gulbuddin Hekmatyar: From Holy Warrior to Wanted Terrorist', *Terrorism Monitor*, 21 September 2006, www.jamestown.org; Burke, p. 72
28. Tariq Ali, 'The Colour Khaki', *New Left Review*, January/February 2003, p. 6
29. Amir Mir, *The True Face of Jehadis: Inside Pakistan's Network of Terror* (Roli Books: New Delhi, 2006), p. 2
30. Kepel, *Jihad*, p. 142
31. Cooley, *Unholy Wars*, p. 55
32. Loretta Napoleoni, *Terror Inc: Tracing the Money Behind Global Terrorism* (Penguin: London, 2004), pp. 114, 108
33. Assem Akram, cited in Labeviere, *Dollars for Terror*, p. 75
34. Burke, p. 58; Napoleoni, p. 115
35. Burke, p. 58
36. Kepel, *Jihad*, p. 145
37. Syed Saleem Shahzad, 'Pakistan turns on itself', www.atimes.com, undated
38. Ronan Gunaratna, *Inside Al Qaeda: Global Network of Terror* (C. Hurst: London, 2003), p. 18; Evan Kohlmann, *Al-Qaida's Jihad in Europe: The Afghan–Bosnian Network* (Berg: Oxford, 2004), p. 42; Burke, *Al-Qaeda*, p. 71
39. Cooley, *Unholy Wars*, p. 81
40. George Crile, *Charlie Wilson's War* (Grove Press: New York, 2003), p. 199
41. Loftus and Aarons, *The Secret War Against the Jews*, p. 398
42. Crile, p. 197
43. Mark Urban, *UK Eyes Alpha: The Inside Story of British Intelligence* (Faber & Faber: London, 1996), p. 36
44. Mir, *The True Face of Jehadis*, p. 2
45. Rahul Bedi, 'Why? An Attempt to Explain the Unexplainable', 14 September 2001, www.janes.com
46. B. Raman, 'Gen. Pervez Musharraf: His Past and Present', 1 July 1999, www.saag.org. According to Raman, a former Indian intelligence officer, Musharraf was involved in the clandestine training of Islamist militants organised in the 'Pakistani Army of Islam'. Musharraf helped select one hundred madrassas and introduced military training into them by serving

and retired army officers. It was from these madrassas that came several future Pakistani terrorist leaders and the Taliban; B. Raman, 'Jaish-e-Mohammed (JEM) – A Backgrounder', 3 October 2001, www.saag.org

47. Pervez Musharraf, *In the Line of Fire: A Memoir* (Simon & Schuster: New York, 2006), p. 208
48. Steve Coll, *Ghost Wars*, p. 135
49. Cooley, *Unholy Wars*, pp. 90–1
50. Cited in Crile, *Charlie Wilson's War*, p. 335
51. Dorril, *Silent Conspiracy*, p. 392; Cooley, p. 96
52. Cited in Sean Kelly, 'Afghanistan – The British Connection', www.solidnet.org
53. Ken Connor, *Ghost Force: The Secret History of the SAS* (Orion: London, 2002), pp. 419–20; 'Scots link to US terror suspect', BBC news, 16 September 2001, www.bbc.co.uk
54. Cooley, p. 93
55. Cooley, pp. 96–7, 108. Little is known about Safi's activities after the war. In 2001, he was put on the UN list of individuals whose assets were frozen due to suspected links to al-Qaida and Taliban terrorism, but died later that year. 'Architect who built Omar's complex says Omar did not marry Bin Laden's daughter', *Newsweek*, 13 January 2002; 'Financial Sanctions: Al-Qaida and Taliban', Bank of England, 25 October 2005.
56. Stephen Grey, 'Mint Tea with the Terrorists', *New Statesman*, 11 April 2005
57. Ibid.
58. Dorril, *Silent Conspiracy*, p. 392
59. Coll, *Ghost Wars*, p. 54; Ahmed Rashid, 'A Warm and charismatic man with little desire', *Telegraph*, 27 October 2001
60. Cooley, pp. 96–7, 108; Rashid, 'A warm and charismatic man'
61. Jonathan Steele, 'Thatcher to meet Afghan guerrilla', *Guardian*, 5 March 1986; By the late 1980s Haq, who had reportedly become more of an Afghan nationalist than an Islamic fundamentalist, was still a darling of Washington, who may have regarded him as a future leader in Afghanistan as US forces prepared to defeat the Taliban in 2001; however, he was executed by the Taliban soon after the beginning of the war in October that year. Rashid, 'A warm and charismatic man'; B. Raman, 'Assassination of Haji Abdul Qadeer in Kabul', 8 July 2002, www.saag.org
62. Defence Intelligence Agency, 'Veteran Afghanistan Traveler's Analysis of Al Qaeda and Taliban Exploitable Weaknesses', 2 October 2001, National Security Archive, 'The September 11th Sourcebooks – Volume VII: The Taliban File', www.gwu.edu
63. Milt Bearden, 'Meet the Pashtuns: Mired in the Tracks of Alexander the Great', *Counterpunch*, 31 March 2004; Coll, pp. 202, 288
64. Urban, *UK Eyes Alpha*, p. 36; Michael Smith, 'SAS to play key role in capturing Bin Laden', *Telegraph*, 17 September 2001; Dorril, *MI6*, p. 752; Burke, *Al-Qaeda*, p. 76; Although Osama Bin Laden was ideologically closer to the Hekmatyar and Sayyaf groups, he was also an admirer of Massoud and reportedly devoted considerable, though ultimately fruitless, efforts to reconciling Massoud's factions with the others. Massoud's forces would go on to fight it out with Hekmatyar's in the brutal civil war that followed the withdrawal of the Soviets, committing numerous atrocities. As a prominent leader of the US and British-

backed Northern Alliance fighting the Taliban in 2001, Massoud was blown up in a bomb attack two days before 9/11. Coll, pp. 237, 123, 151; Crile, p. 198

65. Connor, *Ghost Force*, p. 422
66. John Fullerton, 'H Khan', Reuters 4 February 2002, at www.pakdef.info
67. Prashant Sikshit, 'MANPADS Menace', 27 June 2005, www.ipcs.org; 'Afghan Stinger Buyback Program Underway', 5 February 2005, www.aeronews.net
68. Cooley, p. 63; Hansard, *House of Commons*, 28 July 1989, Col.1164
69. Bergen, *Holy War*, p. 71
70. Ibid., p. 73
71. Ibid., p. 73
72. Mohammed Yousaf and Mark Adkin, *Afghanistan: The Bear Trap* (Casemate: Pennsylvania, 1992), pp. 189–90, 200
73. Rashid, *Taliban*, p. 129; Coll, p. 90, 161
74. Mariam Abou Zahab and Olivier Roy, *Islamist Networks: The Afghan–Pakistan Connection* (C. Hurst: London, 2004), p. 19; Syed Saleem Shahzad, 'Pakistan turns on itself', www.atimes.com, undated
75. Extract from a Foreign Office report from Lahore, 15 January 1957; O. Forster to E. Le Tocq, 30 November 1955, PRO, DO 35/5154
76. Burke, pp. 77–8
77. Ibid., pp. 79–80
78. Robin Cook, 'The struggle against terrorism cannot be won by military means', *Guardian*, 8 July 2005

CHAPTER 9: THE DICTATOR, THE KING AND THE AYATOLLAH

1. See my *The Ambiguities of Power: British Foreign Policy Since 1945* (Zed: London, 1995), p. 212
2. Milton-Edwards, *Islamic Fundamentalism Since 1945*, p. 61
3. Burke, p. 86
4. International Crisis Group, *Pakistan: The Military and the Mullahs*, 20 March 2003, p. 3
5. Kepel, *Jihad*, p. 101
6. Cabinet meeting, 7 July 1977, PRO, CAB/128/62/2
7. House of Commons, *Hansard*, 16 January 1978, Col.47
8. House of Commons, *Hansard*, 6 February 1979, Col.203
9. House of Commons, *Hansard*, 29 January 1980, Col.1118
10. 'Haig to Thatcher', 18 April 1981, www.margaretthatcher.org
11. 'Speech at Banquet Given by Pakistan President (Zia ul Haq)', 8 October 1981, www.margaretthatcher.org
12. Two other organisations were also established at this time. The Sipah-e-Sahaba Pakistan, or SSP, was established in 1984 by a group of Deobandi Muslims backed by the Pakistani state in order to counter the influence of a Pakistani Shia group, the Tehrik Nifaz Fiquah Jaffria (TNFY, since renamed as the Tehrik Fiquah Jaffria, or TFJ). SSP cadres were trained and inducted into Afghanistan to fight Soviet troops. The US was later to support the SSP as a way of countering Shia and Iranian influence in the region, according to some reports. Subsequently, the SSP was accused of involvement in sectarian terrorist violence against Shias in Pakistan and is currently

believed to have 3–6,000 trained activists. Another organisation, the Hizb-ul-Mujahideen (HM) – not to be confused with the HUM – was founded in 1989 by JI leaders as the JI's military wing. Established at the behest of the ISI to 'liberate' Kashmir from Indian control, within a year HM could muster 10,000 cadres to fight in the territory; B. Raman, 'Sipah-e-Sahaba Pakistan, Lashkar-e-Jhangvi, Bin Laden and Ramzi Yousef', 1 July 2002, www.saag.org; Mir, pp. 92–3; B. Raman, 'International Jihadi Terrorism', 6 May 2005, www.saag.org; 'Hizb-ul-Mujahideen', www.globalsecurity.org

13. Mir, *The True Face of Jehadis*, pp. 75–6
14. Mir, pp. 75–6; B. Raman, 'Harkat-ul-Mujahideen', www.ict.org.il
15. Wilson John, 'Lashkar-e-Toiba: New Threats Posed by an Old Organisation', *Terrorism Monitor*, 24 February 2005, www.jamestown.org
16. Mir, pp. 61–2, 122; Zahab and Roy, *Islamist Networks*, p. 53
17. B. Raman, 'International Jihadi Terrorism and Europe – An Indian Perspective', 17 November 2005, www.saag.org
18. Ibid.
19. B. Raman, 'Home-Grown Jihadis (Jundullah) in UK and US', 6 May 2007, www.saag.org
20. Lorenzo Vidino, 'Aims and Methods of Europe's Muslim Brotherhood'
21. Kepel, *Jihad*, pp. 186–7; Vidino, 'Aims and Methods of Europe's Muslim Brotherhood'
22. Although terrorism and radicalisation were major consequences of the Anglo–American cultivation of the Zia regime in the 1980s, there was another potentially great cost. One of the concessions that General Zia extracted from President Reagan in return for Pakistan's cooperation against the Soviets in Afghanistan was the US turning a blind eye to Islamabad's acquisition of the nuclear bomb. This is an issue that goes beyond the scope of this book, but which is hardly negligible given the frightening prospect of a devastating future conflict with a nuclear-armed India. Crile, *Charlie Wilson's War*, p. 463
23. Robinson, *Bin Laden*, p. 97; Gerald Posner, *Why America Slept: The Failure to Prevent 9/11* (Ballantine: New York, 2003), p. 31; Yossef Bodansky, *Bin Laden: The Man who Declared War on America* (Forum: New York, 1999), p. 13
24. Robinson, p. 97; Posner, p. 31; Bodansky, p. 13
25. Dorril, *Silent Conspiracy*, p. 390
26. Bloch and Fitzgerald, *British Intelligence and Covert Action*, p. 133; 'South Yemen sentences 12 to death for sabotage plot', *New York Times*, 8 April 1982; 'South Yemen asks death for 13 in sabotage case', Reuters, 31 March 1982
27. Bob Woodward, *Veil: The Secret Wars of the CIA, 1981–1987* (Simon & Schuster: New York, 1987), p. 398
28. Aburish, *A Brutal Friendship*, pp. 246–7
29. Kepel, *The War for Muslim Minds*, pp. 178–181
30. *The 9/11 Commission Report: Final Report of the National Commission on Terrorist Attacks upon the United States* (W. W. Norton, undated), p. 52
31. Labeviere, *Dollars for Terror*, p. 240; Gunaratna, *Inside Al Qaeda*, p. 20; Kepel, *Jihad*, pp. 79–80

32. 'Speech at Lunch for British Businessmen', 20 April 1981, www.margaretthatcher.org
33. Urban, *UK Eyes Alpha*, p. 236
34. David Leigh and Rob Evans, 'BAE accused of secretly paying £1bn to Saudi prince', *Guardian*, 7 June 2007; Danny Fortson, 'The charges that could torpedo BAE', *Independent*, 10 June 2007; Michael Herman, 'BAE sued over alleged Saudi bribes', *Times*, 20 September 2007
35. Cited in Said Aburish, *Saddam Hussein: The Politics of Revenge* (Bloomsbury: London, 2001), p. 229
36. Graeme Stewart, *Silent Heroes: The Story of the SAS* (Michael O'Mara Books: London, 1997), p. 215
37. Kenneth Timmerman, 'Fanning the Flames: Guns, Greed and Geopolitics in the Gulf War', www.iran.org
38. House of Commons, *Hansard*, 23 November 1992, Col.680; House of Commons, *Hansard*, 20 June 1995, Col.231
39. Chris Blackhurst, 'Government firm "broke Iran embargo"', *Independent*, 17 October 1995
40. Kenneth Timmerman, 'Fanning the Flames', www.iran.org
41. Loftus and Aarons, *The Secret War Against the Jews*, pp. 409, 412, 415
42. Napoleoni, *Terror Inc*, p. 61
43. Loftus and Aarons, pp. 399, 415
44. Ibid., pp. 409, 412, 415
45. Cited in Tim Kelsey and Peter Koenig, 'Was this man Britain's Irangate?', *Independent*, 28 October 1994
46. Loftus and Aarons, pp. 415–6
47. Ibid., pp. 412–6; Kelsey and Koenig
48. Loftus and Aarons, pp. 442, 447, 451, 479
49. Ibid., pp. 442, 447, 451, 479
50. Ibid., pp. 420, 422–3
51. House of Commons, *Hansard*, 18 April 1995, Col.6
52. Loftus and Aarons, pp. 405, 440
53. Ibid., pp. 424, 439, 475
54. The indictment states: 'Since in or about the early 1970s, Monzer Al Kassar ... has been an international weapons trafficker. During this time period, Kassar has been a source of weapons and military equipment for armed factions engaged in violent conflicts around the world. Specifically, Kassar has provided weapons and military equipment to such factions in Nicaragua, Brazil, Cyprus, Bosnia, Croatia, Somalia, Iran and Iraq, among other countries. Some of these factions have included known terrorist organisations, such as the Palestinian Liberation Front (PLF) ... Kassar ... has developed an international network of criminal associates, front companies, and bank accounts in, among other countries, the United Kingdom, Spain, Lebanon, Syria, Iraq, Poland, Bulgaria and Romania. Additionally, Kassar has engaged in money-laundering transactions in bank accounts throughout the world to disguise the illicit nature of his criminal proceeds.' US District Court, Southern District of New York, USA vs. Monzer Al Kassar, at http://hosted.ap.org/specials/interactives/_documents/kassar_indictment.pdf
55. Urban, *UK Eyes Alpha*, p. 96

56. James Ring Adams and Douglas Frantz, *A Full Service Bank: How BCCI Stole Millions Around the World* (Simon & Schuster: New York, 1992), p. 135; Conal Walsh, 'What spooks told Old Lady about BCCI', *Observer*, 18 January 2004; this article was removed from the *Observer* website but is available at http://www.apfn.net/MESSAGEBOARD/01-18-04/discussion.cgi.25.html
57. Adams and Frantz, p. 135
58. Walsh, 'What spooks …', op. cit
59. 'Abu Nidal "behind Lockerbie bombing"', BBC news, 23 August 2002. Another theory alleges that Monzer al-Kassar helped Ahmed Jibril's Popular Front for the Liberation of Palestine General Command group to place a rogue bag onto the flight, and that Jibril had taken on the assignment at the behest of Tehran, seeking to avenge the US downing of an Iranian Airbus passenger jet. See Roy Rowan, 'Pan Am 103: Why did they die?', *Time*, 27 April 1992
60. Dorril, *MI6*, p. 760; Serious Fraud Office, 'Vietnamese Province Victim of a Bogus Rice Export Deal, Case: Hashemi', www.sfo.gov.uk; David Leppard, 'MI6 in on deal for Iran missiles', *Sunday Times*, 4 September 1994; Richard Norton-Taylor and William Raynor, 'Jailed "go-between" on UK–Iran arms deals is freed to keep MI6 secrets out of court', *Guardian*, 6 February 1999
61. David Leppard and Tim Kelsey, 'Tory donor charged over Iran defence deal', *Sunday Times*, 9 February 1997; Tim Kelsey and David Leppard, 'Tory donor has spent lifetime as arms dealer', *Sunday Times*, 9 February 1997
62. Antony Barnett, Yvonne Ridley and Shraga Elam, 'British agents helped Iran to make killer gas', *Observer*, 13 June 1999; Dorril, *MI6*, pp. 767–8
63. Loftus and Aarons, *The Secret War Against the Jews*, p. 436
64. Cited in Craig Unger, *House of Bush, House of Saud* (Gibson Square Books: London, 2006), p. 71; Mike Davis, *Buda's Wagon: A Brief History of the Car Bomb* (Verso: London, 2007), p. 91
65. James Rusbridger, *The Intelligence Game: Illusions and Delusions of International Espionage* (IB Tauris: London, 1991), p. 150
66. Cited in Crile, *Charlie Wilson's War*, p. 201
67. There is considerable evidence that the growth of Hamas was aided by Israel, keen to provide a counter to the secular, nationalist Palestine Liberation Organisation, and to divide its opposition in the occupied territories. The Israeli domestic security service, Shin Beth, had been developing a plan since the early 1970s to support the emergence of organisations likely to compete with and weaken the chief Palestinian nationalist organisation, the PLO. Along with the Saudis, the Israelis began to finance the Palestinian branch of the Muslim Brotherhood and allowed its Islamic centre in Gaza to function along with its nursery schools, hospitals and clinics. The Palestinian Islamists under Sheikh Ahmed Yassin had founded the Islamic Society in 1973 and in February 1988, this became the Movement for Islamic Resistance (or Hamas). The organisation took off after the 1979 Iranian Revolution and in the 1980s had begun to engage in direct competition with the PLO for supremacy in Palestine. Even after the founding of Hamas, there are indications that the Israelis might have backed it. Labeviere, pp. 204–5; Dreyfus, p. 208
68. Kepel, *Jihad*, pp. 8–9
69. Robinson, *Bin Laden*, p. 136

CHAPTER 10: NURTURING AL-QAIDA

1. Kepel, *Jihad*, pp. 219–21
2. Ibid.
3. John Mintz and Douglas Farah, 'In search of friends among the foes', *Washington Post*, 11 September 2004
4. Cited in Dorril, *MI6*, p. 770
5. United States District Court, Southern District of New York, Complaint, 04 Civ.5970, Paras 247–8
6. Urban, *UK Eyes Alpha*, p. 157
7. General Sir Peter de la Billiere, *Storm Command: A Personal Account of the Gulf War* (Harper Collins: London , 1992), p. 116
8. Aburish, *Saddam Hussein*, pp. 308–9
9. Urban, p. 179
10. Posner, *Why America Slept*, pp. 45–6; Atwan, *The Secret History of al-Qaeda*, p. 161. Abdel Bari Atwan suspects this was an 'unwritten truce'
11. Ibid., p. 112
12. Labeviere, *Dollars for Terror*, p. 107
13. Posner, p. 211
14. United States District Court, Southern District of New York, Complaint, 04 Civ.5970, Para 254
15. Jean-Charles Brisard, 'Terrorism Financing: Roots and Trends of Saudi Terrorism Financing', 19 December 2002. A successful law suit was brought against the allegations contained in the report against Khaled Salim bin Mahfouz, in the British High Court in July 2004. See http://www.binmahfouz.info/pdf/faq_4_judgment.pdf. For accusations of these charities' role in terrorist financing, see United States District Court, Southern District of New York, Complaint, 04 Civ.5970, passim
16. David Kaplan, 'The Saudi Connection', *US News and World Report*, 12 July 2003
17. Napoleoni, pp. 146–7, 174–6
18. Ibid., p. 162
19. Ibid., pp. 146–7, 171
20. Coll, *Ghost Wars*, p. 517
21. Cited in Phythian, *The Politics of British Arms Sales Since 1964*, p. 198
22. Ibid., p. 226
23. 'Speech to Chatham House Conference on Saudi Arabia', 4 October 1993, www.margaretthatcher.org
24. Labeviere, p. 226
25. CIA, 'Usama bin Ladin: Islamic Extremist Financier', 1996, National Security Archive, 'The September 11th Sourcebooks – Volume 1: Terrorism and US Policy', www.gwu.edu
26. United States District Court, Southern District of New York, Complaint, 04 Civ.5970, Para 111
27. Ewen Macaskill et al, 'Bin Laden terror network active in 34 countries', *Guardian*, 14 September 2001; Robinson, pp. 167–9
28. Labeviere, p. 101; Roland Jacquard, *In the Name of Osama Bin Laden: Global Terrorism and the Bin Laden Brotherhood* (Duke University Press: Durham, 2002), p. 67
29. Gunaratna, *Inside Al Qaeda: Global Network of Terror*, p. 12

30. Ibid., p. 116
31. United States District Court, Southern District of New York, USA vs Usama bin Laden and others, Indictment, S(9)98Cr.1023 (LBS), para 11, rr
32. Ibid., para 11, jj and ttt
33. Ibid., para 11, rrrr
34. Ibid., para 11, ooooo; Special Immigration Appeals Commission, 'AJOUAOU and AB, B, C and D and Secretary of State for the Home Department', 29 October 2003, para 234, 243, 291
35. Gunaratna, p. 117
36. United States District Court, Southern District of New York, USA v.Usama bin Laden and others, Indictment, S(9)98Cr.1023 (LBS), paras 11, nn, u
37. O'Neill and McGrory, *The Suicide Factory: Abu Hamza and the Finsbury Park Mosque*, p. 112; Duncan Gardham, 'US most wanted terrorist suspect in new extradition fight in Britain', *Telegraph*, 12 February 2009
38. Nick Hopkins and Richard Norton-Taylor, 'Faulty intelligence', *Guardian*, 29 November 2001
39. Ibid.
40. An Egyptian security source said in September 1998 that 'we know them all and have informed the British government of their activities, which include the organisation of meetings and planning acts of subversion in a number of Arab and Islamic countries, including Egypt.' He added: 'We have repeatedly asked Britain not to grant them political asylum or residence permits.' Ahmed Moussa, 'Who are the UK-based militants?', *al-Ahram*, 3 September 1998; Adel Darwish, 'Iyman el-Zawahiri: The terror mastermind of al-Qaeda', 15 February 2002, www.mideastnews.com
41. See Richard Norton-Taylor, 'Blair intervened in deportation process', *Guardian*, 16 November 2004; 'UK: Egyptian National "unlawfully detained" after Intervention by Prime Minister', November 2004, www.statewatch.org
42. Bergen, *Holy War: Inside the Secret World of Osama Bin Laden*, p. 5
43. Steve Coll and Susan Glasser, 'In London, Islamic radicals found a haven', *Washington Post Foreign Service*, 10 July 2005
44. 'US Treasury Designates Two Individuals with Ties to al-Qaida, UBL', 21 December 2004, www.treasury.gov
45. Mahan Abedin, 'The dangers of silencing Saudi dissent', *Asia Times*, undated, www.atimes.com
46. Ibid.
47. Coll, *Ghost Wars*, p. 270
48. 'Interview: Dr Saad al-Faqih', *Middle East Intelligence Bulletin*, November 2003, www.meib.org
49. Mahan Abedin, 'The face of Saudi opposition', *Asia Times*, undated, www.atimes.com
50. Burke, *Al-Qaeda*, p. 140
51. Gunaratna, p. 116
52. O'Neill and McGrory, p. 111
53. David Rose, 'Resentful west spurned Sudan's key terror files', *Observer*, 30 September 2001
54. O'Neill and McGrory, p. 110
55. Hopkins and Norton-Taylor, 'Faulty intelligence'

56. Coll, pp. 271–2
57. Gunaratna, p. 38
58. CIA, 'Usama bin Ladin: Islamic Extremist Financier', 1996, National Security Archive, 'The September 11th Sourcebooks – Volume 1: Terrorism and US policy', www.gwu.edu
59. Jonathan Ford, *Guardian*, 27 May 1995
60. Nick Cohen, 'Saudi dissident goes to court', *Independent*, 7 January 96
61. Phythian, p. 268
62. Mark Hollingsworth, *Saudi Babylon: Torture, Corruption and Cover-Up inside the House of Saud* (Mainstream Publishing: Edinburgh, 2006), p. 171

CHAPTER 11: PAKISTAN'S SURGE INTO CENTRAL ASIA

1. Burke, *Al-Qaeda*, p. 79
2. Cooley, *Unholy Wars*, p. 237
3. Mir, *The True Face of Jehadis*, pp. 5, 76; Yossef Bodansky, 'Pakistan's Kashmir Strategy', www.kashmir-information.com
4. B. Raman, 'Lashkar-e-Toiba: Its Past, Present and Future', Paper No.175, www.saag.org; Bodansky, 'Pakistan's Kashmir Strategy'
5. See submission by Professor Shaun Gregory, Pakistan Security Research Unit, University of Bradford, Foreign Affairs Committee, *Global Security: Afghanistan and Pakistan*, Eighth report, Session 2008–09, July 2009, Ev163
6. Coll, *Ghost Wars*, p. 292
7. Mark Kukis, 'Camp Fire – With Friends Like These …', *New Republic*, 13 February 2006, citing the author Hassan Abbas
8. CIA, 'Harkat ul-Ansar: Increasing Threat to Western and Pakistani Interests', August 1996, National Security Archive, 'Pakistan: "The Taliban's Godfather?"', www.gwu.edu
9. House of Commons, *Hansard*, 5 July 1989, Col.173; 25 July, Col.601; 26 October 1989, Col.599; 25 October 1989, Col.488; 14 May 1990, Col.692; 3 November 1993, Col.282; 28 June 1994, Col.523; 2 November 1994, Col.1194
10. Ibid., 10 May 1989, Col.847
11. Ibid., 25 July 1991, Col.1354
12. Ibid., 25 June 1992, Col.281
13. Ibid., 9 March 1994, Col.254, 29 November 1994, Col.618, 22 March 1993, Col.517
14. Ibid., 2 July 1993, Col.658, 28 June 1994, Col.464
15. Ibid., 9 June 1995, Col.474
16. Dalip Singh and James Clark, 'Britons take war holidays in Kashmir', *Sunday Times*, 21 January 2001
17. Yosri Fouda and Nick Fielding, *Masterminds of Terror: The Truth Behind the Most Devastating Terrorist Attack the World has Ever Seen* (Mainstream Publishing: Edinburgh, 2003), p. 47
18. Nick Fielding, 'The British jackal', *Sunday Times*, 21 April 2002
19. Musharraf, *In the Line of Fire: A Memoir*, p. 225
20. B. Raman, 'Home-Grown Jihadis (Jundullah) in UK and US', 6 May 2007, www.saag.org

21. B. Raman, 'Harkat-ul-Mujahideen: An Update', 20 March 1999, www.saag.org
22. 'Jaish-e-Mohamed', www.globalsecurity.org; B. Raman, 'Harkat-ul-Mujahideen: An Update', 20 March 1999, www.saag.org
23. B. Raman, 'Jihad in US: From Pakistan With Love', 14 June 2005, and 'International Jihadi Terrorism and Europe – An Indian Perspective', 17 November 2005, www.saag.org
24. Yossef Bodansky, 'Islamabad's Road Warriors', www.kashmir-information.com
25. Yossef Bodansky, 'Chechnya: The Mujahidin Factor', January 1998, www.freeman.org
26. Memorandum by BP Amoco, March 1999, in House of Commons, Foreign Affairs Committee, *Sixth Report*, Session 1998–99, 20 July 1999
27. Peter Dale Scott, 'Al Qaeda, US Oil Companies and Central Asia', 30 July 2005, wwwglobalresearch.ca
28. House of Lords, *Hansard*, 29 January 1996, Col.WA95
29. Memorandum by Monument Oil & Gas, 18 March 1999, in House of Commons, Foreign Affairs Committee, *Sixth Report*, Session 1998–99, 20 July 1999
30. Yossef Bodansky, 'Islamabad's Road Warriors'
31. International Crisis Group, *Central Asia: Islamist Mobilisation and Regional Security*, 1 March 2001, p. 3, Appendix A
32. Napoleoni, *Terror Inc.*, p. 120
33. B. Raman, 'Attacks on Uzbeks in South Waziristan', 23 March 2007, www.saag.org
34. Raman, 'Attacks on Uzbeks'; Napoleoni, pp. 120–3
35. Tiffany Petros, 'Islam in Central Asia: The Emergence and Growth of Radicalism in the Post-Communist Era', 2006, www.ndu.edu
36. Robinson, *Bin Laden*, p. 176
37. Napoleoni, pp. 125–6; Chossudovsky, *America's 'War on Terrorism'* (Global Research: Canada, 2005), pp. 29–30; Yossef Bodansky, 'Chechnya: The Mujahidin Factor', January 1998, www.freeman.org
38. Bodansky, 'Chechnya'
39. Ibid.; Napoleoni, p. 126
40. Peter Dale Scott, 'Al Qaeda, US Oil Companies and Central Asia', 30 July 2005, wwwglobalresearch.ca; Mark Irkali et al, 'American Guns, Spies and Oil in Azerbaijan', Alexander's gas and oil connections, 11 October 2005, www.gasandoil.com; Thomas Goltz, 'Soldier, oilman, thief, spy', *Forbes*, 25 September 1997, www.forbes.com
41. Cooley, *Unholy Wars*, pp. 180–1; Dale Scott
42. Cooley, pp. 180–1; Dale Scott
43. Cooley, pp. 180–1
44. Tim Kelsey, 'British mercenaries for Azeri war', *Independent*, 24 January 1994. The report noted that Michael Mates, the Northern Ireland minister, had named Erskine as a 'member of the security services' but the government denied he had ever been a member, but had provided information to the Foreign Office
45. House of Commons, *Hansard*, 31 January 1994, Col.486
46. Douglas Hogg, *Hansard*, House of Commons, 14 February 1994, Col.553

47. Ibid., *Hansard*, 13 April 1994, Col.206
48. Ibid., 15 June 1993, Col.730–1
49. Glen Owen, 'Hookers, spies, cases full of dollars … How BP spent £45m to win "Wild East" oil rights', *Mail on Sunday*, 13 May 2007, found at http://cryptome.org/bp-mi6.htm in August 2007
50. 'BP accused of backing "arms for oil" coup', *Sunday Times*, 26 March 2000. BP denied its involvement in a letter to the *Sunday Times*, 'BP slur', 9 April 2000, saying that 'we do not intrigue to unseat elected governments, we had no conceivable interest in his [Elchibey's] removal, nor did we derive any benefit from it.'
51. Douglas Hogg, House of Commons, *Hansard*, 15 December 1993, Cols.1065–6
52. Dan Morgan and David Ottaway, 'Azerbaijan's riches alter the chessboard', *Washington Post*, 4 October 1998
53. House of Commons, *Hansard*, 25 April 1995, Col.427
54. Mir, *The True Face of Jehadis*, p. 4
55. Musharraf, *In the Line of Fire: A Memoir*, pp. 202, 209
56. Burke, *Al-Qaeda*, p. 116
57. B. Raman, 'Sipah-e-Sahaba Pakistan, Lashkar-e-Jhangvi, Bin Laden and Ramzi Yousef', 1 July 2002, www.saag.org; US Embassy, Islamabad, 'Pakistan Counter-Terrorism', 6 February 1997, National Security Archive, 'Pakistan: "The Taliban's Godfather?"', www.gwu.edu
58. Coll, *Ghost Wars*, p. 296
59. See Rashid, *Taliban*, chapter 12
60. National Intelligence Daily, CIA, 30 September 1996, National Security Archive, 'Pakistan: "The Taliban's Godfather?"', www.gwu.edu
61. US State Department, 'Dealing with the Taliban in Kabul, 28 September 1996, National Security Archive, 'The September 11th Sourcebooks – Volume VII: The Taliban File', www.gwu.edu
62. Rashid, *Taliban*, p. 176
63. Coll, pp. 460–1
64. House of Commons, *Hansard*, 24 July 1996, Col.317
65. Ibid., 31 October 1996, Col.208
66. House of Lords, *Hansard*, 19 February 1997, Col.WA53
67. House of Commons, *Hansard*, 15 June 1997, Col.560
68. Ibid., *Hansard*, 25 March 1998, Col.486
69. Atwan, *The Secret History of al-Qaeda*, pp. 74–5
70. Posner, *Why America Slept*, pp. 117–8, 211
71. Coll, p. 440
72. Defence Intelligence Agency, 'Veteran Afghanistan Traveler's Analysis of Al Qaeda and Taliban Exploitable Weaknesses', 2 October 2001, National Security Archive, 'The September 11th Sourcebooks – Volume VII: The Taliban File', www.gwu.edu
73. See submission by Professor Shaun Gregory, Pakistan Security Research Unit, University of Bradford, Foreign Affairs Committee, *Global security: Afghanistan and Pakistan*, Eighth Report, Session 2008–09, July 2009, Ev163
74. House of Commons, *Hansard*, 5 May 1998, Col.289; House of Lords, 6 April 1998, Col.WA78
75. House of Commons, *Hansard*, 1 June 1998, Col.21

76. See United States District Court, Southern District of New York, Complaint, 04 Civ.5970, para 255
77. Burke, *Al-Qaeda*, p. 167; Rashid, *Taliban*, p. 138

CHAPTER 12: A COVERT WAR IN BOSNIA

1. Kohlmann, *Al-Qaida's Jihad in Europe*, pp. 16–18, 24
2. *The 9/11 Commission Report*, p. 147
3. Ibid., p. 155
4. Cees Wiebes, *Appendix II: Intelligence and the War in Bosnia 1992–1995 – The Role of the Intelligence and Security Services*, chapter 4, section 5 in Netherlands Institute for War Documentation, *Srebrenica: Reconstruction, Background, Consequences and Analyses of the Fall of a Safe Area*, April 2002, www.srebrenica.nl/en
5. Kohlmann, p. 28
6. See various interviews given by Aziz in B. Raman, 'Jihad: After Bosnia and J&K, Hyderabad', 21 May 2005, www.saag.org
7. Kohlmann, p. 125
8. Wiebes, *Appendix II*, chapter 4, section 7
9. Kepel, *Jihad*, p. 248; Kohlmann, pp. 73–4
10. Marcia Kurop, 'Al Qaeda's Balkan links', *Wall Street Journal Europe*, 1 November 2001
11. Robinson, *Bin Laden*, pp. 146–7; Atwan, *The Secret History of Al-Qaeda*, p. 223; Scott Taylor, 'Bin Laden's Balkan connections', *Ottawa Citizen*, 15 December 2001; Kurop, 'Al Qaeda's Balkan Links'
12. Kohlmann, pp. 37–47
13. Ibid., p. 47
14. Wiebes, *Appendix II*, chapter 4, section 2
15. US Senate, Republican Policy Committee, 'Clinton-approved Iranian Arms Transfers Help Turn Bosnia into Militant Islamic Base', 16 January 1997, www.senate.gov
16. Wiebes, *Appendix II*, chapter 4, section 2
17. Ibid.
18. Ibid.
19. Ibid.; 'Allies and lies', BBC news, 22 June 2001, http://news.bbc.co.uk
20. Wiebes, *Appendix II*, chapter 4, section 2
21. Ibid.
22. 'Allies and lies', BBC news, 22 June 2001; See Noel Malcolm's review of General Rose's memoir, http://www.geocities.com/famous_bosniaks/english/fighting_for_peace.html
23. This operative is Tom Carew, a pseudonym for Anthony Sessarego. Sessarego, who has since died, became infamous for recounting in his book, *Jihad!*, which appeared in 2001, how he worked for the SAS in 1980s Afghanistan as a British covert agent supporting mujahideen groups, notably that of Gulbuddin Hekmatyar. It subsequently emerged that Sessarego had never been in the SAS and that his account of his actions in Afghanistan was at best unreliable. Thus I have not drawn upon *Jihad!* for the Afghanistan section of this book. However, there is little doubt that Sessarego was indeed a British covert agent and was in Afghanistan and

also involved in activities elsewhere. Furthermore, there is evidence that his claims of involvement in British secret arms deliveries to the Croats and Muslims are broadly correct. See, for example, Andrew Malone, 'Death of an SAS fantasist', *Daily Mail* online, 27 January 2009

24. Carew, *Jihad!*, pp. 279–80
25. Cited in 'The Small Arms Plague', Norwegian Initiative on Small Arms Transfers, www.nsiat.org
26. Matthew Brunwasser, 'Monzer Al Kassar', May 2002, www.pbs.org/frontlineworld/stories/sierraleone/alkassar.html
27. Wiebes, *Appendix II*, chapter 4, section 2
28. Kohlmann, pp. 74–5
29. See Kohlmann, 'The Afghan–Bosnian Mujahideen Network in Europe', undated, www.fhs.se
30. Brendan O'Neill, 'How we trained al-Qaida', *Spectator*, 15 September 2003; Craif Pyes et al, 'Terrorists use Bosnia as base and sanctuary', *Los Angeles Times*, 7 October 2001
31. B. Raman, 'International Jihadi Terrorism and Europe – An Indian Perspective', 17 November 2005, www.saag.org
32. B. Raman, 'Harkat-ul-Mujahideen: An Update', 20 March 1999, www.saag.org
33. B. Raman, 'Punishment Terrorism', 31 March 2002, www.saag.org
34. B. Raman, 'Daniel Pearl and the London Blasts', www.observerindia.com
35. See Chossudovsky, *America's 'War on Terrorism'*, p. 41
36. Nick Fielding, 'The British jackal', *Sunday Times*, 21 April 2002
37. Musharraf, p. 225
38. Mir, p. 40; Daniel Klaidman, 'US officials are eager to try the main suspect in Daniel Pearl's murder', *Newsweek*, 13 March 2002
39. See: http://www.angelfire.com/bc3/johnsonuk/eng/sos.html; O'Neill and McGrory, *The Suicide Factory*, pp. xiv–xv
40. O'Neill and McGrory, pp. 30–2; Sean O'Neill, 'Abu Hamza "boasted of Bosnia action"', *Times*, 17 January 2006
41. Kohlmann, pp. 138–9
42. House of Commons, *Hansard*, 17 February 1994, Col.938
43. Brendan Simms, *Unfinest Hour: Britain and the Destruction of Bosnia* (Allen Lane: London, 2001), pp. xi, 337, 25
44. Cees Wiebes cited in Brendan O'Neill, '"You are only allowed to see Bosnia in black and white"', 23 January 2004, www.spiked-online.com
45. 'SAS soldier reveals how he helped arm Bosnians', *Sunday Times*, 13 August 2000
46. Wiebes, *Appendix II*, chap 2, Section 4
47. Wiebes, *Appendix II*, chap 2, section 4
48. Kohlmann, *Al-Qaida's Jihad* …, pp. 38–45
49. B. Raman, 'Jihadi Terrorism: The Saudi Connection', 4 September 2003, www.saag.org
50. Stephen Schwartz, 'Wahhabism and al-Qaeda in Bosnia-Herzegovina', *Terrorism Monitor*, 21 October 2004
51. Anes Alic, 'Foreign jihadis face deportation in Bosnia-Herzegovina', *Terrorism Monitor*, 8 November 2007
52. Kohlmann, p. xii

53. Yossef Bodansky, 'Some Call it Peace: Waiting for War in the Balkans', 1996, www.balkania.net
54. Yossef Bodansky, 'Offensive in the Balkans: The Potential for a Wider War as a Result of Foreign Intervention in Bosnia-Herzegovina', 1996, section 7, available online at: http://members.tripod.com/Balkania/resources/geostrategy/bodansky_offensive/index.html
55. Kohlmann, pp. 161–3; Schwartz
56. For sources see my *Web of Deceit*, pp. 38–40
57. House of Commons, *Hansard*, 9 February 1998, Col.11
58. Wiebes, part III, section 4
59. Ibid.
60. Asli Aydintasbas, 'Murder on the Bosphorus', *Middle East Quarterly*, June 2000
61. Human Rights Watch, 'What is Turkey's Hizbullah?', 16 February 2000, www.hrw.org
62. Ibid. Over the years more and more details of the Turkish state's complicity with this group have emerged, mainly from admissions by state officials themselves. A former deputy under-secretary of the MIT, Mehmet Eymur, has said that Hezbollah received the blessing of local police and gendarmerie in southeastern Turkey and that all Hezbollah's activities on behalf of the state were carried out on orders 'from above'. Turkey's 'Batman-gate' scandal, which hit the headlines in 2000, concerned how in 1994, the former governor of Batman province in the southeast, Salih Sahman, set up a 1,000-strong private militia to counter the PKK, importing 1,800 weapons, some of which found their way to Hezbollah. The project to purchase the weapons was approved by Tansu Ciller, the then prime minister. One Hezbollah stronghold was in Batman, a major city in the south east, where much of the conniving with the Turkish police was organised. The police chief there, Ozturk Simsek, recently asserted: 'How can we probe Hizbullah? Their headquarters is right next to the JITEM building', referring to the Gendarmerie Intelligence Agency. 'By action or omission, the Turkish state bears some responsibility for the slaughter committed by Hizbullah,' Human Rights Watch has commented. 'Columnist compares the Turkish Hizbullah with the Lebanese Hizbullah', *Turkish mass media bulletin*, 30 August 2006; Human Rights Watch, 'What is Turkey's Hizbullah?'
63. Suleyman Ozoren, 'Turkish Hizbollah: A case study of radical terrorism', *Turkish Weekly*, 18 April 2007. Now estimated to have thousands of members, the group was recently alleged by the police to have used dungeons and torture cells where the bodies of 100 victims were found, accused of being traitors or of not paying zakat, an Islamic tax. 'Kurdish militant group "Turkish Hezbollah" issuing terrorist threats', Associated Press, 21 December 2006
64. Helena Smith, 'Suicide bombers are buried in Turkey's breeding ground of extremism', *Guardian*, 27 November 2003; Luke Harding, Helena Smith and Jason Burke, 'The softest target', *Observer*, 23 November 2003
65. B. Raman, 'Istanbul Blasts', 21 November 2003, www.saag.org

CHAPTER 13: KILLING QADAFI, OVERTHROWING SADDAM

66. Cooley, *Unholy Wars*, p. 220; Burke, *Al-Qaeda*, p. 73
67. *The 9/11 Commission Report*, p. 123
68. Ibid., p. 123
69. Robin Cook, speech at the Foreign Office, 17 July 1997, www.fco.gov.uk; See my *Web of Deceit*, pp. 363ff for more analysis
70. A. Ibbott, FCO, minute, 7 September 1970, PRO, FCO39/613; Cabinet, Defence and Overseas Policy Committee, 'Anglo–Libyan Relations', Memorandum by Secretary of State for Foreign Affairs, 31 October 1969, PRO, FCO39/389
71. 'From Mujahid to Activist: An Interview with a Libyan Veteran of the Afghan Jihad', 25 March 2005, www.jamestown.org
72. Special Immigration Appeals Commission, Appeal No: SC/42 and 50/2005, 27 April 2005, para 17, www.siac.tribunals.gov.uk
73. Philippe Naughton, 'Liverpool man held after naming on UK terror blacklist', *Times*, 9 February 2006
74. Alison Pargeter, 'LIFG: An organisation in eclipse', *Terrorism Monitor*, 3 November 2005
75. Annie Machon, *Spies, Lies and Whistle-blowers : MI5, MI6 and the Shayler Affair* (Book Guild: Sussex, 2005), pp. 166, 171
76. 'Qadhafi Assassination Plot', http://cryptome.org/qadahfi-plot.htm
77. Ibid.
78. Machon, p. 172
79. Ibid., p. 167
80. Ibid., pp. 167, 250
81. Dorril, *MI6*, p. 793
82. Machon, pp. 247–9
83. Ibid., p. 251
84. Ibid., pp. 248, 273
85. Gary Gambill, 'The Libyan Islamic Fighting Group (LIFG)', *Terrorism Monitor*, 24 March 2005
86. Ibid. In February 2006, the UN ordered the assets of five men believed to be associates of the LIFG to be frozen – all of them were based in Britain, including the LIFG's suspected financier and two men suspected of involvement in the 2003 bombings in Casablanca which killed more than 40 people. Naughton, 'Liverpool man held'
87. Ibid.
88. Bergen, *Holy War*, p. 210
89. Daniel McGrory, 'City was home to terrorist with $25m price on his head', *Times*, 16 January 2003
90. Mark Dooley, 'Our inept response to terrorists living in Ireland must end', *Sunday Independent* (Ireland), 3 July 2005; Gambill
91. Gunaratna, p. 142
92. Martin Bright, 'MI6 "halted bid to arrest Bin Laden"', *Observer*, 12 November 2002
93. See *Web of Deceit*, chapter 1

94. Dorril, *Silent Conspiracy*, pp. 420–1
95. Alec Russell, 'Allawi accused over 1990s bombings', *Daily Telegraph*, 10 June 2004
96. 'Civilian-based National Secular Groups', www.middleeastreference.org.uk
97. Ibid.
98. Jonathan Ford, 'Shutting the door in the face of Islam's bogeymen', *Guardian*, 27 May 1995
99. James Bone, 'MI6 "proposed Iraqi coup" to topple Saddam', *Times*, 18 March 1999
100. AFP, 'Iraqi Opposition to Discuss Armed Resistance', 8 April 1999, www.fas.org
101. Press briefing by FCO Minister, Derek Fatchett, 23 November 1998, www.casi.org.uk
102. House of Commons, *Hansard*, 30 November 1998, Col.97
103. See *Web of Deceit*, pp. 26–8
104. Stratfor, 'Global Intelligence Update', 23 March 1999, www.casi.org.uk
105. Marie Colvin, 'America funds Iraqi guerillas', *Sunday Times*, 24 January 1999; Roula Khalaf, 'US scheme to overthrow Saddam runs into the sands', *Financial Times*, 4 February 1999
106. House of Commons, *Hansard*, 2 March 1998, Col.417
107. 'Representative of Islamic Movement of Iraqi Kurdistan interviewed', *Kurdistan Observer*, 27 January 2003, http://home.cogeco.ca/~observer
108. 'Iraqi Kurdish Islamist leader holds talks with German Foreign Ministry officials', *Kurdistan Observer*, 3 February 2003
109. Human Rights Watch, 'Ansar al-Islam in Iraqi Kurdistan', May 2003, hrw.org
110. 'Osama bin Laden er en god muslim', *VG Nett* (Norway), 9 June 2005, www.vg.no

CHAPTER 14: INTRIGUES IN THE SOUTHERN BALKANS

1. See my *Web of Deceit*, chapter 2
2. Gordon Brown, speech, 10 October 2006, www.hm-treasury.gov.uk
3. US Senate, Republican policy committee, 'The Kosovo Liberation Army: Does Clinton Policy Support Group with Terror, Drug Ties?', 31 March 1999, www.senate.gov; Zoran Kusovac, 'The KLA: Braced to Defend and Control', *Jane's Intelligence Review*, April 1999
4. Agence France Presse, 23 February 1998, cited in US Senate, Republican policy committee
5. House of Commons, *Hansard*, 10 March 1998, Col.317
6. Letter from Derek Fatchett, Foreign Minister, to Chair of House of Lords European Union committee, 20 April 1998, in House of Lords, European Union Committee, Session 1998/99, *European Communities – Report*, 2 February 1999
7. House of Commons, *Hansard*, 27 November 1998, Col.441; 18 January 1999, Col.567
8. See, for example, Home Secretary Jack Straw's parliamentary answer equating the KLA with 'terrorist activity' at: House of Commons, *Hansard*, 9 March 1999, Col.182

9. Neil Mackay, 'Police alert as KLA heroin floods Britain', *Sunday Herald*, 27 June 1999
10. Chris Stephen, 'Bin Laden opens European terror base in Albania', *Sunday Times*, 29 November 1998
11. Chris Stephen, 'US tackles Islamic militancy in Kosovo', *Scotsman*, 30 November 1998; AP, 'Bin Laden operated terrorist network based in Albania', 29 November 1998
12. 'US alarmed as mujahidin join Kosovo rebels', *Times*, 26 November 1998; Jerry Seper, 'KLA rebels train in terrorist camps', *Washington Times*, 4 May 1999; Intelligence sources were also reported stating that the Iranians had sent a 120-man commando unit to Kosovo, including Albanians, Bosnians and Saudis and which was commanded by an Egyptian, Abu Ismail, who served in an Iranian mujahideen unit during the Bosnian War. Iran was by now sending considerable quantities of arms to the KLA, seeing the Kosovo operation – like the Bosnian before it – as a beachhead for the expansion of Iranian influence in Europe. Steve Rodan, 'Kosovo seen as new Islamic bastion', *Jerusalem Post*, 14 September 1998; Milan Petkovic, 'Albanian Terrorists', 1998, www.fas.org
13. Testimony of Ralf Mutschke of Interpol's Criminal Intelligence Division to the House Judicial Committee, US Congress, 13 December 2000, cited in Michel Chossudovsky, 'Regime Rotation in America', 22 October 2003, www.globalresearch.ca
14. Cited in Isabel Vincent, 'US supported al-Qaeda cells during Balkan wars', *National Post* (Canada), 15 March 2002, www.globalresearch.ca
15. House of Commons, *Hansard*, 27 November 1998, Col.441
16. House of Lords, *Hansard*, 18 November 1998, Col.WA168
17. House of Commons, *Hansard*, 9 March 1999, Col.182
18. Yossef Bodansky, 'Some Call it Peace' Part III, section 5
19. Ibid.
20. Tim Judah, *Kosovo: War and Revenge* (Yale University Press, 2000), p. 120, which mentions a meeting but does not name the official. Shaban himself later claimed to have had this meeting; Tom Walker and Aidan Laverty, 'CIA aided guerrilla army', *Sunday Times*, 12 March 2000
21. Ibid., p. 170
22. House of Commons, *Hansard*, 10 May 1999, Col.29
23. House of Lords, *Hansard*, 28 July 1998, Col.WA181
24. House of Commons, *Hansard*, 19 October 1998, Col.958
25. *Scotsman*, 29 August 1999, cited in Chossudovsky, 'Regime Rotation'
26. Philip Sherwell, 'SAS teams move in to help KLA "rise from the ashes"', *Sunday Telegraph*, 18 April 1999
27. Judah, *Kosovo*, p. 172
28. Sherwell, 'SAS teams move in to help KLA'; Ian Bruce, 'SAS faces own trainees in Balkans', *The Herald*, 27 March 2001
29. *The Scotsman*, 29 August 1999, cited in Michel Chossudovsky, 'NATO invades Macedonia', 29 August 2001, www.globalresearch.ca
30. Chossudovsky, 'Regime Rotation in America'
31. House of Commons, *Hansard*, 13 April 1999, Col.25
32. House of Lords, *Hansard*, 11 March 1999, Col.WA47–8; 27 May 1999, Col.WA114

33. James Bissett, 'War on terrorism skipped the KLA', *National Post* (Canada) 13 November 2001, www.globalresearch.ca
34. James Bissett, 'We created a monster', *Toronto Star*, 31 July 2001
35. Nafeez Mosaddeq Ahmed, *The London Bombings: An Independent Enquiry*, (Duckworth: London, 2006), p. 191
36. House of Commons, *Hansard*, 26 April 1999, Col.28
37. Sherwell, 'SAS teams move in to help KLA "rise from the ashes"'; Richard Lloyd Parry, 'War in the Balkans: KLA engaged in fierce fighting with Serb army', *Independent*, 12 April 1999
38. Tom Walker and Aidan Laverty, 'CIA aided Kosovo guerrilla army', *Sunday Times*, 12 March 2000
39. Lloyd Parry, 'War in the Balkans'; George Jones, 'Cook shows support for KLA', *Telegraph*, 31 March 1999
40. B. Raman, 'Punishment Terrorism', 31 March 2002, www.saag.org
41. 'Video of Fox news report, linking terror suspect to British intelligence MI6', 1 August 2005, www.globalresearch.ca
42. David Bamber and Chris Hastings, 'KLA raises money in Britain for arms', *Sunday Telegraph*, 23 April 2000; 'Bush opposes 9/11 query panel', CBS News (US), 23 May 2002
43. 'Video of Fox news report, linking terror suspect to British intelligence MI6', 1 August 2005, www.globalresearch.ca
44. Ibid.
45. Email correspondence with the author, August 2007
46. 'Video of Fox news report, linking terror suspect to British intelligence MI6', 1 August 2005, www.globalresearch.ca
47. The report also noted: 'Questions are also being asked about whether the British did not wish to have Aswat arrested as he was seen as a useful source of information. To some, British intelligence is too willing to let terrorist suspects run in the hope of gathering useful leads and other information.' Richard Woods et al, 'Tangled web that leaves worrying loose ends', *Times*, 31 July 2005
48. 'Britain's first suicide bombers', BBC 2, 11 July 2006
49. 'Kostunica warns of fresh fighting', BBC news, 29 January 2001, www.bbc.co.uk
50. Peter Beaumont et al, '"CIA's bastard army ran riot in Balkans" backed extremists', *Observer*, 11 March 2001; Rory Carroll, 'West struggles to contain monster of its own making', *Guardian*, 12 March 2001
51. 'Albanian rebels, trained by the SAS are gaining ground in Macedonia, aiming for the key city of Tetevo', *Sunday Times*, 18 March 2001
52. UPI, 1 July 2001, cited in Chossudovsky, 'NATO Invades Macedonia'
53. Richard Norton-Taylor, 'Nato pays the price for letting extremists off the hook', *Guardian*, 23 March 2001; Bissett, 'War on Terrorism Skipped the KLA'
54. In May, US diplomat Robert Fenwick secretly met leaders of the KLA and Albanian political parties in Kosovo. A month later, a force of 400 KLA/NLA fighters became surrounded in the town of Aracinovo near the Macedonian capital, Skopje, but as Macedonian forces moved in, they were halted on NATO orders. Instead, US army buses arrived to remove the heavily armed terrorists to a safer area of the country. They

were accompanied by 17 US military advisers from the 'private' military company, MPRI, which had been training the KLA/NLA. 'It was clear the United States was backing the Albanian terrorist cause,' Bissett comments. One of the KLA militants evacuated by the US was Samedin Xhezairi, known as Commander Hoxha, who was the leader of the mujahideen 112th brigade operating in the Tetevo area, and had previously fought in Chechnya and trained in Afghanistan. According to a German TV documentary, broadcast on the mainstream channel, ZDF, Hoxha was an agent working for the German intelligence service, the BND, and an intermediary between Albanian extremists and al-Qaida. By August 2001, the KLA/NLA had established control over nearly a third of Macedonia's territory, largely thanks to arms supplied from the US. Canadian reporter Scott Taylor wrote from Tetevo of a variety of US military supplies including rifles, grenade-launchers, heavy mortars and ammunition which the NLA was using to bombard Macedonian towns. By now, however, it appears that the US had begun trying to rein in its proxy force, presumably under considerable pressure from its NATO allies, and threw its weight behind peace talks. These led to a ceasefire and peace agreement in August, followed by the deployment of a NATO force of 3,000 peacekeepers. The NATO force was meant to 'disarm' the same rebels supported by the US and, before that, also Britain. Bissett, 'War on Terrorism Skipped the KLA'; Mira Beham, 'When Intelligence Officers Fan Flames', 25 November 2004, www.globalresearch.ca; Scott Taylor, 'Macedonia's Civil War: "Made in the USA"', 20 August 2001, www.antiwar.com; Chossudovsky, 'NATO Invades Macedonia'

CHAPTER 15: 9/11 CONNECTIONS

1. Kepel, *Jihad*, p. 375
2. Notably the Project for a New American Century, a grouping of influential right-wing thinkers in US policy-making circles who produced various documents, talks and articles calling for US military expansion and greater US 'global leadership'. See www.newamericancentury.org
3. *Strategic Defence Review: Modern Forces for the Modern World*, July 1998, especially introduction, para 6, 24, 87, 208, and also background papers, http://www.mod.uk/NR/rdonlyres/65F3D7AC-4340-4119-93A2-20825848E50E/0/sdr1998_complete.pdf
4. Defence Committee, *Second Report*, Session 2001–02, 12 December 2001, para 100
5. *Delivering Security in a Changing World, Defence White Paper*, December 2003, especially introduction, paras 1.2, 2.14, 2.7, 3.1, 3.2, 3.5, 4.4, 4.9, 4.10, 4.19
6. Cited in Mir, *The True Face of Jehadis*, p. 247
7. Manoj Joshi, 'India helped FBI trace ISI-terrorist links', *Times of India*, 9 October 2001; Mir, p. 235
8. Stephen McGinty, 'The English Islamic terrorist', *Scotsman*, 16 July 2002; 'Suspected hijack bankroller freed by India in '99', CNN, 6 October 2001; Kathy Gannon, 'Key suspect may have fled the city', Associated Press, 10 February 2002; cited in Chossudovsky, *America's 'War on Terrorism'*, p. 58

9. Mir, p. 236
10. Ibid., p. 218
11. Daniel Klaidman, 'US officials are eager to try the main suspect in Daniel Pearl's murder', *Newsweek*, 13 March 2002; Mir, p. 40
12. Zahid Hussain, *Frontline Pakistan: The Path to Catastrophe and the Killing of Benazir Bhutto* (I. B. Tauris: London), p. 65
13. Paul Watson and Sidhartha Barua, 'Worlds of extremism and crime collide in an Indian jail', *Los Angeles Times*, 8 February 2002
14. Zahid Hussain and Daniel McGrory, 'London schoolboy who graduated to terrorism', *Times*, 16 July 2002
15. David Williams, 'Kidnapper-guy Hotmail.com', *Daily Mail*, 16 July 2002; O'Neill and McGrory, p. 122
16. 'Militant free to return to UK', *BBC News*, 3 January 2000
17. 'Profile: Omar Saeed Sheikh', *BBC News*, 16 July 2002; Ahmed, *The London Bombings*, p. 171; Robert Sam Anson, 'The journalist and the terrorist', *Vanity Fair*, August 2002
18. Anson; Kamran Khan and Molly Moore, 'Pearl abduction was a warning, suspect says', *Washington Post*, 18 February 2002
19. Anson; Nick Fielding, 'The British jackal', *Sunday Times*, 21 April 2002
20. Kamran Khan and Molly Moore, 'Pearl abduction was a warning, suspect says', *Washington Post*, 18 February 2002
21. Rory McCarthy, 'Underworld where terror and security meet', *Guardian*, 16 July 2002
22. Mir, p. 37
23. Ibid., p. 42
24. Cited in Mir, p. 235; Mir, a very informed analyst, also writes: 'Omar Sheikh epitomises the links between Osama Bin Laden, Pakistan's military and intelligence establishments, the 9/11 hijackers, British jehadis and Kashmiri militants. And putting him on death row, and holding him in an isolation cell helps Musharraf keep a key witness out of American, British and Indian hands. But that isolation seems to be one-sided, as Omar seems rather effective in communicating with the outside world. While using the protection of his jail cell, he reportedly keeps in touch with his friends and cohorts and advises them on the future course of action', p. 43
25. Speech in New York, 20 September 2000, reported in *Guardian*, 21 September 2001

CHAPTER 16: LONDONISTAN: A 'GREEN LIGHT' TO TERRORISM

1. Adam Nathan, 'Al-Qaeda London network exposed', *Sunday Times*, 4 January 2004, covering leaked police transcripts of conversations among al-Qaida members; Audrey Gillan et al, 'Allies point the finger at Britain as al-Qaida's "revolving door"', *Guardian*, 14 February 2002
2. Robert Winnett and David Leppard, 'Leaked No 10 dossier reveals Al-Qaida's British recruits', *Times*, 10 July 2005
3. Home Office, *Report of the official account of the bombings in London on 7th July 2005*, HMSO, 11 May 2006, p. 29, emphasis added

4. Crispin Black, *7/7 – The London Bombings: What Went Wrong?* (Gibson Square Books: London, 2006), p. 31
5. Jason Burke, *Observer*, 26 January 2003
6. Vikram Dodd, 'UK failed to act on damning dossier of evidence, says French anti-terror chief', *Guardian*, 8 February 2006
7. Cited in Labeviere, p. 101
8. Cited in Yotam Feldner, 'Radical Islamist profiles (2): Sheikh Omar Bakri Muhammad', Middle East Media and Research Institute (MEMRI), 25 October 2001
9. Neil Doyle, *Terror Base UK: Inside a Secret War* (Mainstream Publishing: Edinburgh, 2006), p. 73
10. Steve Coll and Susan Glasser, 'In London, Islamic radicals found a haven', *Washington Post Foreign Service*, 10 July 2005
11. Ian Cobain et al, 'MI5 decided to stop watching two suicide bombers', *Guardian*, 1 May 2007
12. Michael Clarke, Professor of Defence Studies at King's College, London, notes how the 'covenant of security' is 'favoured by most of the security services – it encourages local communities to join the intelligence effort and allows interesting individuals to be monitored more easily.' 'The contract with Muslims must not be torn up', *Guardian*, 26 August 2005
13. Ibid., p. 288
14. Steve Hewitt, *The British War on Terror* (Continuum: London, 2008), p. 94
15. Ministry of Justice, Immigration Act 1971, Part 1, Section 3 (5) (b), www.statutelaw.gov.uk
16. House of Commons, *Hansard*, 9 December 2002, Col.76
17. O'Neill and McGrory, p. 291
18. House of Commons, Foreign Affairs Committee, *Global Security: The Middle East*, Eighth report, Session 2006/07, 25 July 2007, Ev 53
19. It might also be said that the alternative to housing these dissident groups and individuals in Britain is that they would be based elsewhere and confer the advantages on other states. British declassified files at the end of the war in Yemen in 1970 show that the deposed Imam, who was until then in exile in Saudi Arabia, was expressing interest in 'staying quietly' in Britain. Billy McLean, the Conservative MP with intelligence connections, encouraged then Foreign Secretary Alec Douglas-Home to allow this since 'if circumstances changed in the Yemen he could be a rallying point for those preferring a Royalist solution to a drift to the extreme left', and that 'in any case it was surely better that the Imam should stay quietly in this country than go to (say) Cairo or Baghdad', the home of nationalist regimes. 'Record of a conversation between the foreign secretary and Lieutenant Colonel Neil McLean at the Foreign Office', 31 July 1970, PRO, FCO8/1355
20. Mahan Abedin, 'British intelligence steps up, few oppose', *Daily Star* (Lebanon), 13 March 2004
21. Coll, p. 270
22. Cited in Philipps, p. 93
23. For example, when General Suharto was in power in Indonesia in the 1970s, Britain supported his regime's brutal suppression of the secessionist movements first in East Timor and then in West Papua and Aceh provinces. It was when the nationalist Sukarno was in power in the 1950s

that London and Washington resorted to using Islamist forces, among others, to destabilise his regime by supporting a secessionist movement. In Iraq, Britain supported Baghdad's brutal campaign against the Kurds in the 1960s and again under Saddam in the 1980s, preferring a dictator in Baghdad to a Kurdish state in the north that would encourage Kurdish separatism elsewhere.

24. Cited in Aburish, *House of Saud*, p. 21; D. Riches, minute, 8 August 1958, PRO, FO371/132545
25. Cited in Dorril, *MI6*, pp. 616–7
26. See Saferworld, *The Good, the Bad and the Ugly: A Decade of Labour's Arms Exports*, May 2007, at www.curtisresearch.org
27. Britain also armed both China and Taiwan – to the tune of nearly £500 million each in the Blair years – as tensions between the two often nearly reached the point of war. Again, both countries received similar equipment from Britain that could have aided offensive operations: in 2006, for example, both were granted exports of components for combat aircraft, military communications equipment and components for military transport aircraft. Arms export policies cannot all be put down to profit seeking: they have generally cost the economy more than they have benefitted it, given the huge subsidies from taxpayers to the arms industry.
28. O'Neill and McGrory, pp. 30–2; Sean O'Neill, 'Abu Hamza "boasted of Bosnia action"', *Times*, 17 January 2006
29. Jamie Doward and Diane Taylor, 'Hamza set up terror camps with British ex-soldiers', *Observer*, 12 February 2006; Ahmed Moussa, 'Who are the UK-based militants?', *al-Ahram*, 3–9 September 1998
30. Kohlmann, p. 189
31. Ibid., pp. 127–8, 143, 145–6
32. Ibid., pp. 145–6
33. O'Neill and McGrory, p. 93; Jason Burke, 'AK-47 training held at London mosque', *Observer*, 17 February 2002
34. O'Neill and McGrory, p. xv
35. Richard Woods and David Leppard, 'Focus: How liberal Britain let hate flourish', *Sunday Times*, 12 February 2006
36. O'Neill and McGrory, p. 269
37. Doward and Taylor
38. O'Neill and McGrory, p. 84
39. Daniel McGrory, 'Phone tap evidence links Abu Hamza to murder of hostages', *Times*, 9 February 2006; O'Neill and McGrory, p. 180
40. House of Commons, *Hansard*, 13 November 2001, Col.645W
41. O'Neill and McGrory, p. 294
42. Ibid., pp. xv–xvii
43. Ibid., p. 295
44. Special Immigration Appeals Commission, Omar Mahmoud Mohammed Othman and Secretary of State for the Home Department, Open judgment, SC/15/2002, 8 March 2004, para 20
45. Daniel McGrory and Richard Ford, 'Al-Qaeda cleric exposed as an MI5 double agent', *Times*, 25 March 2004
46. Abdel Bari Atwan, p. 190
47. Special Immigration Appeals Commission, Omar Mahmoud Mohammed

Othman and Secretary of State for the Home Department, Open judgment, SC/15/2002, 8 March 2004, para 1

48. O'Neill and McGrory, p. 67; Simon Freeman, 'Jordan will torture me, says hate cleric fighting deportation', *Times*, 9 May 2006
49. Ibid.
50. Audrey Gillan, 'Detained Muslim cleric is spiritual leader to militants, hearing told', *Guardian*, 20 November 2003
51. Special Immigration Appeals Commission, Omar Othman (aka Abu Qatada) and Secretary of State for the Home Department, SC/15/2005, 26 February 2007, paras 60, 85
52. Special Immigration Appeals Commission, Omar Mahmoud Mohammed Othman and Secretary of State for the Home Department, Open judgment, SC/15/2002, 8 March 2004, para 17; Special Immigration Appeals Commission, Omar Othman (aka Abu Qatada) and Secretary of State for the Home Department, SC/15/2005, 26 February 2007, paras 29, 60
53. Special Immigration Appeals Commission, Omar Mahmoud Mohammed Othman and Secretary of State for the Home Department, Open judgment, SC/15/2002, 8 March 2004, para 17
54. Ibid., para 18
55. Special Immigration Appeals Commission, Omar Othman (aka Abu Qatada) and Secretary of State for the Home Department, SC/15/2005, 26 February 2007, para 22
56. Special Immigration Appeals Commission, Omar Othman (aka Abu Qatada) and Secretary of State for the Home Department, SC/15/2005, 26 February 2007, paras 22–24
57. Camilla Cavendish, 'Lack-of-intelligence services', *Times*, 18 August 2005
58. David Leppard, 'Terror links in Europe: MI5 knew for years of London mosque's role', *Sunday Times*, 25 November 2001
59. Antony Barnett, Martin Bright and Nick Paton-Walsh, 'MI5 wanted me to escape, claims cleric', *Observer*, 21 October 2001
60. Ibid.
61. Kim Willsher and David Bamber, 'French accuse MI5 of failing to help terror hunt', *Telegraph*, 15 September 2002
62. Vikram Dodd, 'Guatanamo Briton claims he spied for MI5', *Guardian*, 22 March 2005
63. David Rose, 'I helped MI5. My reward: brutality and prison', *Guardian*, 29 July 2007. Similarly, another media report noted that while the British government was saying that Qatada's whereabouts were unknown, he was 'actively engaged in a dialogue with British officials that involved Mr al-Rawi'. George Mickum, 'MI5, Camp delta and the story that shames Britain', *Independent*, 16 March 2005
64. Bruce Cumley, 'Sheltering a puppet master?', *Time*, 7 July 2002
65. Government letter cited in Special Immigration Appeals Commission, Omar Mahmoud Mohammed Othman and Secrteary of State for the Home Department, Open judgment, SC/15/2002, 8 March 2004, para 3
66. O'Neill and McGrory, p. 108; Daniel McGrory et al, 'Bin Laden's 'ambassador' arrested', *Times*, 25 October 2002; Philippe Naughton, 'Cleric accused over Madrid released as Spain grieves', *Times*, 11 March 2005

67. Paul Lewis and Alan Travis, 'Radical preacher released on 22-hour curfew', *Guardian*, 18 June 2008
68. George Mickum, 'MI5, Camp Delta and the story that shames Britain', *Independent*, 16 March 2005. Al-Rawi has said that he tried to 'help with steps necessary to get a meeting between Abu Qatada and MI5. I was trying to bring them together. MI5 would give me messages to take to Abu Qatada and Abu Qatada would give me messages to take back to them.'
69. George Mickum, 'After five years of torture, Bisher is slowly slipping into madness', *Guardian*, 9 January 2007; David Pallister and Vikram Dodd, 'UK resident to be freed from Guantanamo', *Guardian*, 30 March 2007. MI5 denounced al-Rawi after the refusal of his colleague, Jamil el-Banna, to work for the organisation. See David Rose, 'I helped MI5. My reward: brutality and prison'
70. David Bamber and Chris Hastings, 'KLA raises money in Britain for arms', *Sunday Telegraph*, 23 April 2000
71. Doyle, p. 73; O'Neill and McGrory, pp. 105–6
72. See speech by Andrew Dismore, *Hansard*, House of Commons, 16 October 2001, Col.1085
73. Doyle, p. 74
74. Ibid., p. 61
75. Qunitan Wiktorowicz, *Radical Islam Rising: Muslim Extremism in the West* (Rowman & Littlefield: Maryland, 2005), p. 66; Doyle, p. 72
76. Cited in Doyle, p. 77
77. Ibid., p. 191; Jamestown Foundation, 'Al-Muhajiroun in the UK: An Interview with Sheikh Omar Bakri Mohammed', 23 March 2004, www.jamestown.org
78. Cited in 'Britain bars freed cleric Bakri', CNN, 21 July 2006
79. Sam Knight, 'Terror gang hatched international plot to bomb UK', *Times*, 21 March 2006; Sam Knight, 'Al Qaeda supergrass "trained British terror gang"', *Times*, 23 March 2006
80. Nicola Woolcock, 'The al-Qaeda supergrass who wanted to wage war in Britain', *Times*, 24 March 2006
81. Press Association, 'Terror accused "ran away" to join jihad', 14 September 2006
82. Jonathan Calvert, 'July 7 ringleader linked to Tel Aviv suicide bombers', *Sunday Times*, 9 July 2006
83. Ian Cobain and Nick Fielding, 'Banned Islamists spawn front organisations', *Guardian*, 22 July 2006
84. One wonders how many more individuals being protected by MI5 there were, or are. There is certainly a long list of militants who have escaped prosecution by the British authorities. These include: The Algerian Rachid Ramda, noted above, had come to Britain in 1992 fleeing from Algeria after police there linked him to terrorist attacks. In 1995, it is alleged that Ramda led a gang which exploded a bomb packed with nails and bolts on the Paris underground, killing eight people. The French authorities passed Ramda's name to MI5 in 1994 and later stated that had the British acted, the bombings could have been averted. After the Paris blast, French authorities repeatedly sought Ramda's extradition but this was only granted in December 2005. His extradition had been rejected in the High Court in

2002. 'Can you imagine how the British would react if France caught the alleged moneyman behind the July 7 bombings, and then years later he was still fighting extradition?', a former officer with France's external security service has been quoted as saying. (O'Neill and McGrory, pp. 113–4; Simon Freeman, 'Mastermind of Paris metro bombings jailed', *Times*, 29 March 2006); The Moroccan, Mohammad Guerbouzi, a leader of the Group of Islamic Combatants of Morocco, was sentenced *in absentia* in Morocco in December 2003 for a series of bombings but has lived in London for over a decade and is now a British citizen. Extradition requests from Spain and Morocco have been refused, the British authorities saying that they 'have not been presented with sufficient evidence that he was involved in any terrorist attack'. (Mark Townsend et al, 'The secret war', *Observer*, 21 March 2004); The Syrian, Mustafa Setmariam Nasar, one of those suspected of being behind the 2004 Madrid train bombing, is an associate of Abu Qatada and Abu Musab al-Zarqawi, and lived in Neasden, northwest London from June 1995. Spanish investigators believe he set up a 'sleeper' cell of terrorists in Britain. He was questioned twice by British intelligence officials and arrested by British police following the 1995 Paris bomb attacks, but released. Nasar has claimed that while in London he engaged only in journalism, and that 'all these activities were well-known to the British security forces'. He also claims that 'an agent [presumably meaning a British agent] once asked me to share some of my expertise in making explosives for the purpose of the Paris bombings' – though this may simply be propaganda. Before coming to London, Nasar had joined a group associated with the Syrian Muslim Brotherhood in the 1980s and had then fought in the anti-Soviet jihad in Afghanistan. From 1988, he trained elite fighters for al-Qaida in military strategy and the use of explosives. Nasar was captured in Pakistan in 2005. (Nick Fielding and Gareth Walsh, 'Mastermind of Madrid is key figure', *Times*, 10 July 2005; Craig Whitlock, 'Architect of new war on the West', *Washington Post Foreign Service*, 23 May 2006; 'Abu Musab al-Suri's final "Message to the British and the Europeans"', August 2005, www.globalterroraltert.com; Atwan, pp. 228–9); The Egyptian, Yasser al-Sirri, accused of attempting to assassinate Egypt's prime minister in 1993, was granted asylum in Britain and set up the Islamic Observation Centre (IOC), an Egyptian Islamist opposition group. Al-Sirri was arrested in London in late 2001 since assassins posing as journalists who killed Afghan leader Ahmed Shah Massoud, on the eve of 9/11, used accreditation from the IOC. Al-Sirri was arrested in Britain but a hearing concluded that there was no case to answer; al-Sirri was immediately re-arrested on a US extradition warrant but in 2002 the Home Secretary refused authority to proceed, citing no evidence to support the allegations against him. (Bergen, pp. 202–3; Mohamad Bazzi, 'Britain still hub for Islamic militants', *Newsday*, 14 April 2005; Special Immigration Appeals Commission, 'AJOUAOU and AB, B, C and D and Secretary of State for the Home Department', 29 October 2003, para 203)

CHAPTER 17: 7/7 AND THE LONDON–ISLAMABAD AXIS

1. House of Commons, *Hansard*, 6 March 2002, Col.299; 29 October 2002,

Col.756W; 9 September 2004, Col.1381W; House of Lords, 10 December 2003, Col.WA67

2. House of Commons, *Hansard*, 2 November 1999, Col.82
3. Ibid., 24 July 2002, Col.1324W
4. 'Profile: General Pervez Musharraf', 24 September 2001, www.bbc.co.uk
5. Ibid., 24 July 2002, Col.1324W, and 2 July 2002, Col.254W
6. Ibid., 1 March 2002, Col.1648W
7. Richard Norton-Taylor, 'Show of force overture to covert campaign', *Guardian*, 20 September 2001
8. House of Commons, *Hansard*, 11 February 2002, Cols.17–18
9. Ibid., 24 July 2002, Col.1324W
10. Ibid., 10 June 2002, Col.609
11. See Pakistan section in FCO, *Strategic Export Controls Report 2002*, 1 July 2003, www.fco.gov.uk
12. House of Commons, *Hansard*, 10 June 2002, Col.609
13. Ibid., 24 July 2002, Col.1324W
14. FCO, Memorandum to the House of Commons, Foreign Affairs Committee, January 2007, FAC, *Fourth report of session 2006–07*, 18 April 2007, Ev.35
15. See ICG, *Pakistan: Karachi's Madrassas and Violent Extremism*, 29 March 2007 and various other ICG reports on Pakistan
16. Mir, *The True Face of Jehadis*, pp. 136–7
17. Ali Dayan Hasan, Human Rights Watch, 'Popular resistance to Musharraf's rule has seemingly caught the US off-guard', *Los Angeles Times*, 27 June 2007, www.hrw.org
18. ICG, *The State of Sectarianism in Pakistan*, 18 April 2005, p. i
19. Zahab and Roy, pp. 43–4, 76–80
20. ICG, *The State of Sectarianism in Pakistan*, 18 April 2005, p. 1
21. Ibid., p. 63; The JEM, meanwhile, is widely regarded as having been created by the ISI to operate in Kashmir and was also considered to have close links to al-Qaida. Musharraf did, however, ban the JEM in 2002 and the following year it was discovered to be involved in twin attacks on Musharraf's life in the northern city of Rawalpindi, prompting a further clampdown by the authorities; it has since renamed itself, to escape terrorist designations, and split into other factions. Zahab and Roy, pp. 29, 31, 43, 54; Mir, *The True Face of Jehadis*, p. 45; Bergen, p. 221
22. Zahab and Roy, pp. 22–3, 42, 53
23. Ibid., pp. 43, 54; Mir, p. 45
24. B. Raman, 'Musharraf Releases Bin Laden's Close Associate', 5 December 2006, www.saag.org; Mir, pp. 78–80. The HUM has renamed itself the Jamiat ul-Ansar but also uses the name Harkat ul-Mujahideen al-Alami
25. House of Commons, *Hansard*, 12 December 2000, Col.477
26. House of Lords, *Hansard*, 30 May 2002, Col.1512
27. House of Commons, *Hansard*, 10 June 2002, Cols.595–6, 605
28. Ibid.
29. Daniel McGrory et al, 'Top al-Qaeda trainer "taught suspects to use explosive"', *Times*, 12 August 2006
30. Ian Cobain et al, 'Intelligence bungles in build up to 7/7 attacks', *Guardian*, 13 May 2006
31. David Leppard, 'Iraq terror backlash in UK "for years"', *Times*, 2 April 2006

32. Home Office and Foreign Office, 'Young Muslims and Extremism', April 2004, pp. 4–5, leaked on *Times* online website, www.timesonline.co.uk
33. Steve Coll and Susan Glasser, 'In London, Islamic radicals found a haven', *Washington Post Foreign Service*, 10 July 2005
34. Daniel McGrory and Michael Theodoulou, 'Suicide bomber's video confession blames Iraq war', *Times*, 2 September 2005
35. Home Office, *Report of the Official Account of the Bombings in London on 7th July 2005*, HMSO, 11 May 2006, p. 19
36. Paul Whiteley, 'Baghdad backlash', *Guardian*, 6 May 2003; Burridge, Evidence to the Defence Committee, 11 June 2003, www.parliament.uk
37. Ian Cobain et al, 'MI5 decided to stop watching two suicide bombers', *Guardian*, 1 May 2007; David Leppard, 'MI5 knew of bomber's plan for holy war', *Sunday Times*, 22 January 2006
38. Mir, p. 258
39. Intelligence and Security Committee, *Report into the London Terrorist Attacks on 7 July 2005*, Cm.6785, May 2006, p. 27; Home Office, *Report of the Official Account of the Bombings in London on 7th July 2005*, pp. 21, 27
40. Sandra Laville, '7/7 and 21/7 began at al-Qaida camp, court told', *Guardian*, 24 March 2007
41. 'The five found guilty yesterday', *Guardian*, 1 May 2007; 'The Pakistan connection', *Guardian*, 28 September 2006
42. Agencies, 'UK al-Qaida man "hoped to kill thousands"', *Guardian*, 6 November 2006
43. Jason Bennetto, 'Forty-year jail term for British al-Qaida terrorist', *Independent*, 8 November 2006
44. Rachel Williams, 'July 7 plot accused tell of times with Taliban', *Guardian*, 21 May 2008; Philip Johnston and Paul Stokes, 'Mystery over London bomber's "£120,000 estate"', *Daily Telegraph*, 7 January 2006
45. Mir, pp. 75–6; B. Raman, 'Harkat ul-Mujahideen', www.ict.org.il
46. Arif Jamal and Somini Sengupta, 'Suspect spotted at militant training', *New York Times*, 27 July 2005
47. Gethin Chamberlain, 'Investigators reveal London bomber's links to al-Qaeda', *Scotsman*, 16 July 2005; 'UK blast suspect met Islamabad church bomber', *Dawn* (Pakistan), 16 July 2005
48. B. Raman, 'Home-Grown Jihadis (Jundullah) in UK and US', 6 May 2007, www.saag.org
49. Sean O'Neill and Roger Boyes, 'Link between British suspect and 9/11 conspirator explored', *Times*, 15 August 2006
50. Gethin Chamberlain, 'Attacker "was recruited" at terror group's religious school', *Scotsman*, 14 July 2005; Declan Walsh, 'Musharraf's terrorist claims are dismissed', *Guardian*, 27 July 2005
51. Chamberlain, 'Investigators reveal London bomber's links to al-Qaeda'
52. Zahab and Roy, pp. 76–80; 'Foreign Secretary interview on the Andrew Marr show', 28 April 2008, www.fco.gov.uk
53. Isambard Wilkinson, 'Al Qaida presence in Pakistan "huge concern"', *Telegraph*, 12 May 2007
54. House of Commons, *Hansard*, 21 July 2005, Col.2104W
55. 'Musharraf doing excellent job in terror fight: Rumsfeld', *Daily Times*

(Pakistan), 4 June 2006; ICG, *Winding Back Martial Law in Pakistan*, 12 November 2007, p. 7

56. House of Commons, *Hansard*, 18 April 2006, Col.10W
57. Mark Kukis, 'Camp Fire – With Friends Like These ...', *New Republic*, 13 February 2006
58. Human Rights Watch, *'With Friends Like These ...': Human Rights Violations in Azad Kashmir*, and *'Everyone lives in fear': Patterns of impunity in Jammu and Kashmir*, both September 2006, www.hrw.org; Human Rights Watch also claims that the militant camp structure in Kashmir that existed in the 1990s under ISI control was formally closed down in the aftermath of 9/11 and due to the peace process with India, meaning that the levels of infiltration into Indian Kashmir have decreased somewhat. However, the United Jihad Council: 'still has machine guns, assault rifles, mortars, explosives, mines, rockets and some sophisticated military equipment supplied by the Pakistani military, including night-vision equipment ... Weapons and training continue to be provided to the militants by Pakistan'.
59. Amir Mir, 'General Musharraf's commitment to wipe out jihadis badly exposed', *South Asian Tribune*, 2 August 2005
60. Rajat Pandit, 'London bomber trained at Pak jehadi camp', *Times of India*, 30 July 2005
61. ICG, *Winding Back Martial Law in Pakistan*, 12 November 2007, p. 7
62. Cited in Neil Mackay, *The War on Truth* (Sunday Herald Books: Glasgow, 2006), p. 458
63. Daniel McGrory et al, 'Top al-Qaida trainer "taught suspects to use explosive"', *Times*, 12 August 2006
64. House of Commons, *Hansard*, 14 June 2007, Col.1217W
65. 'Press conference with the Pakistani President', 19 November 2006, www.pm.gov.uk
66. Ali Dayan Hasan, 'Pakistan's moderates are beaten in public', *International Herald Tribune*, 15 June 2005, www.hrw.org; The Musharraf regime also took very few steps to confront the madrassas – of which there are over 10,000 in Pakistan educating perhaps over a million students – which provide the breeding ground for jihadists and a centre for recruitment. Much of their funding comes from Saudi Arabia, importantly, and many are controlled by the HUM and LET terrorist groups. A 2007 report by the International Crisis Group on the madrassas in Karachi noted that, five years on from Musharraf's pledge to clamp down on Islamic extremism, 'the Pakistani government has yet to take any of the overdue and necessary steps to control the religious extremism in Karachi and the rest of the country'. It also noted that 'Musharraf's periodic declarations of tough action, given in response to international events and pressure, are invariably followed by retreat'. The continuation of the madrassa structures allows the jihadist groups to continue to recruit, fundraise and remain active. B. Raman, 'Pakistani madrassas: Questions and answers', 5 August 2005, www.saag.org; International Crisis Group, *Pakistan: Karachi's Madrassas and Violent Extremism*, 29 March 2007, p. i
67. House of Commons, *Hansard*, 11 June 2007, Col.632; 22 January 2007, Col.1455W

68. International Crisis Group, *Pakistan: Karachi's Madrassas,* p. 17
69. Cited in Isambard Wilkinson and Damien McElroy, 'Running Karachi – from London', *Telegraph*, 15 May 2007
70. Ayaz Amir, 'A love–hate relationship', *Dawn*, 12 November 2004
71. Isambard Wilkinson and Massoud Ansari, 'Pakistan on the brink of disaster as Karachi burns', *Telegraph*, 12 May 2007
72. House of Commons, *Hansard*, 11 June 2007, Col.628ff
73. David Miliband, 'Miliband in Pakistan – Press Conference', 26 July 2007, www.fco.gov.uk
74. ICG, *Winding Back Martial Law in Pakistan*, 12 November 2007, p. 1
75. Jason Burke, 'Musharraf wins but faces fight for power', *Guardian*, 7 October 2007
76. 'Prime Minister urges Pakistan on to democratic future', 28 December 2007, www.pm.gov.uk
77. Some links between the 7/7 bombers and the British intelligence services have been reported, but which in my view remain murky and inconclusive. Two particular individuals have been the subject of much speculation on some internet sites. First, there is the curious case of Haroon Rashid Aswat. As noted in chapter 14, the former US Justice Department prosecutor and terrorism expert, John Loftus, has claimed that Aswat was one of the British volunteers who took part in the jihad in Kosovo in 1999. Moreover, Loftus called Aswat a British 'double agent' in a US TV interview soon after 7/7, saying that he was being pursued by the police but protected by MI6. ('Video of Fox news report, linking terror suspect to British intelligence MI6', 1 August 2005, www.globalresearch.ca). Aswat had been one of Abu Hamza's aides at the Finsbury Park mosque, acting as his spokesman and running its day to day affairs (O'Neill and McGrory, p. 191). Mohamed Siddique Khan, the ringleader of the 7/7 bombers, came from the same town – Dewsbury, in Yorkshire – as Aswat, and arrived at the mosque in 2002 carrying a letter of introduction addressed to him (O'Neill and McGrory, p. 191). In the weeks before 7/7, Aswat was reportedly under surveillance in South Africa by the US authorities who wanted to arrest and question him – perhaps by 'extraordinary rendition', thus taking him to Guantanamo Bay – about his alleged involvement in a plan to set up a military training camp for jihadists in the US in 1999. The South Africans relayed this request to the British who were reluctant to arrest him because of his status as a British citizen. However, the *Times* noted that: 'Questions are also being asked about whether the British did not wish to have Aswat arrested because he was seen as a useful source of information. To some, British intelligence is too willing to let terrorist suspects run in the hope of gathering useful leads and other information.' (Richard Woods et al, 'Tangled web that still leaves worrying loose ends', *Times*, 31 July 2005). Aswat was then reported to have 'either slipped his surveillance or was allowed to move on from South Africa'. (Woods et al). There were media reports soon after 7/7 that Aswat had had numerous telephone conversations with the London bombers just before the attacks, and that he was being held in Pakistan about to flee across the border into Afghanistan (See, for example, Zahid Hussain et al, 'Top al-Qaeda Briton called Tube bombers before attack', *Times*, 21 July 2005). However, some

media soon reported that the man being held in Pakistan turned out to be a case of mistaken identity (Ian Cobain and Ewen Macaskill, 'Man held in Zambia', *Guardian*, 29 July 2005). Rather, Aswat had moved from South Africa to Zambia, where he was seized on 21 July and subsequently questioned by British and US investigators (Woods et al; Agencies, 'Zambia to deport terror suspect', *Guardian*, 3 August 2005). However, on 31 July, it was reported that US intelligence sources were still saying they believed Aswat 'assisted or masterminded' the bombings and that it was likely that the US National Security Agency had been monitoring his calls. In contrast, British investigators were saying that the telephone calls may have been made to a phone linked to Aswat rather than Aswat himself and indeed that 'he is not considered a priority in their criminal investigation into' 7/7. The *Times* added, cryptically: 'senior Whitehall officials also deny 'any knowledge' that he might be an agent for either MI5 or MI6' (Woods et al). By early August 2005, British counter-terrorism officials were repeatedly saying that there was no evidence linking Aswat to 7/7 and that they were 'irritated by repeated suggestions in the US that he was connected to the bombings' (Duncan Campbell and Richard Norton-Taylor, 'UK officials denied access to detained Briton', *Guardian*, 1 August 2005). Aswat was then deported from Zambia on 7 August and arrested by British police on a US warrant. In mid-August he was in court challenging the US extradition request, and Aswat's name disappeared from the 7/7 enquiries. Two years later, in late 2006, he lost the battle in the British courts to avoid extradition to the US (Agencies, 'UK terror suspects lose extradition battle', *Guardian*, 30 November 2006). There is also the case of Omar Saeed Sheikh and various suggestions in the media that Sheikh may have been involved with the 7/7 bombers, but with not much further information. Some 'well-informed sources in Pakistan' have claimed that he had met two of the perpetrators of 7/7 in his jail in Sindh province during their visit to Pakistan and that it was he who had motivated them to launch the bombings (B. Raman, 'Bojinka II, Pakistan and Musharraf, 12 August 2006, www.rediff.com). The Pakistani press reported in June 2006 that Sheikh was being questioned by Pakistani authorities at the behest of British intelligence, who wanted to know whether he had met any of the 7/7 bombers during his stay in London (Amir Mir, 'Daniel Pearl Killer Grilled for 7/7', 29 June 2006, www.dnaindia.com). Sheikh was a key operative in the JEM, with whom one of the London bombers appeared to have strong connections. A US media report noted soon after 7/7 that the British police in Pakistan had traced a telephone call from one of the 7/7 bombers to Masood Azhar, the leader of the JEM. (Chossudovsky, *America's 'War on Terrorism'*, p. 330, citing *Christian Science Monitor*, 1 August 2005) Azhar had set up the JEM in February 2000 and has close connections to Omar Saeed Sheikh; he was the General-Secretary of the HUA when Sheikh went to join the Bosnian jihad in 1993

78. Bin Laden's organisation may have managed and carried out only a small number of attacks itself, such as the 1998 US embassy bombings, the attack on the USS Cole in Yemen in 2000 and 9/11, according to some analysts. Other terrorist attacks, such as in India, Bali, Casablanca, Mombasa, Istanbul, Madrid, London and elsewhere, have been carried out either by

local branches of al-Qaida, largely on their own initiative, or by non-Arab organisations with little or no formal connections to al-Qaida other than sharing its ideology, or, as appears in the London case, by loose groups of individuals not formally part of any organisation as such but taking inspiration from a variety of groups and the idea of global jihad. See B. Raman, 'London blasts: An analysis', 9 July 2005, www.saag.org

CHAPTER 18: ALLIANCES OF MODERATION

1. Department of Trade and Industry, *Our Energy Future – Creating a Low Carbon Economy*, February 2003, section 6
2. *The National Security Strategy of the United Kingdom*, Cm.7291, March 2008, pp. 18–20, 31, 44–7
3. Gordon Brown, speech, 12 November 2007, www.pm.gov.uk
4. James Randerson, 'UK's ex-science chief predicts century of "resource" wars', *Guardian*, 13 February 2009
5. House of Commons, Foreign Affairs Committee, Global Security: The Middle East, *Eighth report*, Session 2006/07, 25 July 2007, Ev 55
6. 28 November 2007, Evidence to House of Commons, Foreign Affairs Committee, 'Global security: Iran', *Fifth report*, Session 2007/08, 20 February 2008, Ev.78
7. Ibid., Ev.72
8. William Lowther, 'US funds terror groups to sow chaos in Iran', *Telegraph*, 25 February 2007'; Tim Shipman, 'Bush sanctions "black ops" against Iran', *Telegraph*, 27 May 2007
9. House of Commons, 'Pakistan's political and security challenges', *Research Paper 7/68*, 17 September 2007, p. 18; Declan Walsh, 'Arrested in Afghanistan', *Guardian*, 2 October 2006; Raja Karthikeya, 'Jundullah a wedge between Iran, Pakistan', *Asia Times*, 7 August 2009; Ghulam Hasnain and Dean Nelson, 'Gunfire over the Pakistan border rattles Iranian leaders', *Times*, 4 March 2007
10. 'The secret war against Iran', ABC news, 3 April 2007. It has been reported on some internet sites that several of the terrorists arrested in Britain in 2006 for planning to bomb transatlantic airliners were reportedly trained in Jundullah camps in the Waziristan area of Pakistan, and also that Matiur Rehman, a leading figure in Jundullah, is suspected of masterminding the plot. However, this Jundullah is a different organisation than the Iranian/Baluchi organisation and is a pan-Pakistani offshoot of Baitullah Mehsud's Taliban faction.
11. William Lowther, 'US funds terror groups to sow chaos in Iran', *Telegraph*, 25 February 2007
12. 'Did British bomb attacks in Iran provoke hostage crisis?', *Independent*, 1 August 2009
13. Tim Shipman, 'Bush sanctions "black ops" against Iran', *Telegraph*, 27 May 2007
14. Eli Lake, 'Israel waging "secret war with Iran"', *New York Sun*, 15 September 2008
15. Uzi Mahnaimi, 'MI6 chief visits Mossad for talks on Iran's nuclear threat', *Sunday Times*, 4 May 2008

16. Gordon Thomas and Camilla Tominey, 'Saudis will let Israel bomb Iran nuclear site', *Daily Express*, 27 September 2009
17. Tony Blair, speech, 1 August 2006, www.pm.gov.uk
18. Ibid.
19. Government response to House of Commons, Foreign Affairs Committee, Global security: The Middle East, October 2007, para 118
20. House of Commons, Foreign Affairs Committee, Global Security: The Middle East, para 215
21. Miliband interview with CNN, 28 November 2007, www.fco.gov.uk
22. Gunaratna, p. 43
23. Home Office/Foreign Office, Working with the Muslim Community: Key messages, July 2004, cited in Martin Bright, *When Progressives Treat with Reactionaries: The British State's Flirtation with Radical Islamism*, Policy Exchange, 2006, p. 64
24. A. McKee to M. Nevin, 19 July 2005, in Bright, *When Progressives* ..., pp. 44–6
25. A. McKee to P. Goodenham et al, 7 June 2005, in Bright, *When Progressives...*, pp. 37–40
26. R. Murphy and B. Eastwood, 'We must talk to political Islamists in the Middle East – and not just in Iraq', undated, in Bright, *When Progressives* ..., pp. 51–2
27. D. Plumbly to J. Sawers, FCO, 23 June 2005, in Bright, *When Progressives* ..., p. 41
28. J. McGregor to Foreign Secretary, 17 January 2006, in Bright, *When Progressives* ..., pp. 47–9
29. Westminster Foundation for Democracy, *Annual Review 2005/06*, p. 9, www.wfd.org.uk
30. House of Commons, *Hansard*, 12 May 2006, Col.627W
31. Ibid., 23 May 2006, Col.1326
32. Ibid.
33. Government response to Foreign Affairs Committee, Global Security: The Middle East, October 2007, para 86; Some British officials had also argued to allow into the country Sheikh Yusuf al-Qaradawi, the Qatar-based spiritual leader of the international Muslim Brotherhood. Mockbul Ali, an Islamic Issues Adviser to the Foreign Office, argued in 2005 that Qaradawi's visit might be useful 'given his influence in relation to our foreign policy objectives'. Ali quotes the Political Director of the Foreign Office, John Sawers, as having said: 'Having individuals like Qaradawi on our side should be our aim. Excluding them won't help'. Ali stated that Britain did not agree with Qaradawi's views on Iraq or Israel but that 'to act against Qaradawi would alienate significant and influential members of the global Muslim community', and that 'he is the leading mainstream and influential Islamic authority in the Middle East and increasingly in Europe, with an extremely large popular following', involved 'in a number of high profile mainstream Muslim bodies and initiatives'. Qaradawi's most recent visit to London was in 2004 at the invitation of Mayor of London, Ken Livingstone, which was seen as controversial in light of Qaradawi's support for suicide bombings in Israel. In an interview with the Guardian in October 2005, Qaradawi insisted that such suicide attacks were a justified form of jihad,

maintaining that they are targeted at combatants only: 'Sometimes they kill a child or a woman. Provided they don't mean to, that's OK, but they shouldn't aim to kill them'. He has also justified the notorious verse in the Koran which allows for the 'beating' of wives, and expressed opposition to gay rights. In fact, Qaradawi has been a regular visitor to Britain, undertaking five trips between 1995 and 1997, for example. Ali noted that 'he has previously been visiting the UK for the last 10 years without incident'. In July 2006, the Foreign Office also funded a conference on Muslims in Europe, held in Istanbul, and paid Qaradawi's expenses to attend. At the conference he was met by Frances Guy, Britain's former ambassador to Yemen and head of the Foreign Office's Engaging with the Islamic World Group. M. Ali to J. Sawers, 14 July 2005, in Bright, *When Progressives ...*, pp. 53–4; Madeleine Bunting, 'Friendly fire', *Guardian*, 29 October 2005; Labeviere, pp. 139, 146; Kepel, *The Roots of Radical Islam*, p. 154; Karen McVeigh and Will Woodward, 'Tories accused of anti-Muslim bias', *Guardian*, 31 January 2007; John Ware, 'UK "hosted controversial cleric"', BBC news, 11 July 2006; Benedict Brogan, 'Taxpayers fund radical Muslim cleric's Turkey trip', *Daily Mail*, 13 July 2006

34. The Bush administration increased contacts with the Syrian National Salvation Front, a coalition grouping comprising the Brotherhood and a faction led by Abdul Halim Khaddam, a former Syrian Vice-President who defected in 2005. A delegation of the Front's members met officials from the US National Security Council in 2005 while a former senior CIA officer told journalist Seymour Hersh in early 2007 that Washington was providing political and financial support to the Front, with the Saudis 'taking the lead with financial support'. (Seymour Hersh, 'The Redirection', *New Yorker*, 5 March 2007.) US government contacts with the Syrian Brotherhood were nothing new. The Washington Post has reported that 'for years the State Department and CIA officials have met with Brotherhood activists in Egypt, Kuwait, Jordan, the Palestinian territories and elsewhere to track currents within Islamic politics'. The Bush administration also stepped up contacts with the Egyptian Brotherhood, though these appeared more limited, presumably due to Washington's need to be seen to be backing President Mubarak. In April 2005, al-Sharq al-Awsat, the Arabic newspaper based in London, reported that the State Department had drawn up a memo calling for dialogue with the Egyptian Brotherhood. In early 2007, the US ambassador in Cairo hosted a reception where some representatives of the Muslim Brotherhood were present. John Mintz and Douglas Farah, 'In search of friends among the foes', *Washington Post*, 11 September 2004; Baer, pp. 87–8, 94–5; 'US reaching out to Muslim Brotherhood: Report', 3 April 2005, www.islamonline.net; Eli Lake, 'Bush weighs reaching out to "brothers"', *New York Sun*, 20 June 2007
35. Martin Bright, 'I am no Islamophobe', 14 July 2006, www.commentisfree.guardian.co.uk
36. Bright, *Observer*, 30 July 2006
37. D. Plumbly to J. Sawers, FCO, 23 June 2005, in Bright, *When Progressives ...*, p. 41
38. A. McKee to M. Nevin, 19 July 2005, in Bright, pp. 44–6
39. J. McGregor to Foreign Secretary, 17 January 2006, in Bright, pp. 47–9

40. House of Commons, Foreign Affairs Committee, Global Security: The Middle East, para.152; Derek Plumbly, interview, 8 January 2008, www.fco.gov.uk
41. Cited in Evgenil Novikov, 'Muslim Brotherhood in Crisis?', *Terrorism Monitor*, 26 February 2004
42. For example, former CIA officer, Robert Baer, has described US contacts with the Brotherhood in Syria, as well as in Libya and Lebanon, in the mid-1980s, after then Syrian President Assad, father of the current President, had virtually crushed the movement in a brutal crackdown in 1982. Baer refers to the Brothers as 'surrogates' for the Reagan administration's battle against Syria and Iran at the time. He also admits to designing a 'false flag' operation to place explosives on the cars of Syrian diplomats and then fabricate a communiqué claiming the attacks had been carried out by Hezbollah, to provoke Assad cracking down on it. Although the plan was rejected by his superiors, Baer states that a similar operation was authorised 'to irritate Assad' but does not give details. Baer also met with Libyan members of the Muslim Brotherhood while in Sudan in the mid-1980s, putting out feelers to them for helping to overthrow Qadafi. Baer's account leaves it unclear as to further US planning, but implies that senior CIA and political figures would have worked with anyone to get rid of Qadafi. The Khartoum CIA station chief at the time was Milt Bearden, who had moved on from overseeing CIA operations in the Afghan jihad. Baer, pp. 87–8, 94–5
43. Nasser Salem, 'Muslim Brotherhood reasserting its leadership of Syria's fractured opposition', 16 September 2002, www.muslimmedia.com
44. 'Excerpts from the NSF press conference', *Syria Monitor*, 6 June 2006, http://syriamonitor.typepad.com
45. Mahan Abdein, 'The battle within Syria: An interview with Muslim Brotherhood leader Ali Bayanouni', *Terrorism Monitor*, 11 August 2005
46. 'Foreign Secretary in Syria', 18 November 2008, www.fco.gov.uk
47. A. McKee to M. Nevin, 19 July 2005, in Bright, pp. 44–6
48. House of Commons, *Hansard*, 27 February 2006, Col.301W
49. Hazel Blears, speech, 25 February 2009, www.communities.gov.uk
50. House of Commons, *Hansard*, 10 February 2003, Col.581W
51. Tony Blair, speech, 21 March 2006, www.pm.gov.uk
52. An article in the establishment US journal, *Foreign Affairs*, commissioned by the US National Intelligence Council, noted that US policy towards the Brotherhood was contested between those officials who viewed the organisation as part of the global jihadist network and those who stressed its moderating influence and popular support in key Muslim countries. The article sided with the latter argument, and called on the US to develop a 'conversation' with the Brotherhood since it 'presents a notable opportunity' in the US search for 'Muslim moderates'. Leiken and Brooke argue that the Brotherhood has eschewed revolution and 'depends on winning hearts through gradual and peaceful Islamization', seeking a compact with the powers that be and 'offering a channel for discontent while slowly expanding its influence'. Yet even these authors also noted that there was 'slim evidence' that the Brotherhood has ever pondered what it would do if it achieved power – to embrace or abolish democracy. They also stated: 'If a

Muslim Brother wishes to commit violence, he generally leaves the organisation to do so. That said, a number of militants have passed through the Brotherhood since its inception, and the path from the Brotherhood to jihad is not buried in sand'. Finally, Leiken and Brooke asserted that although the Brotherhood expressly denies its organisation is anti-semitic, their literature 'has expressed hatred for all Jews not just Zionists'. (Robert Leiken and Steven Brooke, 'The Moderate Muslim Brotherhood', *Foreign Affairs*, March/April 2007). Yusuf al-Qaradawi outlined in a 1990 book the importance of dawa – dialogue – and other peaceful means to achieve the Islamic movement's goals. Qaradawi condemned the 9/11 attacks since, he told the author Gilles Kepel, the terrorists had brought opprobrium upon all of Islam in the West and threatened the progress of conversion and the strengthening of Islamist political action within the community. The attacks thus set back the Muslim Brothers' missionary effort in the West and its strategy since the late 1980s of rooting themselves in Western civil society, where many Muslims now lived and which is therefore considered part of the land of Islam. This view contrasts to the jihadists who view the Brothers as 'deviants' and demand that European Muslims adopt a self-imposed apartheid and isolate themselves from the European infidels. (Kepel, *The War for Muslim Minds*, pp. 253–5) Yet a key aspect of Qaradawi's thinking, which has been called for by the European Fatwa Council, an influential Islamic legal organisation, is that sharia law be applied to Muslims living on European soil. In his 1990 book, Qaradawi also called for a separate society for Muslims within the West which would establish 'your own "Muslim ghetto"'. Lorenzo Vidino of Tufts University, who has extensively analysed Brotherhood activities in Europe, notes that Qaradawi's treatise 'corresponds to what the international network of the Muslim Brotherhood has been doing in the West for the past fifty years', which is aiming at 'the introduction of sharia law within the Muslim communities of Europe'. The Brotherhood's strategy in Europe, Vidino notes, is not currently to challenge the establishment since it is too weak, but is one of 'befriending the establishment' by setting up organisations that engage in dialogue with national governments. (Lorenzo Vidino, 'Aims and Methods of Europe's Muslim Brotherhood'). The Brotherhood's agenda in public, speaking to an English-language audience, is stated to be one of finding peaceful ways of achieving reform, participating wherever possible in the political process by engaging in elections. Yet several analysts have pointed to statements made by Brotherhood leaders on its Arabic language website. Muhammad Akef, the Supreme Guide of the Muslim Brotherhood, reportedly declared in February 2007 that 'the jihad will lead to smashing Western civilisation and replacing it with Islam which will dominate the world', and that 'Muslims are obliged to continue the jihad that will cause the collapse of Western civilisation and the ascendance of the Muslim civilization on its ruins'. The Brotherhood's official website articulates its goal as to liberate 'the Islamic homeland' from foreign rule and to establish an Islamic state that will implement sharia law. In turn, other Muslim lands will be liberated until all are brought together in a union. For some analysts, the nature of the Brotherhood is very clear. Alain Chouet, a former head of the French secret service, the DGSE, regards the Brotherhood as remaining a 'fascist movement' true to its roots of having supported the Nazi regime in the 1930s. 'Like every fascist movement on the trail of power, the Brotherhood has achieved perfect fluency in double-speak', Chouet asserts. The 'democratic conversion' of its leaders 'should not fool anyone'. (Rachel Ehrenfeld and Alyssa Lappen, 'The Muslim Brotherhood's Propaganda Offensive', 2 April 2007, www.americanthinker.com; Lorenzo Vidino, 'Aims and methods of Europe's Muslim Brotherhood'; Alain Chouet, 'The Association of Muslim Brothers: Chronicle of a Barbarism Foretold', 6 April 2006, www.esisc.org). As for the Brotherhood's links to terrorism, the organisation regularly publicly condemns al-Qaida and has often been publicly outspoken against terrorism. The Brotherhood in Egypt renounced violence in the 1970s and has since participated in electoral politics and other formal institutional bodies. (Chris Zambelis, 'Egypt's Muslim Brotherhood: Political Islam without al-Qaeda', *Terrorism Monitor*, 26 November 2007). The US Council on Foreign Relations, an academic body with close links to the US foreign policy establishment, states that the Brotherhood's links to terrorism are 'unclear'. Some analysts say that the Brotherhood acts as a 'stepping stone' for individuals to join jihadist groups. (Mary Crane, 'Does the Muslim Brotherhood have ties to terrorism?', Council on Foreign Relations, 5 April 2007, www.cfr.org). Certainly, as we have seen in earlier sections, individuals such as Abdullah Azzam and Ayman al-Zawahiri have 'progressed' from membership of the Muslim Brotherhood to greater militancy; at the same time, they have recognised the ideological roots of leading Brotherhood thinkers in much al-Qaida theology. We have also seen how the Afghan jihad in the 1980s took off partly by utilising the resources and networks of the Muslim Brotherhood. Some figures associated with the Brotherhood are alleged to have been involved in funding terrorism. In November 2001, for example, the US Treasury designated two key figures in the al-Taqwa bank, dubbed the 'bank of the Muslim Brotherhood', as financiers of terrorism. (Lorenzo Vidino, 'The Muslim Brotherhood's Conquest of Europe', *Middle East Quarterly*, Winter 2005, www.meforum.org) The chief of the US Treasury's terrorist finance unit has been quoted saying that the Brotherhood 'are a political movement, an economic cadre and in some cases terrorist supporters… They operate business empires in the Western world, but their philosophy and ultimate objectives are radical Islamist goals that in many ways are antithetical to our interests. They have one foot in our world and one foot in a world hostile to us'. (Cited in John Mintz and Douglas Farah, 'In search of friends among the foes', *Washington Post*, 11 September 2004). Syrian businessmen closely linked to the Syrian Muslim Brotherhood are alleged to have run a network of companies in Spain and Germany that financed al-Qaida activities in Europe and even employed some of the 9/11 hijackers. (Lorenzo Vidino, *Al Qaeda in Europe: The New Battleground of International Jihad* (Prometheus: New York, 2006), p. 91). Terrorism expert Ronan Gunaratna notes that 'organisationally, Al Qaeda is the natural offshoot of the Muslim Brotherhood' and that 'it built on the Brotherhood, drawing on its committed followers, its structures and its experience'. Al-Qaida is also similarly 'organised along the lines of a broad-based family clan with its constituent multinational members designated as "brothers", a term commonly used by religious Muslims when referring to each other'. (Gunaratna, p. 96) Yet al-Qaida is clearly very different to the Muslim Brotherhood in the extent of its militancy, and in actually carrying out acts such as 'martyrdom', of which the Brotherhood simply (sometimes) speaks. Al-Qaida condemns the Brotherhood for participating in elections and lending legitimacy to apostate governments. For some individuals, it may be the specific failure of the Brotherhood to change regimes that has led many to the militancy of al-Qaida and other jihadist groups.

53. Napoleoni, p. 164
54. Cited in Hollingsworth, p. 102
55. Kepel, *The War for Muslim Minds*, pp. 191–2
56. Congressional Research Service, 'Saudi Arabia: Terrorist Financing Issues', 1 March 2005, US Library of Congress, p. 16
57. 'Update on the global campaign against terrorist financing', Second Report of an Independent Task Force on Terrorist Financing sponsored by the Council on Foreign Relations, 15 June 2004, p. 20
58. David Kaplan, 'The Saudi Connection', *US News & World Report*, 12 July 2003
59. osh Meyer, 'Saudi Arabia is prime source of terror funds, US says', *Los Angeles Times*, 2 April 2008
60. Hollingsworth, p. 230
61. See Atwan, *The Secret History of Al-Qaeda*, p. 168
62. Ibid., p. 169. For speculation that BBC reporter Frank Gardner's attackers may have been tipped off by Saudi officials, see Tom Walker and Nicholas Hellen, 'BBC man fled for a mile before killing', *Sunday Times*, 13 June 2004, and Patrick Barret, 'Scotland Yard joins hunt for BBC killers', *Guardian*, 9 June 2004
63. Ned Parker, 'Saudis' role in Iraq insurgency outlined', *Los Angeles Times*, 15 July 2007
64. Donna Abu-Nasr, 'Saudi network backs Iraq insurgency', Fox news, 28 February 2005
65. Associated Press, 'Officials say Saudis major provider of finance to Iraqi Sunni insurgents', 7 December 2006
66. Neil Partrick, Evidence to Foreign Affairs Committee, Foreign Policy Aspects of the War Against Terrorism, 21 June 2006, Ev.187
67. Seymour Hersh, 'The Redirection'. It is also noteworthy that fighters from the Pakistani terrorist group, Lashkar-e-Toiba (LET), have also turned up in Iraq. With the LET now acting as one of the world's most important terrorist organisations, some analysts argue that its most important infrastructure outside Pakistan is in Saudi Arabia, from which its terrorist activities in South and Southeast Asia are managed. Hafez Mohammed Saeed, the amir of the Jamaat-ud-Dawa, the political wing of the LET, is a strong supporter of the Saudi monarchy and is said to have received funds from Saudi intelligence, while the Saudi authorities have turned a blind eye to LET activities on their soil. According to B. Raman, one militant responsible for infiltrating LET fighters into Saudi Arabia was Saleh Mohammed al-Oufi, a leading figure in al-Qaida. Al-Oufi had previously joined the Pakistani terrorist group, HUA, and had been part of the Pakistani contingent infiltrated by the ISI into the Bosnian jihad in

the 1990s. Mir, *The True Face of Jehadis*, p. 71; B. Raman, 'LET: Al Qaeda's Clone', 2 July 2003; B. Raman, 'Saudi Arrests of Jihad Suspects', 30 April 2007, www.saag.org; B. Raman, 'Al Qaeda in Saudi Arabia', 27 June 2004, www.saag.org

68. FCO, 'Engaging with the Islamic World Programme', www.fco.gov.uk
69. Statements by the queen and prime minister, 1 August 2005, www.fco.gov.uk
70. Anton La Guardian, 'New Saudi envoy to London has Bin Laden links', *Telegraph*, 19 October 2002; David Leigh, 'Saudi arms deal inquiry closes in on secret papers', *Guardian*, 20 November 2006; Dorril, *Silent Conspiracy*, p. 292
71. Hollingsworth, Saudi Babylon, pp. 46–7. In 2003 the Saudis agreed to give clemency to a group of Britons held and tortured for nearly three years in Saudi jails; they had been unjustly accused of a bombing campaign in the country which Saudi officials were perfectly aware was the responsibility of al-Qaida. Hollingsworth's book documents how the British government virtually abandoned the prisoners in order to appease their allies in Riyadh. Indeed, it is significant that the Britons were finally released as part of a deal – in exchange for the US releasing five Saudi members of al-Qaida who had been held at Guantanamo Bay. Hollingsworth, passim and p. 200
72. Jack Straw, speech, 16 January 2006, www.fco.gov.uk
73. Jack Straw, speech, 18 April 2006, www.fco.gov.uk
74. Jack Straw, speech, 23 February 2005, www.fco.gov.uk
75. Kim Howells, speech, 29 October 2007, www.fco.gov.uk
76. Foreign Secretary joint press conference with Saudi Foreign Minister Price Saud al-Faisal, 23 April 2008, www.fco.gov.uk
77. 'Long history of friendship with Saudi Arabia', 20 November 2008, www.fco.gov.uk
78. Defence Secretary visits Riyadh', 9 November 2009, www. ukinsaudiarabia.fco.uk
79. Foreign Affairs Committee, *Foreign Policy Aspects of the War against Terrorism*, 21 June 2006, p.48
80. David Leigh, Richard Norton-Taylor and Rob Evans, 'MI6 and Blair at odds over Saudi deals', *Guardian*, 16 January 2007; Michael Peel and Jimmy Burns, 'BAE probe "had widened to MoD staff"', *Financial Times*, 16 January 2007
81. Cited in David Leigh, Rob Evans and David Gow, 'BAE bosses named as corruption suspects', *Guardian*, 17 January 2007; David Leigh and Richard Norton-Taylor, 'Lives at stake if inquiry had upset Saudis, says Goldsmith', *Guardian*, 18 January 2007; Leigh, Norton-Taylor and Evans, 'MI6 and Blair at odds over Saudi deals'
82. SABB notes, 'Saudi-British Trade Relations', 30 October 2007, www.sabb.com; 'UK Saudi Relations', undated, www.ukinsaudiarabia.fco.gov.uk
83. Gordon Brown, speech, 21 June 2006, www.hm-treasury.gov.uk
84. Gordon Brown, speech, 13 June 2006, www.hm-treasury.gov.uk
85. Ed Balls, speech, 30 January 2007, www.hm-treasury.gov.uk
86. Ed Balls, speech, 30 October 2006, www.hm-treasury.gov.uk
87. Roula Khalaf, 'City acts to cash in on booming Gulf', *Financial Times*, 17 June 2006
88. Richard Orange, 'The petrodollars power', *The Business*, 3 January 2007

89. Douglas Alexander, speech, 29 November 2004, www.fco.gov.uk
90. Gordon Brown June press conference, 12 June 2008, www.pm.gov.uk

CHAPTER 19: ALLIED TO THE ENEMY: IRAQ AND AFGHANISTAN

1. Sabrina Tavernise, 'Iraqi dead may total 600,000, study says', *New York Times*, 10 October 2006; Opinion Research Business, 'January 2008 – Update on Iraqi casualty data', www.opinion.co.uk
2. Eric Herring, 'UK Operations in Iraq', UK Watch, 12 October 2007
3. ICG, *Shiite Politics in Iraq: The Role of the Supreme Council*, 15 November 2007, p. 8
4. Mike O'Brien, House of Commons, *Hansard*, 18 March 2003, Col.722
5. Robert Dreyfus, 'How the Bush administration and the neocons got into bed with Iran's agents in Iraq', *The American Prospect*, 20 May 2007
6. ICG, Shiite Politics in Iraq, p. 10
7. Ibid., p. 22
8. Jack Straw, Evidence to Foreign Affairs Committee, 15 March 2006, Q230, www.parliament.uk; Des Browne, House of Commons, *Hansard*, 1 February 2007, Col.387
9. House of Commons, *Hansard*, 12 December 2006, Col.729
10. ICG, *Shiite Politics in Iraq*, p. 16
11. Reidar Vissar, 'The Sadrists, the Bush administration's narrative on Iraq and the Maysan operations', 3 July 2008, www.historiae.org
12. ICG, *Shiite Politics in Iraq*, p.23
13. ICG, *Where is Iraq Heading? Lessons from Basra*, June 2007, pp. 1–12
14. Ibid., pp. 11–12
15. Michael Knights and Ed Williams, *The Calm Before the Storm: The British Experience in Southern Iraq*, Washington Institute for Near East Policy, February 2007, p. 15
16. Knights and Williams, pp. 34, 25
17. Michael Evans, 'Army tells its soldiers to "bribe" the Taleban', *Times*, 16 November 2009
18. ICG, *Where is Iraq Heading?*, p. 13
19. Ibid., pp. i, 15
20. Knights and Williams, p. 33
21. 'Retired US general criticises British', United Press International, 23 August 2007
22. Ian Black, Ewen Macaskill, 'MoD denies deal over withdrawal from Basra', *Guardian*, 31 August 2007. The deal was so obvious that even the BBC covered it, confirming the agreement in the TV programme, Panorama. See 'The battle for Basra palace', BBC1, 10 December 2007
23. John Hutton, House of Commons, *Hansard*, 4 November 2008, Col.304W
24. Richard Norton-Taylor, 'British to step up detainee release after militia talks', *Guardian*, 8 September 2007
25. Ibid.
26. Deborah Haynes and Michael Evans, 'Secret deal kept British army out of battle for Basra', *Times*, 5 August 2008
27. Jock Stirrup, 'Exit Iraq, heads high', *Guardian*, 18 December 2008

28. 'Joint Statement on Basra', 30 October 2007, www.fco.gov.uk; Gordon Brown, statement to parliament, 8 October 2007, www.pm.gov.uk
29. Richard Norton-Taylor and Matthew Taylor, 'British troops officially end combat operation in southern Iraq', *Guardian*, 30 April 2009
30. Kim Sengupta, 'After six years, one month and 11 days, Britain ends its military mission in Iraq', *Independent*, 1 May 2009
31. Patrick Cockburn, 'Britain bows out of a five-year war it could never have won', *Independent*, 17 December 2007
32. Knights and Williams, p. 16
33. ICG, *Shiite politics in Iraq*, p. 24
34. Reidar Visser, 'The Surge, the Shiites and nation building in Iraq', *Terrorism Monitor*, 13 September 2007
35. Dreyfus, 'How the Bush administration and the neocons got into bed with Iran's agents in Iraq'; Juan Cole, 'The Iraqi Shiites', *Boston Review*, October/November 2003
36. Zaki Chehab, 'Sunni vs Shia', *New Statesman*, 12 February 2007
37. Jim Rutenberg and Mark Mazzetti, 'President links Qaeda of Iraq to Qaeda of 9/11', *New York Times*, 25 July 2007
38. John Burns and Alissa Rubin, 'US arming Sunnis in Iraq to battle old Qaeda allies', New York Times, 11 June 2007
39. Ali al-Fadhily and Dahr Jamail, '"Awakening" forces arouse new conflicts', Inter Press Service, 26 December 2007
40. Martin Chulov, 'Iraq bombs linked to Sunni militias who fought against al-Qaida', *Guardian*, 7 April 2009
41. 'Ground control', *Times*, 21 June 2007
42. Gordon Brown, Press conference, 8 October 2007, www.pm.gov.uk; emphasis added
43. HM Government, *UK Policy in Afghanistan and Pakistan: The Way Forward*, April 2009, p. 8; Richard Norton-Taylor, 'More troops sent to fight Taliban', *Guardian*, 17 June 2008
44. 'Foreign Secretary William Hague: "What we want is a situation in Afghanistan where our own national security and that of our allies is protected"', 20 November 2010, www.fco.gov.uk
45. House of Commons, Defence Committee, UK Operations in Afghanistan, *Thirteenth Special Report of Session 2006–07*, 9 October 2007, Ev 2
46. David Batty, 'PM rejects Afghan president's denigration of UK forces', *Guardian*, 25 January 2008
47. Talatbek Masadykov et al, 'Negotiating with the Taliban: Toward a Solution for the Afghan Conflict', *Crisis States Working Paper Series*, No.2, LSE, London, January 2010, p. 3
48. ISAF, *Commander's Initial Assessment*, 30 August 2009, p. 1
49. Michael Flynn, *State of the Insurgency: Trends, Intentions and Objectives*, ISAF, 22 December 2009; International Council on Security and Development, press release, 10 September 2009, www.icosgroup.net
50. Flynn, *State of the Insurgency*
51. House of Commons, Defence Committee, UK Operations in Afghanistan, *Thirteenth Special Report of Session 2006–07*, 9 October 2007, para 94
52. 'Operations in Afghanistan: British Casualties', undated, www.mod.uk
53. Talatbek Masadykov et al, 'Negotiating with the Taliban: Toward a Solution

for the Afghan Conflict', *Crisis States Working Paper Series*, No.2, LSE, London, January 2010, p. 4

54. Flynn, *State of the Insurgency*
55. World Bank, 'Afghanistan Country Overview 2010', www.worldbank.org; World Bank, *Interim Strategy Note for Islamic Republic of Afghanistan for the Period FY09-FY11*, 5 May 2009, p. 8; 'UNICEF: More than half of Afghan children suffer from malnutrition', Health News, 11 November 2009, www.rawa.org
56. 'Afghanistan civilian casualties: What are the real figures?', *Guardian*, 19 November 2009; United Nations Assistance Mission in Afghanistan, *Annual Report 2010*, p.i
57. UNAMA figures cited in Simon Rogers, 'Afghanistan civilian casualties: what are the real figures?', Guardian, 19 November 2009; United Nations Assistance Mission in Afghanistan, *Afghanistan Annual Report on Protection of Civilians in Armed Conflict, 2009*, p. 16.
58. House of Commons, Defence Committee, UK operations in Afghanistan, Ev 5
59. Human Rights Watch, 'Afghanistan: Conference Should Link Rights to Security', 26 January 2010, www.hrw.org
60. ISAF, *Commander's Initial Assessment*, 30 August 2009, p. 1–2
61. Johann Hari, 'The three fallacies that have driven the war in Afghanistan', *Independent*, 21 October 2009
62. William Hague, 'Progress in Afghanistan is the "top foreign policy priority for the Government"', 27 October 2010, www.fco.gov.uk
63. '"A remarkable record of service" from Marines in Afghanistan', 4 November 2010, www.fco.gov.uk
64. 'Foreign Secretary Hague statement on Afghanistan', 21 July 2010, www.fco.gov.uk
65. House of Commons, Foreign Affairs Committee, 'The UK's Foreign Policy Approach to Afghanistan and Pakistan', *Fourth Report of Session 2010-11*, 9 February 2011, pp.24, 29
66. Imtiaz Ali, 'The Haqqani network and cross-border terrorism in Afghanistan', *Terrorism Monitor*, 24 March 2008
67. Cited in Syed Saleem Shahzad, 'Taliban's new commander ready for a fight', *Asia Times*, 20 May 2006
68. Ibid.
69. Milt Bearden, 'Meet the Pasthuns', *Counterpunch*, 31 March 2004; Declan Walsh and Richard Norton-Taylor, 'Taliban sets out demands to Afghan President', *Guardian*, 15 October 2007
70. 'Afghan warlord "aided Bin Laden"', BBC news, 11 January 2007
71. Cooley, p. 63; House of Commons, *Hansard*, 28 July 1989, Col.1164
72. Mark Mazzetti and Eric Schmitt, 'US says agents of Pakistan aid Afghan Taliban', *New York Times*, 22 December 2009; Kaushik Kapisthalam, 'Musharraf and his Taliban "pals"', *Asia Times*, 19 July 2005
73. Muhammad Tahir, 'Gulbuddin Hekmtayar's return to the Afghan insurgency', *Terrorism Monitor*, 29 May 2008
74. David Miliband, speech, 17 August 2009, www.fco.gov.uk
75. Foreign Affairs Committee, Global Security: Afghanistan and Pakistan, *Eighth report*, Session 2008–09, July 2009, Ev86

76. David Miliband, speech, 17 August 2009, www.fco.gov.uk
77. David Miliband, interview, 1 December 2009, www.fco.gov.uk
78. Foreign Affairs Committee, Global Security: Afghanistan and Pakistan, *Eighth report*, Session 2008–09, July 2009, Ev86
79. 'Army tells soldiers fighting in Afghanistan to buy off Taliban "with bags of gold"', *Daily Mail*, 17 November 2009
80. Mark Sedwill, speech, 6 August 2009, www.fco.gov.uk
81. Foreign Affairs Committee, Global Security: Afghanistan and Pakistan, *Eighth report*, Session 2008–09, July 2009, Ev86
82. Kim Sengupta, 'Karzai to brief PM on secret Taliban talks', *Independent*, 13 November 2008
83. Richard Norton-Taylor, 'Britain and US prepared to open talks with the Taliban', *Guardian*, 28 July 2009
84. Syed Saleem Shahzad, 'US gets cosy with Taliban's point man', *Asia Times*, 18 June 2004
85. Australian parliament, House of Representatives, Committee report, 'Jamiat ul-Ansar', undated, www.aph.gov.au
86. Syed Saleem Shahzad, 'US gets cosy with Taliban's point man'
87. Foreign Office minute, 18 March 2004, Response to Freedom of Information Act request from Foreign Office to the author, 16 November 2011
88. 'Obama reaches out to religious parties in Pakistan', *Dawn*, 19 August 2009
89. Ben Farmer, 'Taliban fighters to be lured from fighting with cash', *Telegraph*, 11 November 2009
90. Jon Boone, 'US pours millions into anti-Taliban militias in Afghanistan', *Guardian*, 22 November 2009
91. Richard Norton-Taylor, 'Money talks in Afghanistan, says army counterinsurgency manual', *Guardian*, 17 November 2009
92. 'Army tells soldiers fighting in Afghanistan to buy off Taliban "with bags of gold"', *Daily Mail*, 17 November 2009
93. Farmer, 'Taliban fighters'
94. Address to the IISS, 21 September 2007, www.mod.uk
95. Bob Ainsworth, speech, 8 July 2009, www.mod.uk
96. Bob Ainsworth, speech, 15 September 2009, www.mod.uk
97. Ibid.
98. General David Richards, speech, 17 September 2009, www.mod.uk
99. Foreign Affairs Committee, Global security: Afghanistan and Pakistan, *Eighth report*, Session 2008–09, July 2009, Ev75. The war is NATO's first 'out of area' operation, and is 'a test of the alliance's political will and military capabilities', a recent US Congressional report notes. It adds that 'the allies wish to create a "new" NATO, able to go beyond the European theatre and combat new threats such as terrorism'; CRS report for Congress, *NATO in Afghanistan: A Test of the Transatlantic Alliance*, 6 May 2008, Summary
100. General Sir Richard Dannatt, speech, 15 May 2009, www.mod.uk
101. Declan Walsh, 'US aid will not stop Pakistan supporting militants', *Guardian*, 30 November 2010
102. Mark Mazzetti and Eric Schmitt, 'US says agents of Pakistan aid Afghan Taliban', *New York Times*, 26 March 2009
103. Barnett Rubin, 'Saving Afghanistan', *Foreign Affairs*, January/ February 2007

104. See submission by Professor Shaun Gregory, Pakistan Security Research Unit, University of Bradford, Foreign Affairs Committee, Global Security: Afghanistan and Pakistan, *Eighth report*, Session 2008–09, July 2009, Ev162
105. Declan Walsh, 'Taliban attacks double after Pakistan's deal with militants', *Guardian*, 29 September 2006
106. Mark Mazzetti and Eric Schmitt, 'US says agents of Pakistan aid Afghan Taliban'. *New York Times*, 26 March 2009
107. Cited in Foreign Affairs Committee, Global security: Afghanistan and Pakistan, *Eighth report*, Session 2008–09, July 2009, para 231
108. David Miliband, speech, 17 November 2009, www.fco.gov.uk
109. Walsh, 'Pakistan sheltering Taliban, says British officer', *Guardian*, 19 May 2006
110. See submission by Professor Shaun Gregory, Ev161
111. Kim Sengupta, 'Pakistanis accused of aiding Taliban with missile parts', *Independent*, 13 March 2006
112. Ewen Macaskill, 'Pakistan to "weed out" Taliban sympathisers', *Guardian*, 2 August 2008
113. Peter Beaumont and Mark Townsend, 'Pakistani troops "aid Taliban"', *Guardian*, 22 June 2008
114. Gordon Brown, press conference in Islamabad, 14 December 2008, www.number10.gov.uk
115. Jeremy Page, 'Britain to train Pakistan's Frontier Corps troops in Baluchistan', *Times*, 9 October 2009
116. Tariq Mahmud Ashraf, 'Pakistan's Frontier Corps and the War Against Terrorism – Part Two', *Terrorism Monitor*, 11 August 2008
117. Foreign Affairs Committee, Global Security: Afghanistan and Pakistan, *Eighth report*, Session 2008–09, July 2009, para 170; emphasis added
118. Ibid., Ev 60 and 59
119. See submission by Professor Shaun Gregory, Ev162. In June 2007, the leading Pakistani intelligence agencies produced a paper on the growing influence of 'Talibanisation' in the Northwest Frontier province, which concluded that thirteen districts were affected by varying degrees of militancy and extremism. Hassan Abbas, a former police chief in the province and now a Fellow at Harvard University's Kennedy School of Government, has noted that Islamabad has not countered this Talibanisation because it 'must have concluded earlier that Pakistan would yet again need a "working relationship" with the Taliban to pursue its interests in Afghanistan and to compete with Indian and Iranian goals in the region'. Hassan Abbas, 'Is the NWFP Slipping out of Pakistan's Control?', *Terrorism Monitor*, 26 November 2007
120. ICG, *Pakistan's Tribal Areas: Appeasing the Militants*, 11 December 2006, p. 13
121. ICG, *Pakistan's Tribal Areas*, p. i
122. In 2004 the Pakistani military, supported by the US and a 100-strong SAS contingent, deployed 80,000 troops in the FATA to deny al-Qaida and some Taliban militants safe haven and to end their cross-border attacks. But the operations, which involved indiscriminate attacks on civilians and caused high Pakistani army casualties, failed to dislodge the insurgents. So the Musharraf regime completely reversed its policy, and

tried to appease the militants by signing a peace deal with pro-Taliban forces in South Waziristan, a region of the FATA, in April 2004. During the ceremony for this 'the [Pakistani army's] corps commander's pro-jihad speech ... reinforced perceptions that the military had surrendered to the militants', the International Crisis Group (ICG) notes. The peace deal soon broke down as renewed fighting ensued and the centre of militancy essentially shifted to North Waziristan, where another 'peace' deal was signed in September 2006. The agreement was that Pakistan would stop operations against the pro-Taliban militants in exchange for their promise to stop attacks on government officials and cross-border forays into Afghanistan. Initially supported by both the US and Britain, the deal soon – somewhat predictably – resulted in an increase in cross-border attacks into Afghanistan and was widely seen as empowering the Taliban. The deal 'effectively allowed the Taliban and its allies to control the area and has given them free rein to commit abuses', Human Rights Watch notes. The deal 'appears to have empowered the Taliban, most likely contributing to its resurgence', the ICG agreed. Within nine months, by mid-2007, the deal appeared dead, as Taliban forces accused the government of attacking them. This was just after Musharraf had ordered the storming of the Red Mosque in Islamabad, in response to its seizure by Islamist militants. In May 2008, the Musharraf regime signed another peace deal with the Taliban, this time in the neighbouring Northwest Frontier province: in exchange for the government withdrawing troops and introducing sharia law in one part of the province, the Taliban would end suicide bombings and attacks on government buildings. ICG, *Pakistan's Tribal Areas*, pp. 16, 19. Human Rights Watch, 'Pakistan: Improved Security got Civilians in Tribal Areas', 23 February 2007, www.hrw.org; See also Khalid Hasan, 'NATO seen following Waziristan lead', *Daily Times* (Pakistan) 17 October 2006; Declan Walsh, 'Pakistan makes peace deal to end pro-Taliban violence', *Guardian*, 22 May 2008

123. Foreign Affairs Committee, Global Security: Afghanistan and Pakistan, *Eighth report*, Session 2008–09, July 2009, para 149
124. Ishtiaq Mahsud, 'Pakistan fights militants inside 3 fronts', Associated Press, 19 October 2009
125. Rosa Prince, 'David Cameron: Pakistan is promoting the "export of terror"' *Daily Telegraph*, 28 July 2010
126. 'Transcript of a press conference given by the Prime Minister David Cameron and Prime Minister of Pakistan in Islamabad', 5 April 2011, www.pm.gov.uk
127. 'Transcript of the opening remarks given by Prime Minister David Cameron at the press conference with President Barack Obama at Lancaster House', 25 May 2011, www.pm.gov.uk
128. Cited in Foreign Affairs Committee, Global Security: Afghanistan and Pakistan, *Eighth report*, Session 2008–09, July 2009, para 231
129. House of Commons, *Hansard*, 18 April 2006, Col.10W

CHAPTER 20: GOOD AND BAD REVOLUTIONS: THE ARAB SPRING

1. David Cameron, Speech to Lord Mayor's Banquet, 15 November 2010, www.pm.gov.uk
2. Prime Minister, *A Strong Britain in an Age of Uncertainty: The National Security Strategy*, October 2010, p.4
3. 'Foreign Secretary: "For the first time in decades our diplomatic reach will be extended not reduced"', 11 May 2011, www.fco.gov.uk
4. David Lidington, Speech, 5 April 2011, www.fco.gov.uk
5. David Cameron, Speech to Lord Mayor's Banquet, 15 November 2010, www.pm.gov.uk
6. William Hague, Speech, 10 May 2011, www.fco.gov.uk
7. William Hague. Speech, 17 November 2010, www.fco.gov.uk
8. David Lidington, Speech, 5 April 2011, www.fco.gov.uk
9. *Hansard*, House of Commons, 14 September 2010, Col.722; Foreign Secretary interview with Sky News, 17 October 2010, www.fco.gov.uk
10. Nick Hopkins, 'UK military steps up plans for Iran attack amid fresh nuclear fears', Guardian, 2 November 2011
11. Ken Dilanian, 'US grants support to Iranian dissidents', *USA Today*, 25 June 2009; Jason Ditz, 'Clinton: US supported Iran protesters "behind the scenes"', 9 August 2009, www.antiwar.com; Mark Mazzetti, 'U.S. Is Said to Expand Secret Actions in Mideast', *New York Times*, 24 May 2010
12. Lord Howell, Speech, 14 June 2011, www.fco.gov.uk
13. Lord Howell, Speech, 22 February 2011, www.fco.gov.uk
14. Lord Howell, Speech, 22 September 2010, www.fco.gov.uk
15. Lord Howell, Speech, 22 February 2011, www.fco.gov.uk
16. Lord Howell, Speech, 30 May 2011, www.fco.gov.uk
17. Lord Howell, Speech, 22 February, www.fco.gov.uk
18. *Hansard*, House of Commons, 11 February 2011, Col.442
19. Lord Howell, Speech, 3 February 2011, www.fco.gov.uk
20. *Hansard*, House of Lords, 11 February 2011, Col.495
21. David Lidington, Speech, 5 April 2011, www.fco.gov.uk
22. 'British Foreign Secretary William Hague visits Cairo', 3 November 2010, www.fco.gov.uk
23. 'Change of Her Majesty's Ambassador to Egypt', 22 June 2010, www.fco.gov.uk
24. Campaign Against the Arms Trade, 'UK arms sales to Middle East include tear gas and crowd control ammunition to Bahrain and Libya', 17 February 2011, www.caat.org.uk
25. 'Joint UK-France-Germany statement on Egypt', 29 January 2011, www.fco.gov.uk
26. *Hansard*, House of Lords, 31 January 2011, Cols.1225-6
27. *Hansard*, House of Lords, 31 January 2011, Col.1235
28. *Hansard*, House of Commons, 31 January 2011, Col.594
29. Chris McGreal, 'Tony Blair: Mubarak is "immensely courageous and a force for good"', Guardian, 2 February 2011

30. 'Foreign Secretary: "We are on the side of a stable democratic future for Egypt"', 6 February 2011, www.fco.gov.uk
31. *Hansard*, House of Commons, 16 February 2011, Col.819W; William Hague, *Hansard*, House of Commons, 14 February 201, Col.720
32. 'Foreign Office minister promotes democracy; meets with Egypt's MB', 3 March 2011, www.ikhwanweb.com. The Foreign Office website states: 'Foreign Office Minister Alistair Burt will meet the Egyptian Prime Minister, other senior members of the transitional government and leading members of the political opposition during the 2 day visit'. 'Foreign Office Minister visits Egypt', 09 March 2011, www.fco.gov.uk
33. 'MB Chairman inaugurates MB centre in Alexandria', 1 April 2011, www.ikhwanweb.com; 'Jonny Paul, 'British gov't slammed for visit to Muslim Brotherhood', Jerusalem Post, 19 April 2011
34. 'Jonny Paul, 'British gov't slammed for visit to Muslim Brotherhood', *Jerusalem Post*, 19 April 2011
35. Al-Sayyed Al-Abbadi, 'Foreign Office Visits MB in Alexandria', 4 April 2011, www.ikhwanweb.com
36. Edmund Blair, 'UK prime minister in Egypt, won't meet Brotherhood', Reuters, 21 February 2011
37. James Kirkup, 'Cameron arrives in Egypt to push for democracy', *Daily Telegraph*, 21 February 2011
38. Noha Samir, 'No threat from growth of Mulsim Brotherhood's role', 27 June 2011, www.masress.com
39. 'Foreign Secretary: "We are on the side of a stable democratic future for Egypt"', BBC1 interview, 6 February 2011, www.fco.gov.uk
40. 'UK ambassador congratulates FJP Secretary General', 4 December 2012, www.masress.com; 'FJP receives British ambassador in Cairo', 4 December 2011, www.ikhwanmisr.net
41. Craig Whitlock, 'U.S. reexamining its relationship with Muslim Brotherhood opposition group', *Washington Post*, 2 February 2011; 'Egypt's Muslim Brotherhood welcomes idea of U.S. contacts', Haaretz, 30 June 2011; 'US ready to cooperate with Egypt's Muslim Brotherhood', *Al Ahram*, 22 July 2011
42. An English version of the manifesto is available at http://www.scribd.com/doc/73955131/FJP-Program-En (accessed 6 January 2012), p.24
43. Martin Bright, 'Britain's former spy chief: MI6 kept secrets from Israel, Hamas Iran's puppet', *Jewish Chronicle*, 31 March 2011
44. Jason Burke, 'Guantánamo Bay files: Pakistan's ISI spy service listed as terrorist group', *Guardian*, 25 April 2011
45. *Hansard*, House of Lords, 11 February 2011, Col.490
46. 'PM's interview at the G8 Summit in Deauville', 26 May 2011, www.pm.gov.uk. See Peter Dale Scott, 'The Libyan War, American Power and the Decline of the Petrodollar System', April 29, 2011, www.globalresearch.ca
47. 'British military officers to be sent to Libya', BBC news, 19 April 2011
48. 'Foreign Secretary updates Parliament on the Middle East and North Africa', 13 October 2011, www.fco.gov.uk; William Hague, 'Supporting the Libyan National Transitional Council', 13 May 2011, www.fco.gov.uk; Virginia Wheeler and Tom Newton Dunn, 'Brit held with SAS in Libya was spy', *Sun*, 7 March 2011; Julian Borger and Martin Chulov, 'Al-Jazeera

footage captures "Western troops on the ground" in Libya', Guardian, 30 May 2011

49. Eli Lake, 'Libya rebels will receive $25M from U.S.', *Washington Times*, 20 April 2011
50. Charles Levison and Matthew Rosenberg, 'Egypt Said to Arm Libya Rebels', *Wall Street Journal*, 17 March 2011; Robert Fisk, 'Libya in turmoil: America's secret plan to arm Libya's rebels', *Independent*, 7 March 2011
51. John Pilger, 'David Cameron's gift of war and racism, to them and us', 6 April 2011, johnpilger.com; Patrick Martin, 'Mounting Evidence of CIA Ties to Libyan Rebels', 4 April 2011, www.globalresearch.ca
52. Charles Levison, Ex-Mujahedeen Help Lead Libyan Rebels', *Wall Street Journal*, 2 April 2011; Praveen Swami, Nick Squires and Duncan Gardham, 'Libyan rebel commander admits his fighters have al-Qaeda links', *Daily Telegraph*, 25 March 2011
53. Patrick Cockburn, 'The shady men backed by the West to displace Gaddafi', *Sunday, Independent*, 3 April 2011
54. Praveen Swami, Nick Squires and Duncan Gardham, 'Libyan rebel commander admits his fighters have al-Qaeda links', *Daily Telegraph*, 25 March 2011
55. Richard Spencer, 'Libya: the West and al-Qaeda on the same side', *Daily Telegraph*, 18 March 2011
56. Alexander Cockburn, 'Libya rebels: Gaddafi could be right about al-Qaeda', First Post, 24 March 201, www.thefirstpost.co.uk
57. Eli Lake, '"Freelance jihadists" join Libyan rebels', *Washington Times*, 29 March 2011
58. Martin Bright, 'Britain's former spy chief: MI6 kept secrets from Israel, Hamas Iran's puppet', *Jewish Chronicle*, 31 March 201; Robert Winnett and Duncan Gardham, 'Libya: al-Qaeda among Libya rebels, Nato chief fears', *Daily Telegraph*, 29 March 2011
59. *Hansard*, House of Commons, 30 March 2011, Col.351
60. Personal correspondence from Ministry of Defence to the author, 2 November 2011
61. Daya Gamage, 'Libyan rebel commander admits link to al-Qaeda: Chad President says al-Qaeda acquired weapons in rebel zone', *Asian Tribune*, 28 March 2011
62. Ian Black, 'Qatar admits sending hundreds of troops to support Libya rebels', *Guardian*, 26 October 2011
63. Ian Black, 'Qatar admits sending hundreds of troops to support Libya rebels', *Guardian*, 26 October 2011
64. 'Pgymy with the punch of a giant', *Economist*, 5 November 2011
65. Nic Robertson and Paul Cruickshank, 'New jihad code threatens al Qaeda', CNN, 10 November 2009
66. 'Gadafi: The end game', Press release, 28 November 2011, http://www.talkafrique.com/news-flash/gaddafi-the-game-press-release
67. Nick Mcdermott, 'Paraded on Libyan TV, the rebel "Al Qaeda fighter" from Britain', *Daily Mail*, 16 March 2011; Channel Four News, 15 March 201, http://www.channel4.com/news/british-libyan-detained-by-gaddafi, 'British-Libyan detained by Gaddafi'
68. Ian Birrell, 'MI6 role in Libyan rebels' rendition "helped to strengthen

al-Qaida', *Guardian*, 24 October 2011; Martin Chulov, 'Libyan commander demands apology over MI6 and CIA plot', *Guardian*, 4 September 2011

69. Terry Macalister, 'Secret documents uncover UK's interest in Libyan oil', *Observer*, 30 August 2009
70. Jason Allardyce, 'Lockerbie bomber "set free for oil"', *Sunday Times*, 30 August 2009
71. 'Libya and Britain: the new special relationship', *Sunday Times*, 6 September 2009
72. Jonathan Russell, 'British business's taste for Libyan oil money exposed', *Daily Telegraph*, 27 February 2011
73. Ian Drury, 'The "dirty secret" of British arms sales to Libya just months before Gaddafi slaughtered pro-democracy protesters, *Daily Mail*, 5 April 201; Campaign Against the Arms Trade, 'New report shows that UK kept exporting arms to Libya through 2010', 21 April 2011, www.caat.org.uk
74. Campaign Against the Arms Trade. 'MPs' damning report on arms export controls highlights flaws in UK policies', 5 April 2011, www.caat.org.uk
75. Abdel Bari Atwan, 'Libya is all about logistics now', *Guardian*, 15 April 2011
76. 'Growth of Resource Nationalism in Libya', *Daily Telegraph*, 31 January 2011
77. Alex Spillius, 'Wikileaks: Saudis "chief funders of al-Qaeda"', *Daily Telegraph*, 5 December 2010; 'US embassy cables: Hillary Clinton says Saudi Arabia "a critical source of terrorist funding"', *Guardian*, 5 December 2010
78. 'US embassy cables: Hillary Clinton says Saudi Arabia "a critical source of terrorist funding"', *Guardian*, 5 December 2010
79. 'US embassy cables: Hillary Clinton says Saudi Arabia "a critical source of terrorist funding"', *Guardian*, 5 December 2010
80. Congressional Research Service, *Qatar: Background and US Relations*, Report RL31718, January 2008, front cover
81. 'State Visit of The Emir of Qatar', 26 October 2010, www.fco.gov.uk
82. 'Joint statement between the Prime Minister of the UK and the Emir of Qatar', 26 October 2010, www.pm.gov.uk
83. 'Press conference with Prime Minister of Kuwait', 22 February 2011, www.pm.gov.uk
84. 'Prime Minister's speech to the National Assembly', 22 February 2011, www.pm.gov.uk
85. Alistair Burt, Speech, 21 October 2010, www.fco.gov.uk
86. 'Prime Minister's speech to the National Assembly', 22 February 2011, www.pm.gov.uk'; See also the comment of Lord Howell: 'But if this is a time of fast-moving events, it is also a time when wise reflection is needed, on how to meet the aspirations of the people of the Middle East can be met, acknowledging that there are no simple or single answers, and that there are many ways for nations to achieve and maintain legitimacy, by their own pattern of participation and consent'. Lord Howell, Speech, 30 May 2011, www.fco.gov.uk
87. 'Press conference with Prime Minister of Kuwait', 22 February 2011, www.pm.gov.uk
88. 'Press conference with Prime Minister of Kuwait', 22 February 2011, www.pm.gov.uk
89. Alan Duncan, Speech, 21 October 2010, www.fco.gov.uk
90. 'UK Saudi relations', undated, http://ukinsaudiarabia.fco.gov.uk

91. Personal correspondence from Foreign Office, Information Rights Team to the author, 11 November 2011
92. Lord Howell, Speech, 30 May 2011, www.fco.gov.uk
93. 'UK Saudi relations', undated, http://ukinsaudiarabia.fco.gov.uk
94. 'UK Saudi relations', undated, http://ukinsaudiarabia.fco.gov.uk
95. 'Amnesty links British jets to Saudi attacks in Yemen', *Guardian*, 24 August 2010; Amnesty International, 'Yemen: Exclusive new images show scale of destruction from Yemeni and Saudi bombardments', 6 April 2010
96. William Hague, 'Libya Contact Group: Chair's statement', 13 April 2011, www.fco.gov.uk
97. 'Dialogue Is the Best Solution, Says HRH Crown Prince', Bahrain News Agency, 9 March 2011, http://www.bna.bh
98. Mahmood Rafique, 'HM the King receives Peter Ricketts', 9 March 2011, http://twentyfoursevennews.com/
99. Finian Cunningham, 'Bahrain: Western Complicity in Saudi-Backed War Crimes', 6 April 2011, www.globalresesearch.ca
100. Pepe Escobar, 'Exposed: The US-Saudi Libya deal', *Asia Times*, 2 April 2011; Finian Cunningham, 'Bahrain: Western Complicity in Saudi-Backed War Crimes', 6 April 2011, www.globalresesearch.ca; Craig Murray, 'The invasion of Bahrain', http://www.craigmurray.org.uk, 14 March 2011
101. Campaign Against the Arms Trade, 'Saudi Arabia uses UK-made armoured vehicles in Bahrain crackdown on democracy protesters', 16 March 2011, www.caat.org.uk
102. Jamie Doward and Philippa Stewart, 'UK training Saudi forces used to crush Arab spring', *Guardian*, 28 May 2011
103. Campaign Against the Arms Trade, 'Saudi Arabia uses UK-made armoured vehicles in Bahrain crackdown on democracy protesters', 16 March 2011, www.caat.org.uk
104. Amnesty International, 'Bahrain: international pressure needed to halt human rights crisis - new report', 21 April 2011
105. Finian Cunningham, 'Bahrain and Libya: US-NATO Colludes with Islamic Extremism, 14 April 2011, www.globalresearch.ca; Ian Black, 'Bahrain protests: "The repression is getting worse"', Guardian, 8 August 2011
106. Amnesty International, 'Bahrain: Emergency law's renewal signals more repression', 4 May 2011
107. William Hague, 'The UK will be an active and distinctive voice in the Middle East', 14 February 2011, www.fco.gov.uk
108. Joint statement: PM and His Majesty the King of Bahrain, 15 July 2010, www.pm.gov.uk
109. 'Foreign Secretary welcomes HRH Crown Prince of Bahrain to the UK', 1 December 2010, www.fco.gov.uk
110. William Hague, 'Bahrain: "We urge all sides to avoid violence and the police to exercise restraint"', 17 February 2011, www.fco.,gov.uk
111. 'Cameron calls for restraint on all sides in Bahrain', 16 March 2011, www.pm.gov.uk
112. 'Oral Evidence Taken before the Foreign Affairs Committee', Q38, 40, 16 March 2011, www.parliament.uk
113. See, for example, *Hansard*, House of Commons, 17 March 2011, Col.505. Hague said: 'It is important not to view Bahrain and Libya as analogous. In

the case of Bahrain, the Government have genuinely offered dialogue with opposition groups and offered a referendum on a new constitution'.

114. Ian Black, 'Bahrain urged to deliver human rights reforms as King visits London', *Guardian*, 12 December 2011
115. 'Statement on PM's meeting with King of Bahrain', 12 December 2011, www.pm.gov.uk
116. Human Rights Watch, 'Bahrain: Release people jailed for speaking out', 6 December 2011

Index